# Property and Casualty Insurance

License Exam Manual

7th Edition

Dearborn

PASSTRAK™

Dearborn™

*This text is updated periodically to reflect changes in laws and regulations. To verify that you have the most recent update, you may call Dearborn at 1-800-423-4723.*


Published by Dearborn Financial Institute, Inc.®



Printed in the United States of America.

**Library of Congress Cataloging-in-Publication Data**

Passtrak property and casualty insurance : license exam manual.—7th ed.
p. cm.
ISBN 0-7931-8801-6 (pbk.)
1. Insurance, Property—United States—Examinations, questions, etc. 2. Insurance, Casualty—United States—Examinations, questions, etc. I. Title: Pass Trak property and casualty insurance. II. Title: Property and casualty insurance.
HG8531.P37 2004
368'.0076—dc22 2004003289

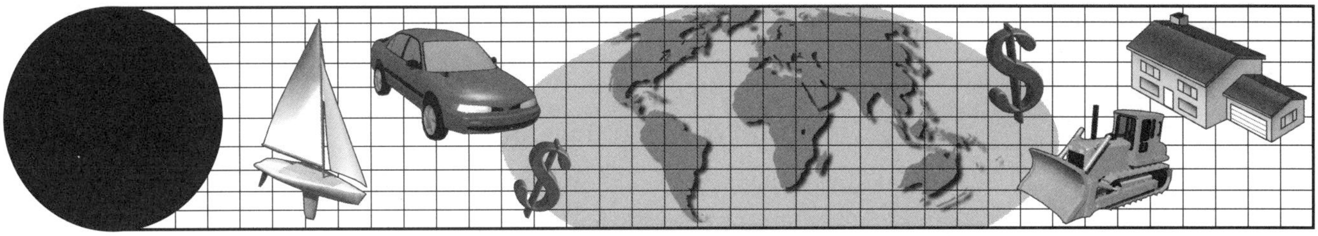

# Contents

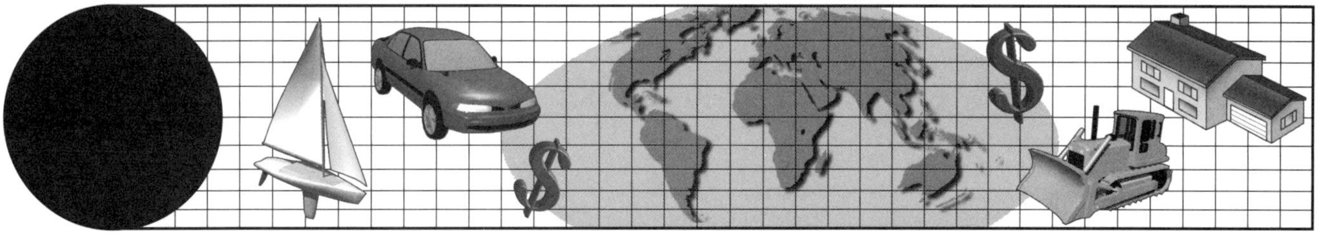

# Acknowledgments

The publisher would like to acknowledge the following individuals for their contributions to the development of this text:

John Berti, Insurance Training Manager (New York)
Barb Gavitt, Dearborn Midwest Regional Trainer
Diane M. Lamyotte, CPCU, AU, Content Reviewer
Barbara Meyer, Dearborn Midwest Regional Trainer
Anne Shropshire, CLU, Associate Publisher

Their efforts have resulted in a text that we believe will be an excellent source of knowledge and information about property and casualty insurance in these early years of the new millennium.

Arthur G. Carvajal, Esq.
Senior Legal Editor

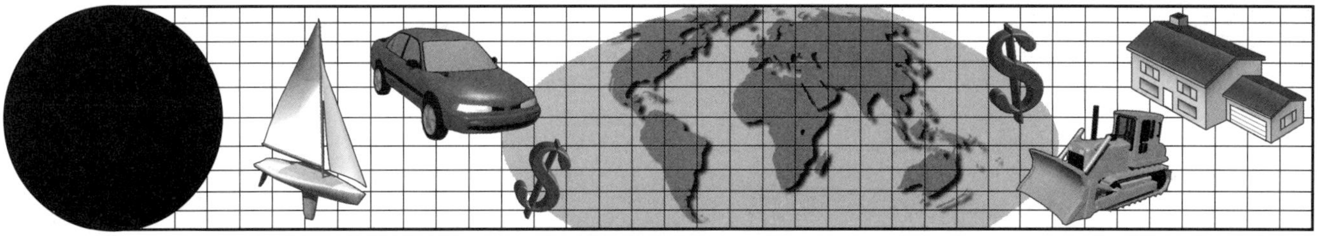

# Introduction

Thank you for purchasing *PASSTRAK Property and Casualty Insurance License Exam Manual*. This brief introduction will help you get the most out of this book when preparing for your state licensing examination.

Most states require individuals to obtain some education in insurance before taking a state licensing exam. All states require individuals to take an exam to become licensed as an insurance agent or producer. Some individuals may be exempt from this licensing exam, usually on the basis of prior insurance education or experience. You can contact your state's department of insurance to determine its precise licensing requirements.

### *How to Use the License Exam Manual*

*PASSTRAK Property and Casualty Insurance License Exam Manual* consists of Units, Unit Tests, and Practice Final Exams.

Here is an effective way to maximize your comprehension of this text:

1. Read the entire text, or at least the units that deal with the line of insurance you are studying. If you are studying for a property insurance licensing examination, study those units that cover property insurance and general insurance topics. If you are preparing to take a combined property and casualty insurance exam, study the entire book.
2. Throughout the text, you will see three special types of notes to help your comprehension. These notes have a specific purpose and are denoted with different text markers:

✓ ***Take Note:*** This note highlights an important point of fact, law, policy, or practice that you should understand. Reading the Take Note sections by themselves after you have read the book provides a quick review of these important points just before you take the licensing exam.

**Test Topic Alert!**

This note alerts you to important information that frequently appears in the licensing exam. This information comes directly from the instructor and highlights an important point that you should remember for the exam.

✓ ***For Example:*** This note illustrates the operation of important concepts and principles. It applies a principle or concept to a realistic situation.

3. Each unit contains periodic Quick Quizzes to ensure that you understand and retain the material covered in the preceding section.
4. We have noted the policy form numbers of the Insurance Services Office (ISO), which publishes the standard policy forms used by many insurance carriers (e.g., PP 00 01 06 98).
5. At the end of each unit, you will find a unit exam. This review test covers all of the topics presented in the preceding Unit. If you have mastered the Quick Quizzes, you should have no trouble successfully completing the unit exam.
6. Finally, when you have finished reading the course and have mastered the Quick Quizzes and unit exams, you are ready to take the final exams at the end of the book. If you are studying for a property insurance license, take the property insurance final exam. If you are studying for a casualty insurance license, take the casualty insurance final exam. If you are studying for both lines, take both final exams. You should get at least 80% of the questions correct after careful study of this book.

The state insurance licensing exam is not easy. You must display considerable knowledge of the topics presented in this textbook and the law supplement, which covers state insurance laws and regulations. (If you do not have this law supplement for your state, contact Dearborn's customer service department at 1-800-423-4723.) If you understand the information in this book and in the law supplement thoroughly, you will be well prepared to take the licensing exam.

Part One

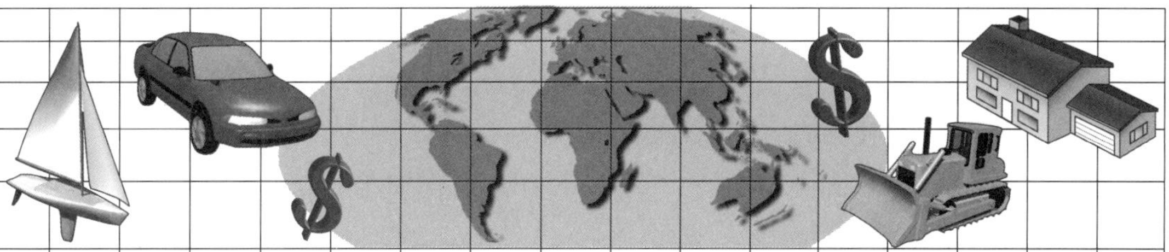

# Principles of Property and Casualty Insurance

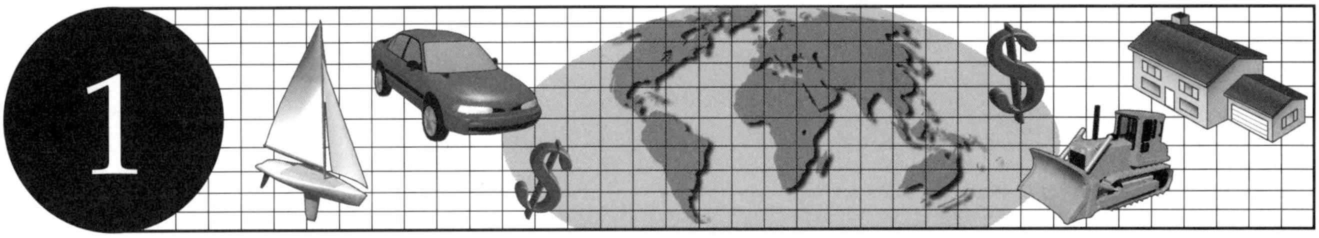

# The Purpose of Property and Casualty Insurance

## INTRODUCTION

This unit lays the foundation for your study of property and casualty insurance by defining and explaining many of the terms used throughout this text and throughout your career as an agent, a broker, or a producer. The number of insurance terms and concepts introduced throughout this text may seem overwhelming as you begin your study. The more you read, use, and discuss the basic insurance terms and concepts, the easier it will be to understand the more complex insurance concepts addressed in later units of this course. The more you learn about the important regulatory nuances of the insurance industry, the better equipped you will be to address the needs of your future clients.

## UNIT OBJECTIVES

When you have completed this unit, you should be able to:

- explain the importance of insurance in the economy of the United States;
- define *risk* and distinguish between pure risk and speculative risk;
- identify the methods used to handle risk;
- explain why insurable interest and the principle of indemnity are important to the insurance industry; and
- define *peril*, *hazard*, and *loss* and give an example of each.

# History of Insurance

The insurance industry's history dates back many centuries to when wealthy Chinese merchants along the Yangtze River decided that it was too risky to place all their merchandise on a single vessel and sail it down the river. Instead, they split the shipment into smaller portions and placed them on several boats. They knew that it was unlikely all the vessels would sink or suffer damage, and that if one did sink the majority of the cargo would reach its destination safely. Although this arrangement was not formally called *insurance,* it was the forerunner of the modern insurance company, as it recognized the importance of spreading risk.

The more formalized insurance arrangements we are familiar with today actually began at a coffeehouse owned by Edward Lloyd near London, England. In the late 1600s, wealthy merchants gathered at the coffeehouse to discuss their latest ventures, which often involved shipments across the oceans, increasingly to the new world. Concerned that they could be wiped out financially if an entire shipment was lost, they began to make arrangements with each other to share their risks of loss. When a shipment was scheduled to depart, the owner posted a notice with a complete description of the cargo and vessel at the coffeehouse. Other merchants looked at the description and signed their names beneath with a percentage of the cargo they were willing to pay for if the vessel were lost. When 100% of the cargo was "insured" in this manner, the vessel sailed. These individuals became known as **underwriters**. If the voyage was successful, each underwriter received a bonus, or **premium**. If, however, the vessel did not reach its destination, the underwriters made good the loss to the shipper.

This, of course, was the beginning of **Lloyd's of London**, an institution that has continued to operate in much the same way for more than 300 years and after which many of our United States insurance customs and practices are patterned. Lloyd's remains a major participant in the worldwide insurance industry.

# The Role of Insurance: Costs and Benefits

The products and services the insurance industry provide offer many positive aspects. Today's insurance functions primarily as a means to reimburse people when their property is damaged or they suffer some other unforeseen loss. Insurance helps individuals and business owners resume their normal standard of living and operations, which actually benefits society as a whole.

✓ ***For Example:*** If your home burns down and you have no means to pay for the repairs, it is unlikely you would have the funds to make other purchases. Not only would you be affected, but also others from whom you ordinarily buy things. A negative ripple effect on the economy occurs. The proceeds of an insurance policy benefit everyone by restoring the insured person or organization to the same financial condition as before the loss.

Another way insurance benefits society is by encouraging activities and devices that reduce the amount of losses and their economic impact.

✓ ***For Example:*** It has been proven that seat belts and other passive restraints in automobiles significantly reduce the extent of injuries suffered by vehicle occupants involved in auto accidents. Insurance companies were a major force behind requiring seat belts as standard equipment in all vehicles. Or you may have noticed the "UL Approved" label on an appliance you own. UL stands for Underwriters Laboratories, an insurance industry think tank that develops safety standards for items used in residences and businesses.

Although these examples represent more recent efforts of insurers to eliminate or reduce the amount of loss and human suffering, such efforts have long been a part of the insurance industry.

Of course, insurance is not without its costs. In addition to the obvious consumption of resources, human and otherwise, insurance also can create a situation where losses become more likely to occur.

✓ ***For Example:*** Who would be tempted to burn down his house if he had to bear the financial burden? The use of insurance has caused some unscrupulous people to commit the crime of **arson**, simply to access the insurance policy proceeds. This is considered a cost of insurance because a loss would not occur unless a person could collect on the insurance policy. In other words, arson would not exist without insurance.

Similarly, some people are not as careful to prevent losses when they have insurance. They don't cause the loss intentionally, as the arsonist does, but they are indifferent as to whether a loss occurs. You may have heard someone say, "So what if something happens to my property? That's what I have insurance for!" This indifference to loss leads to damage and injury that could be prevented; thus, it, too, is considered a cost of insurance.

✓ ***Take Note:*** While insurance provides benefits by eliminating losses, reducing anxiety, serving as a basis for the extension of credit, and paying for losses, it is not without its costs. In addition to the physical and human resources consumed in the insurance industry, insurance also creates some losses that would not occur otherwise, such as an arson-caused fire or a carelessly discarded match.

## Concept of Risk Management

### Risk

Any introduction to insurance requires a clear understanding of the concept of risk. Many insurance professionals use the word *risk* to refer to an insured or a prospect for insurance, or to the peril that is being insured. They will say that a particular person or property is a good risk or a bad risk, meaning that they have evaluated the underwriting characteristics of that person or property for a particular insurance policy.

This usage differs from the strict insurance definition; **risk** means the uncertainty regarding financial loss.

✓ ***Take Note:*** Risk = uncertainty regarding financial loss

To understand this strict insurance definition, consider what happens when an individual decides to burn down his own home. When gasoline is sprayed on the house and a torch is applied, the loss is certain. The event is purposeful in nature, and no uncertainty exists. Therefore, there is no risk (in insurance terms) of loss by fire.

However, when a house fire is started by faulty electrical circuitry or a lightning strike, the event is sudden and unexpected. The owner of the house and the financial institution that holds the loan on the house both suffer a financial loss. The loss is uncertain and accidental; therefore, a risk exists and the loss is covered by insurance.

**Loss** is defined for insurance purposes as unintended, unforeseen damage to property, injury, or the amount the insurance company is obligated to pay for personal injury.

✓ ***For Example:*** The wearing out of clothing represents destruction or decline in value; however, for insurance purposes, it is not loss because it is the expected or intended consequence of wearing the clothes.

### Types of Risk

Two kinds of risk exist—speculative and pure.

- **Speculative risk** involves three possible outcomes: loss, no loss, or profit. Investing in the stock market is an example of speculative risk. One might profit when the value of the stock rises, lose when it declines, or break even if no change occurs. Speculative risks are not insurable.
- **Pure risk** involves only two possible outcomes: loss or no loss, with no possibility of gain or profit. The risk associated with the chance of being robbed is an example of pure risk. No opportunity for gain exists if the robbery does not occur—only an opportunity for loss if it does. Only pure risks are insurable.

**Test Topic Alert!**

A pure risk involves only the chance of a loss, never the chance of a gain. Insurance is designed to protect against a pure risk.

The purpose of insurance is to protect the insured against losses caused by pure risk. While speculative risk concerns individuals and businesses, the potential for economic gain makes it an improper subject for insurance, which is designed to reimburse people who experience financial loss.

### Exposure

In the context of insurance, **exposure** is the possibility of a loss. It simply means the degree to which a person or property is vulnerable to risk or to the possibility of loss from a risk.

✓ ***For Example:*** A construction company usually experiences greater exposure than an accounting firm.

## Risk Management

To achieve greater security, individuals, families, businesses and institutions have five basic ways to handle risk. This can be remembered using the acronym TRAIL:

- **T**ransfer (other than insurance);
- **R**etention;
- **A**voidance;
- **I**nsurance; and
- **L**oss control.

### Transfer (Other Than Insurance)

Some risks, or loss exposures, may be transferred to another person or entity. For example, a construction contract may transfer certain construction risks to a subcontractor, such as when an electrician agrees to reimburse a general contractor for certain injuries that occur at the job site while the electrician performs his duties.

**Retention**

A risk also may be retained. If a person wants to accept responsibility for the risk, he may choose to retain all or part of that risk. Retention may be **passive** (the company or person is not aware that the risk exists, does not insure it and must pay if a loss occurs), or it may be **active** (the company or person is aware of the risk and accepts it). A deductible is an example of active retention because the insured agrees to retain part of the loss in order to reduce the premium.

**Avoidance**

The most obvious method of risk treatment is simply to avoid as many risks as possible. By choosing not to drive or own an automobile, a person could avoid the associated risks. By never flying, a person could eliminate the risk of being involved in an airplane crash. Clearly, few risks can be handled in this manner.

**Insurance**

Insurance is a financial device for transferring or shifting risk from an individual or entity to a large group with the same risk. This is accomplished through a contract, the **insurance policy**, with an insurance company. Under this arrangement, the individual, along with other insureds, pays a sum to the insurance company. In turn, the insurance company agrees to pay an amount of money (reimbursement) to the individual, or on behalf of the individual, if the events described in the policy occur.

**Test Topic Alert!**

Insurance is used to indemnify, or restore, a policyholder to a preloss condition.

The individual accepts a known cost, the **premium**, in exchange for payment of a large, uncertain financial loss. The insurance company combines, or pools, a large number of similar units (homes, autos, businesses, etc.) and thus can predict losses within these units. This principle, known as the **law of large numbers**, simply states that as the number of observations of an event increase, the closer the predicted outcome will be to the actual outcome. Insurers know, within a very narrow margin, how many homes will be damaged each year by fire. However, they do not know which homes will be damaged. This uncertainty introduces risk and makes the insuring of homes for loss by fire possible.

**Loss Control**

Losses can be reduced or prevented using a variety of loss control techniques. Air bags in automobiles reduce the amount of injury suffered by vehicle occupants in the event of a collision. Sweeping the produce aisle in the supermarket prevents someone from being injured on a slippery floor. Loss control is an important part of risk management, regardless of whether the risks are transferred to an insurance company.

**Quick Quiz 1.1** Each of the following is an example of a way to treat risk. Match the method with the description.

A. Transfer
B. Retention
C. Avoidance
D. Insurance
E. Loss control

1. Accepting a large deductible and paying claims out of your own resources

2. Reducing or preventing losses by installing safety devices

3. Signing a contract and having another party agree to pay losses on your behalf

4. Agreeing to pay a certain sum in order to transfer risks to another firm

5. Quitting smoking so you don't develop lung cancer

***Answers***

*1. B. Retention*

*2. E. Loss control*

*3. A. Transfer*

*4. D. Insurance*

*5. C. Avoidance*

# Fundamental Insurance Concepts

## Insurable Interest and Indemnity

**Insurable interest** means having a relationship to property such that a loss of, or damage to, the property results in a financial loss to an individual or organization. Such an interest generally comes about through:

- owning property;
- having a relationship with the named insured (family member, employee, etc.);
- holding a mortgage or lien on property; or

- having care, custody, or control of other people's property.

**Test Topic Alert!**

An insurable interest is a relationship between a person and a property such that if a loss occurs, the person is harmed financially. An insurable interest must exist at the time of the loss for payment to be made.

The loss could result from physical destruction, negligence, court action, or taking the owner's property improperly.

Generally, state law requires that the buyer of insurance, as well as other insureds on the contract, have an insurable interest at the time of application for the insurance policy and at the time of a loss (claim). However, insurable interest need not be maintained throughout the life of the contract.

✓ ***For Example:*** A loan can be paid off, extinguishing the lender's interest. The policy does not have to be cancelled nor the name of the lender removed, but it will not receive any benefits under the policy because its insurable interest has ended.

## Requirements of an Insurable Risk

Not all pure risks are insurable. Insurance companies generally are unwilling to insure unusual risks or those that represent a potential for catastrophic loss. Certain requirements must be met for a risk to be insurable from a company's viewpoint. The acronym CANHAM will help you remember them:

- **C** Chance of loss must be **calculable** by the insurer;
- **A** Premiums must be **affordable**;
- **N** Loss must be **noncatastrophic**;
- **H** Large number of **homogeneous** (similar) exposures must exist;
- **A** Loss must be **accidental** from the insured's standpoint; and
- **M** Loss must be **measurable** (number and amount).

✓ ***Take Note:*** A few exceptions to these requirements apply. Certain natural disasters that may cause widespread damage, such as floods, brush fires, hail, and earthquakes, may appear to be uninsurable. However, coverage can be purchased through certain specialty insurers or particular government programs.

## The Principle of Indemnity

One of the foundations upon which the property and casualty industry is built is the **principle of indemnity**. This is similar to insurable interest, but rather than defining under what circumstances a policyholder can collect on an insurance policy, the principle of indemnity determines how much he can collect. Under this rule, insurance policies are considered to be contracts of indemnity, meaning they are designed to put someone back in the same general financial condition he was in before the loss.

✓ ***Take Note:*** In other words, a person shouldn't be able to profit by collecting on insurance. The elimination of gain also supports the idea that insurance is designed to insure only pure risk situations.

## The Law of Large Numbers

The mathematical principle of probability is called the law of large numbers. In insurance, a prediction must be made from past loss experience or statistical analysis of the number of losses to be expected within a group of exposures. The law of large numbers tells us that actual losses will be more accurate as the number of units of exposure increases.

**Small Certain Loss Replaces Large Uncertain Loss**

The theory of insurance is that in paying the relatively small premium, each policyholder has benefitted by exchanging the uncertainty of a large future loss for the certainty of a small immediate consideration (the premium paid).

✓ ***For Example:*** Assume 1,000 homes in an area are each worth $50,000. Also assume that statistics show that five of these homes can be expected to burn this year. If each of 1,000 homeowners contributes his share ($250) of the expected $250,000 loss into a fund at the beginning of the year, an adequate insurance pool will exist to pay for the losses if they occur. Similarly, an insurer issues to a large number of homeowners policies insuring against the same type of risk. The insurer knows how many homes may be destroyed by fire in a single year, but not which homes will suffer the loss.

## Quick Quiz 1.2

1. To be commercially insurable, a risk must possess which of the following characteristics?

   A. The risk must be unique.
   B. The chance of loss must be calculable.
   C. The loss must occur during the policy period.
   D. The loss must affect only a small number of insured people.

2. Which of the following situations does NOT create an insurable interest?

   A. Being named in someone's will as an heir
   B. Holding a mortgage or lien on property
   C. Having custody or control of someone else's property
   D. Owning property

3. The law of large numbers states that the larger

   A. the number of insureds, the more likely they will have losses
   B. a company, the more profit it will make
   C. the chance of loss, the higher the premium
   D. the number of insureds, the easier it is to estimate their losses

## Answers

1. **B**. *The requirements for insurability are that the risks be similar, the losses accidental, measurable, calculable and non-catastrophic, and that premiums be affordable.*
2. **A**. *Insurable interest arises out of ownership of property, among other things. Simple expectation of ownership, such as in a will, is not sufficient to create the insurable interest until the actual title to property passes.*
3. **D**. *The law of large numbers states that as the number of observations or exposures increases, the more closely estimated losses will reflect actual losses.*

## Peril/Cause of Loss

**Peril**, the actual cause of a loss, is identified or referred to in the policy. Perils include such events as fire, wind, hail, and collision with another car.

### Specified or Named Peril Policy

A **named peril policy** only provides coverage if a loss is caused by one of the perils specifically named or identified in the policy, such as fire, wind, or hail. If a peril is not listed, it is not covered. The policy may also specifically exclude certain causes of loss or certain property. Policies also can exclude perils only under certain conditions or cover them only under certain conditions.

✓ ***For Example:*** Vandalism is a covered cause of loss in most property insurance policies. However, coverage for vandalism often is excluded when a building has been vacant for more than 60 days preceding the loss.

When a policy is issued on a named peril basis, the burden of proof in the event of loss rests with the insured. He must demonstrate that the loss was caused by one of the listed perils to have coverage.

### Open Perils or Special Form Policy

The insuring agreement of an **open perils policy** is stated in very broad terms: the policy provides coverage for risks of direct physical loss or damage except from those causes of loss specifically excluded (e.g., intentional losses, earthquakes). Because the intent of most property policies is to provide a broad array of coverages, it is easier to identify those few situations in which coverage will not apply than the reverse. For an open perils policy, the burden of proof in the event of a loss is on the insurer. To deny coverage, the insurer must demonstrate that the cause of loss was one of the listed exclusions.

✓ ***Take Note:*** The term *all risk* should not be used in any written or oral communication with an insured. This has become insurance industry shorthand for an open perils or a special form policy, but the term can be misleading to a policyholder who might expect his policy to cover every type of loss situation.

## Hazard

**Hazards** are situations or factors that increase the possibility of a loss occurring (called the **frequency of loss**) or increase the probable size of a loss (called the **severity of loss**).

Hazards may be classified as:

- **Physical**—Material, structural, or operational characteristics of a risk itself, such as an improperly installed wood stove or worn-out brakes
- **Moral**—Dishonest tendencies on the part of the insured toward the occurrence of a loss, staging a car accident, or committing arson
- **Morale**—Careless attitude or general indifference on the part of the insured toward the occurrence of loss
- **Legal**—Susceptibility to legal action (such as a lawsuit) and jury verdicts that increase the amount of damages awarded

**Test Topic Alert!** A hazard increases the possibility or the probable size of a loss.

## Loss

The probability that an event will occur is called a **chance of loss** or an **exposure to loss**. Losses can be classified as either direct or indirect, with insurance policies designed to cover either or both types of loss.

### Direct Loss

**Direct loss** refers to actual physical loss, destruction, or damage to property—for instance, the loss caused by a fire as well as other damage for which the fire was the proximate cause, such as water damage from putting out the fire.

### Indirect Loss

**Indirect loss** is a financial loss incurred as a result of direct damage to property. For a business, this includes loss of profits, rent, and continuing or extra expenses necessary to keep the business operating after a direct loss.

✓ ***For Example:*** In the case of a personal dwelling, indirect loss involves the possible loss of rent from a rental unit in the dwelling or the extra expenses the homeowner incurs from living in a motel while his home is being repaired after a direct loss.

Indirect losses may be covered during the time it takes to repair direct damage to the property. Such losses are referred to as **consequential losses**; that is, they are the consequence of a direct loss. They also may be referred to as **time element losses** because the losses occurred over a period of time.

## Proximate Cause

**Proximate cause** is the uninterrupted sequence of events that produces a loss due to negligence, injury, or damage. In other words, there is an unbroken chain of cause and effect between the occurrence of an insurance peril and the damage to property.

Suppose a fire in one part of a building caused damage to wiring that in turn caused a short circuit. The short circuit then caused damage to machinery in another part of the building. In this example, fire was the proximate cause of damage to the machinery.

✓ ***For Example:*** The story of Mrs. O'Leary and her cow that caused the Great Chicago Fire is a classic example of proximate cause. The cause (cow kicking over the lantern) that sets in motion an unbroken chain of events leading to a loss (fire damage) is considered the proximate cause of the loss.

# Unit Test One

1. Uncertainty regarding loss is the definition of
   A. insurance
   B. risk
   C. hazard
   D. peril

2. Insurance was first arranged at Edward Lloyd's coffeehouse during the
   A. 1500s
   B. 1600s
   C. 1700s
   D. 1800s

3. The benefits of insurance include each of the following EXCEPT
   A. payment of losses
   B. economic benefits
   C. premiums
   D. loss control

4. The purpose of insurance is to
   A. eliminate risk
   B. transfer risk
   C. increase hazards
   D. reduce hazards

5. Which of the following is an example of a pure risk?
   A. Deciding to manufacture a new drug
   B. Purchasing a piece of real estate
   C. Threat of fire damage to property
   D. Playing the lottery

6. Insurance has which one of the following purposes?
   A. It eliminates risk by accumulating funds.
   B. It makes risk predictable by transferring funds.
   C. It eliminates risk by transferring funds.
   D. It transfers risk by accumulating funds.

7. An insured's acceptance of a large deductible is an example of which method of handling risk?
   A. Loss control
   B. Retention
   C. Insurance
   D. Avoidance

8. Which of the following is an example of a peril?
   A. Gasoline stored on a property
   B. Earthquake along a fault line
   C. Indifference to a danger
   D. Bodily injury

9. Which of the following is NOT an example of a hazard?
   A. Oily rags stacked in a corner of a building
   B. Homeowner's carelessness because he has insurance
   C. Fire that destroys personal property in a building
   D. Insured who sets fire to his or her own building

10. The term *insurable interest* refers to the
    A. relationship between an insured and his agent
    B. charges a person pays when financing insurance
    C. amount of insurance a person has
    D. financial loss a person will suffer when an event occurs

11. To have an insurable interest in property, the insured must
    A. have some current relationship to the property
    B. have had a past financial relationship to the property
    C. be the sole owner of the property
    D. be the person who purchases insurance on the property

12. Which of the following does NOT create an insurable interest?
    A. A repair person places a lien on an electrical appliance for payment of service charges.
    B. A bank takes the pledge of an automobile as security for a loan.
    C. An accounting firm leases a copy machine under contract.
    D. A grandfather names his grandson as his sole heir.

13. To be insurable from an insurance company's standpoint, which of the following statements regarding losses must be TRUE?
    A. They must be catastrophic.
    B. They must be accidental.
    C. They must be intentional.
    D. They must be random.

14. Under the law of large numbers, what happens to estimated losses when the number of observations increases?
    A. Increase
    B. Decrease
    C. Stay the same
    D. More predictable

15. Another term for the premium paid for an insurance policy is
    A. comparison
    B. consideration
    C. constitution
    D. condemnation

16. Under a named peril policy, the burden of proof in the event of a loss rests with the
    A. insured
    B. insurer
    C. claims adjuster
    D. appraiser

17. Each of the following is an example of a type of hazard EXCEPT
    A. physical
    B. legal
    C. mental
    D. morale

18. Which of the following is an example of a direct loss?
    A. Loss of rental income after a building is destroyed
    B. Loss of income when a store must shut down following a theft
    C. Loss due to fire damage to a building
    D. Loss due to amounts spent on hotels following fire damage to a home

19. When determining the cause of a loss, an insurance company considers the
    A. approximate cause
    B. proximate cause
    C. proxy cause
    D. appropriate cause

20. Which of the following is considered a hazard?
    A. Lightning
    B. Fire
    C. Trash
    D. Explosion

# Unit Test One Answers & Rationale

1. **B.** Risk is defined as uncertainty regarding financial loss.

2. **B.** Edward Lloyd's London coffeehouse was significant in insurance development during the 1600s.

3. **C.** Premiums are not considered a benefit of insurance, but rather a cost.

4. **B.** Insurance in and of itself does not eliminate risk, but transfers it to insurers. While it also attempts to reduce hazards, that is not the primary purpose of insurance.

5. **C.** A pure risk is one in which there is no potential for gain, only loss or no loss.

6. **D.** Insurance does not eliminate risk; it allows an insured to transfer risk to an insurance company, which accumulates funds to pay losses when they occur.

7. **B.** When an insured agrees to pay all or any part of losses that take place, he uses the risk management technique of retention. A deductible is partial retention.

8. **B.** Gasoline and indifference are hazards, and bodily injury is a consequence of a loss, not its cause. Earthquake is a peril.

9. **C.** Fire is a cause of loss or peril, not a hazard.

10. **D.** Insurable interest is the measure of loss to the insured in financial terms.

11. **A.** Property and casualty insurance requires that an insurable interest be present at the time a person applies for a policy.

12. **D.** An expectation of a future financial interest in property does not create a current insurable interest.

13. **B.** To be insurable to the underwriter, losses must not be catastrophic or intentional; in fact they must be accidental from the insured's standpoint.

14. **D.** The law of large numbers states that as the number of observations increases, the ability to predict the outcome is more precise.

15. **B.** Legal contracts require consideration, or something of value to be exchanged between the parties. For the insurer, it is the promise to pay; for the insured, it is the premium.

16. **A.** In a named peril policy, the insured must prove that a cause of loss is one of the listed perils in order to have coverage.

17. **C.** The hazards in insurance include physical, moral, morale and legal.

18. **C.** Fire damage is a direct loss, while loss of rents, income or additional expenses is indirect or consequential.

19. **B.** In determining coverage, an insurer looks for the proximate cause of the loss, or the cause that sets in motion an unbroken chain of events leading to the loss.

20. **C.** Fire, lightning, and explosion are examples of perils. Trash is a hazard because it increases the likelihood that a loss will occur.

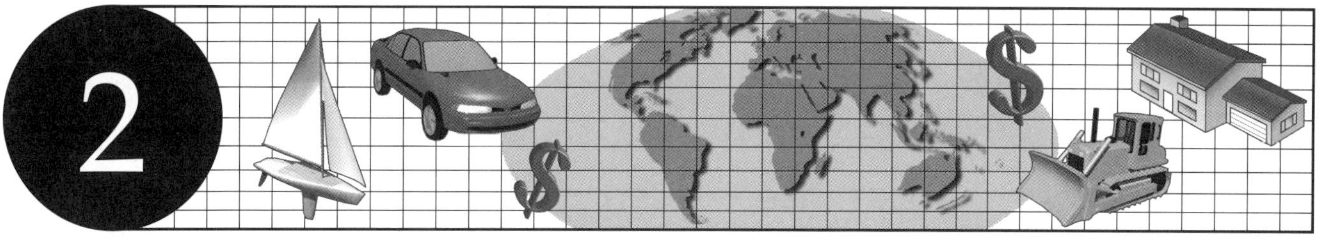


# The Insurance Industry

## INTRODUCTION

The insurance industry is one of the most highly regulated in the United States. This is because insurance is considered to be affected with the public interest, meaning that insurance companies and their representatives are charged with the responsibility of protecting consumers. To ensure that no abuses occur, the insurance departments in the various states oversee the market conduct of insurance companies and their agents in terms of the sale of insurance, the claims process, and a number of other areas. In addition, the misdeeds of companies and agents are subject to legal action. Any conduct or practice may result in a court review to determine its appropriateness. When lawmakers believe that insurance professionals have not behaved in the public's best interest, they may pass laws that dictate the proper method for dealing with consumers.

## UNIT OBJECTIVES

When you have completed this unit, you should be able to:

- identify the three methods used to regulate the insurance industry;
- distinguish between admitted and nonadmitted insurers and between authorized and unauthorized insurers;
- explain the different classifications of insurers, based on their principal locations, their organizational structures, and their distribution systems;
- distinguish between the authority of an agent and a broker; and
- describe the two major functional areas for an insurance company.

# Regulation of the Insurance Industry

The insurance industry in the United States has been regulated primarily by the states rather than the federal government. Insurance regulation began when state legislatures granted charters to new insurers, which authorized their formation and operation. The case of *Paul v. Virginia* in 1869 was a landmark Supreme Court decision establishing the states' right to regulate insurance. The Supreme Court ruled that insurance was not interstate commerce and that the states, rather than the federal government, had the right to regulate the insurance industry. This decision held for about 75 years until it was reversed by the Supreme Court in 1944.

In the case of *United States v. Southeastern Underwriters Association (SEUA),* the Court reversed its earlier decision by ruling that insurance is interstate commerce. SEUA, a cooperative rating bureau, was found guilty of price fixing and other violations of the Sherman Antitrust Act. In the SEUA case, the Supreme Court ruled that insurance was interstate commerce when conducted across state lines and was subject to federal regulation. The Court's decision caused confusion and turmoil throughout the insurance industry.

In response, Congress passed the **McCarran-Ferguson Act (Public Law 15)** in 1945. This law recognized that state regulation of insurance was in the public's best interest and thus exempted the insurance industry from the federal regulation required for most interstate commerce industries. However, the act did give the federal government the right to apply antitrust laws to the extent that such business (insurance) is not regulated by the state level (federal flood insurance programs, for example). To avoid federal intervention, each state has revised its insurance laws to conform with these requirements.

## Methods for Regulating Insurers

Three principal methods are used to regulate insurance companies: legislation, courts and state insurance departments.

### Legislation

Each state has developed laws that regulate the formation and operation of insurance companies. These laws determine how insurance professionals are licensed, what financial requirements an insurer must meet to maintain solvency, how rates are determined, how sales and claims are handled, and how consumers are protected.

In addition to state laws, insurers are also subject to regulation by some federal laws and agencies. For example, the **Securities and Exchange Commission (SEC)** regulates the sale of insurance company securities to the general public. The **Federal Trade Commission (FTC)** regulates mail-order insurers in those states where they are not licensed to do business.

Laws also may be made by public referendum or popular vote. These laws hold the same authority as those developed through the legislative process. California's Proposition 103, for example, which mandated a rate reduction for good drivers who purchased personal automobile policies, was enacted through the state's voter initiative process rather than through the state legislature.

### Courts

State and federal courts may hand down decisions regarding the constitutionality of state insurance laws, an insurer's interpretation of policy clauses and provisions and decisions about the legality of a state insurance department's administrative actions. Various court decisions can affect the ways in which an insurance company handles its operations and markets its insurance products. Judicial review of voter-approved laws dealing with insurance also has become more common.

### State Insurance Departments (Regulation)

Each state has an insurance department, division, or bureau that (in most states) is headed by an **insurance commissioner** or **superintendent** or a **director of insurance**. Depending on the state, the head of this department either is appointed by and at the will of the governor or is an elected official. The commissioner administers state insurance laws and wields considerable power over companies doing business in that state. The commissioner's duties include investigating the practices of anyone engaged in the business of insurance, holding hearings, issuing cease-and-desist orders, approving policies and rates, investigating policyholder complaints, and revoking or suspending an insurer's license to do business. However, the extent of these duties varies between states.

Insurance commissioners belong to an association called the **National Association of Insurance Commissioners (NAIC)** that meets periodically to discuss insurance industry problems, draft model laws, and work for adoption of these laws by state legislatures. Most states accept all or part of the NAIC's recommendations, even though it has no legal authority to force states to accept its recommendations. The NAIC also accredits states for following a majority of its proposed legislation.

## Licensing of Insurers

To transact insurance, an insurer must comply with certain state regulations. An **insurer** is any person or company engaged as the principal party in the business of entering into insurance contracts. This includes stock and mutual insurance companies, fraternal benefit societies, health maintenance organizations, and nonprofit corporations offering dental, hospital, and medical services.

Each state has requirements for the formation and licensing of insurance companies. Such companies receive a **charter** or **certificate of authority** from the state that authorizes the insurer's formation and legal existence. No individual, association, or corporation may engage in the business of insurance unless it is issued a certificate of authority. If the state insurance department is satisfied that an insurer applying to do business in the state has complied with the law fully, it issues a certificate to transact insurance business. Each certificate of authority remains in effect until revoked, cancelled, or suspended according to law.

When an insurer has received a charter or certificate from its state, the company is referred to as an **admitted insurer**. An insurer, for a variety of reasons, may wish to do business in a state as a **nonadmitted insurer**, which generally fall into two categories: authorized and unauthorized. An **authorized nonadmitted insurer** has been approved to transact insurance in a state, but must do so only through a licensed surplus lines broker. An **unauthorized nonadmitted insurer** may not transact insurance in a state.

## Surplus Lines

In most cases, insurance business is placed with an admitted insurer, or a company licensed to do business in the state. However, it is possible that insurance is unavailable in the standard market or from admitted companies. This can occur when an applicant possesses such unusual risk characteristics that standard insurers are unwilling or unable to accommodate the placement of the insurance. This business is referred to as **surplus lines** or **excess** insurance because it is often beyond the capacity of standard insurers.

Some lines of business are placed routinely in the surplus lines market. Aviation liability, products liability, earthquake liability, and professional liability are examples of surplus lines risks. Each state insurance department determines which types of risks may be "exported" to the excess and surplus lines market. With this accomplished, business is arranged using a licensed surplus lines agent or broker. The surplus lines broker can be thought of as a wholesaler because he passes products from the company to the retail agent. In this sense, the lines broker is an agent's agent.

If surplus lines business ultimately is placed with a nonadmitted insurer, a disclosure usually must be provided to the policyholder. This is because a state's insurance guarantee association, which provides insolvency protection to policyholders, is not available for nonadmitted insurers.

## Quick Quiz 2.1

1. The three methods used to regulate insurance companies are __________, __________, and __________.
2. Insurers that have received certificates of authority from their states are called __________ insurers.
3. Nonadmitted insurers must place business through a ____________________.

### *Answers*

1. *legislation, courts, state insurance departments*
2. *admitted*
3. *surplus lines broker*

# Licensing of Agents, Brokers, and Producers

A producer is a person who sells insurance to or negotiates insurance for the public. Most producers are categorized as agents or brokers, but insurance company employees and others also may be producers. Many states are now converting to a single license, which no longer provides a clear distinction between agent and broker, at least in terms of licensing. The title on the license may read *producer, solicitor,* or *broker-agent.*

No person or corporation may transact insurance with or on behalf of an insurer unless that person or corporation has been issued a license. In most states, an applicant must complete a specific course of study, apply for a license, then pass a written examination, usually under the direction of the state insurance department. The purpose of the examination is to ensure that the applicant possesses some knowledge of insurance law and of the insurance contracts he intends to sell. The license is considered a safeguard for the insured. After the producer is licensed, the state insurance commissioner has the power to revoke or suspend that license if the agent is found to be incompetent or dishonest.

## Agent

The definition of **agent** varies by state. In general, an agent is any person who (1) solicits insurance on behalf of any insurance company, (2) takes or transmits (other than for himself) an insurance application or policy, (3) examines any risk, or (4) receives, collects, or transmits any premium. The agent is the insurance company's legal representative. Under the legal doctrine of **respondeat superior,** a principal is considered legally responsible for the wrongful acts of its agent.

A property and liability insurance producer generally has the authority to immediately bind the company for certain types of coverage. In most cases, the agent issues a verbal or written **binder of insurance,** which serves as temporary evidence of insurance until the policy is issued.

An agent may bind the principal (the insurance company) if he possesses express, implied, or apparent authority and **express authority** is given to the agent by the insurer, usually in a contract called the **agency agreement**. **Implied authority** is additional power that is not expressed specifically, but is customarily given to an agent (collecting premiums, for example). Implied authority is derived from express authority and is necessary to carry out the express authority; one never exists without the other. **Apparent authority** is power that the public has reason to believe the agent possesses. It is not up to the insurance-buying public to determine whether an actual agency relationship exists between an insurance company and a producer. If the authority is apparent and the consumer acted on that assumption, the principal (insurance company) is obligated to the consumer. The principal may, of course, seek indemnity from the producer. This also is referred to as **authority by estoppel**.

✓ ***Take Note:*** Although it is common to refer to nearly all insurance producers as agents, an agent is the legal representative of the insurance company and owes certain duties to the principal. These duties include loyalty, obedience, and full disclosure. Violation of these duties provides a company with a legal cause of action.

## Broker

A **broker** is a person who represents the insured rather than the insurance company. A broker can solicit or accept applications for insurance, then attempt to place the business with an insurer directly or through an agent. A broker cannot legally bind insurance and coverage is not in force until the company accepts the business. The only exception to the broker's authority to act on behalf of an insurance company is the collection of premiums, where the broker is considered to be acting as an agent. Single-producer licenses have blurred the distinction between agents and brokers. The specifics of a situation determine whether the producer was acting as an agent or a broker for a particular transaction.

## Producer/Solicitor

A **producer** or **solicitor** is the legal representative of an agent or a broker and generally has no contract with any insurer. A producer or solicitor often can represent only one agent or broker at a time.

## Countersignature

Unless excluded by law, an insurance contract that covers liability or property must be countersigned by a resident agent of the company in the state where the policy is sold. A **resident agent** is an agent domiciled in the state where the policy is sold. Some agents hold nonresident licenses for the other states in which they do business regularly.

## Duties to the Applicant and Insured

In general, the producer represents the insurance company when soliciting applications and binding coverage, recording transactions, collecting premiums, and issuing policies. However, the producer also has duties to the applicant and insured. In addition to the contractual duties with respect to fulfilling the terms of the insuring agreement, the producer also acts as a **fiduciary** in regards to an applicant or insured. A fiduciary is a person who is entrusted with another's money or confidence. A fiduciary is expected to be trustworthy, act in good faith and with candor, and preserve confidential information. An insurance producer is in a fiduciary relationship with an applicant or insured with respect to any premiums received, as that money is entrusted to the producer to be transferred to the insurer. The producer also is in a fiduciary relationship with the insurer because he is entrusted to collect premiums and pay them to the insurer, and to transfer the insurer's payments on a claim to the insured.

# Organization of the Insurance Industry

## State of Domicile

In the United States, insurers are classified by their **states of domicile** (the states where the insurers are chartered or incorporated) and are considered domestic, foreign, or alien companies or insurers.

### Domestic Insurance Company

A **domestic insurer** is an insurance company incorporated and formed under the laws of the state in which it is domiciled.

✓ ***For Example:*** An insurer formed under Connecticut laws is said to be a domestic insurer when conducting business in Connecticut.

**Foreign Insurance Company**

A **foreign insurer** is one domiciled and organized under the laws of one state, but licensed to do business in another state.

✓ ***For Example:*** An insurer formed under Michigan laws but licensed to do business in Illinois is said to be a foreign insurer when conducting business in Illinois.

**Alien Insurance Company**

An **alien insurer** is an insurance company formed under the laws of a country other than the United States.

✓ ***For Example:*** A company domiciled in Toronto, Canada, doing business in Colorado would be an alien insurance company.

## Legal Forms of Organization

**Stock Companies**

Most insurance companies are organized as **stock companies**. Similar to shareholders in other businesses, insurance company shareholders appoint directors, officers, and others to manage the day-to-day operations of the companies they own. Stock insurers write about 75% of the property and casualty insurance in the United States.

**Mutual Companies**

Under the other major form of legal ownership—the **mutual company**—the people or businesses the company insures are also the owners. Unlike a stock company, the mutual company has no shareholders and the policyowners themselves bear any profit or loss the company experiences. Mutual company directors and officers are chosen by the policyholders. Mutual insurers write about 25% of United States property and casualty insurance.

**Lloyd's of London**

Another type of insurer is **Lloyd's of London**. Although it is not really an insurance company, Lloyd's attempts to make a profit for its members, who are called **names**. The names are organized into syndicates or groups to underwrite risks. Lloyd's operates on many of the same principles as a stock exchange in that it matches buyers wishing to secure insurance with sellers who wish to underwrite the risks.

Both stock and mutual companies and Lloyd's are considered **proprietary** because they attempt to profit for their owners. Others types of insurers focus on providing benefits to policyholders. These types of insurers are referred to as **cooperative**. They consist of reciprocals, health associations, and health service plans.

**Other Private Insurers**

A **reciprocal insurer** is an unincorporated group of people who provide insurance to each other. They are not referred to as policyholders, but as members or subscribers. To purchase the insurance products reciprocals offer, individuals or organizations first must demonstrate that they are members of the group. A reciprocal also is called an **interinsurance exchange**.

✓ ***For Example:*** Many states allow the purchase of personal lines insurance through automobile associations or auto clubs. To purchase their insurance, a person first must become a member of a club. Then, he agrees to exchange promises to insure with the other members of the club.

A **health association** or **health service plan** focuses on delivering hospital, medical, or dental benefits to its members. Rather than paying the bills for services obtained from others, the association actually provides the services using prepaid plans. The best known of these types of insurers are the **Blues**—Blue Cross and Blue Shield.

**Fraternal benefit societies** provide limited insurance benefits to their members, usually restricted to life and health insurance. They are not as popular as they once were, having been formed to promote the maintenance of ethnic and religious groupings.

## Government Insurers

At times, the private insurance marketplace leaves policyholder needs unmet. Particularly when coverage is mandated by law, such as workers' compensation or personal automobile insurance, the government becomes the insurer of last resort. In other cases, such as flood insurance, nuclear energy liability insurance, crop insurance, or unemployment compensation, the only insurer interested in underwriting these risks is the government. Thus, governmental insurance is an important and necessary complement to the private insurance market.

## Risk Retention Groups and Risk Purchasing Groups

Widespread unavailability of insurance in the 1980s led Congress to pass legislation creating two new avenues for businesses and individuals to secure much needed insurance coverage. A **risk retention group (RRG)** is a liability insurance company owned by its policyholders. The policyholders must possess similar liability risks and the RRG must be licensed as an insurer under the laws of at least one state. A **risk purchasing group (RPG)** is formed to purchase liability insurance on behalf of its members. Unlike a risk retention group, the RPG merely buys insurance and need not be licensed as an insurer.

## Quick Quiz 2.2

Match the terms in column one with their definitions in column two:

1. Stock company
2. Domestic insurer
3. Alien insurer
4. Mutual company
5. Foreign insurer

A. Company licensed to do business in your state
B. Company owned by its policyholders
C. Company licensed in another state
D. Company owned by shareholders
E. Company licensed in another country

***Answers*** *1.* ***D*** *2.* ***A*** *3.* ***E*** *4.* ***B*** *5.* ***C***

## Marketing and Distribution

In addition to being categorized based on form of organization and legal status, insurance companies also can be classified based on how their products are sold or distributed and by whom. Some companies use the **independent agency** model for selling their products. Under this system, a company finds agents in various geographic areas who agree to sell the insurer's policies in exchange for a percentage of each premium, called a **commission**. Most commercial insurance policies are distributed by independent insurance agencies. Rather than represent a single insurance company, independent agents work on behalf of many companies and select the company that best suits a customer's needs.

Other companies have a dedicated agency force that does not represent any other insurers. In other words, these **exclusive agents** have a contract with a single insurance company, and they can offer only that company's products.

✓ ***For Example:*** State Farm is an exclusive agency company because each local State Farm agent is under an exclusive contract with that organization.

Another type of insurance company, a **direct writer** or **direct response company**, may not have any local agents. All its products and services are offered from the company's home office and the company takes care of all service. The individuals who sell and service the policies are employees of that company and typically are paid salaries rather than commissions.

✓ ***For Example:*** GEICO and USAA are direct writing insurance companies.

✓ ***Take Note:*** No single best method exists for a company to distribute its products. In fact, many insurers now use a combination of methods. In some areas or for some products, they may employ the independent agency system. In other cases, they may act as direct writers. Many companies are also exploring the Internet as a distribution option.

# Insurance Company Operations

## Underwriting

**Underwriting** usually is defined as the selection, classification, and acceptance or rejection of a proposed insured according to the insurer's underwriting standards. Top-level management determines the company's overall underwriting philosophy, including which classes of business or property are acceptable, and outlines this philosophy in detail in an **underwriting guide**. This manual usually includes the lines of insurance the company wishes to pursue, acceptable and prohibited business, amounts of insurance that may be written, rates and forms to be used, types of business that require approval by a senior underwriter, and many other underwriting details.

The **underwriter** is the person who actually selects the applicants, prices coverage, and determines policy terms. In many instances, the agent is the first underwriter for new business. In essence, the agent is a **field underwriter** for the insurance company, determining whether business will be acceptable to the insurance company. It is usually the agent who selects the insured and, in many cases, quotes the premium the insured will pay. After the agent submits an application to the company, the **line underwriter** (usually located in the home office) makes the final determination about whether the risk can be written and at what premium. **Staff underwriters** are employed in the company's home office to help line underwriters implement the company's underwriting guidelines.

The underwriting process consists of four basic steps:

- gathering necessary underwriting information;
- making the underwriting decision;
- implementing the decision; and
- monitoring the decision.

## Rate Making

One of the most important parts of an underwriter's job is to determine the proper pricing for insurance products. Insurance rates are regulated by state insurance departments to make sure the rates are adequate to pay losses and cover expenses. In addition, the departments check to make sure the rates are not excessive (rates must be reasonable) or unfairly discriminatory (not significantly different for two insureds with essentially the same degree of risk). However, because a company does not know in advance how many claims and expenses it will incur for a certain period, it is difficult to determine how much a particular insurance product should cost.

### Rate Regulation

In addition to requirements mandating that insurance rates be adequate, not excessive and not unfairly discriminatory, rates are subject to additional regulation. States vary in the degree of regulation they apply to the rating of different lines of insurance. The types of rate laws in effect follow.

#### *Prior Approval*

Under this system, all rates must be filed with an insurance department and are subject to approval before their use. This is the most restrictive form of regulation.

#### *File and Use*

This type of rating law requires an insurance company to file its rates, but the company is permitted to use them before their approval. If the rate filing is subsequently disapproved, the company must adjust any policies that have been issued with the new rate.

#### *Open Competition*

Some states have adopted a competitive rating systems, which means they encourage competition and rely on it to lead to fair and adequate rates for insurance coverages. Although such a system does not require rate filings, an insurance department monitors rates to see that they continue to be adequate and not excessive.

#### *Mandatory Rates*

In a limited number of states, rates for some types of insurance are mandated by law. A rating bureau develops the rates, and insurers must use these rates in pricing policies.

### Rate

The **rate** is the amount of dollars and cents charged for a particular amount of insurance.

✓ ***For Example:*** The rate charged for a fire policy might be $.50 per $100 of value. If the insured wishes to cover property valued at $50,000, the annual premium would be $250 ($.50 × 500 hundreds = $250).

Rates for different coverages are based on different factors. In fire insurance, for example, rates are based on such factors as construction, property location, and local fire protection classifications. In automobile insurance, rates are based on the driver's age, use of car, and type of car. In workers' compensation, rates are based on the employee's job duties.

Rates are applied to **exposure units** or an **exposure base**. In fire insurance, an exposure unit is a portion of the value insured (such as each $100). In liability insurance, the exposure unit might be every $100 or $1,000 in sales or revenue. In workers' compensation, rates are applied to every $100 of payroll.

**Premium** The **premium**, which is calculated from the rate, is the total cost for the amount of insurance coverage (or limit of liability) purchased.

✓ ***For Example:*** Assume the workers' compensation rate for clerical workers is $.60 per $100 of payroll. If a business has a total annual payroll of $100,000 for its clerical workers, its workers' compensation premium would be calculated as follows:

$100,000 ÷ $100 = $1,000
$1,000 × .60 = $600

Premiums can be further modified by applying credits or debits based on a policyholder's loss experience, safety efforts, or unique risk characteristics.

## Loss Ratios/Expense Ratios

The quality of a company's underwriting is determined in part by its loss ratios and expense ratios. A **loss ratio** is determined by dividing total losses by total premiums received. The resulting information may be used to make decisions about whether to continue an agent's (or agency's) contract, whether to revise underwriting guidelines, or whether to discontinue writing a certain line of business.

An **expense ratio** is determined by dividing an insurer's total operating expenses by total premiums. By adding the company's loss ratio to its expense ratio, an additional ratio (the **combined ratio**) is determined. The insurer breaks even if the combined ratio is 100%. If the combined ratio is less than 100%, an underwriting profit has occurred. If the combined ratio is more than 100%, an underwriting loss has occurred.

✓ ***Take Note:*** In addition to an underwriting profit, an insurance company earns a return on its investments. An underwriting loss may be offset by an investment profit, meaning the insurance company may lose money on underwriting insurance, but remain profitable overall. Investment profits normally are not contemplated in determining adequacy of insurance rates.

## Loss Reserves

Property and casualty insurers must maintain certain funds or **loss reserves** for the estimated cost of settling claims that already have occurred, but that have not yet been paid as of a certain date. A loss reserve is particularly important for casualty insurers because liability losses, which include bodily injury, may take several years to settle. When settlement is finally made, an insurer must have the funds available to make the claims payment.

The size of the loss reserve may be determined in one of four ways:

- **Case reserve**—A loss reserve is established for each claim when it is reported.
- **Average value method**—A loss reserve is established based on the average settlement for a particular type of claim.
- **Loss ratio method**—A loss reserve is established by formula based on the expected loss ratio for a particular line of business or class of insureds.
- **Tabular method**—A loss reserve is established based on the estimated length of an insured's or a claimant's life, the estimated length of disability, etc.

Companies are required by law to maintain minimum reserves on their balance sheets. These reserves ensure that the premiums collected in the present will be available to pay losses in the future.

## Solvency and Capacity

Insurers receive premiums in return for the promise to pay for losses in the future. Because the money received from the public is received in a fiduciary capacity, it must be held in trust to meet these future obligations. Therefore, it is vital that insurers guard against insolvency.

State laws impose capital and surplus requirements on insurers, require the preparation of annual financial statements, and mandate periodic examinations of the insurers' operations. State insurance departments attempt to rehabilitate companies whose financial situations falter and attempt to liquidate the companies if the insurers become insolvent. Most states also have **insurance guaranty associations**, which provide insolvency funds for partial repayment of unpaid claims when an admitted insurer is declared insolvent.

To further ensure company solvency, a limit is placed on the amount of business an insurer may write. This limit, called an insurer's **capacity**, is determined by the company's level of capital and surplus. In this case, *surplus* refers to assets exceeding liabilities on the insurer's balance sheet.

### Rating Services

The financial strength and stability of an insurance company are two vitally important factors to potential insurance buyers and to insurance companies themselves. Guides to insurance companies' financial integrity and claims-paying ability are published regularly by various rating services, such as A.M. Best, Standard & Poor's, Moody's and Fitch's.

✓ ***For Example:*** In *Best's Insurance Reports*, companies are rated A++ to A+ (superior), A to A– (excellent). B++ to B+ (very good), B to B– (good), C++ to C+ (fair), C to C– (marginal), D (below minimum standards), E (under state supervision), F (in liquidation) and S (suspended). Experts generally recommend that insurance buyers purchase policies from companies that have ratings of A++ to A– (under the Best rating system) because these ratings indicate a strong ability to meet obligations to policyholders (See Figure 2.1 *Insurance Company Rating Systems.*)

## Reinsurance

**Reinsurance** provides insurance protection to an insurance company should a loss occur. In this way, it serves as the insurance company's insurer.

Insurance companies (or primary insurers) write insurance policies to protect insureds should a loss occur. Under state law and for sound business operations, insurance companies cannot carry on their books larger amounts at risk than they can expect to cover with their surpluses. Therefore, insurers turn over specified proportions of the risks they accept from policyholders to reinsurance companies. This is called **ceding risk**. The methods used to determine what part of the risk goes to a reinsurer vary based on the contract between the primary insurance company and the reinsurer. This contract is called the **treaty**.

The two types of reinsurance treaties are:

- **facultative**—the primary insurer makes reinsurance arrangements on a case-by-case basis; and
- **automatic**—a portion of every risk the primary insurer accepts is ceded to the reinsurer, subject to the specific terms in the contract or treaty.

Reinsurance treaties can be arranged in a variety of ways, depending on the primary insurer's needs. Sometimes the insurer needs surplus relief, which is required when the insurer wishes to expand its writing of primary insurance. Other times the need is to protect against catastrophic losses, such as earthquakes or hurricanes. Some additional terms concerning reinsurance follow:

**FIGURE 2.1 Insurance Company Rating Systems**

**A.M. Best Company**

| | |
|---|---|
| A++, A+ | Superior; very strong ability to meet obligations |
| A, A– | Excellent; strong ability to meet obligations |
| B++, B+ | Very good; strong ability to meet obligations |
| B, B– | Good; adequate ability to meet obligations |
| C++, C+ | Fair; reasonable ability to meet obligations |
| C, C– | Marginal; currently has ability to meet obligations |
| D | Below minimum standards |
| E | Under state supervision |
| F | In liquidation |
| S | Suspended |

**S&P**

| | |
|---|---|
| AAA | Superior; highest safety |
| AA | Excellent financial security |
| A | Good financial security |
| BBB | Adequate financial security |
| BB | Adequate financial security; ability to meet obligations may not be adequate for long-term policies |
| B | Currently able to meet obligations, but highly vulnerable to adverse conditions |
| CCC | Questionable ability to meet obligations |
| CC, C | May not be meeting obligations; vulnerable to liquidation |
| R | Under a court order of liquidation; in receivership |

**Moody's**

| | |
|---|---|
| Aaa | Exceptional security |
| Aa | Excellent security |
| A | Good security |
| Baa | Adequate security |
| Ba | Questionable security; moderate ability to meet obligations |
| B | Poor security |
| Caa | Very poor security; elements of danger regarding payment of obligations |
| Ca | Extremely poor security; may be in default |
| C | Lowest security |

**Fitch's**

| | |
|---|---|
| AAA | Highest claims-paying ability; negligible risk |
| AA+, AA, AA– | Very high claims-paying ability; moderate risk |
| A+, A, A– | High claims-paying ability; variable risk over time |
| BBB+, BBB, BBB– | Below average claims-paying ability; considerable variability in risk over time |
| BB+, BB, BB– | Uncertain claims-paying ability |
| CCC | Substantial claims-paying ability risk; likely to be placed under state supervision |

- **Quota share**—The primary insurer and reinsurer agree to share the amount of insurance, premium, and loss on some percentage basis
- **Surplus treaty**—The reinsurer agrees to accept some amount of insurance on each risk exceeding a designated amount, up to some specified limit, retained by the primary insurer
- **Excess loss treaty**—The reinsurer pays only when a loss exceeds a certain amount, for any one piece of property or in any one occurrence
- **Pooling**—Each member of a group assumes a percentage of every risk written by a member of the pool

## Quick Quiz 2.3

1. An insurance company that uses no local agents to sell or distribute its products is a(n)

   A. independent agency company
   B. direct writer
   C. captive company
   D. exclusive agency company

2. The underwriting process involves each of the following EXCEPT

   A. gathering information
   B. binding coverage
   C. making decisions to modify coverage
   D. marketing the company's products

3. The premium for workers' compensation is determined by applying a rate to the insurer's

   A. number of employees
   B. payroll
   C. sales
   D. receipts

### Answers

*1.* ***B.*** *An insurance company that sells products directly from the company office with no agents is referred to as a direct writer or direct response company.*

*2.* ***D.*** *The underwriting process involves gathering necessary information, making the underwriting decision, implementing the decision, and monitoring the decision.*

*3.* ***B.*** *The rates for workers' compensation apply to total payroll regardless of the number of employees. Sales and receipts are most often used as a rating base in liability insurance.*

# Unit Test Two

1. Each of the following is a method used to regulate insurance companies EXCEPT
   A. legislation
   B. courts
   C. NAIC
   D. state insurance departments

2. When an insurance company becomes authorized to do business in a particular state, it receives a(n)
   A. appointment
   B. certificate of authority or charter
   C. article of incorporation
   D. authorization

3. Which of the following statements about nonadmitted insurers is TRUE?
   A. They may not do business in the United States.
   B. They may place business only through other insurance companies.
   C. They may operate only as reinsurers.
   D. They may be authorized or unauthorized.

4. All of the following lines of business are placed routinely in the surplus lines market EXCEPT
   A. boiler and machinery
   B. aviation
   C. earthquake
   D. professional liability

5. The entity used to place insurance in the surplus lines market is referred to as a(n)
   A. special lines broker
   B. surplus lines broker
   C. export broker
   D. excess broker

6. A producer may include any of the following EXCEPT a(n)
   A. insurance agent
   B. insurance broker
   C. stock broker
   D. solicitor

7. To obtain an insurance license, an applicant must perform all of the following EXCEPT
   A. pass an examination
   B. complete an application
   C. complete a course of study
   D. complete college

8. To be considered an agent, a person must perform all of the following EXCEPT
   A. take applications for insurance
   B. collect and remit premiums
   C. adjust and pay claims
   D. solicit insurance on behalf of a company

9. The three types of authority given to agents are
   A. express, implied, and appealing
   B. express, compliance, and apparent
   C. implied, apparent, and agreed
   D. express, implied, and apparent

10. The type of authority given to an agent in his agency contract is
    A. apparent
    B. implied
    C. express
    D. inherent

11. The type of authority the public has reason to believe an agent possesses is
    A. inherent
    B. applied
    C. implied
    D. apparent

12. The difference between an agent and a broker is that the agent is authorized to act on behalf of a(n)

    A. brokerage
    B. customer
    C. state
    D. insurance company

13. An agent who conducts business in another state on a regular basis is referred to as a(n)

    A. resident alien
    B. nonresident agent
    C. resident agent
    D. unauthorized agent

14. An insurer incorporated and formed under the laws of the state in which it is domiciled is what type of company?

    A. Domestic
    B. Resident
    C. Foreign
    D. State

15. A company authorized to do business in a state but formed under the laws of a country other than the United States is an

    A. authorized insurer
    B. alien insurer
    C. admitted company
    D. unauthorized company

16. Each of the following is an example of a proprietary insurer EXCEPT

    A. Lloyd's of London
    B. a mutual company
    C. a stock company
    D. a reciprocal insurer

17. An insurer that is unincorporated and refers to its policyholders as members or subscribers is a

    A. mutual company
    B. reciprocal insurer
    C. stock insurer
    D. proprietary insurer

18. The government may write insurance for which of the following types of risks?

    A. Crop insurance
    B. Unemployment insurance
    C. Flood insurance
    D. All of the above

19. An agent who represents a single insurance company under contract is referred to as what type of agent?

    A. Captive
    B. Exclusive
    C. Independent
    D. Restricted

20. When an insurance company distributes its products directly to consumers via phone, mail or other means, it is called a(n)

    A. exclusive writer
    B. independent company
    C. direct writer
    D. soliciting company

21. An insurance company underwriter may take one of several actions when reviewing applications for insurance. Which of the following is NOT an example of an appropriate underwriting action?

    A. Deciding which applicants to insure
    B. Determining the proper classification for a risk
    C. Deciding how much to charge applicants based on their income
    D. Determining which applicants do not qualify for the company's products

22. When determining the amount to charge prospective policyholders, a company must follow basic guidelines concerning rates that include all of the following EXCEPT

    A. rate adequacy
    B. absence of discrimination
    C. rate reasonableness
    D. absence of unfair discrimination

23. States use various types of approval systems when evaluating an insurance company's rates. Which of the following is an example of a state rate law?

    A. Prior approval
    B. File and use
    C. Open competition
    D. All of the above

24. Assuming a rate of $1 per $1,000 of insurance, a policy covering a building valued at $250,000 would produce a premium of

    A. $25
    B. $250
    C. $2,500
    D. $25,000

25. Manitoba Mutual's most recent accounting year produced the following results:

| | |
|---|---|
| Expenses | $35 million |
| Premiums | $100 million |
| Losses | $70 million |

    The company's combined ratio is

    A. 35%
    B. 70%
    C. 75%
    D. 105%

26. Using the information in Question 25, Manitoba Mutual is experiencing an

    A. underwriting profit
    B. accounting profit
    C. underwriting loss
    D. expense loss

27. Property and casualty insurers must create reserves to pay for claims that may arise in the future. Which of the following is NOT an example of a method used to establish loss reserves?

    A. Average value
    B. Expected settlement
    C. Loss ratio
    D. Tabular

28. The amount of insurance a company can write based on its financial status is referred to as

    A. solvency
    B. adequacy
    C. capacity
    D. fiduciary

29. The mechanism used to expand the capacity of a primary insurer to write more business is called

    A. retrocession
    B. reinsurance
    C. remediation
    D. reengineering

# Unit Test Two Answers & Rationale

1. **C.** Insurance is regulated by legislation, courts and state insurance departments. The NAIC, while influential, has no authority to regulate insurers.

2. **B.** The document given to an insurer authorizing it to transact insurance in a state is known as a certificate of authority or charter.

3. **D.** Either nonadmitted insurers are authorized to do business in a state using licensed surplus lines brokers or they are unauthorized and may not transact business at all in that state.

4. **A.** Certain special lines of insurance are exported routinely to the surplus lines market. Aviation, products liability, earthquake, and professional liability are examples of exported business.

5. **B.** State law requires that insurance placed in the nonadmitted market be handled by a licensed surplus lines broker.

6. **C.** *Producer* is the general term applied to someone who sells insurance. He may be licensed as an agent, a broker, or a solicitor, depending on circumstance and state law.

7. **D.** While applicants for insurance licenses must complete an application, take an exam, and complete a course of study before the exam, they need not have a college degree.

8. **C.** Agents are involved in taking applications for insurance, transmitting them to insurers, examining risks, and collecting premiums. Company representatives or independent contractors working for an insurer adjust and pay claims.

9. **D.** The authority an agent possesses is either expressed in a contract, called the agency agreement, implied by necessity to carry out duties expressly authorized, or apparent to the buying public by virtue of the agent's conduct.

10. **C.** The authority an agent possesses is either expressed in a contract, called the agency agreement, implied by necessity to carry out duties expressly authorized, or apparent to the buying public by virtue of the agent's conduct.

11. **D.** The authority an agent possesses is either expressed in a contract, called the agency agreement, implied by necessity to carry out duties expressly authorized, or apparent to the buying public by virtue of the agent's conduct.

12. **D.** A broker transacts insurance with an insurance company on behalf of her clients, while an agent is an insurer's legal representative.

13. **B.** A nonresident agent is licensed in one state, but conducts business in another state, often requiring countersignature.

14. **A.** An insurer is classified as domestic (domiciled in its state), foreign (domiciled in another state), or alien (domiciled in another country).

15. **B.** An insurer is classified as domestic (domiciled in its state), foreign (domiciled in another state), or alien (domiciled in another country).

16. **D.** A reciprocal insurer is considered a cooperative insurer attempting to provide products and services to its members rather than profits for the owners.

17. **B.** A reciprocal insurer is considered a cooperative insurer attempting to provide products and services to its members rather than profits for the owners.

18. **D.** The government frequently provides insurance in cases where it is needed and

commercially uninsurable, such as unemployment, flood, crop, workers' compensation, and nuclear energy.

19. **B.** An agent who represents only one company under contract is an exclusive agent.

20. **C.** A company that uses a direct method of distribution by phone, mail or other means, rather than by using agents, is a direct writer.

21. **C.** Determining prices based on an applicant's income is considered unfair discrimination and is not an appropriate (or legal) underwriting action.

22. **B.** Insurance is inherently discriminatory, classifying risks based on similar characteristics and chances of loss; however, it is not intended to be unfairly discriminatory.

23. **D.** The types of rating laws in effect are prior approval, file and use, open competition, and mandatory rates.

24. **B.** 250,000 divided by 1,000 is 250. 250 times a rate of $1 equals $250.

25. **D.** 35 million divided by 100 million produces an expense ratio of 35%. 70 million divided by 100 million produces a loss ratio of 70%. 35% added to 70% (combined ratio equals loss plus expense) equals 105%.

26. **C.** An underwriting loss occurs when the combined total of claims paid and expenses incurred exceeds the amount of premiums received.

27. **B.** The methods insurers use to set loss reserves are case reserve, average value method, loss ratio method, and tabular method.

28. **C.** Insurers may expand premiums based on the amount of policyholder surplus, or assets exceeding liabilities, that they possess.

29. **B.** Reinsurance, the insurance company's insurance policy, allows the primary insurer to transfer risk to the reinsurer. This lessens its potential liabilities, allowing it to write more primary insurance.

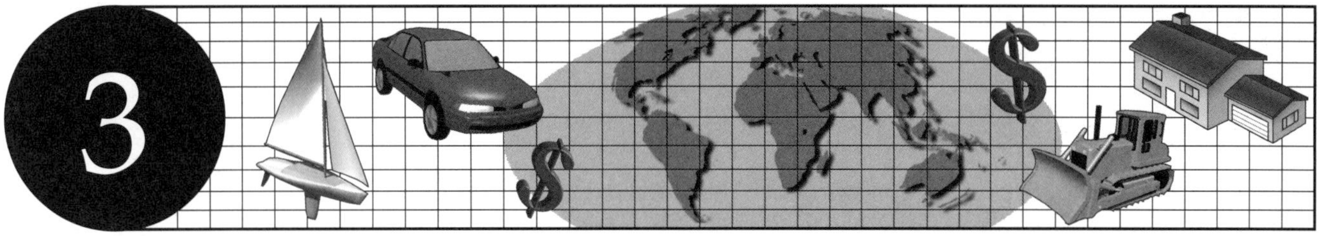


# Contract Law and the Insurance Industry

## INTRODUCTION

The insurance contract spells out the legal responsibilities and obligations of both the insurer and the policyholder. Although they have been modernized in recent years, insurance policies are still complex legal documents that require careful study and analysis. Mastering the art of insurance policy language is one of the skills required of a true insurance professional.

This unit provides an overview of the legal concepts involved in insurance contract formation and offers a foundation for the study of specific policy provisions contained in Unit 4. It also reviews some of the more common insurance policy provisions that may be found in many insurance contracts.

## UNIT OBJECTIVES

When you have completed this unit, you should be able to:

- distinguish between representations and warranties in insurance applications;
- differentiate between representation, concealment, and fraud as they relate to insurance contract formation;
- identify the major parts of an insurance policy;
- list the essential elements of a valid contract; and
- explain the characteristics of insurance contracts.

# Applications for Insurance

## Application

An **application** is the form on which the prospective insured states or declares facts the insurance company requests. The insurance company underwrites the risk based on these facts and decides whether to accept the application, modify the coverage that was requested or decline the application. The application usually is considered the offer to purchase an insurance policy.

## Representations, Warranties, and Concealment

### Representations

A **representation** is a written or an oral statement the applicant makes that is true to the best of his knowledge or belief.

**Test Topic Alert!**

A representation is a factual statement on an application that is made to the best of one's knowledge. The person making the statement does not warrant that it is actually true, but only that it is true to the best of that person's knowledge and belief.

If the statement turns out to be false, the **misrepresentation** may provide grounds for the insurer to cancel the contract or deny a claim. Such action, however, can occur only if the misrepresentation involves a material fact. A **material fact** is a statement that may have caused the insurance company to reject the application or issue the policy on substantially different terms if the insurance company had known the correct information.

In some cases, an insurance company elects to void an insurance contract. To void a contract is to cancel retroactively to the original effective date. In general, the misrepresentation must be made with fraudulent intent before the insurer can use it as grounds to void the policy. Some states also mandate that a misrepresentation or the concealment of a material fact must contribute to the loss before it can be grounds for voiding the policy.

✓ ***For Example:*** If an insured represented to an insurance company that he had an alarm system and a burglary occurred, the company could deny the loss if, in fact, no alarm existed.

In other states, the law prevents the voiding of certain insurance contracts. Nevertheless, these states allow the policies to be canceled and claims denied based on misrepresentation.

**Warranties** When a representation is made a part of the insurance contract, usually by physical attachment of the application to the policy, the insured's statements become **warranties**. Warranties also include promises of the insured that are set forth in the policy. For example, a promise by the insured to maintain a burglar alarm in proper working order at all times is a promissory warranty. A breach of a warranty, meaning that the statement is not correct, may give grounds for cancellation of a policy, and unlike representations, it may do so without reference to the materiality of the statement or promise. Therefore, a warranty must be absolutely true.

Because of the severity of the legal doctrine of warranties, courts and state law have tended to modify its strict application. Courts may require that the breach of warranty materially increase the risk before it can be used to void an insurance policy. In some cases, a policy itself may state that the statements in the application, a copy of which is attached to the policy, are only representations and not warranties. In some states, statements made on applications are considered representations, not warranties.

Other requirements may include that the breach of warranty can be used to cancel a policy only if it increased the risk of loss or only if it contributed to the loss. Because of the confusion that may result from using warranties in a policy, an insurer may, instead, include an **exclusion** in the policy.

✓ ***For Example:*** An exclusion may indicate that coverage is not applicable while any burglar alarm equipment is in disrepair or not properly connected. Or, if the equipment is not working properly, the company may limit coverage to some stated percentage of normal limits of liability.

**Concealment** Not only must the applicant disclose accurate information, he also has the obligation to voluntarily reveal material facts that may affect the underwriting of insurance if the company could not be expected to know about them. Failure to disclose such facts may constitute a **concealment**, and willful concealment of a material fact gives the insurer grounds for cancelling the policy or denying a claim.

✓ ***Take Note:*** Material facts normally are extraordinary facts known to the applicant, that would not commonly be asked about on a standard application.

✓ ***For Example:*** If an insured regularly permitted a local scout troop to use his property to camp and conduct exercises, the insurance company would not be expected to know this or ask questions to determine whether this were the case. The applicant would have to disclose this fact to the company. Similar to laws regarding warranties, state laws have modified the general concealment doctrine by requiring that the fact concealed contribute to the loss before it can be grounds for canceling the policy.

**Fraud** Fraud is an intentional misrepresentation of the facts. Insurance fraud has become a serious problem in recent years. An insurance contract requires that an applicant deal in good faith with the insurance company in providing necessary underwriting information. In many cases, neither the company nor the agent actually has seen or inspected the property to be insured. The issuance of a policy presumes that any losses will be fortuitous, not within the policyholder's control. When a policy has been issued with the intent to commit insurance fraud, the insurer may rescind the contract, effectively saying that it never was recognized as valid. Insurance fraud is a felony in most states, and insurance companies have been much more aggressive in pursuing legal action against people who commit this crime.

### Waiver and Estoppel

A **waiver** is the voluntary relinquishment of a known right and waiver may be intentional or unintentional.

✓ ***For Example:*** If an insurance company sends out a renewal policy, it has waived its right to refuse renewal coverage.

**Estoppel** means that when something is allowed to occur repeatedly, the defenses to it are waived. Estoppel prevents an insurance company from reasserting a right it has waived previously.

✓ ***For Example:*** An insurance company that continually accepts late payments from the insured is estopped from denying coverage when a policy could be cancelled because of nonpayment.

### Parol Evidence Rule

Another rule of law in insurance contracts is the **parol evidence rule**, which provides that any oral statements leading up to a contract should be incorporated into the contract if they are to affect its terms. An insurance company that seeks to deny coverage based on a statement the insured made before contract formation will be estopped from using this defense to defeat the contract.

### Doctrine of Reasonable Expectation

The **doctrine of reasonable expectation** states that if an insurance policy's terms are ambiguous, they are to be interpreted in a way that meets the reasonable expectations of the insured. This means that the insured should recover what a reasonable person would expect to recover under similar circumstances. Insurance producers should be careful not to overstate the coverage that a policy offers. Such statements can give the insured a false impression of the coverage.

## Quick Quiz 3.1

1. When an applicant for insurance hides a material fact from the insurer, this is called __________.
2. When an applicant intentionally misrepresents the facts on an application, it is referred to as __________.
3. When the facts stated on an application do not accurately reflect the true situation, it is called __________.
4. To avoid paying claims under a policy, an insurer must demonstrate that a fact withheld, omitted or misstated was of a __________ nature.
5. When an insurer gives up a right possessed, it is referred to as __________ and the insurer is __________ from reasserting that right.

### *Answers*

1. *concealment*
2. *fraud*
3. *misrepresentation*
4. *material*
5. *waiver, estopped*

# Parts of an Insurance Policy

The four basic parts of a policy are: declarations, insuring agreement, conditions, and exclusions. They can be remembered by the acronym **DICE**:

- **D**eclarations (or simply Dec Page);
- **I**nsuring Agreement;
- **C**onditions; and
- **E**xclusions.

Not all policies are arranged the same way, but all contain the four basic policy parts. In addition, most policies include a section containing important definitions and endorsements, or amendments to the basic policy.

## Declarations, Declaration Page, or Dec Page

The **Declarations Page** contains the statements, or at least some of them, the insured made on the application; information about the risk; and other pertinent data, such as insured's name, effective date of coverage, deductible, premium amounts, coinsurance percentage, and location of the property. The who, what, where, when, and how much are spelled out in the Declarations. This information personalizes an insurance policy.

## Insuring Agreement

The **insuring agreement** contains the insurance company's promise to pay for loss, if it should result from the perils insured against. In addition, the insured promises to pay the appropriate premium. Both cases are promises of utmost good faith concerning the consideration, or promises of value. This section also indicates what coverages the contract offers.

## Conditions

The **Conditions** spell out, in detail, both the insurer's and the insured's rights and duties. These conditions relate to the insured's duties in the event of loss, change of risk or exposure, as well as the process to be followed if a disagreement occurs about the value of a loss. This section does not give or exclude coverage; it simply sets forth the ground rules or administration of the policy itself. Think of this section as the strings attached to the promises set forth in the insuring agreement.

✓ ***For Example:*** Property insurance policies often require the insureds to report theft losses to the police.

## Exclusions

In the **Exclusions**, the insurance company states what perils or property it will not cover or under what situations the coverage does not apply. The Exclusions must be read in conjunction with the Insuring Agreement (the section in which the perils insured against are described). Perils generally are excluded because they are uninsurable, such as catastrophic events like war or flood, or because the basic premium does not contemplate the exposure, such as automobile coverage under a homeowner's policy.

## Definitions

A contract normally does not include a Definitions section. However, most insurance policies contain a glossary of terms. The purpose of this section is to clearly establish the specific meanings of certain words used in the policy versus their meanings when used commonly.

## Endorsements

An **endorsement** is a form attached to a policy that changes the policy to fit special circumstances. Such modification of the contract is not permitted unless the insurance company approves it in writing. An endorsement may be attached at the beginning of the policy or added during the policy's term.

## Binders

A **binder** is a temporary contract, issued for a short period of time (30 to 60 days), that a company uses as evidence of insurance until the final contract is delivered. The binder is usually in writing, although some states permit it to be oral. The binder issued by the company or by an agent on behalf of the company is accepted by the insured with the understanding that it provides the same coverage as the policy form that the company will issue.

**Test Topic Alert!** A binder is temporary proof of coverage until the policy is issued. It can provide immediate coverage.

## Quick Quiz 3.2

Match the following terms with their definitions. One term does not match any definition given.

Binder
Insuring agreement
Exclusion
Condition
Declarations
Endorsement
Definition

1. __________ A policy provision that eliminates coverage under certain situations
2. __________ Temporary evidence of insurance pending policy issuance
3. __________ A term that has been given a specific meaning within an insurance policy
4. __________ A document attached to a policy that modifies the terms and conditions
5. __________ The portion of a policy that broadly defines the obligations of the parties
6. __________ A policy provision that details the rights and duties of each party to the contract

***Answers***

*1. Exclusion*

*2. Binder*

3. *Definition*
4. *Endorsement*
5. *Insuring Agreement*
6. *Condition*

## General Contract Law

Generally, any valid contract, including an insurance policy, has four basic elements:

- competent parties;
- legal purpose;
- offer and acceptance; and
- consideration.

### Competent Parties

Parties to a contract must have a legal capacity to contract. Certain parties cannot enter into a contract, but generally have the authority to void the contract. Such persons include minors, insane persons, convicts, aliens, and persons otherwise unable to make an informed decision. In most cases, insurance companies do not have legal capacity to enter into insurance contracts until they are licensed or admitted by their states.

### Legal Purpose and Public Policy

A contract's purpose must be legal and not against public policy. For instance, a contract to have a person killed is not legally binding or valid.

### Offer and Acceptance

Every contract should contain one party's offer and another party's acceptance of that offer. Usually, the application for insurance is considered an offer the buyer makes, and a binding contract does not exist until the insurance company accepts that offer. Property and casualty agents usually have the authority to bind coverage—that is, to accept insurance on behalf of their companies.

FIGURE 3.1 Elements and Characteristics of a Property and Casualty Insurance Contract

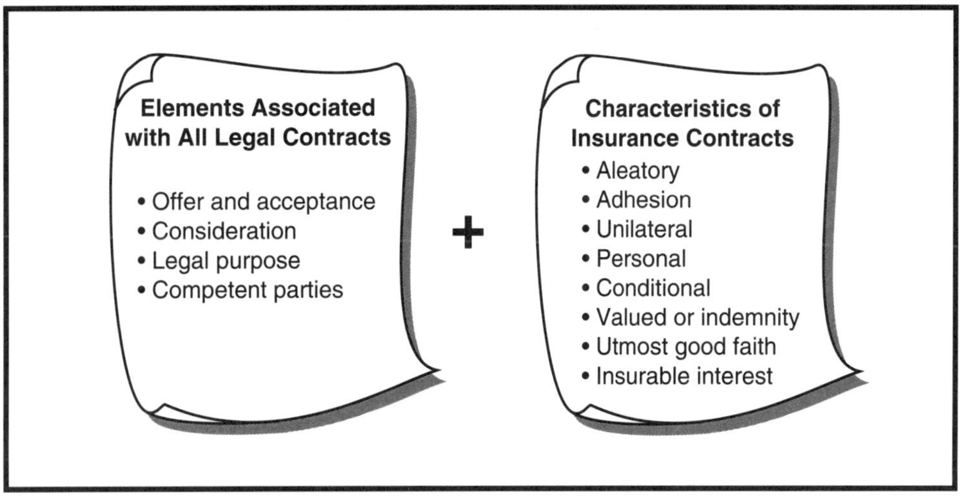


## Consideration

Each party to a contract may give **consideration**—that is, an exchange of values. In an insurance policy, the insured's consideration is payment of the premium. The company's consideration is the promise to pay in case of a covered loss.

# Special Legal Characteristics of Insurance Policies as Contracts

All legal contracts share certain characteristics. As legal contracts, insurance policies are characterized by the following legal doctrines.

## Contract of Adhesion

An insurance contract is drawn up by the insurer and is either accepted or rejected by the applicant. The applicant cannot modify or alter the contract. This type of contract is referred to as a **contract of adhesion**. Because the insurer alone draws up the contract, courts generally have held that any ambiguity in the contract should be interpreted in favor of the insured. An ambiguity exists whenever a term in the policy could be interpreted in two different ways.

## Unilateral Contract

An insurance contract is also a **unilateral contract,** which means only one party (the insurer) makes a legally enforceable promise (to pay a claim). The insured can stop paying the premium at any time.

## Aleatory Contract

**Aleatory** means that the outcome of the contract is affected by chance and that the consideration given up is unequal. The insured pays a relatively small premium and receives no dollars back if no loss occurs. If a loss does occur, however, the insurer may pay a claim that exceeds the premium dollars received.

## Personal Contract

A policy for property and casualty insurance is a **personal contract** between the insured and insurer. It may not be transferred to another person or organization without the insurer's written consent.

## Conditional

An insurance contract is **conditional** because the insurer's promise to pay is conditioned upon several things: the occurrence of an insured event, the insured's fulfillment of the policy terms, and the existence of insurable interest.

## Utmost Good Faith

An insurance contract requires **utmost good faith** between the parties. This means that each party can rely on the other's statements and representations. No attempt to conceal information or deceive the other party should occur.

## Indemnity

Insurance is a contract designed to reimburse an insured who suffers a loss. In some cases, such as in liability insurance, payments are made on the insured's behalf. The insurance contract intends to put the insured back in the same financial condition he enjoyed before a loss, no better and no worse. Many policy provisions support the concept of **indemnity** in insurance contracts.

# Insurance Contract Provisions

## Sources of Underwriting Information

The primary source of information is the application containing an insured's statements. The agent, broker or producer who sees the applicant or property is another source of information.

**Investigations** or **inspection reports**, sometimes referred to as **consumer reports**, are another source of information. Data that may be collected about an insured include financial status, occupation, character, and the alleged use of alcoholic beverages. Some state and federal laws prevent certain personal information from being used as underwriting criteria.

An insurer also may request information from the motor vehicle department regarding an individual's driving history. Inspections, including photographs by an agent or by a company inspector, also may be obtained to determine suitability of a property for fire or liability insurance. Inspections of premises by independent companies may also be made.

## Fair Credit Reporting Act

The **Fair Credit Reporting Act** is a federal law requiring that an applicant for insurance be advised that a consumer report may be requested, if such is the case. The applicant must also be informed of the scope of the investigation the insurance company may request. If coverage is denied or restricted solely on the basis of the report, the applicant must be supplied with the name and address of the reporting company that collected the information. The applicant has the right to obtain from this company a copy of the information in its files. The consumer may dispute any information in the report. The reporting company then must reinvestigate and change its report, if so indicated.

## Insured

The **insured** (sometimes referred to as the **named insured**) is that party to an insurance arrangement whom the insurance company agrees to indemnify for losses and to whom the company provides benefits or renders service. A policy may consider, by definition, persons other than the named insured as persons insured under the policy. The spouse of the named insured, without having their name appear in the policy, may be an insured by virtue of their relationship to the named insured. Some policies also refer to the **first named insured**. This is literally the first person or entity listed on the Declarations Page. The first named insured is the only one authorized to change the policy, receive claim payments or premium refunds, or cancel the policy. In addition, this person is responsible for paying the premium.

## Duties of the Insured

The insured's duties may be a separate section of a policy. Nevertheless, they are part of the policy conditions. These duties include notifying the insurance company in case of loss, furnishing proof of loss, and protecting property from further damage.

## Notice of Claim

The insurance company requires **notice** of any loss within a specified time. This notice allows the insurer to begin its investigation and claim processing. The company may send a claims form to be completed by the insured. The insured also is responsible for turning over any legal documents, including those related to lawsuits, to the insurer promptly upon receipt.

## Proof of Loss

The **proof of loss** (the properly completed claim form) is a formal statement made by the insured to the insurance company regarding a loss. It is usually in the form of an affidavit, and its purpose is to give the insurer sufficient information about the loss to enable it to determine its liability under the policy. The proof of loss contains such items as time and cause of loss, interest of the insured or other persons who may be partial owners of the property, identification of all liens on the property, other insurance, if any, and an inventory of damaged property.

## Mortgagee Clause

The **mortgagee clause** (standard mortgage clause), or **lien holder's endorsement,** is a provision noting that any loss payment will be payable to the mortgage or lien holder as its financial interest may appear (balance due on the loan) and that the mortgage holder's right of recovery will not be defeated by any act or negligence of the insured. This clause may be attached to or made a part of the policy covering the mortgaged property. The clause also gives the mortgagee other rights and privileges, including the right to 10 days' prior notice of policy cancellation by the insured or insurer and the right to sue the insurer in its own name, rather than through the insured, in the event of a dispute.

## Loss Payable Clause

Property insurance policies contain a provision that authorizes the insurer to make a loss payment to an entity (called a **loss payee**) other than the insured to the extent that the loss payee has an insurable interest in the property.

Loss payees typically include automobile lienholders and property mortgagees that have loaned money to the insured to purchase property. The extent of a claim for damage to property is measured by the amount of the loss suffered by the property owner.

## No Benefit to Bailee

**Bailees**, or persons temporarily holding property of others, often accept by bailment contract or common law some risks from the property owners. Liability for damage to the property held is shifted from the property owner to the bailee. For example, when a customer leaves a coat to be dry cleaned, the dry cleaner takes temporary possession of that coat. The dry cleaner, called the bailee, will often provide a receipt when accepting a bailor's property. The bailee must exercise a high degree of care in protecting property in their care, custody, or control.

Liability policies usually exclude coverage for damage to property in the insured's care, custody or control. The **No Benefit To Bailee exclusion** in liability policies prohibits the bailee from collecting from the property owner's liability policy should a loss occur. In some cases, liability policies can be endorsed to afford protection. Sometimes separate property or inland marine insurance policies are purchased, covering only property held under contract.

## Appraisal

Most property-related policies provide that if the insurer and the insured cannot agree on the value of a loss, the matter will be submitted to disinterested parties for resolution. This process is known as **appraisal**. The insured chooses one appraiser and the insurance company the other. The two appraisers then choose a third party, known as an **umpire**. Each party pays the cost of the appraiser it selects and splits the fee for the umpire and other appraisal costs. Majority rule determines the value of the loss to be paid.

This procedure is not used to determine whether a loss is covered, only the value of the loss. Policy provisions dictate coverage. Any dispute as to coverage is a matter for a civil court to resolve.

## Assign/Assignment/Transfer of the Insured's Interest in the Policy

A policy for property and casualty insurance is a personal contract between the insured and the insurance company, often insuring a described piece of property or personal risk. Because the insurer wants a chance to investigate a person before issuing a policy to him, a provision in the contract usually allows **assignment** to another person only if the insurer agrees to it in writing. Generally, the insured may assign proceeds of a loss settlement without permission from the insurer. An example would be when a person signs over an insurance claim check to a lender.

## Subrogation and Insurer's Right to Recover Payment

When a company pays the insured for a loss for which some person other than the policyholder is responsible, the insurer has the right to recover its loss from the negligent party. This is the right of **subrogation**. The insurer steps into the insured's place to take legal action against the negligent party, but only to the extent of the amount the insurance company paid the to the insured. The insurance company also may recover the insured's deductible, but it has no responsibility to do so. The insured must do everything necessary to secure these rights for the insurer and must do nothing after a loss to impair these rights.

**Test Topic Alert!**

Subrogation allows an insurance company to collect damages paid to the insured from a negligent third party.

This principle is designed to prevent the insured from collecting from the insurance company, then taking his own legal action against the party who caused the loss and collecting from that party as well. This violates the principle of indemnity.

**Test Topic Alert!**

A person is negligent if he fails to act as a reasonable and prudent person would under the circumstances.

## Pro Rata Liability

If more than one insurance company has a policy covering the same property (building, auto for physical damage, etc.) or if two or more policies apply to a liability claim, each company pro rates its payment for the loss. This also may be expressed as a clause in the contract that reads: "The company's share is the proportion that its limit of liability bears to the total of all applicable limits whether collectible or not." This usually is found in the Other Insurance section of the contract.

✓ ***For Example:***

| | |
|---|---|
| Total Insurance | $1,000,000 |
| Loss | $ 300,000 |
| Proportionate Share Policy | |

| | Limits | | Share of Loss |
|---|---|---|---|
| Company A | $ 500,000 | (½) | $150,000 |
| Company B | $ 250,000 | (¼) | $ 75,000 |
| Company C | $ 250,000 | (¼) | $ 75,000 |
| | $1,000,000 | | $300,000 |

Each company pays only its share. If one company is insolvent, the other companies will pay only their pro rata share of the loss. They will not pay the insolvent company's share.

# Unit Test Three

1. Statements a person makes in an application for insurance that he or she claims are true to the best of his knowledge are

   A. warranties
   B. concealments
   C. representations
   D. misrepresentations

2. Statements made in an insurance application are considered to be

   A. warranties
   B. representations
   C. possible concealments
   D. guarantees

3. Deliberate failure to reveal material facts that would affect the validity of a policy of insurance is known as

   A. inducement
   B. concealment
   C. collusion
   D. rebating

4. An insurance contract can be modified by a(n)

   A. condition
   B. addendum
   C. memorandum
   D. endorsement

5. Which of the following statements about the principle of subrogation is CORRECT?

   A. It prevents the insured from collecting twice for a loss.
   B. It sometimes conflicts with the principle of indemnity.
   C. It increases the cost of insurance.
   D. It applies only in ocean marine insurance.

6. When an insurer sues a negligent third party to recover a loss paid to an insured, the company is exercising its right of

   A. assignment
   B. arbitration
   C. estoppel
   D. subrogation

7. The mortgage clause in a property insurance policy does each of the following EXCEPT

   A. guarantees that the lending institution may act for itself in paying a premium
   B. guarantees that claim payments will be divided as the interests of the insured and mortgagee appear
   C. acts as a separate agreement between the mortgagee and the insurance company
   D. guarantees that the policyholder will make mortgage payments on time

8. Which of the following defines an insurance binder?

   A. Always issued before a policy is issued
   B. Form of agreement that cannot be oral
   C. Form of agreement that grants temporary insurance protection until replaced by a policy
   D. Form of agreement that determines whether a company issues a policy

9. The intentional misrepresentation of material facts in an insurance application is called

   A. misrepresentation
   B. misunderstanding
   C. fraud
   D. concealment

10. Which of the following statements regarding the parol evidence rule is CORRECT?
    A. It requires substantial evidence before convicted criminals can be released from prison.
    B. It prevents an insurance company from using oral statements unless they are incorporated into a contract.
    C. It provides a means by which an insured can demonstrate that he did not commit fraud in applying for insurance.
    D. It allows an insurance company to relinquish a right it has possessed previously.

11. The part of an insurance contract that expresses the statements made by an applicant for insurance is known as the
    A. conditions
    B. expressions
    C. declarations
    D. agreements

12. When an insurance company requires that insured property be located within a certain geographic area to be compensated for a loss, this is an example of a policy
    A. exclusion
    B. condition
    C. warranty
    D. definition

13. The part of a policy that reflects changes that have been made since the beginning of the policy period is called a(n)
    A. endorsement
    B. amendment
    C. restriction
    D. exclusion

14. To have a legally valid contract, each of the following must be present EXCEPT
    A. consideration
    B. competent parties
    C. notarization
    D. acceptance of an offer

15. In an insurance contract, the consideration that the insurer exchanges is the
    A. offer to reinstate
    B. premium
    C. policy
    D. promise to pay

16. When an insurance policy contains ambiguous wording, which of the following represents the legal doctrine that the courts apply in interpreting the contract?
    A. Estoppel
    B. Insurable interest
    C. Adhesion
    D. Utmost good faith

17. The legal doctrine that holds that the parties to a contract may give up unequal consideration is called
    A. adhesion
    B. aleatory
    C. alienation
    D. ad hoc

18. Which of the following is required to transfer a property and casualty insurance policy from one party to another?
    A. Written consent
    B. Payment of premium
    C. Binding arbitration
    D. All of the above

19. Which of the following is NOT an example of a source of underwriting information used by property and casualty insurance companies?
    A. Investigative report
    B. Driving record obtained from the motor vehicle department
    C. Confidential medical report
    D. Application completed by the insured's agent

20. The federal law that protects the privacy rights of applicants for insurance and requires that companies disclose the reasons for rejecting applicants is the

    A. Americans with Disabilities Act
    B. Privacy Act
    C. Fair Claims Act
    D. Fair Credit Reporting Act

21. The form that may be required when an insured submits a claim to the insurance company is the

    A. witness statement
    B. proof of loss
    C. claimant form
    D. appraisal form

22. One of an insurance contract's provisions that helps support the principle of indemnity is

    A. subrogation
    B. arbitration
    C. appraisal
    D. consent

23. Mr. and Mrs. Smith agreed that they needed to secure an insurance policy for their new home. Each approached a different agent and company and purchased the following insurance:

| | |
|---|---|
| Mr. Smith | $300,000 |
| Mrs. Smith | $400,000 |

    They later suffered a loss of $70,000 when a fire damaged their home. What is the total obligation of Mrs. Smith's insurer?

    A. $30,000
    B. $40,000
    C. $70,000
    D. $400,000

# Unit Test Three Answers & Rationale

1. **C.** Warranties are statements that are absolutely true and must continue to be so during a contract. Representations are statements that are true to the best of someone's knowledge. State law generally makes the statements made in the process of obtaining insurance representations rather than warranties.

2. **B.** Warranties are statements that are absolutely true and must continue to be so during a contract. Representations are statements that are true to the best of someone's knowledge. State law generally makes the statements made in the process of obtaining insurance representations rather than warranties.

3. **B.** Failure to reveal facts an applicant knows and should disclose is considered concealment.

4. **D.** Insurance contracts can be modified in writing only. The document attached to a policy making a change is called an endorsement.

5. **A.** Subrogation is important to support the principle of indemnity because it prevents an insured from collecting from his insurer, then collecting a second time from the party that caused the loss.

6. **D.** The transfer of an insured's right to recover from a third party to the insurance company following payment of a claim is known as subrogation.

7. **D.** Nothing guarantees that a mortgage holder will make payments to the bank or lending institution. Mortgage clauses protect these institutions by allowing them to pay premiums to keep coverage in force and have claim payments payable to them. The mortgage clause functions as a separate agreement between an insurer and a lending institution.

8. **C.** A binder is temporary evidence that insurance has been placed pending issuance of the policy contract. It may be written or oral.

9. **C.** Fraud is the intentional misrepresentation of facts by an applicant for insurance or in the process of settling a claim.

10. **B.** The parol evidence rule mandates that the statements leading up to the formation of an insurance contract must be incorporated into the contract to be binding on the applicant.

11. **C.** The items that the applicant declares (represents) to be true are placed on the front, or declarations, page of the insurance policy.

12. **B.** Conditions are the *ifs*, *whiles*, and *but nots* of an insurance contract. They are strings attached to the promise. Most policies require that losses occur in a certain area before payment is made. Losses that occur while outside the specified area are not covered. These are conditions on the insurer's promise to pay losses.

13. **A.** Insurance contracts can be modified in writing only. The document attached to a policy making a change is called an endorsement.

14. **C.** A legal contract's requirements are offer and acceptance (agreement), consideration, competent parties and legal purpose.

15. **D.** Consideration is merely something of value exchanged in a contract. For the insured this is the premium, and for the insurer it is the promise to pay future claims.

16. **C.** The doctrine of adhesion places the burden of clear language on an insurer and requires that ambiguities be construed favorably toward policyholders.

17. **B.** *Aleatory* is a term used to define an unequal exchange between two parties to a contract. In insurance, the insured must pay a certain

sum, called the premium, that is potentially much smaller than the amount he or she might collect from the insurer in the event of a loss.

18. **A.** A property and casualty insurance policy is considered a personal contract and cannot be transferred without the insurer's written consent.

19. **C.** A confidential medical report is an important underwriting item for life or health insurance, but almost never is appropriate for property and casualty products.

20. **D.** The Fair Credit Reporting Act is a federal law that requires that applicants for insurance be told (1) that consumer reports might be obtained and (2) the exact scope of any investigative reports that may be conducted in connection with an application for insurance.

21. **B.** A proof of loss is a sworn, properly completed claim form signed by an insured before payment of a loss.

22. **A.** Subrogation is important to support the principle of indemnity because it prevents an insured from collecting from his insurer, then collecting a second time from the party that caused the loss. The transfer of an insured's right to recover from a third party to the insurance company following payment of a claim is known as subrogation.

23. **B.** The pro rata liability clause states that a company's share is the proportion that its limit of liability bears to the total of all applicable limits, whether or not collectible. In this case, Mrs. Smith's policy is $400,000/$700,000, or $\frac{4}{7}$ of the total amount of insurance. Four-sevenths of a loss of $70,000 is $40,000.

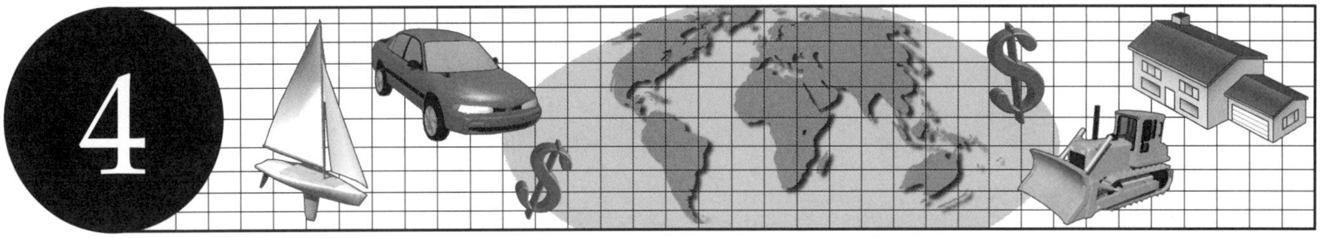


# Contract Terms and Definitions

## INTRODUCTION

Insurance policy terms and conditions vary based on the type of insurance involved. Some terms are used exclusively in property insurance, others in casualty and some in both areas. While most modern insurance policies contain a Definitions section, or an internal glossary, the vast majority of terms in an insurance contract are not defined within the policy, leaving them open to misunderstanding and misinterpretation. It is important, therefore, to understand the various provisions contained in insurance policies and the intent behind their inclusion in the forms. Policy terms and conditions are not designed to be incomprehensible, although they can seem that way at times—not only to consumers, but also to insurance professionals.

This unit will discuss some of the major contract terms and definitions nearly all individual policies contain.

## UNIT OBJECTIVES

When you have completed this unit, you should be able to:

- describe the various types of insurance and their purposes;
- explain the operation of various insurance policy provisions;
- define some of the important terms insurance policies contain; and
- distinguish between property and casualty insurance provisions.

# Types of Insurance

Traditionally, insurance coverage has been categorized as property, casualty, life, and health. This text is concerned only with property and casualty insurance.

## Property Insurance

**Property insurance** protects against losses due to fire and other causes, such as windstorm, hail, or theft, to items of real and personal property. Such insurance is designed primarily to protect against direct financial loss resulting from damage to or destruction of the property itself, but also may include consequential losses that result from damage to property. The major types of property insurance follow:

- **Fire and allied (related) lines insurance**. Covers property at specified locations; and
- **Marine insurance**. Protects against loss of property in the course of transportation—in other words property not at a specific location (sometimes referred to as **floaters**). Marine insurance is further divided into:
  - **Ocean marine**. Covers all types of oceangoing vessels, cargo (import and export shipments) and shipowner's liability; and
  - **Inland marine**. Covers domestic shipments; instruments of transportation and communication such as bridges, tunnels, and radio towers; and personal property floater risks.

## Casualty Insurance

**Casualty insurance** was developed after fire, marine, and life insurance. It is a broad term that encompasses all types of coverage that are not part of property, marine, or life insurance. **Liability insurance**, one of the major components of the casualty insurance category, pays for loss due to the insured's negligence. This negligence may come from some responsibility imposed by law or assumed by contract. The insurance company makes the payment to a third party on behalf of the insured. Casualty insurance also includes personal automobile protection, workers' compensation, burglary, robbery, theft, and fidelity and surety bonds.

### Package Policies

Before 1950, insurance was written on a **mono-line basis**. In other words, a company wrote only one line of coverage, either property or liability. This was due to the fact that insurers were authorized as either property or casualty companies. Starting in the 1950s, and following changes in state laws, insurance companies began writing package policies that combined property coverages with liability. Policies that include several types of insurance are **multiple-lines,** or simply **multi-lines**. Sometimes these contracts are referred to incorrectly as **multi-perils**, which really just means that more than one peril is covered in the policies.

✓ ***Take Note:*** Have you ever wondered why different types of insurance are referred to as *lines* of business? This term comes from the fact that each insurer must file an annual statement with the insurance departments of the states in which they operate. Included in this report is a line-by-line listing of each type of coverage written, thus the name.

## Property and Casualty Classifications

The person who owns an office building and the person who owns a home face many of the same property risks, such as fire, lightning, wind, and theft, as well as liability arising from negligent conduct. Nevertheless, some differences in the risks exist. Therefore, insurance policies also are categorized as **commercial lines** (business) and **personal lines** (nonbusiness).

Many of the insuring agreements, conditions and exclusions in the two categories, or lines of insurance, are similar; however, certain features are unique to each. Some of the common features were presented in Unit 3. Unique property descriptions or causes of loss found in specific contracts will be presented as various policies are described later in this text.

# Provisions Common to Property and Casualty Insurance

Some of the contract provisions that might be found in either a property or casualty policy include the following.

## Limit of Liability

The **limit of liability** is the maximum amount an insurance company will pay in case of a loss; sometimes it is referred to as the policy's **face amount**. Despite a maximum amount payable for a loss, a policy may impose internal or sublimits of insurance—such as $2,000 for loss by theft of firearms in a homeowner's policy, regardless of larger limits of insurance on the home and personal property.

### Property Insurance

In **property insurance**, the limit of liability is stated as a single dollar amount. A homeowner's policy that insures the house for $100,000 will pay no more than $100,000 for damage or destruction of the house (less the appropriate deductible). This limit applies for any one occurrence, with no limit on how many times the company may have to pay for separate occurrences during the policy period.

### Liability Insurance

In **liability insurance**, a policy may cover several categories of claims stemming from different types of activity of the insured: **bodily injury (BI) liability**, **property damage (PD) liability**, **personal injury liability**, and **advertising injury**. The policy will pay no more than the stated amount per occurrence. The limit of insurance for bodily injury, property damage, advertising injury or personal injury may be expressed as one amount (a **combined single limit**), such as $300,000 per occurrence for bodily injury, property damage or both combined. Or it may be expressed as a **split limit**, such as 100/300/50, which indicates $100,000 per person and $300,000 per occurrence for bodily injury and $50,000 per occurrence for property damage.

### Aggregate Limits

A policy also may have an annual **aggregate limit**, which is the maximum amount the policy will pay in any one policy year for all occurrences. This aggregate limit may be for one coverage or all coverages under the policy.

✓ ***Take Note:*** Because an aggregate limit is a maximum amount that the insurer will pay in any single policy year, it is actually possible for the insured to run out of insurance. This is called **exhausting the aggregate**. When the aggregate is depleted but some coverage remains, the aggregate is said to be **impaired**. Aggregate limits can be reduced only by the actual payment of claims, not by reserves set to settle claims in the future.

### Limits Per Occurrence

The limit of liability (whether per occurrence or aggregate) applies regardless of the number of:

- persons or organizations insured under the policy;
- persons or organizations who have sustained injury or damage; or
- claims made or suits brought because of injury or damage.

Thus, if someone names an insured and a spouse in a claim under a homeowner's policy, the limit of insurance applies to that one occurrence, not separately to both the insured and the spouse.

### Test Topic Alert!

The most an insurance company will pay on any loss is the amount of the loss or the policy limit, whichever is lower.

### Duty to Defend Provision

Under the terms of the Duty to Defend provision under a liability policy, the insurer has an obligation to defend the insured in a suit brought by a third party. For occurrences covered by the policy, a defense must be provided even if a suit is found to be groundless or false. However, there is no duty to defend a suit if the complaint or petition fails to state facts that potentially bring the case within the coverage of the policy.

In most policies, the defense expenses are covered in addition to policy limits; however, some policies include this expense in the limit, which reduces the amount available for damages by the costs of defense.

## Deductibles

In most cases, a **deductible clause** is included in a policy. This clause requires the insured to pay a small portion of the loss, with the insurance company paying the remainder. Companies include deductibles for two reasons: (1) to place a certain amount of responsibility on the insured to minimize losses and avoid hazards and (2) to avoid paying small claims that are disproportionately expensive to handle.

It is important to remember that when a loss occurs, any deductible is subtracted after the loss payment is estimated. If the loss is less than the deductible, no payment is made.

✓ ***For example:*** Assume an insured has a homeowner's policy with a $250 deductible. A small fire causes damages totaling $200. In this case, the insured would pay for the damages and collect nothing from the insurer. If, however, the damages were $2,000, the insured would pay the $250 deductible and the insurer would pay the remaining $1,750.

Deductibles in liability insurance are relatively uncommon, except for larger accounts. When they are used, they often are limited to property damage claims and may be required by underwriters if there has been a history of frequent, small PD losses.

## Accident

An **accident** is a sudden, unforeseeable, unintended event causing loss or damage. An accident must be identifiable as to a specific time and place. The explosion of a steam boiler in an apartment building, a collision between two vehicles, and a slip and fall in a retail store are all examples of accidents.

## Occurrence

The term **occurrence** includes an accident as well as continuous or repeated exposure to the same conditions, which results in injury to persons or damage to property neither expected nor intended from the insured's standpoint.

✓ ***For Example:*** If a contractor damages a gas pipe, causing it to leak, and people working in the area are injured after inhaling the fumes, this is an occurrence.

## Cancellation

**Cancellation** occurs when the insurance company or the insured terminates a contract before its normal expiration. Termination is carried out in accordance with provisions in the contract, by mutual agreement or by statute, and must comply with various time limits and notification requirements set by state law.

### Refund of Premium

**Refund of premium** after cancellation may be on a *short rate* or *pro rata* basis, depending on which party cancelled the policy. The portion of the premium the insurer retains is called the **earned premium**. The portion refunded to the policyholder is the **unearned premium** or **return premium**. Premiums are calculated by three methods, as described below.

#### *Pro Rata Cancellation*

**Pro rating** the premium is the method used to calculate the premium refund when the insurance company initiates cancellation. Under this method, the premium refund equals the premium paid for the unexpired term of the policy. In other words, the insured pays premium for the period he had coverage and gets a full refund for the period he did not have coverage.

#### *Short Rate Cancellation*

**Short rate** is the method used when a policyholder cancels his policy before it reaches its natural expiration. In this case, the company pays a return premium less than the pro rata part that remains unearned. The insured pays a penalty of roughly 10% of the unearned premium for cancelling early. This amount withheld from the return premium is designed to compensate the insurer for its policy issuance and administrative expenses.

#### *Flat Cancellation*

When a policy is terminated on its effective date, it is called a **flat cancellation**. The entire premium is refunded to the policyholder.

## Renewal and Nonrenewal

### Renewal

**Renewal** is the continuation of a policy about to expire. This may be accomplished by issuance of a new policy, a renewal receipt, or a certificate, to take effect upon expiration of the prior policy. Though a new policy number may be issued, the coverage is considered continuous and, thus, a renewal.

### Nonrenewal

**Nonrenewal** means that the insurance company will not renew or continue the policy beyond the expiration date.

Most states have laws with specific requirements governing the sending of either a notice of nonrenewal or an offer of renewal when the renewal offer is for a policy with less favorable provisions than the original policy. State laws specify the contents of such nonrenewal notices.

## Quick Quiz 4.1

1. A type of policy that combines both property and liability coverage is referred to as

   A. package
   B. bundle
   C. floater
   D. multi-peril

2. A limit of insurance that determines the maximum amount that can be paid in any one policy year is a(n)

   A. occurrence limit
   B. face amount
   C. aggregate limit
   D. single limit

3. A policy that the insurance company cancels results in which type of return premium computation?

   A. Short rate
   B. Pro rata
   C. Flat
   D. None of the above

## *Answers*

1. ***A.*** *A policy that combines two lines of coverage is referred to as multi-line. When the two lines are property and liability, the policy is called a package.*
2. ***C.*** *An aggregate limit is the maximum amount the insurer will pay in any one policy year, regardless of the number of occurrences.*
3. ***B.*** *When the insurance company cancels a policy prior to its normal expiration date, the full unearned premium is returned to the policyholder. This is referred to as a pro-rate or pro-rata cancellation.*

# Property Insurance Policy Provisions

## Basis of Payment for Loss of the Insured Property

A policy may pay the insured on the basis of the following:

- **Actual cash value (ACV)**—the sum of money required to pay for damage to or loss of property. This sum is the property's current replacement cost minus depreciation caused by obsolescence or wear and tear to the property. ACV also may be defined as the current fair market value (FMV) in some states.
- **Replacement cost**—the full amount necessary to replace or repair the damaged property to its condition before the loss. Replacement cost is generally more than the actual cash value because the insurer settles without a deduction for depreciation. Generally, however, the insured must in fact replace the property with like kind, quality, and quantity before the claim is fully recovered.

**Test Topic Alert!**

Replacement cost – depreciation = actual cash value (ACV) or fair market value (FMV)

## Vacancy and Unoccupancy

The use to which a building is put also affects coverage. Different risks arise when a building is occupied, unoccupied, or vacant.

- **Occupied**—A building that is being used is considered occupied. For example, a building with a bank or a retail store is an occupied building.
- **Unoccupied**—A building is unoccupied if no one is currently in it, but furnishings are present and the occupants intend to return, such as when a family takes a vacation.
- **Vacant**—A building that is not currently being used and does not have enough furnishings to function in its normal capacity is considered vacant.

Certain policies or specific coverages may become ineffective if a building has been unoccupied or vacant for a specified period of time. Some of these restrictions will be noted as specific policies are reviewed.

**Abandonment** of a premises occurs when the owner gives up all right, title, claim, and possession of the property, but does not transfer it to another person. The owner gives up the property without any intention to reclaim it or resume ownership or possession of it in the future.

## Loss Valuation

In insurance terms, *valuation* is the assessment of the value or worth of something, usually by appraisal; the determination of the value of insured property. Valuation of potential property loss is part of the risk management process. The valuation of the property may be based actual cash value, replacement cost, agreed value, market value, or a number of other determinations. Once loss exposures are identified and valued, funding for a potential loss, including transfer of risk, can be developed.

**Agreed Value** is an agreement between the insurer and the insured that the limit of insurance on a scheduled item of property equals the property's value. For some items, such as jewelry and fine arts, the insurer may require an appraisal.

Property insurance policies sometimes provide for loss adjustment on the basis of **functional replacement cost,** which is the minimum cost to replace the damaged property with property that performs the same functions, though it may be less expensive than the original. For example, a brick warehouse may be replaced with a concrete tilt-up building which is less expensive but functions in the same manner.

## Coinsurance

When applied to real property insurance, a **coinsurance clause** requires a policyholder to carry insurance equal to a specified percentage of the total value of the property being insured.

✓ ***For Example:*** If property is valued at $100,000 and the coinsurance clause is 80%, the policyholder must carry at least $80,000 of coverage to satisfy the coinsurance clause requirement.

Because property losses typically are only partial losses, property owners are inclined to carry just partial insurance on their property. To distribute the cost of insurance more equitably among insureds, however, many companies include coinsurance clauses requiring policyholders to carry minimum amounts of insurance. A reduced rate is granted on a policy that carries a coinsurance clause. However, if the insured fails to maintain the required insurance and a loss occurs, the insurance company imposes a penalty. The insured becomes a coinsurer in the loss and must participate in the loss.

✓ ***Take Note:*** The insured must agree to maintain insurance at least equal to the stated percentage of the value of the insured property. This means that the amount of insurance must equal or exceed the required percentage at the time of loss. If this requirement has not been met, the insured may not fully recover the loss even though the loss is for less than the policy amount.

The insured and the insurer may agree to the value of the property. This value is established before the policy is written.

The following coinsurance formula is used to determine the amount that an insurance company will pay for a covered loss:

$$\frac{\text{Amount of insurance carried}}{\text{Amount of insurance required}} \times \text{loss - deductible (if any)} = \text{amount paid}$$

The calculation for the example above would be as follows:

$$\frac{\$40,000}{\$80,000\ (80\%\ \text{of}\ \$100,000)} \times \$10,000 - \$250 = \$4,750$$

## Application of the Coinsurance Formula and Deductible

Assume that an insured owns an office building valued at $200,000. His insurance policy carries an 80% coinsurance clause. Therefore, according to the clause, the insured must maintain a policy for at least $160,000 ($200,000 × 80% = $160,000).

The following examples illustrate how the coinsurance formula affects the claim settlement when the insured suffers a fire loss of $100,000.

✓ ***For Example:***

$$\frac{\text{Amount carried}}{\text{Amount required}} \times \text{loss} - \text{deductible} = \text{amount paid}$$

*Example 1*

| | |
|---|---|
| Property Value (ACV) | $200,000 |
| Coinsurance | 80% |
| Insurance Carried | $160,000 |
| Loss | $100,000 |

$$\frac{\$160,000}{\$160,000} \times \$100,000 = \$100,000 \text{ settlement}$$

*Example 2*

| | |
|---|---|
| Property Value (ACV) | $200,000 |
| Coinsurance | 80% |
| Insurance Carried | $160,000 |
| Deductible | $500 |
| Loss | $100,000 |

$$\frac{\$160,000}{\$160,000} \times \$100,000 - \$500 = \$99,500 \text{ settlement}$$

*Example 3*

| | |
|---|---|
| Property Value (ACV) | $200,000 |
| Coinsurance | 80% |
| Insurance Carried | $100,000 |
| Deductible | $500 |
| Loss | $100,000 |

$$\frac{\$100{,}000}{\$160{,}000} \times \$100{,}000 = \$62{,}500$$

$62,500 – $500 = $62,000 settlement

***Note:*** The insured is penalized for being underinsured when the loss occurred. In addition to the $500 deductible, the insured must pay the remaining $37,500 the insurance company won't pay, for a total of $38,000 in out-of-pocket expenses.

*Example 4*

| | |
|---|---|
| Property Value (ACV) | $200,000 |
| Coinsurance | 80% |
| Insurance Carried | $250,000 |
| Deductible | $500 |
| Loss | $100,000 |

*If the amount carried equals or exceeds the amount required, it is not necessary to use the coinsurance formula on the loss.*

***Note:*** The insurer pays a settlement of $99,500 because the insured cannot collect more than the actual loss. Remember, the purpose of insurance is not to enrich the insured, but to indemnify the insured, or to "make whole" by returning the insured property to the condition it was in before the loss.

## Pair and Set Clause

The **pair and set clause** in an insurance contract establishes the conditions that apply when a single item of a pair or set is lost or destroyed. The clause generally provides that the insurer (1) may repair or replace the lost part, thereby restoring the pair or set to its value before the loss or (2) may elect to pay the difference between the actual cash value of the property before the loss and after the loss. This provision is designed to prevent the insured from collecting for a total loss when only part of a pair or set is the subject of the loss.

✓ ***For Example:*** If only one of a pair of diamond earrings is lost, the insurer may elect to replace the lost earring or pay the difference between the value of the pair and the residual value of the single earring. Only the insurer may determine the method of settlement.

## Right of Salvage/Salvage

An insurance company has the right to any **salvage** when it settles a loss. The company may take possession of the damaged property and pay the insured the appropriate value of the loss. It then can sell or otherwise dispose of this salvage property to reduce the claim's overall cost. However, the insured cannot require the company to take the salvage nor can he abandon the property to the insurer.

✓ ***For Example:*** In the case of an auto accident, the insurance company may total the vehicle by paying the actual cash value to the policyholder. The company then becomes the legal owner of the salvage (in this case, the damaged car) and may dispose of it as the company sees fit. In some cases, the salvage actually is sold to the insured.

## Burglary

**Burglary** is defined as the breaking and entering into the premises of another with felonious, wrongful, or criminal intent to take property and with visible sign of forced entry. By definition, burglary involves forcible entry, although some policies also cover forcible exit.

## Robbery

**Robbery** is the felonious, wrongful, or criminal taking, either by force or by fear of force, of the personal property of another. This act of forcibly taking property from someone commonly is known as a hold-up.

## Theft and Larceny

**Theft** is any act of stealing, including larceny, burglary, and robbery. In general, it is the taking of someone else's property without the owner's permission. **Larceny** is the unlawful taking of the personal property of another without his consent and with the intent to deprive him or her of the ownership or use of that property.

## Mysterious Disappearance

**Mysterious disappearance** is the disappearance of insured property in an unexplained manner. An example would be noting one day that a stone is missing from your ring or discovering that the watch you put on your dresser three days ago isn't there. Mere loss of property, such as an article dropped from a boat, is not included in this definition because the disappearance is not mysterious. This coverage is included under a limited number of policies or endorsements.

## Inflation Guard/Automatic Increase in Insurance

Property polices may include automatically or by endorsement a provision whereby insurance limits are increased to compensate for inflation. For example, the limit of insurance on a building may be increased at the end of a given period of time, say quarterly, or even daily, based on a fixed percentage determined at the beginning of the policy term. This provision is designed to prevent underinsurance that occurs when the replacement cost or actual cash value of property increases due to inflation.

## Inherent Vice

**Inherent vice** is a defect or cause of loss arising out of the nature of certain goods. For example, a star sapphire might become cloudy over time, or the rubber moldings on a car might deteriorate after awhile if the car is kept in a very warm climate. Losses due to inherent vice are usually not covered by property insurance policies.

## Blanket Policy

A **blanket insurance policy** covers more than one type of property in a single location, or one or more types of property at more than one location. This is in contrast to specific insurance, which covers a single type of property at a single location.

# Liability Insurance Policy Provisions

Liability insurance is designed to pay damages on behalf of the insured to others who have been injured or had property damaged as a result of an action or inaction by the insured. This responsibility may (1) arise out of negligence, (2) be imposed by law, or (3) be assumed by contract.

### Categories of Liability Exposures

The four general classifications of liability exposures are noted below. Specific policies covering these exposures will be presented throughout this manual:

- **General liability**—the exposure arising from the use and maintenance of premises, the operations involved in conducting a business or both.
- **Personal liability**—the exposure arising from the nonbusiness activities of an individual and family, with certain exceptions. Automobiles are not included in this category; they make up their own.

- **Professional liability**—the exposure arising from the conduct of a profession, such as from practicing medicine, law, engineering, architecture, insurance, or accountancy.
- **Vicarious liability**—arises from one person's legal responsibility for the negligent behavior of another, as in the case of a parent who is held responsible for the vandalism his child causes.

## Types of Injury or Damage Arising from Liability

### Bodily Injury

As used in liability insurance, **bodily injury** means bodily harm, sickness, or disease, including required care, loss of services, loss of income, and death that results therefrom to a person other than the insured.

### Property Damage

For purposes of liability insurance, **property damage** means injury to, destruction of, or loss of use of tangible property. It also may include loss of use of tangible property that has not been physically injured.

### Personal Injury

As used in liability insurance, **personal injury** means injury to one's mental or emotional well-being arising out of one or more of the following offenses:

- false arrest, detention, or imprisonment, or malicious prosecution;
- libel, slander, or defamation of character; or
- invasion of privacy, wrongful eviction, or wrongful entry.

### Advertising Injury

**Advertising injury** is injury arising out of any of the following:

- oral or written publication of material that slanders or libels a person or an organization or that disparages a person's or an organization's goods, products or services;
- oral or written publication of material that violates a person's right of privacy;
- misappropriation of advertising ideas or style of doing business; or
- infringement of copyright, title, or slogan.

✓ ***Take Note:*** The four types of injury that arise from liability—bodily injury, property damage, personal injury, and advertising injury—represent the coverage typically provided by a personal or business liability policy.

## Compensatory Damages

**Damages**, in contrast to damage, is compensation or indemnification awarded by a court of law to any person who has suffered loss or damage as the result of the unlawful act or omission of another party. Damages are usually expressed in monetary terms, and are awarded as compensation for injuries sustained as the result of another's tortious act or breach of contract.

**General damages** arise as the direct result of a wrong act, and are presumed to have been the necessary result of the injury. They arise without regard to the character, condition, or circumstances of the party injured.

In contrast, **special damages** arise from the particular injury sustained, and are not presumed to be the necessary result of the injury. They depend on the character, condition, and circumstances of the injured party.

## Punitive Damages

**Punitive damages** are awarded to an injured party in addition to any compensation that will cover his loss or injury. These damages are awarded in cases where the wrong committed against the injured party was violent, malicious, oppressive, fraudulent, or wicked. Also called **exemplary damages**, they are intended to punish the wrongdoer or make an example of him for similar wrongdoers.

## Negligence and Liability

Wrongs that an individual may commit can be classified into two categories. The first is a **public wrong** or a criminal act. This is a wrong against society, such as murder or arson, that is punishable by the courts.

The second type of wrong that an individual can commit is a **private** or **civil wrong**, which is an infringement by one person on the rights of another individual. This infringement also is called a **tort**.

✓ ***For Example:*** A drivers license gives you the privilege to drive on the street in your car. You do not have the right to drive at an excessive speed (civil wrong or tort) and strike another vehicle or pedestrian (public wrong or crime), causing injury or damage.

These rights and duties arise from common law, case law (rulings by judges or court decisions), the constitution, legislative statute, or regulation. Remedies for persons whose rights are infringed upon include direct reasonable action or judicial and civil action, which may include a monetary award, an injunction or restitution.

## Absolute Liability, Strict Liability, and Negligence

**Absolute**, or **strict, liability** assigns liability to a party without regard to the party's fault or negligence. The doctrine imposes liability on a party who engages in an inherently dangerous activity and causes injury as the result of that dangerous activity. For instance, a demolition company that uses explosives to demolish a building may be held strictly liable for any injuries it causes to passersby who are injured by the blast. Similarly, the doctrine imposes liability on a party who sells a defective product that is unreasonably dangerous to a consumer's personal safety if that product causes injury to the ultimate user.

### Negligence

The legal doctrine of **negligence** is based on the principal that every person has a duty to act carefully toward others and in a manner that does not injure others. Negligence arises from the failure of a person to fulfill this duty. It is the failure to do something that a reasonable person under similar circumstances would do. It also is the act of doing something that a reasonable person under similar circumstances would *not* do.

### Contributory Negligence

Just as people have a duty to act carefully toward others to avoid injuring them, people also have a duty to protect themselves from injury. In some states, a person who is sued for negligence may raise the defense of **contributory negligence**, arguing that the plaintiff's own negligence was a proximate cause of his injury.

### Comparative Negligence

Most states have **comparative negligence** statutes, under which the extent of a person's negligence is measured in terms of a percentage. A person who suffered personal injury or property damage may sue to recover the costs of the damage. If the person sues another party for money damages and wins, the amount of the award will be reduced by the percentage of that person's own comparative fault, or negligence. Some states will apportion the award strictly according to these percentages.

In other states, a person who is 50% or more at fault for the damages may receive a smaller award. In still other states, that person would be barred from recovering anything because he or she was mostly responsible for the injury.

# Unit Test Four

1. If an insured suffered a loss of one earring from a pair, the insurance company probably would offer to settle in which of the following ways?
   A. Pay the entire value of the pair of earrings
   B. Pay a portion of the total value
   C. Pay 1⁄10 of the value on the basis that one earring remains
   D. Pay nothing because the entire set was not lost

2. An insured owns a commercial building with a value of $100,000. He takes out an insurance policy for $60,000 with an 80% coinsurance clause and later suffers a $12,000 loss. Based on this information, he will be paid
   A. $7,200
   B. $9,000
   C. $9,600
   D. $12,000

3. Which of the following is the purpose of coinsurance?
   A. To encourage an insured to carry insurance equal to a high percentage of his property's value
   B. To allow rate credits for high amounts of insurance
   C. To punish an insured for not knowing the insurable value of a building
   D. To make an insured share in every loss to encourage loss control

4. An insurer that cancels a policy must refund the unused portion of the premium on a
   A. pro rata basis, returning all unearned premiums
   B. pro rata basis, returning all earned premiums
   C. short rate basis, returning all unearned premiums
   D. short rate basis, returning all earned premiums

5. Failure to exercise the care that circumstances require is called
   A. legal liability
   B. negligence
   C. disregard
   D. malfeasance

6. A policy that covers many causes of loss is referred to as
   A. multi-line
   B. monoline
   C. multi-peril
   D. allied line

7. A limit in a liability policy that includes coverage under both bodily injury and property damage is called a(n)
   A. single limit
   B. blanket limit
   C. aggregate limit
   D. combined single limit

8. Which of the following describes an aggregate limit?
   A. Maximum amount payable in any policy year
   B. Maximum amount of insurance that can be purchased
   C. Limit that applies to bodily injury claims
   D. Maximum amount of any occurrence

9. An insurance policy has been issued with a limit of $100,000 for any one occurrence. After an accident, the injured parties make the following demands:

| | |
|---|---|
| Party A | $25,000 |
| Party B | $50,000 |
| Party C | $50,000 |

The maximum amount the insurance company will pay for the accident is

A. $25,000 for A; $37,500 for B; $37,500 for C
B. $25,000 for A; $50,000 for B; $25,000 for C
C. $25,000 for A; $50,000 for B; $50,000 for C
D. $100,000 apportioned among A, B and C

10. Which of the following is NOT a reason to include deductibles in insurance policies?

A. To punish insureds who don't purchase enough insurance
B. To have insureds share losses to minimize their occurrence
C. To encourage loss control
D. To avoid expensive small claims

11. When the insured cancels an insurance policy before its normal expiration date, this type of cancellation is called

A. flat
B. pro rata
C. short rate
D. mid-term

12. When a policy is canceled on its effective date, the amount returned to the insured is the

A. unearned premium
B. entire premium
C. earned premium
D. short rate premium

13. Under a property insurance policy, the insured receives what type of payment that takes into account physical depreciation?

A. Replacement cost
B. Market value
C. Actual cash value
D. Appraised value

14. For insurance purposes, when a building is completely void of any furnishings or equipment, it is considered

A. vacant
B. unoccupied
C. occupied
D. abandoned

15. The purpose of a coinsurance clause in property insurance policies is to

A. reward policyholders who overinsure their buildings
B. encourage policyholders to maintain enough insurance
C. prevent payment in full for any loss
D. make policyholders share in any losses

16. When an insured leaves a valuable ring on a counter at the airport and returns to find the ring is gone, the cause of loss is

A. robbery
B. burglary
C. mysterious disappearance
D. theft

17. A clause in a policy that automatically adjusts the amount of insurance when building costs increase is called a(n)

A. inflation guard
B. escalation clause
C. building cost modifier
D. agreed value clause

18. Which of the following is NOT a way that legal responsibility may arise?
    A. Out of negligence
    B. Imposed by law
    C. Assumed by contract
    D. Out of habit

19. Each of the following is an example of a classification of liability exposures EXCEPT
    A. general
    B. personal
    C. financial
    D. professional

20. Advertising injury involves which of the following?
    A. Oral or written publication of material that slanders or libels a person or an organization
    B. Oral or written material that violates a person's right of privacy
    C. Misappropriation of advertising ideas or style of doing business
    D. All of the above

21. To establish that a tort has been committed, a party must prove which of the following?
    A. Negligence
    B. Actual damages or loss
    C. Violation of statute
    D. Commission of public wrong

22. When one person causes an injury but the legal responsibility is imputed to another, this is a situation of
    A. vicarious liability
    B. comparative negligence
    C. strict liability
    D. negligence per se

23. The inability to recover damages when a person is partially responsible for his or her own injuries or damage is a legal doctrine called
    A. last clear chance
    B. negligence per se
    C. comparative negligence
    D. contributory negligence

24. In a pure comparative negligence state, if a person suffers $50,000 in injuries but is 40% responsible due to his own behavior, the maximum amount that person could recover from another party is
    A. $30,000
    B. $40,000
    C. $50,000
    D. None of the above

# Unit Test Four Answers & Rationale

1. **B.** A policy's pair and set clause takes into account the value of the items before the loss and their residual value following the loss, providing payment to the insured of a portion of the total value.

2. **B.** A building valued at $100,000 requires insurance of $80,000 (80% of $100,000) to comply with the coinsurance provision. Because in this case the insured purchased only $60,000 of coverage, the insurer will pay $60,000/$80,000 or (¾) of each loss. Three-fourths of $12,000 is $9,000.

3. **A.** Because most losses are small, insureds may be inclined to carry only minimal insurance, resulting in rate inequities. Through the use of a coinsurance clause, insurance companies encourage policyholders to carry an amount of insurance closer to the full value of their properties.

4. **A.** When a policy is cancelled at the company's request, the insurer returns all premiums for the unused portion of the policy. The premium is pro rated based on the exact number of days coverage was in effect.

5. **B.** Negligence is defined as the failure of a prudent person to exercise the proper degree of care required by the circumstances.

6. **C.** When two or more causes of loss are combined in a single policy, it is referred to as multi-peril. Multi-line refers to a policy that combines several types of coverage, such as property and liability.

7. **D.** A liability policy that contains one limit for two types of losses, such as bodily injury and property damage, is called a combined single limit.

8. **A.** The maximum amount that a liability policy will pay in a given policy period, regardless of the number of claims submitted, is the aggregate limit.

9. **D.** In this case, the policy limit of $100,000 is insufficient to pay all the claimants' demands ($125,000). Therefore, the loss will be apportioned among the victims and paid up to the $100,000 limit.

10. **A.** Deductibles serve to eliminate small losses, to encourage insureds to use loss control by having them participate in losses and to encourage insureds to prevent losses.

11. **C.** When the insured elects to cancel a policy mid-term, the insurer requires reimbursement for costs incurred in issuing the policy. Therefore, in addition to the pro rated amount of premium for the number of days the coverage was in effect, the insurer withholds a certain percentage of the premium to offset expenses. This is called a short rate cancellation.

12. **B.** A policy canceled on its effective date is referred to as a flat cancellation. Because, in effect, no coverage was ever in force, the entire premium (consideration) is returned to the insured to reinforce that the contract is null and void.

13. **C.** The definition of actual cash value is replacement cost of the property minus physical deterioration.

14. **A.** A building that is without enough furnishings to conduct the operations for which it is intended is considered vacant.

15. **B.** Because most losses are small, insureds may be inclined to carry only minimal insurance, resulting in rate inequities. Through the use of a coinsurance clause, insurance companies encourage policyholders to carry an amount of insurance closer to the full value of their properties.

16. **C.** Because the insured does not know exactly what happened to the ring, it cannot be

presumed to have been stolen; thus, it constitutes a mysterious disappearance.

17. **A.** An inflation guard often is added to a property insurance policy to offset the increases that occur in building costs during the policy year.

18. **D.** Legal responsibility can arise only out of statute (criminal) or tort (civil) or by contract.

19. **C.** The classes of liability exposures are general, personal, automobile and professional.

20. **D.** Advertising injury involves each of the items listed as well as infringement of copyright, title or slogan.

21. **B.** One of the elements of a tort action is that a private wrong has been committed and that the aggrieved party suffered a loss because of it.

22. **A.** Vicarious liability occurs when one person is held legally responsible for the negligent behavior of another, such as a parent who is held responsible for the vandalism his child causes.

23. **D.** Through the defense of contributory negligence, any negligence on the part of the injured party that contributed to his own injury will defeat or reduce the amount that the injured party can collect.

24. **A.** Under pure comparative negligence, the amount that a party can collect is reduced by the percentage that the person contribute to his or her own injuries or damages. Thus, $50,000 in damages for which the party is 40% responsible means the person cannot recover $20,000 (40% of $50,000), but may recover the remaining $30,000.

Part Two

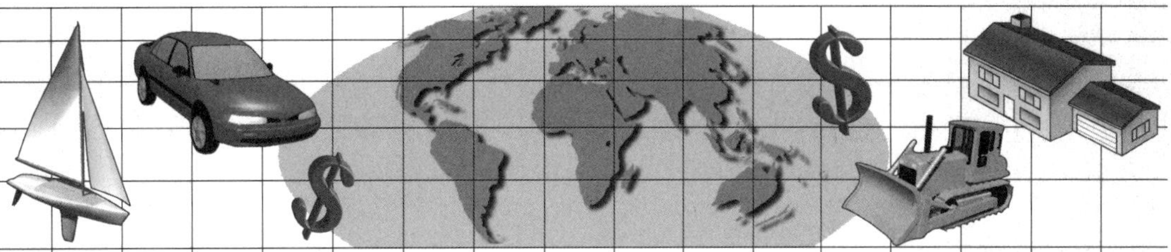

# Principles of Casualty Insurance

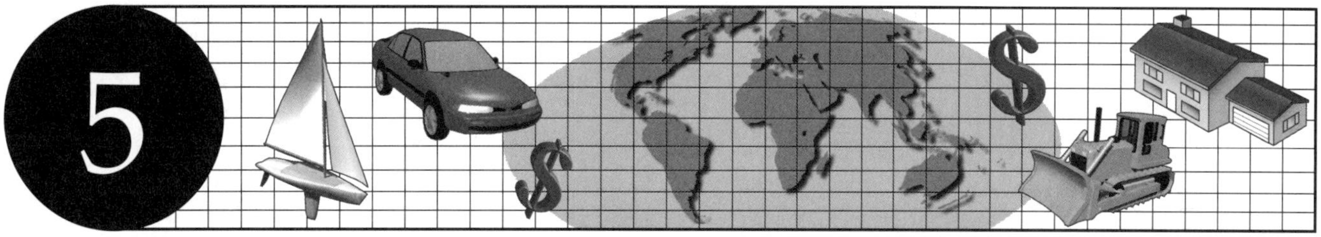


# Commercial General Liability Insurance

## INTRODUCTION

Liability insurance is designed to pay on behalf of an individual, a business, or an organization the actual damages that the insured becomes legally obligated to pay. With the number of lawsuits filed daily and the ever-increasing size of the judgments awarded, liability insurance is a necessity for businesses and professionals, as well as for many individuals.

This unit presents the risk exposures that a business may face and general liability insurance that provides protection for those risks are presented. In addition, the Commercial General Liability (CGL) policy and its coverage for bodily injury, and property damage, personal and advertising injury, and medical payments are reviewed in detail.

## UNIT OBJECTIVES

When you have completed this unit, you should be able to:

- explain the situations that create liability exposures for an insured;
- distinguish between occurrence- and claims-made policies;
- explain the purpose of extended reporting periods, or tails;
- describe the coverages the CGL policy provides;
- describe CGL policy exclusions;
- determine who a CGL policy insures;
- describe how the limits apply under the CGL policy;
- explain the conditions and definitions the CGL policy contains; and
- identify the CGL policy's major endorsements.

# General Liability

A business, regardless of its nature (retail merchant, manufacturer, contractor, or insurance agent), will be exposed to claims by third parties for injury to persons or property arising out of, or in the course of, doing business. The source of bodily injury and property damage will vary depending on the nature of the business. The business also may be exposed to claims for personal injury (libel and slander) and advertising injury. It is the purpose of liability insurance to pay on behalf of the insured for such injuries or damages.

**Test Topic Alert!** Business owners can be legally liable for four losses: bodily injury, property damage, personal injury, and advertising injury.

## General Liability Insurance

**General liability insurance** is written to cover two major risk exposures: premises and operations and products and completed operations.

For each type of risk, coverage may be written for events that occur within the policy period (**occurrence form**) or events for which a claim must be reported during the policy period (**claims-made form**).

**Test Topic Alert!** The four main business exposures are premises, operations, products, and completed operations.

## Premises and Operations Exposure

### Ownership and Maintenance of Premises

The owner or tenant of a building can be held liable if a member of the public (third party) is injured or the third party's property is damaged as a result of a condition of, or arising out of the use of, the premises. It is easy to see how such conditions as a loose stair tread and a wet floor could cause a person to fall and be injured or cause the person's property to be damaged.

✓ ***For Example:*** A customer dropping off a watch for cleaning trips on a loose carpet and drops the watch. She may suffer bodily injuries as well as damage to the watch.

### Conduct of Business Operations

Liability also arises in the course of a business's daily operations. A firm may be liable if a member of the public is injured or his property is damaged either (1) on the premises where the business is conducted or (2) away from the premises by an activity of the owner or an employee.

✓ ***For Example:*** A stock clerk, while stocking shelves in a grocery store, drops a box on a customer, causing bodily injury to the customer. An insurance agent, while calling on a client, puts his briefcase on the client's dining room table, causing property damage when the table is scratched. In both examples, some business activity takes place (operations) that causes the injury or damage.

## Products and Completed Operations Liability

**Products Liability** A manufacturer or distributor of a faulty product that injures someone or damages someone's property may be held legally liable. Depending on the circumstances of the case, the person injured may seek recovery based on the legal doctrine of negligence, breach of warranty, or strict liability.

- **Negligence**. Negligence may arise because of poor product manufacture or design or improper warning about dangerous qualities.

✓ ***For Example:*** A machine's safety device is removable. If a person is injured after taking off the safety device, the manufacturer may be negligent for designing a safety device that is removable.

- **Breach of warranty**. A product is sold with an implied warranty that it is fit for its intended purpose. If it causes injury during its use or consumption, the implied warranty was breached and liability can result.
- **Strict liability**. Under the doctrine of strict liability, the person injured must prove that the:
  - manufacturer or supplier knew or should have known that the product was defective when it left the manufacturer's or supplier's custody or control;
  - defective condition made the product unreasonably dangerous; or
  - defective product was the proximate cause of the injury.

**Test Topic Alert!** Liability payments always are made to a third party, the injured party.

**Completed Operations Liability** **Completed operations liability** exposure arises when a business (such as a contractor) completes operations away from the premises it owns, rents, or controls. When work off premises is completed or abandoned and someone is injured or his property is damaged, this is a completed operations exposure.

✓ ***For Example:*** A contractor completes a building and turns it over to the retail merchant who owns the building and will conduct business in it. After the building is transferred and occupied, the roof leaks, causing damage to inventory. This is a completed operations liability exposure and the contractor is liable.

By contrast, if someone is hurt or their property damaged while the contractor is in the process of building the structure, it is a business operations exposure, described previously.

## Distinction of Cause of Loss

It is necessary to distinguish between premises and operations losses and products and completed operations losses; in some cases, because of the manner in which limits apply under a policy. The distinction is based on the following:

- Coverage under products liability depends on whether the loss occurred away from the insured's premises and after the insured relinquished physical possession of the product.
- Operations are completed when:
  - the contract is complete;
  - one job site of several is complete;
  - a completed portion of work has been put to its intended use; or
  - operations may require further work, but are otherwise complete.
- Completed operations always must be away from the named insured's premises.
- The completed operations hazard does not include:
  - operations in connection with the transporting of property unless it arises out of a condition in or on a vehicle created by loading or unloading; or
  - the existence of tools, uninstalled equipment or abandoned or unused materials.
- Separate aggregate limits apply to premises and operations and products and completed operations.

## Vicarious or Contingent Liability

The general rule is that the principal that engages an independent contractor is not liable for the independent contractor's torts (civil wrongs). Some exceptions to this general rule exist, and the liability of the agent (contractor or subcontractor) is imposed on the principal (person, firm, or entity that engaged the contractor or subcontractor) in some circumstances. In other words, the principal is vicariously liable for the agent's actions.

✓ ***For Example:*** The principal may be liable when he or she is negligent in:

- selecting a contractor;
- giving instructions; or
- failing to stop any unnecessarily dangerous practices that come to his attention.

In addition, an employer who engages an independent contractor to do work that is inherently dangerous to others is subject to liability caused by the independent contractor's negligence. Examples of such inherently dangerous work are blasting and excavating in or near a public highway.

Vicarious liability also may be called **contingent liability**.

### Contractual Liability

A business may assume liability for negligent acts of another through a written or an oral contract. When such a contract exists, the business has taken upon itself another's liability.

✓ ***For Example:*** In a construction contract, the landowner may want the general contractor to sign a hold harmless agreement. By signing such an agreement, the general contractor assumes (holds harmless) the landowner's liability during the construction period.

## General Liability Policy

Through the years, the coverage parts just discussed became known as the **Comprehensive General Liability (CGL) policy**. This original CGL policy was replaced by a simplified commercial lines program in January 1986. The Insurance Service Office (ISO) developed a package program with one part known as the **Commercial General Liability (CGL) policy**.

✓ ***Take Note:*** There is a difference in the full title of this policy, but identical abbreviations are used to designate the forms.

### Commercial General Liability Coverage Form (CG 00 01 10)

The CGL policy covers four major exposures, including medical payments, in three coverage sections:

- **Coverage A**—for bodily injury and property damage resulting from the premises, operations, products, and completed operations (among other coverages, it includes blanket contractual liability, fire legal liability, host liquor liability, nonowned watercraft liability, and limited worldwide products liability);

- **Coverage B**—for personal and advertising injury, including protection for such offenses as defamation (libel, slander), false arrest, and advertising liability; and
- **Coverage C**—for medical expenses resulting from accidental bodily injury on or away from the premises.

✓ ***Take Note:*** The policy starts with very broad coverage that can be narrowed by endorsement.

**Premiums and Exposures**

Unlike in other policies, the exposures used to determine general liability insurance premiums are variable, such as payroll and sales. A policy covers exposures that are identified at the time the policy is taken out, and an advance premium is paid based on an estimate of those exposures. At the end of the year, based on an audit, the premium is adjusted for the actual exposures that were present during the policy term.

## Quick Quiz 5.1

Identify the types of liability exposure (as listed below ) the following situations represent:

Premises
Operations
Products
Completed Operations

1. __________ A department store customer trips over a vacuum cleaner cord and injures her hip.
2. __________ A restaurant customer finds a piece of glass in a hamburger.
3. __________ After a plumber installs a new sink in an office building, the sink falls from the wall, injuring one of the office workers.
4. __________ An employee drops a pallet of bricks onto the hood of a vehicle parked at a job site.
5. __________ A visitor at a county fair steps in a pothole in the parking lot and twists her ankle.
6. __________ A backhoe operator hits a city-owned water pipe while digging a trench.

***Answers***

1. *Premises*
2. *Products*

3. *Completed operations*
4. *Operations*
5. *Premises*
6. *Operations*

## Occurrence Form

The commercial general liability policy can be written on an occurrence or a claims-made form. Policies providing coverage on an occurrence basis pay if an insured is legally liable for injuries or damage that occurred during a policy period, even if a claim is submitted after the policy has expired. When an injury or damage is immediately obvious, this type of coverage poses no problem for the insurance company.

Some types of injuries or damages, however, are latent and not discovered until many years after a policy has expired. For a disease that takes a long period of time to develop symptoms, the problem is further complicated by the fact that it may be difficult to determine when the injury in fact occurred. Possibilities include:

- when the person was first exposed to a hazardous condition (the exposure theory);
- while the disease was developing; and
- when the disease first manifested itself (the manifestation theory).

As we have stated, with the occurrence policy, coverage applies if the damage occurred, started, or was discovered when the policy was in force—even if the policy has since expired. This raises an important issue. A business may have had several liability policies over the years. In this case, the problem is determining when the event occurred in order to know which policy applies. Obviously, if many insurers are involved, each may have its own opinion of when the event occurred and whether that insurer's policy was effective at the time of the event.

✓ ***For Example:*** Employees who worked with asbestos in the 1950s did not know they had contracted asbestosis until 20 or 30 years later. The damage was triggered in the 1950s, so the policy in force then was responsible for providing the coverage. (A **trigger** is what must happen during the policy period for coverage to become available for a particular instance of bodily injury or property damage). Consequently, insurers found themselves paying damages in the 1980s for losses that originated 30 years earlier and that were absolutely unanticipated. Furthermore, claims costs were significantly higher in the l980s than in the l950s, when the policy rates were set. Obviously, the rates charged in the 1950s did not anticipate the eventual costs. Moreover, many of the policies had long since expired so insurers had no chance to recoup the losses. Finally, because a trigger often could not be determined, the courts required many of the policies in effect during this period to pay claims for which they may not have been responsible.

## Claims-Made Form

To avoid such surprises, the insurance industry developed a **claims-made form**. This type of policy involves two triggers—when the claim occurs and when the claim is first made. The claim must be made during the policy period; the injury or damage must have occurred after the policy's retroactive date but before the policy expires.

A claims-made policy sets two important dates in addition to the policy's inception date.

### Retroactive Date

The first is the **retroactive date**, which can be:

- the same as the policy's inception date;
- a specified earlier date; or
- no retroactive date.

The retroactive date also can restrict coverage to:

- all events after the retro-date;
- events at a specific location; or
- a specific event.

The retroactive date is designed to accept a claim that occurred before the contract's inception date, but that has not yet been investigated by any insurer.

✓ ***For Example:*** An applicant takes out a policy on January 1, 2004, with Insurer A for the period 1/1/04 through 1/1/05. The policy has a retroactive date of 9/1/03. If a claim is made during 2004 for an injury that occurred on or after 9/1/03, Insurer A is responsible for the claim if no other investigation of the claim has occurred and the insured is legally liable. If the injury occurred before 9/1/03, the retroactive date, Insurer A is not responsible.

### Extended Reported Period

The second date is the **extended reporting period**, which is important in the claims-made form for claims first reported after the policy expired for bodily injury or property damage that occurred before termination of the policy expired, but after its retroactive date. In effect, it extends the time, after policy expiration, during which a claim can be made so that possible coverage gaps almost always are eliminated.

✓ ***Take Note:*** An extended reporting period, also called a **tail**, is a common provision in a claims-made policy. It does not extend the period of time in which occurrences may take place, merely the time frame for reporting those claims to the insurance company.

### *Basic Extended Reporting Period (Basic Tail)*

Two types of extended reporting period exist. The **basic extended reporting period (basic tail)** is included in the CGL policy form. It covers claims made up to five years after the end of the policy period as long as an occurrence is reported to the insurer no later than 60 days after the end of the policy period. The bodily injury or property damage must have occurred before the end of the policy period and after the retroactive date.

The basic tail contains one additional provision: coverage applies to all other claims reported to the insurer within 60 days after the policy period. This means that coverage exists for unknown or unreported claims first made in the 60 days following policy expiration. No charge is imposed for the basic tail.

**Test Topic Alert!** Professional liability policies usually are sold as claims-made forms.

### *Supplemental Extended Reporting Period (Supplemental Tail)*

The insured also may purchase, by endorsement, a **supplemental extended reporting period (supplemental tail)**. The insured must request to purchase the supplemental tail in writing within 60 days after policy expiration. When added to the policy, the supplemental tail contains its own aggregate limit equal to the expired policy's aggregate. Coverage under the supplemental tail begins when the coverage provided by the basic tail runs out. The reporting period under the supplemental tail has no time limit. Therefore, it is sometimes referred to as the **forever tail**.

The premium for the tail is determined at the time the endorsement is requested. However, it may not exceed 200% of the original annual premium for liability coverage. The premium is fully earned, and the endorsement cannot be cancelled. (Some states also limit the amount of premium that insurers may charge for this extended reporting period. Please refer to your state study manual for state-specific information.)

✓ ***For Example:*** An applicant takes out a policy on January 1, 2004 with Insurer A for the period 1/1/04 through 1/1/05. The policy has a supplemental extended reporting period. If a claim occurs on 4/14/04, but is not discovered nor reported until 6/30/06, the policy issued by Insurer A provides coverage. (The basic tail does not provide coverage because it only extends the five-year reporting period for claims reported in the first 60 days after policy expiration.)

## Quick Quiz 5.2

For each of the following situations, identify which policy, if any, applies to the loss.

| | |
|---|---|
| Policy A occurrence form | 7/1/03–7/1/04 |
| Policy B claims-made form | 7/1/04–7/1/05 (7/1/03 retroactive date, no endorsements) |
| Policy C occurrence form | 7/1/05–7/1/06 |

1. __________ A person injured in an accident on May 1, 2003, files a claim on August 15, 2003.
2. __________ A person injured in an accident on September 15, 2003, files a claim on July 25, 2004.
3. __________ A person injured in an accident on July 15, 2004, files a claim on August 10, 2004.
4. __________ A person injured on September 10, 2004, files a claim on August 1, 2005. This is the first notice of the occurrence.

### *Answers*

1. *None. Policy A only applies to events that occur between 7/1/03 and 7/1/04. This event took place prior to that time.*
2. *Policy A. Since Policy A is an occurrence policy, there is no time limit for when claims can be presented as long they occurred between 7/1/03 and 7/1/04. Policy B could also apply: the claim was made during its term, the occurrence took place after the retroactive date.*
3. *Policy B. Both the occurrence and the claim took place under Policy B's term, meeting both coverage triggers under that policy.*
4. *Policy B. Since the claim was unknown during the first 60 days after the expiration of Policy B, it would be covered by the automatic mini tail or extended reporting period of that policy. It would not be covered under Policy C because the occurrence took place prior to the inception date of that policy.*

## Commercial General Liability Policy

The CGL policy has five sections: Coverages, Who Is an Insured, Limits of Insurance, Conditions, and Definitions. A description of each section follows.

## Section I—Coverages

The CGL provides three coverages:

- bodily injury and property damage liability;
- personal and advertising injury liability; and
- medical payments.

### Coverage A: Bodily Injury and Property Damage

The insurance company pays those sums that the insured becomes legally obligated to pay as damages because of bodily injury or property damage. The bodily injury or property damage must be caused by a covered occurrence and must take place within the coverage territory during the policy period. **Coverage territory**, the geographical limits to which the coverage extends, is defined in the policy.

Property damage includes injury to tangible property, including loss of use of that property. It also includes loss of use of the tangible property that is not physically damaged.

✓ ***For Example:*** If property damage to a neighboring building makes access to an insured's property impossible, the policy pays even though the insured's structure incurs no physical damage.

The insurance company has the right and duty to defend any suit seeking bodily injury or property damage even if such suit is groundless. This right extends to arbitration proceedings. The insurer pays for defense costs in addition to the limit of liability, but only until the limit of liability is used up.

The claims-made form states that any claim for bodily injury or property damage must be made during the policy period. If a person has two or more claims under the same occurrence, the first claim's date is the applicable date, A claims-made policy has a retroactive date and an extended reporting date, as previously discussed. It also sets one automatic extended reporting period of 60 days. A supplemental extended reporting period is available by endorsement for an additional premium.

### Exclusions

Coverage A of the CGL policy has 15 exclusions:

1. **Expected or intended liability**. The CGL policy provides no coverage for bodily injury or property damage that is expected or intended from the standpoint of the insured. However, bodily injury resulting from using reasonable force to protect persons or property is therefore, covered.
2. **Contractual liability**. The CGL policy does not cover damages the insured is obligated to pay because he assumes liability under a contract. Exceptions to this exclusion are for tort liability assumed under an insured contract (such as a hold harmless agreement) or a situation in which the insured would be liable even without a con-

tract. The following are insured contracts, either oral or written, for which coverage would apply:
- municipal indemnity agreements;
- easement agreements:
  (1) easement or license agreements in connection with vehicle or pedestrian private railroad crossings at grade; or
  (2) other easement agreements;
- elevator maintenance agreements;
- leases of premises;
- railroad sidetrack agreements; and
- any part of any other contract pertaining to the insured's business under which the insured assumes the tort liability of another. (**Tort liability** means liability imposed by law in the absence of any contract or agreement. It includes liability for negligence or assault.)

✓ ***Take Note:*** The insured contracts under a CGL policy can be remembered using the mnemonic acronym LEASE:

- **L**ease of premises
- **E**asement
- **A**greement to indemnify a municipality
- **S**idetrack agreement
- **E**levator maintenance agreement

This broad wording provides almost blanket contractual liability coverage. Coverage can, by endorsement, be reduced to incidental contracts.

3. **Liquor liability.** The CGL policy does not cover liability incurred because the insured is in the business of manufacturing, distributing, selling, or serving liquor. Many states have **dram shop acts** or alcoholic beverage acts that give an injured person the right to recover from someone who served or contributed to the intoxication of a person, such as a bartender might do. Under this exclusion then, a bartender or similar person is not eligible for liability coverage under CGL insurance. However, **host liquor liability** is part of the liability policy. A casual host who simply serves alcohol is provided with liquor liability coverage under the policy.
4. **Workers' compensation**. There is no coverage under the policy for benefits payable under workers' compensation, disability benefits, or unemployment compensation laws.
5. **Employer's liability.** The CGL policy excludes coverage for bodily injury to the insured's employees for injuries arising out of or in the course of employment by the insured. As a result, this exclusion prohibits claims by spouses or families and so-called third-party-over actions. (A **third-party-over action** occurs when an employee sues a manufacturer for injuries caused by a product of that manufacturer, such as a machine, and the manufacturer subsequently sues the employer for negligence in operating or maintaining the machine.) These types of claims are covered under a workers' compensation or employer's liability policy.

6. **Pollution.** The policy does not cover cleanup costs or bodily injury and property damage arising out of the actual or alleged discharge, disposal or escape of pollutants. An endorsement that is part of the policy does provide coverage for damages caused by heat, smoke, or fumes from a hostile fire on the premises. Pollution coverage is discussed in more detail at the end of this unit.
7. **Auto, aircraft, or watercraft.** Liability arising out of the ownership, maintenance, operation, entrustment, loading, unloading, or use of any automobile, aircraft, or watercraft is not covered in the CGL policy. The intent of this exclusion is to rule out legal liability other policies cover. However, this exclusion does not eliminate coverage for:
   - watercraft of any size while ashore on premises owned or rented to the named insured;
   - watercraft the named insured does not own, but rents or borrows, provided it is:
     (1) less than 26 feet long; and
     (2) not being used to carry people or property for a charge;
   - an auto parked on the public ways (sidewalks, land, streets, etc.) next to the premises the named insured owns or rents as long as the auto is not owned by, rented to, or loaned to the insured (thus, damage to an auto caused by a valet while he was parking a customer's auto at a restaurant would be covered); or
   - operation of mobile equipment.
8. **Mobile equipment**. The policy provides no coverage for mobile equipment while it is being transported by an auto owned or operated by or rented or loaned to an insured or while it is being used in an organized racing, speed or demolition contest.
9. **War**. Liability arising out of war, insurrection, or rebellion is excluded even if it arises from liability assumed under a contract.
10. **Care, custody, or control.** The CGL policy excludes coverage for damage to property owned by, rented by, or otherwise in the care, custody, or control of the insured. An insured should have property insurance to cover such property. This also excludes damage to premises sold to, given by, or abandoned by the insured unless the premises were the insured's work and never occupied, rented, or held for rental by the named insured. However, the policy would cover bodily injury or property damage to others for defects the seller inadvertently failed to mention to the buyer. (The latter is sometimes called **premises alienated** by the insured.) Also, the CGL policy does not cover property on which work is being performed.
11. **Damage to the insured's product.** Excluded from the policy is property damage to the insured's product or any part of it arising out of that product. Repair or replacement of the insured's work is excluded. In a situation where A makes a product that is a component in a product B makes, A does not have coverage for its part, but should have coverage to protect B for damage to the whole product caused by A's component.
12. **Property damage to the insured's work.** This provision excludes coverage for the cost of replacing, repairing, or otherwise redoing the

insured's or the insured's employees' faulty work, including loss of use of the named insured's work. This exclusion does not apply if a subcontractor performed the work.

✓ ***For Example:*** A TV repairperson comes to a house and fixes the TV on the premises. After that person leaves, however, the TV starts a fire, which ultimately burns down the house. The CGL policy covers the damage to the house, but not the TV. Similarly, suppose a contractor builds a roof over a pedestrian walkway, and three months after the work is completed, the roof collapses. The CGL policy does not pay for rebuilding the roof; however, if a person was injured when the roof fell, that loss is covered.

13. **Property damage to impaired property.** The CGL policy provides no coverage for loss to others caused by property not actually damaged, but not working properly (impaired property), arising out of a deficiency or condition in the insured's work or product or of a failure to perform a contract according to its terms. In other words, this policy does not guarantee products or workmanship.

✓ ***For Example:*** Impaired property exists, for instance, when an insured installs a faulty valve in a piece of equipment that makes the equipment unusable. By removing and repairing or replacing the valve, the machine can operate. Therefore, it is impaired property and excluded from coverage. If, however, the insured sells fruit to an ice cream manufacturer and after the batches of ice cream are made it is discovered that the fruit was tainted, the damage to the ice cream is covered under property damage.

14. **Product recall (the sistership exclusion).** The policy excludes damage for loss or cost to the insured for recalling or replacing products or for redoing completed operations. Also excluded is loss of use of a product due to a known or suspected defect. A very limited number of insurers provide product recall coverage.
15. **Personal and advertising injury.** The CGL excludes coverage for bodily injury arising out of personal and advertising injury.

## Quick Quiz 5.3

For each of the following situations, which exclusion under the CGL policy eliminates coverage?

1. __________ An employee of the insured is injured when a machine malfunctions.

2. __________ A piece of equipment, borrowed from another firm, is damaged.

3. __________ A restaurant employee intentionally strikes a patron.

4. __________ A night club sells beer to a customer, who subsequently injures someone in an automobile accident.

5. __________ A manufacturer makes a gauge that must be removed from a boat because it is defective

## Answers

1. *Exclusion #4. Injuries for which benefits are payable under a workers' compensation, disability benefits, or unemployment compensation law.*
2. *Exclusion #10. Damage to property owned by, rented by, or otherwise in the care, custody, or control of the insured.*
3. *Exclusion #1. Bodily injury or property damage that is expected or intended from the standpoint of the insured.*
4. *Exclusion #3. Coverage does not apply to an insured in the business of manufacturing, distributing, selling, or serving liquor.*
5. *Exclusion #13. There is no coverage for loss to other's property if it is not damaged, but simply "impaired" because it contains a defective product of the insured's.*

### Fire Legal Liability

A statement in the exclusions indicates that all of the exclusions (except #1 and #2) do not apply to fire damage to property rented to the named insured. The two exclusions that do apply are intentional injury and contractual liability.

Therefore, for a tenant to have coverage in case he causes a fire to rented property, the fire must be unintentional and the tenant must be the negligent party. The CGL policy excludes coverage for damage caused by a tenant's negligence, when such damage affects areas of the property within the tenant's control. The tenant must purchase a fire legal liability insurance policy for that coverage.

### Coverage B: Personal and Advertising Injury Liability Coverage

The insurance company pays those monetary sums that the insured becomes legally obligated to pay as damages because of:

- personal injury arising out of the conduct of the insured's business, excluding advertising, publishing, broadcasting, and telecasting by the insured; or
- advertising injury in the course of advertising the insured's goods, products, or services to which the insurance applies.

The company has the right and duty to defend any suit seeking damages up to the policy limits. The company may investigate and settle any claim at its discretion.

**Personal injury** means injury other than bodily injury arising out of:

- false arrest, detention, or imprisonment;
- malicious prosecution;
- wrongful entry into or eviction of a person from a room, dwelling, or premises that the person occupies;
- oral or written publication of material that slanders (spoken material) or libels (written material) a person or an organization, or that disparages a person's or an organization's goods, products, or services; or
- oral or written publication of material that violates a person's right of privacy.

**Advertising injury** means injury arising out of oral or written publication of material that:

- slanders or libels a person or an organization;
- violates a person's or an organization's ideas or style of doing business;
- misappropriates an person's or an organization's ideas or style of doing business; or
- infringes on a person's or an organization's copyright, title or slogan.

## Exclusions

The following exclusions apply to Section B coverage:

- Injury arising out of the willful violation of laws
- Liability assumed under contract or arising from a breach of contract
- Publication of material known to be false, or published before the policy period
- Failure of goods, products, or services
- Incorrect description of price of goods, products, or services
- Offense committed by an insured in the business of advertising, broadcasting, publishing, or telecasting
- Criminal acts
- Infringement of copyright, patent, trademark, or trade secret
- Electronic chatrooms or bulletin boards
- Unauthorized use of another's name or product
- Pollution

## Coverage C: Medical Payments Coverage

In **Coverage C**, the insurance company pays reasonable expenses for bodily injury to a third party caused by an accident:

- on the premises that the insured owns or rents;
- on ways next to the premises the insured owns or rents; or
- because of the insured's business operation.

These medical expenses are paid regardless of fault. However, it should be noted that medical payments are not made unless the circumstances of the occurrence are covered under the bodily injury liability coverage if negligence is determined. In addition, the expenses must be incurred within the coverage territory and reported to the insurance company within one year from the date of any accident.

**Test Topic Alert!**

Medical payments coverage is for the bodily injury of a third party, claimed as a premises and operations loss only.

**Exclusions**

Section C offers no coverage for:

- bodily injury to any insured;
- bodily injury to any employee of the insured (covered by workers' compensation);
- bodily injury to a tenant of the insured;
- injuries incurred while a person takes part in athletics;
- damages sustained in accidents excluded under Coverage A; and
- war.

**Supplementary Payments for Coverages A and B**

The insurance company pays certain costs independent of the policy's liability limits. These costs include:

- all expenses the insurance company incurs (including defense costs, expenses for investigating the claim, costs taxed against the insured, and interest on judgments);
- up to $250 for bail bonds and release of attachment bonds (the insurance company provides the money, but the insured or an attorney must apply for the bonds); and
- reasonable expenses the insured incurs when the insurance company requests the insured's assistance in investigating or defending any claim or suit (including up to $250 per day for time away from work).

**Test Topic Alert!**

Supplementary payments for court-related costs always are paid in addition to the policy limits.

Finally, many states require that all costs for defense fall outside of (in addition to) the limits of liability shown on the declarations page.

## Section II—Who Is an Insured

If the business is a sole proprietorship, the **insured** is the designated person and spouse, but only for business acts. If the business is a partnership or a joint venture, the partners or coventurers and their spouses are the insureds—but, again, only for business acts.

If the business is a corporation, the executive officers and directors are the insureds only for their business acts. The stockholders are also insureds, but only in relation to their possible liability as stockholders.

Employees other than executive officers also are insured for liability for acts they commit within the scope of their employment. An employee is not an insured for causing bodily or personal injury to a fellow employee because such injury covered is under workers' compensation.

An employee is not covered for bodily or personal injury that arises when the employee provides or fails to provide professional health care services. Individuals who provide health care services must carry their own medical malpractice coverage.

## Section III—Limits of Insurance

The CGL policy sets six limits of insurance:

- General aggregate limit (sum of all medical damages under coverage C plus the damages under Coverages A and B; excludes injury and damages included in the products and completed operations hazard)
- Products and completed operations aggregate limit
- Personal and advertising injury limit
- Each occurrence limit (maximum under one limit)
- Fire damage limit (maximum payable for property damage to rented premises for a single fire)
- Medical expense limit (maximum payable because of bodily injury to one person)

## Section IV—Conditions

This section of the CGL policy deals with a number of issues, from bankruptcy to legal actions.

### Bankruptcy

Bankruptcy or insolvency of the insured or of the insured's estate does not relieve the insurer of any obligation.

### Duties in the Event of Occurrence, Claim, or Suit

In the event of an occurrence, a claim or a suit, the insured's duties include:

- notifying promptly the insurer of an occurrence that may result in a claim (including how, when, and where the occurrence took place and the names and addresses of any injured persons and witnesses);
- providing prompt written notice of a claim or suit;
- providing immediate notice to the insurer of receipt of demands, notices, summonses, or other legal papers the insured receives in connection with a claim or suit; and
- cooperating and assisting in the investigation of a claim.

Except at his own cost, no insured voluntarily makes a payment, assumes any obligation, or incurs any expense, other than for first aid, without the insurer's consent. If the insured does so, the policy is not void but the insurance company is not obligated to cover this particular occurrence.

Furthermore, if an insured fails to notify promptly the insurer of an occurrence that may result in a claim, the insurer will probably reserve its right to refuse coverage without voiding the policy.

**Legal Action against the Insurer**

The insured must comply fully with all terms of the policy before taking legal action against the insurer. A party may sue the insurer to recover damages against an insured in the form of a settlement or judgment. Such a settlement or judgment can amount to no more than the policy limits.

**Other Insurance**

Generally, the CGL policy is the primary policy. In some situations, however, it is the excess policy. If there two policies exist, each with a provision making it primary, the method of sharing will be as follows:

If all other insurance permits contribution by equal shares, the policy will follow that approach; and if any other insurance does not permit contribution by equal shares, contribution will be by limits (pro rata to the total amount available).

**Premium Audit**

The premium paid is an advance premium as a deposit premium only. At the end of the policy period, or during periods stated in the contract, the insurer audits the insured's basis of premium (sales, payroll, etc.) and computes the earned premium for that period.

**Representations**

Statements the insured makes are **representations**—that is, statements of fact that are substantially true to the best of the insured's knowledge and belief.

**Separation of Insureds**

Except with respect to the limits of insurance, the CGL policy applies separately to each insured against whom a claim is made or a suit is brought. In other words, the limit of insurance is paid only once per occurrence regardless of the number of claimants or the number of persons insured. For other costs, such as defense costs, each insured is separate.

**Transfer of Rights of Recovery against Others to the Insurer**

If the insured has rights to recover from a third party all or part of any payment the insurer has made, those rights are transferred to the insurer. The insured must do nothing to impair those rights. At the insurer's request, the insured must bring suit or transfer those rights to the insurer. This transfer of rights is known as **subrogation.**

## Section V—Definitions

Other key definitions that arise in CGL policies are explained below.

**Advertisement** is any notice published to the general public or segment of it about goods, products, or services to attract customers. This includes content placed on the Internet. With respect to websites, it includes only that part of a site that is about the insured's products, goods, or services that is designed to attract customers.

**Bodily injury** means bodily injury, sickness, or disease a person sustains, including death resulting from any of these at any time.

**Coverage territory** includes:

- the United States (including its territories and possessions), Puerto Rico, and Canada;
- international waters or airspace, provided the injury or damage does not occur in the course of travel or transportation to or from any place not included in the paragraph above; or
- all parts of the world if:
  - the injury or damage arises out of goods or products the insured makes or sells in the territory described above, or the activities of a person whose home is in the territory described above, but who is away for a short time on the insured's business; and
  - the insured's responsibility to pay is determined in a suit on the merits, in the territory described above, or in a settlement the insurer agrees to.

**Employee** includes a leased worker, but not a temporary worker.

**Impaired property** means tangible property, other than the insured's product or work, that cannot be used or is less useful because:

- it incorporates the insured's product or work that is known or thought to be defective, deficient, inadequate or dangerous; or
- the insured has failed to fulfill the terms of a contract or an agreement if the property can be restored to use by the repair, replacement, adjustment or removal of the insured's product or work or fulfillment of a contract or an agreement.

**Loading or unloading** means handling of property:

- after it is moved from the place where it is accepted for movement into or onto an aircraft, a watercraft, or an auto;
- while it is in or on an aircraft, a watercraft, or an auto; or
- while it is being moved from an aircraft, a watercraft, or an auto to the place where it is finally delivered.

Loading or unloading does not include the movement of property by means of a mechanical device other than a hand truck that is not attached to the aircraft, watercraft, or auto.

**Mobile equipment** includes:

- bulldozers, farm machinery, forklifts, and other vehicles designed for use principally off public roads;
- vehicles maintained for use solely on or next to premises the insured owns or rents;
- vehicles that travel on crawler treads;
- vehicles, whether or not self-propelled, maintained primarily to provide mobility to permanently mounted power cranes, shovels, loaders, diggers, or drills or to road construction or resurfacing equipment such as graders;
- other vehicles that are not self-propelled and are maintained primarily to provide mobility to permanently attached equipment such as air compressors, pumps, generators, "cherry pickers", and similar devices used to raise or lower workers; and
- other vehicles maintained primarily for purposes other than the transportation of persons or cargo.

Certain self-propelled vehicles with permanently attached equipment are not mobile equipment, but are considered autos. This includes equipment designed primarily for snow removal, road maintenance equipment and "cherry pickers."

✓ ***For Example:*** When equipment operates as a "cherry picker" lifting workers or materials at a construction site, the CGL policy provides coverage. However, when it operates as an auto, ferrying workers or materials from one construction site to another, the CGL does not provide coverage. Instead, an auto policy applies.

**Occurrence** means an accident, including continuous or repeated exposure to substantially the same general harmful conditions.

**Property damage** means physical injury to tangible property, including all resulting loss of use of the property. All such loss is considered to occur at the time of the physical injury that caused it. Property damage also means loss of use of tangible property that is not physically injured.

**Your product** means:

- any goods or products, other than real property, the insured sells, manufactures, handles, distributes, or disposes of, others trading under the insured's name, or a person or an organization whose business or assets the insured has acquired; and
- containers (other than vehicles), materials, parts, or equipment furnished in connection with such goods or products.

The term **your product** includes:

- warranties or representations made at any time with respect to the fitness, quality, durability, performance or use of a product; and
- the providing of or failure to provide warnings or instructions.

**Your work** means:

- work or operations performed by the insured or on his or her behalf; and
- materials, parts or equipment furnished in connection with such work or operations.

The term your work includes:

- warranties or representations made at any time with respect to the fitness, quality, durability, performance, or use of the insured's work; and
- the providing of or failure to provide warnings or instructions.

## Endorsements to the CGL Policy

The CGL policy can be modified to meet a policyholder's needs by adding endorsements. Some of the more commonly used endorsements follow.

### Deductible Liability Insurance

Although liability insurance usually is issued without a deductible, at times one is desired or necessary from an underwriting standpoint. This endorsement applies a per claim or per occurrence deductible to bodily injury, property damage or both.

### Additional Insured Endorsements

A broad array of endorsements is designed to add coverage for additional interests under the CGL policy.

### Exclusion—All Hazards in Connection with Designated Premises

This endorsement eliminates coverage for certain locations. This may be done to accommodate an underwriter that does not wish to take on the exposures presented or a policyholder who has insured the location under another policy. Separate endorsements function in a similar manner to exclude coverage for designated products or services of the insured.

### Liquor Liability

When the insured is engaged in the business of serving or furnishing alcoholic beverages, the exclusion in the form can be deleted by using this endorsement.

## Coverage for Pollution

As noted earlier, the CGL policy contains an exclusion for pollution and clean-up costs that is nearly absolute. The ISO has developed two separate coverage forms for dealing with pollution exposures:

- Pollution Liability Coverage Form (Designated Sites); and
- Pollution Liability Limited Coverage Form (Designated Sites).

Both of these coverage forms are issued on a claims-made basis. The major difference between them is that the limited form does not include any coverage for pollutant clean-up costs. Although the ISO has made these forms available, they are used very little in the marketplace. Environmental impairment liability insurance, which includes pollution, is a highly specialized field and is written by only a few insurance companies using special forms.

# Unit Test Five

1. Which of the following is NOT an occurrence as defined in a liability policy?
   A. Running out of gas while driving
   B. Continuous discharge of chemicals that damage a crop
   C. Motor vehicle accident
   D. Person who slips on a wet floor

2. Which of the following statements about the commercial general liability policy is CORRECT?
   A. It does not cover assault because it is intentional.
   B. It covers assault and battery under certain conditions.
   C. It does not cover assault and battery if committed by the insured.
   D. It covers assault and battery only if committed by the insured's employees.

3. Legal liability is determined by
   A. custom and practice
   B. voluntary settlement between the parties
   C. applying the law to the facts of the case
   D. agreement between two parties in an accident

4. Each of the following is a duty of the insured in the event of an occurrence, a claim or a suit EXCEPT
   A. promptly notifying the insurer of an occurrence that may result in a claim
   B. at his own expense, making any reasonable settlement with the injured party
   C. forwarding any legal papers, including suits, to the insurance company
   D. cooperating with the insurer in the defense of a claim

5. Under the commercial general liability policy, if the insured receives notice of a claim or suit, he must notify the insurer of this action
   A. within 5 days
   B. as soon as practical
   C. promptly
   D. immediately

6. Each of the following is a covered territory under the CGL policy EXCEPT
   A. Canada
   B. Mexico
   C. Puerto Rico
   D. New Mexico

7. Under the CGL policy, mobile equipment includes which of the following?
   A. Land motor vehicle designed for use on public roads
   B. Vehicle designed for use principally off public roads, such as a bulldozer or forklift
   C. Vehicle operated exclusively on public roads
   D. Vehicle being towed by a covered vehicle

8. Which of the following is NOT a supplementary payment the CGL policy provides?
   A. Cost of bonds
   B. Interest on judgments
   C. Costs of investigation and defense
   D. Medical payments

9. Mobile equipment may include which of the following?
   A. Equipment not subject to motor vehicle registration
   B. Licensed vehicles
   C. Snow removal equipment
   D. Road maintenance equipment

10. When an insured settles a liability claim with a third party, which of the following are options for the insurer?
    A. It may void the policy and refund the premium.
    B. It may reimburse the insured's actual out-of-pocket expenditures.
    C. It may not have to pay liability damages or the insured's defense costs.
    D. It may not provide coverage for future liability losses.

11. Which of the following statements defines subrogation?
    A. The insurance company may recover costs from a third party, assuming that party was responsible for the accident.
    B. The insured can collect for the loss from his or her own insurance company and also from the party responsible for the loss.
    C. The insurance company may collect from a responsible party, then reimburse the insured.
    D. The responsible party must pay the insured before the insurance company will pay.

12. For an event to qualify as an occurrence under a liability policy, which of the following statements must be TRUE?
    A. It must have been expected by the claimant.
    B. It must not have been expected or intended from the insured's standpoint.
    C. It must be unexpected and unintended from the claimant's standpoint.
    D. It must have occurred while the insured was not present.

13. A condition of the commercial general liability policy is that in the event of a covered loss, the insured must do which of the following?
    A. Obtain legal counsel on behalf of the insurance company
    B. Immediately send to the insurer copies of any demands, notices, summons or legal notices
    C. Respond to legal notices within a prescribed period
    D. Make contact with the claimant to determine liability

14. A laundromat might purchase a CGL policy to protect against which of the following situations?
    A. Employees leaving to continue the same business elsewhere, resulting in a loss of customers
    B. Loss of revenues if the electricity goes off as a result of the utility's negligence
    C. Burning of a person in a restroom from hot water
    D. Damage to property from ruptured water pipes

15. Which of the following is included under the commercial general liability policy as premises and operations coverage?
    A. Guest slips on carpet in the insured's apartment building
    B. Insured is injured while repairing the roof
    C. Customer becomes ill after eating at the insured's restaurant
    D. Roof begins to leak after the insured installs new shingles

16. The commercial general liability policy covers which of the following accidents?
    A. Injury to a customer that is never reported to the company
    B. Injury caused by an employee to a customer while acting within the scope of employment
    C. Injury to an employee of the insured while acting within the scope of employment
    D. Injury caused by an employee while on vacation

17. A commercial general liability policy covers the policyholder for contractual liability arising from all of the following EXCEPT a(n)
    A. easement agreement
    B. railroad sidetrack agreement
    C. elevator maintenance agreement
    D. escrow agreement

18. If the owner of a large apartment building purchases commercial general liability coverage, he or she has coverage in which of the following situations?
    A. Tenant is injured while participating in an athletic event off the owner's premises.
    B. Tenant who is also a caretaker-janitor is injured while cleaning a hallway.
    C. Tenant is injured when a fixture falls on him while he cleans his apartment.
    D. Tenant refuses to leave the premises after failure to pay rent.

19. If an owner has leased her entire building to a responsible party, with the lease requiring the lessee to carry liability insurance, which of the following statements is CORRECT?
    A. The owner cannot be sued for injury or damage because the tenant occupies the building.
    B. The owner need not carry liability insurance because she is protected adequately by the lessee's insurance.
    C. The owner should carry liability insurance because all parties normally are named in any suit.
    D. The owner need not carry liability insurance because it is not available to landlords.

20. Which of the following is NOT included as an insured contract in the commercial general liability policy?
    A. Railroad sidetrack agreement
    B. Lease of premises
    C. Easement
    D. Claim service agreement

21. An insured under a CGL policy has coverage for all of the following EXCEPT a(n)
    A. small child falling into an excavation
    B. employee injured when temporary steps collapse
    C. adult injured while touring a home under construction
    D. vandal hurt on the premises who files an action against the contractor

22. A heating contractor who installed a furnace in a suburban home agreed to service the furnace periodically under a service contract. In this case, his CGL policy would cover each of the following accidents EXCEPT one that

    A. results from faulty installation of the furnace requiring reinstallation
    B. occurs during a service call
    C. results from a malfunction of the heater
    D. results from his completed work

23. The commercial general liability policy provides protection for each of the following EXCEPT liability arising

    A. out of the insured's activities at an insured location
    B. from accidents caused by the insured's past activities away from the premises
    C. out of the use of any products sold, for accidents occurring away from the premises
    D. out of an accident the insured caused intentionally

# Unit Test Five Answers & Rationale

1. **A.** An accident is an event that can be identified as to time and place. An occurrence includes an accident as well as an event that occurs over time. Running out of gas, while unfortunate, is not accidental.

2. **B.** The CGL policy covers assault and battery as long as the insured did not cause the injury or damage intentionally.

3. **C.** Legal liability arises out of statute, common law, or contractual assumption. In each case, liability must be examined in light of the facts by a claims adjuster, judge or jury.

4. **B.** The insurance contract precludes the insured from settling with third parties without the insurer's permission.

5. **C.** The CGL policy requires prompt notice of any incident that may give rise to a claim, but does not define prompt.

6. **B.** The CGL policy coverage territory does not include Mexico because American insurance is considered invalid in that country.

7. **B.** The definition of mobile equipment under the CGL policy includes vehicles designed for use principally off public roads, used solely on the insured's property, that travel on crawler treads or are used to provide mobility to other equipment.

8. **D.** Medical payments, a separate coverage under the CGL policy, is not included in supplementary payments.

9. **A.** The definition of mobile equipment specifically eliminates coverage for snow removal and road maintenance equipment. Licensed vehicles are covered under the definition only if they are maintained for use solely on or next to premises the insured owns or rents.

10. **C.** The insured may not make any settlements without the insurer's consent. If he does so, the insurer may deny both payment of the claim and the defense of any suits.

11. **A.** Subrogation involves the transfer of the insured's rights of recovery against others to the insurance company in exchange for payment of the loss by the insurer.

12. **B.** The first exclusion under the CGL policy eliminates coverage for insured's bodily injury or property damage that is expected or intended from the insured's standpoint.

13. **B.** Under the condition pertaining to duties in the event of occurrence, claim, or suit, the CGL policy requires immediate notice for any demands, notices, summons, or other legal papers due to the time-sensitive nature of these items.

14. **C.** The CGL policy covers bodily injury and property damage as well as personal and advertising injury. It does not extend coverage for consequential losses or for losses to property.

15. **A.** Premises and operations coverage applies to occurrences that take place on property the insured owns, rents, or controls or that arise from current activities. Coverage does not apply to the insured.

16. **B.** The CGL policy requires prompt notice of claims. Coverage does not apply to injuries to employees on or off the job.

17. **D.** Insured contracts under the CGL policy include leases, easements, agreements to indemnify municipalities, sidetrack agreements, and elevator maintenance agreements only.

18. **C.** The CGL policy pays for bodily injury or property damage that arises out of the premises. Injuries to employees are excluded.

19. **C.** It is in the owner's best interest to carry liability insurance for the protection it gives in the event of a lawsuit which names the owner as a defendant.

20. **D.** Insured contracts under the CGL policy include leases, easements, agreements to indemnify municipalities, sidetrack agreements, and elevator maintenance agreements only.

21. **B.** Employees are excluded from liability coverage because they would receive payments from workers' compensation.

22. **A.** The CGL policy excludes coverage for property damage to the insured's work.

23. **D.** The first exclusion under the CGL policy eliminates coverage for insured's bodily injury or property damage that is expected or intended from the insured's standpoint.

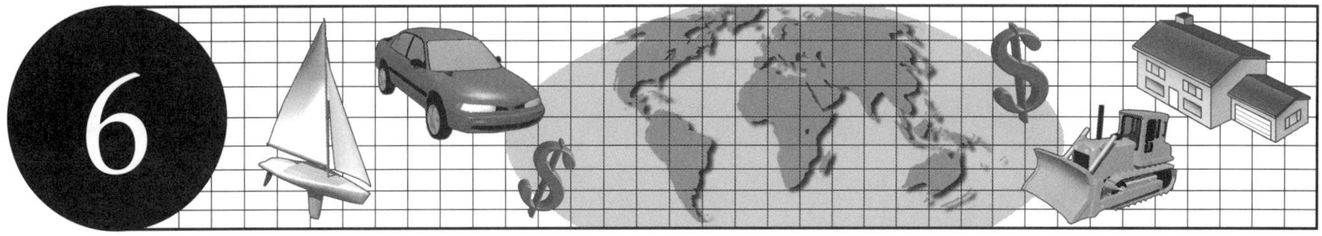


# Professional Liability Insurance and Umbrella Policies

## INTRODUCTION

A professional is a person who possesses the special knowledge and skills necessary to render a service. The knowledge and skills come from that person's education and experience in a particular branch of science or learning.

Such professionals must attain and maintain a minimum standard of special knowledge and ability and must exercise reasonable care in performing their services. A person who fails in this regard can be held liable to a client if the client is injured or damaged by such failure. Professional liability insurance protects professionals against claims for damages arising out of their providing, or failing to provide, services. The policies are referred to as malpractice and errors and omissions liability insurance.

## UNIT OBJECTIVES

When you have completed this unit, you should be able to:

- identify the exposures to loss individuals in various professions face;
- describe the basic provisions professional liability policies contain;
- discuss the major types of professional liability policies, including their insuring agreements and exclusions;
- explain the professional liability exposures of insurance agents and brokers;
- discuss the reasons for umbrella policies for individuals, businesses, and other organizations; and
- explain the common features umbrella policies contain.

# Duties of Professionals

Professionals have two types of duties:

- **contractual obligations**; and
- **tort obligations**.

## Contractual Obligations

A professional, such as a doctor or an engineer, who agrees to perform particular services for a client creates a contract, essentially a promise to provide competent work or service. The law recognizes that such a promise establishes duties that the professional must fulfill. Should the professional fail to fulfill those duties, the law provides a remedy.

If a professional fails to perform contractual obligations as promised and a client suffers an injury or damage, the client is entitled to be placed as nearly as possible in the same position he would have been in had the contract been performed. To place the client in this position, a court awards him damages. Damages are usually some form of monetary compensation.

Professional liability insurance protects professionals such as physicians, attorneys, engineers, accountants, insurance agents and brokers, or architects against claims for damages arising out of the services they provide—or fail to provide—when practicing their professions.

## Tort Obligations

Torts are civil wrongs. Defamation, assault and battery, fraud, false arrest, and negligence are examples of torts. If a person fails to perform a common or statutory law duty, the injured party may seek damages from that person. The law imposes a general duty upon everyone to avoid causing harm to others.

In the case of a professional, this harm may be caused by acting negligently in rendering professional services, or by failing to act when there is a duty to do so. Thus, the question is whether a **prudent person**, in exercising the degree of care required of a professional under similar circumstances, would have acted—or failed to act—in the same manner. If the professional's action or inaction harmed the client, the professional may be liable to the client. Monetary damages are often the award given in these situations.

# Types of Professional Liability Insurance

## Professional Liability Policies

Professional liability policy provisions differ from those of the commercial general liability policy in several ways. A brief discussion of the general nature of professional liability insurance follows.

### Insuring Agreement

The **Insuring Agreement** of a professional liability policy provides the coverage grant and describes the nature of the coverage being extended. It typically includes a description of the acts or services covered, the persons or organizations covered, the coverage territory, the damages to which coverage applies, and the applicability of defense costs. It also may contain a statement of the claims settlement procedures that are followed if a loss occurs. Important parts of the insuring agreement are the clauses relating to the insurer's liability limit and the policy deductible.

✓ ***Take Note:*** Unlike the CGL policy, which provides coverage for bodily injury, property damage, and personal injury, a professional liability policy typically covers wrongful acts, errors, or omissions the insured commits. In some cases, such as medical malpractice and architects' and engineers' policies, bodily injury is a covered cause of loss due to the nature of the profession.

### Limits of Liability

Four basic approaches are used in setting the limits in a professional liability policy. The first method involves a single, aggregate limit—the maximum amount the insurer will pay on the insured's behalf during the policy period. This aggregate may apply to both damages and defense costs. The second method is to issue the policy with a per-claim limit and an annual aggregate. Often the per-claim limit is the same as the aggregate, making the policy function in fundamentally the same manner as it does under the first method. The third approach is to impose an annual aggregate that is some multiple of the per-claim limit. Finally, the policy may have a per-claim limit only, with no annual aggregate. This approach, usually reserved for medical professional policies, benefits the policyholder by not restricting the number of claims that can be brought during the policy term.

### Deductible

It is common for a professional liability policy to have a deductible provision. The deductible usually applies per wrongful act because a single misdeed could result in multiple claims under the policy. The insurer generally pays the third party the full amount of the settlement (subject to the policy limit), then seeks reimbursement of the deductible from the insured.

### Exclusions

Four general types of exclusions exist in a professional liability policy. The first two are mostly nonnegotiable, meaning the insurer usually is unwilling to delete them.

### *Uninsurable Exposures*

The first type of exclusion involves uninsurable exposures, such as fraud or criminal acts by the insured. It is obvious why these acts are excluded. However, the insurance company may provide defense coverage for alleged fraudulent acts or alleged crimes associated with the coverage the policy establishes.

### *Other Coverage*

The second type of exclusion involves exposures that are better covered under other types of policies, such as general liability or workers' compensation policies. Occasionally, this exclusion can be problematic for both the insurer and the insured. For example, the bodily injury exclusion often found in professional liability policies is included because bodily injury, such as a slip and fall at the insured's premises, would be covered under a general liability policy. It does not occur because of the rendering or failing to render a professional service. At the same time, the general liability policy would include an exclusion that exempts from coverage a bodily injury that results from the providing of professional services.

✓ ***For Example:*** A dentist's patient slipped and fell on a carpet in the dentist's office. A contributing factor to the fall is thought to be the after-effects of an anesthetic used in a dental procedure. In cases such as this, it is possible the carrier for the professional liability coverage and the insurer of the general liability coverage might deny coverage or both could be forced to share the loss. This type of loss illustrates the fact that while exclusions and policy wording in general are drawn very carefully to minimize misunderstandings, even a carefully written insurance contract can be subject to contention and disagreement between the parties to the contract.

✓ ***Take Note:*** The remaining types of exclusions are negotiable and often can be modified or removed from the policy at the insurer's discretion. If the exclusions are removed, the insurer may wish to increase the premium.

### *Additional Exposures*

The third type of exclusion covers exposures arising out of a particular facet or portion of the professional's work or service that the insurance company does not wish to include. Sometimes these are highly specialized areas of a profession that require extraordinary skill or special training. Often an insurer excludes such a specialty for the average practitioner in a profession, but agrees to delete the exclusion for a practitioner who has the necessary advanced training and experience.

✓ ***For Example:*** An attorney's professional liability policy often excludes legal work involving the transfer of securities because it is highly specialized and involves exposure to very substantial and costly claims. If a particular attorney, however, is highly trained and experienced in this area of law, the insurer may delete the exclusion on his policy, often in exchange for a higher premium charge to the insured.

### *Contractual Liability*

The fourth type of exclusion involves contractual liability. It is a fairly common business practice in some professions to assume the liability of others under a contract; however, many professional liability policies exclude the assumption of another's liability under contract. The purpose of the exclusion is to allow the insurance company to evaluate in advance the types of contracts the insured enters into. In this way, the insurer can assess the exposure before accepting it. This also allows the insurer to determine whether an additional premium charge is necessary whether it is not an exposure that the insurance company wishes to undertake.

## Settlement

Defense, settlement, and supplementary payments for professional liability policies are similar to those for general liability policies. A significant exception used to be that many professional liability policies contained a provision stating that an insurer was precluded from settling a claim or suit unless it had the insured's written consent. This provision was designed to prevent an insurer from making an unwarranted settlement that could affect the professional's reputation adversely. Today this provision is frequently eliminated in policies.

The treatment of defense costs in malpractice and errors and omissions policies often differs from that of defense costs in general liability. Professional liability policies often establish the payment of defense costs within the limit of liability rather than in addition to (outside of) the limit.

## Quick Quiz 6.1

1. One of the unique features of a professional liability policy is that unlike other liability policies, coverage applies to __________ __________ of the insured.

2. The four basic types of exclusions under a professional liability policy are:
   ____________________
   ____________________
   ____________________
   ____________________

3. True or false? Defense costs under a professional liability policy usually are paid outside the limits of liability.

### Answers

1. *wrongful acts*
2. *Uninsurable exposures, those exposures that are better covered by other policies, particular facets or portions of the insured's service or profession, and contractual liability*
3. *False*

## Medical Malpractice

**Medical malpractice insurance** is a form of protection for various medical-related institutions and medical professionals where the exposure is bodily injury to a client. The injury may involve rendering a service or failing to render a service. These policies are issued to:

- hospitals;
- physicians, surgeons, and dentists;
- nurses;
- opticians;
- optometrists;
- chiropractors;
- veterinarians; and
- pharmacists.

Medical malpractice policies usually are written on a claims-made basis rather than on an occurrence form.

## Legal Malpractice

**Legal malpractice insurance** protects attorneys and law firms that perform legal services for clients. It also protects them from claims by third parties who were the intended beneficiaries of the legal services, but not the actual clients.

The injury in a legal malpractice claim involves the loss or compromise of a client's legal right due to the attorney's or law firm's negligence in performing—or failing to perform—its professional duties. It also may involve a monetary loss.

## Errors & Omissions (E&O)

**Errors and omissions (E&O) insurance** relates to other types of professionals, such as architects, engineers, insurance agents, and accountants. In fact, the list of professionals who may obtain insurance in the nonmedical and non-legal professional liability lines is almost limitless. Unlike medical malpractice policies, errors and omissions policies generally exclude bodily injury and damage to tangible property because the profession's E&O policies cover usually generate claims for financial damages. However, the nature of a profession ultimately determines the nature of malpractice claims, and the insuring agreement of the professional liability policy reflects that fact.

✓ ***For Example:*** The form covering architects and engineers covers claims for bodily injury and property damage because errors or omissions in the design of buildings or products often lead to bodily injury or property damage.

As with medical and legal malpractice insurance, E&O coverage is for rendering or failing to render a service. Errors and omission policies generally are written on a claims-made form rather than an occurrence form.

## E&O Coverage for Insurance Agents and Brokers

Two sources of professional liability claims against insurance agents and brokers exist. The first is insurance companies an agent represents. If the agent exceeds his or her authority and causes an insurance company to suffer a loss by paying a claim that should not have been covered, the insurer sues the agent to recover the loss. The second source of E&O claims against insurance agents and brokers is their clients. Some of the common causes of claims are failure to secure insurance coverage, failure to renew and failure to advise of the need for coverage.

✓ ***For Example:*** A customer calls to add a vehicle to her automobile policy. If the agent fails to do so, a claim that occurs might not be covered. In this case, the client would have a cause of action against the agent or the E&O insurer for the amount of the uncovered loss. If, on the other hand, the agent adds the vehicle to the insured's policy, but it violates an agreement the agent has with the insurance company, the claim would be paid, but the company would have a cause of action against the agent for reimbursement of the loss.

The major causes of errors and omissions losses for insurance agents and brokers follow.

### Claims Made by Clients

- Failure to place coverage promptly
- Failure to place requested coverage
- Failure to increase or update coverage
- Failure to recommend needed coverage
- Failure to explain coverage limitations
- Clerical error or misunderstanding
- Verbal extension of nonexistent coverage
- Inadvertent cancellation or failure to renew

- Failure to advise of cancellation, nonrenewal or material restrictions
- Failure to place coverage with a solvent insurer

**Claims Made by Insurers**

- Failure to follow underwriting guidelines or exceeding authority
- Failure to exercise reasonable diligence in discharging insurer's duties
- Failure to act in the insurer's best interest
- Failure to revise coverage upon request
- Failure to cancel coverage upon request
- Failure to disclose material information

Errors and omissions coverage for insurance agents and brokers is important for firms of all sizes. Such policies protect agencies from the variety of E&O claims listed above. Usually, a deductible applies under a policy to encourage the agent to engage in some form of loss control that will reduce or eliminate E&O claims. Loss control activities, which can have a significant positive impact in reducing errors and omissions losses for agents and brokers, includes documentation of policies and procedures, audits to ensure adherence to standards, and use of checklists to reduce the possibility of overlooking important steps in an insurance transaction.

# Other Professional Liability Policies

## Directors' and Officers' Liability

Corporations are owned by stockholders and operated by boards of directors. The management of a corporation includes the board of directors, executive officers, and high-ranking employees. Corporate officers and directors may be sued for breach of corporate duties.

Directors and officers are said to have the fiduciary duties listed below:

- Duty to exercise reasonable care (the care a prudent officer or director would exercise in similar circumstances)
- Duty of loyalty to the corporation (officer or director cannot secretly seize for himself a business opportunity that properly belongs to the corporation)
- Duty of loyalty to the stockholders (officer or director may not use insider information and must exercise confidentiality)
- Duty to disclose material facts to people who have the right to know
- Duties under Employee Retirement Income Security Act of 1974 (ERISA), which imposes statutory duties on all persons deemed fiduciaries within a very broad definition of the concept

A **fiduciary** is a person who occupies a position of special trust and confidence, as in handling or supervising the affairs or funds of another. Trustees, executors, administrators, and corporate directors are fiduciaries. The mere fact that somebody trusts someone else, however, does not establish a fiduciary relationship. The relationship must fit a recognized legal category. True fiduciaries often must meet certain statutory tests and may not engage in defined acts.

Tort actions against officers and directors are based on negligence and intentional interference, resulting in:

- derivative suits by stockholders, wherein the damages go directly to the corporation, not to the stockholders as plaintiffs; and
- nonderivative suits by outsiders, which competitors or others initiate for tortuous acts or omissions.

Directors and officers may be held liable for acts of misfeasance, nonfeasance or malfeasance.

- **Misfeasance** is the performance of an act in an improper manner.
- **Nonfeasance** is a person's failure to perform an act he or she has a duty to perform.
- **Malfeasance** is the commission of an illegal act.

**Directors' and officers' (D&O) liability insurance** is a two-part contract:

- **Part I** covers the individual directors and officers. It also provides personal liability protection for the directors and officers when they are not indemnified by the corporation.
- **Part II** insures the corporation for company reimbursement. It repays the corporation for money paid to directors or officers for personal expenses associated with a claim.

## Coverage

The D&O form is a claims-made policy, and coverage begins only if the claim is first made against the insured during the policy period. If the claim is received before the policy period begins or after the policy expires, no coverage exists.

The key coverage of the D&O policy is wrongful acts resulting from any actual or alleged error, misstatement or misleading statement or omission, neglect, or breach of duty.

## Exclusions

Several exclusions exist for D&O liability insurance:

- libel or slander, dishonest acts, bodily injury, sickness, disease or death of any person; and
- all pollution events, sudden, accidental or otherwise.

## Employment Practices Liability

The 1980s and 1990s saw a dramatic rise in the number of lawsuits brought against employers and potential employers for discrimination, harassment and wrongful termination. This exponential increase is due to a couple of factors: the enactment or broadening of many federal laws dealing with employment-related issues and the increasing tendency of employees to seek legal remedies. All of this led to the creation of a new insurance product.

Until the Civil War, few laws were on the books that dealt with employment-related issues. Passage of the Civil Rights Act of 1866 signaled the beginning of federal legislation aimed at preventing race-based discrimination in the workplace. However, despite this new law, employers essentially remained free to hire and fire at will and they did so with some impunity. The Civil Rights Act of 1964 represented a dramatic change in thinking about employment relationships and it—along with the subsequent body of legislation passed since then—has changed the shape of the employer-employee relationship forever. No business or nonprofit organization is immune from lawsuits pertaining to employment discrimination, harassment, or wrongful termination.

This situation and employers' increasing desire to protect their assets have led to the development of a new insurance product designed to fill gaps that exist in general liability, workers' compensation, directors' and officers' liability and other products with respect to employment-related claims.

✓ ***Take Note:*** Landmark legislation that deals with employment practices liability includes the:

- Civil Rights Act of 1866;
- Equal Pay Act of 1964;
- Civil Rights Act of 1964;
- Age Discrimination Act of 1967;
- Pregnancy Discrimination Act of 1978;
- Civil Rights Act of 1991;
- Americans with Disabilities Act of 1992; and
- Family Medical Leave Act of 1993.

### Insurance Coverage for Employment-Related Practices

Before the introduction of specific policies to deal with employment-related claims, employers often sought relief under their standard business insurance policies. In some cases, insurers defended or paid claims under these policies, but only reluctantly. When standard policies were developed, the body of law and the number of suits related solely to employment practices were unknown. Although few of the policies contained exclusions for these types of losses, coverage clearly was not contemplated either the contract language or the pricing structures. Standard policies still may provide some limited coverage, however, depending on the allegations a lawsuit contains. It is a good idea to forward any employment-related suits to all potential insurers.

**General Liability** The commercial general liability policy, or its counterpart in the **Business Owner's Policy (BOP)**, covers bodily injury as well as personal injury. It is somewhat unusual for an employment practices suit to raise issues that would be covered under either of these coverage parts, but it is possible, particularly in cases of sexual harassment, wrongful discharge, or discrimination. Some courts have ruled that emotional distress and mental anguish constitute bodily injury and therefore might be covered by the liability policy. Others have taken the opposite position. Even if a court rules that mental anguish and emotional distress are bodily injury, they still must be caused by an occurrence to have the liability policy apply. Additionally, exclusions for employers' liability and intentional acts typically are part of the contract as well, so even absent a specific exclusion for employment-related claims, it is unlikely that the general liability policy will respond.

Personal injury coverage is limited to false arrest, detention, imprisonment, malicious prosecution, wrongful eviction or entry, invasion of the right to private occupancy, libel, and slander. Because this essentially is a named peril coverage, it is unlikely that coverage would apply.

### *Workers' Compensation and Employers' Liability*

To trigger coverage under a workers' compensation policy, there must be bodily injury and an accident. Therefore, the same coverage limitations that exist under the liability policy nearly always preclude coverage under workers' compensation as well.

The employers' liability portion of a workers' compensation policy might provide some coverage. However, most policies now contain broad exclusions pertaining to **employment practices liability (EPL)** claims.

### *Directors' and Officers' Liability*

Organizations purchase Directors' and Officers' (D&O) coverage to protect boardmembers and corporate officers from suits alleging mismanagement. Because these policies vary widely, it is difficult to say with certainty whether any coverage for an EPL suit, or at least a defense, would be provided, but the possibility exists.

Because the body of EPL common law constantly changes and evolves, it is difficult to make definitive statements about the presence or absence of coverage under these standard policies. It is certain, however, that virtually every business or organization can benefit from the purchase of a separate, specific EPL policy.

## Employment Practices Liability Insurance

The rapid increase in both the number and size of EPL claims in recent years coupled with the limitations in standard policies has given rise to the development of **employment practices liability insurance (EPLI)**. Beyond providing asset protection to an organization, EPLI also establishes much-needed loss control and prevention. It is unlikely that an underwriter will even consider an employer that does not have an up-to-date employee handbook and a well-written policy covering sexual harassment and discrimination. Some insurers even provide assistance in updating and enhancing current policies.

No standard EPLI policy exists, although one recently has been developed by the Insurance Standards Office (ISO). As the market has emerged, companies have designed their own forms in light of recent legal developments and the needs of their customers. Some policies are issued on a stand-alone basis, and others are attached to general liability or D&O policies. Regardless of how coverage is provided, many similarities between the contracts exist.

### *Coverage*

Nearly all EPLI policies are written on a claims-made basis; thus, coverage under a policy is triggered by the filing of a claim during the policy period. It is important to distinguish between the **coverage trigger** and actually having coverage under a policy. A coverage trigger is merely a set of circumstances or requirements that must be met to activate the policy's coverage. It depends on when the alleged wrongful employment practice took place, when the claim is made, what constitutes a claim, and what the claim reporting requirements the policy establishes. A claim under EPLI also includes notification that a complaint has been filed with the Equal Employment Opportunities Commission (EEOC). Coverage still may be denied based on the specific facts contained in any legal action and the policy language.

**Test Topic Alert!**

Almost all employment practices liability insurance policies are written on a claims-made basis. Coverage is triggered when a claim is filed during the policy period.

✓ ***Take Note:*** The insuring agreement of an EPLI policy typically covers wrongful acts, including sexual harassment, discrimination, and wrongful discharge. Some policies merely state that they will pay damages that arise out of a wrongful employment practice. Obviously, the broader and less specific the definition of a wrongful act, the better for the policyholder.

Another area some policy insuring agreements address is third-party liability. Employees are not the only ones who successfully pursue claims for employment practices liability. Customers, vendors, patients, clients, and other nonemployees (both current and past) also can bring claims and third-party liability coverage is designed to pay these losses as well.

An important part of the EPLI policy is the section entitled *Who Is Insured.* Because many EPLI claims involve not only individual managers, supervisors, or co-workers, but also the firm for negligent management or supervision, all potential defendants should be included for coverage. Most EPLI policies include as insureds the business entity, shareholders, directors and officers, supervisors and managers, nonmanagerial employees, and former employees.

Limits of liability are available in a range from $5 million for small employers up to $200 million for large companies. These limits usually apply per claim, but an aggregate limit also may be the same as the per-claim limit or a multiple of it. It is not uncommon in EPL insurance to include the defense costs in the limits. Unlike standard liability policies that establish defense as a supplementary payment and therefore have no limits, EPLI includes defense as part of damages, so it is subject to the per-claim limit. Some policies cover defense only, and others may set separate defense and damages limits.

Another difference EPLI policies and standard liability policies is the inclusion of a deductible in EPLI. Sometimes referred to as a **retention clause**, these provisions require the insured to absorb a flat amount of each loss. Deductibles can range from $2,500 to $250,000 per claim. Generally speaking, the higher the limit, the higher the deductible.

### *Self Insured Retention (SIR)*

Other EPLI contracts use a **self-insured retention (SIR)** concept. Although both an SIR and a deductible require the insured to pay a portion of losses, a functional difference exists: The insured usually must pay the SIR before the insurer pays anything. A deductible, on the other hand, usually is collected from the insured after the insurer has paid the full amount of the loss.

**Test Topic Alert!**

An EPLI policy can include a deductible or a self-insured retention (SIR) amount. The principal difference between the deductible and the SIR is that the insured pays the deductible after the insurer pays for the loss; the insured pays the SIR before the insurer pays anything.

An EPLI policy also may require the policyholder to pay a percentage of any claims exceeding the deductible or SIR. This is referred to as **coinsurance**, but unlike the concept in property insurance, this type of coinsurance is merely an additional deductible expressed as a percentage of the loss. Coinsurance percentages may range from 5% to 20% or higher, depending on the risks presented and the firm's loss history. It is thought that the presence of a coinsurance participation encourages the insured to use good loss control measures and cooperate with the insurer more fully in the event of a claim.

### *Exclusions*

Of course, like all liability policies, EPLI has its own exclusions. Many are identical to those found in other standard liability policies. Of particular interest in EPLI policies are exclusions for mergers or consolidations, willful failure to comply with the law, retaliatory actions, strikes and lockouts, assault and battery and employee benefits liability.

## Liquor Liability/Dram Shop Liability

Many states have special laws called **dram shop acts** that provide a right of action against a seller of alcoholic beverages if the purchaser injures a third party. The laws vary greatly in detail, with some applying only in situations where liquor is sold to a minor or an intoxicated person. In other states, the law recognizes a separate and independent cause of action on the part of the victims' dependents. Even if a state does not have a statute that pertains to the disbursement of alcoholic beverages, liability may be imposed under common law.

✓ ***Take Note:*** You will recall that the CGL policy contains an exclusion for liquor liability and that an endorsement is available to provide coverage. While this may happen, separate, stand-alone policies also are designed to provide the coverage. When a liquor liability or dram shop liability policy is used, it often is issued on a claims-made basis, although occurrence form policies also are available.

## Quick Quiz 6.2

1. The duties of a corporate director or officer include all of the following duties EXCEPT

   A. loyalty
   B. utmost care
   C. reasonable care
   D. full disclosure

2. Directors and officers may be held liable for each of the following acts EXCEPT

   A. misfeasance
   B. malfeasance
   C. tortfeasance
   D. nonfeasance

3. An employment practices liability exposure exists due to the enactment of various federal laws and statutes. Which of the following is NOT a law that creates an employment practices exposure?

   A. Family and Medical Leave Act
   B. Equal Pay Act
   C. Americans with Disabilities Act
   D. Workers' compensation statutes

4. Some of the common features of an EPLI policy are

   A. claims-made coverage
   B. aggregate limits
   C. deductible, self-insured retention, or coinsurance (participation)
   D. all of the above

**Answers**

*1.* ***B****.* *The duties owed by directors and officers to the corporation are reasonable care, loyalty to the corporation, loyalty to shareholders, disclosure of material facts, and duties imposed by ERISA.*

*2.* ***C****.* *Directors and officers of corporations many be held liable for misfeasance, nonfeasance, or malfeasance.*

*3.* ***D****.* *Workers' compensation laws create a statutory obligation of an employer to provide medical, loss of income, and other benefits, but insulate them from tort actions brought against them by employees.*

*4.* ***D****.* *Although there are no standard EPLI policies, most are issued on a claims-made basis, contain annual aggregate limits, and require the insured to participate in all losses using either a deductible, self-insured retention, or participation percentage, or some combination of such participation methods.*

## Umbrella Liability Policies

An **umbrella policy** is a catastrophic liability contract that provides high limits of coverage, usually with broader coverage than underlying policies, for insureds subject to liability claims of excess proportions. In many cases, professional or business insureds are primary targets for large settlements and are especially interested in this type of extra insurance protection.

Umbrella policies are designed to provide coverage either above the limits of the underlying insurance or above the SIR amount (the amount of loss the insured is willing to absorb without insurance protection). Some umbrella policies are written as **following form coverage,** which means they do not provide coverage broader than the primary insurance. In other words, if the underlying contract is a claims-made form, the umbrella also acts as a claims-made form. These types of policies often are called **excess liability, following form excess liability,** or **straight excess** to indicate that they do not give additional coverage, merely higher limits. Other policies are designed to fill in coverage gaps by providing coverage not included in the primary (or underlying) coverage.

Umbrella policies were developed to provide business firms and individuals with broader than primary coverage. In general, umbrella policies provide limits of insurance exceeding underlying coverage. However, umbrella policies can drop down to provide coverage for claims the underlying policies do not cover.

✓ ***For Example:*** Perils such as slander and libel typically are excluded under primary liability policies, but may be covered under umbrella policies.

No standard form exists for umbrella liability; insurers develop their own. In general, umbrella liability covers general liability, automobile liability, and other separate basic liability contracts.

## Commercial Umbrella Policies

**Commercial umbrella policies** usually provide a minimum of $1 million of insurance, but typically are written with limits of $10 million or more. These policies are intended to cover insurance gaps caused by oversight or those losses typically not fully insured under traditional policies. If no primary insurance exists, the required self-insured retention is usually $25,000 or equal to what a traditional insurance contract would have required.

**Test Topic Alert!**

Commercial umbrella policies cover insurance gaps caused by oversight or those losses typically not fully insured under traditional policies.

Commercial umbrellas are commonly written on a worldwide basis for products liability, which is an important coverage for companies selling to international markets. In addition, commercial umbrella policies may cover blanket contractual liability (for both oral and written contracts), incidental malpractice, nonowned aircraft, nonowned watercraft, and employees' liability coverage, which means employees become part of the definition of named insured.

✓ ***Take Note:*** The majority of commercial umbrellas have a Difference in Conditions section allowing for proper coordination between the contracts.

## Personal Umbrella Policies

**Personal umbrella policies** are designed to protect individuals against catastrophic lawsuits or judgments. Most companies provide coverage ranging from $1 million to $10 million, typically including liability exposures associated with the ownership of private homes, boats, autos, and sport and recreational vehicles.

Personal umbrella policies offer insurance exceeding any basic underlying policies that may apply. They are not substitutes for primary personal liability insurance. Personal umbrellas are intended to be used for losses that exceed primary limits and to cover those losses not covered by primary insurance because they just can't happen—yet they sometimes do.

**Test Topic Alert!**

Personal umbrella policies cover individuals against catastrophic lawsuits or judgments. They cover losses that exceed the limits of primary personal liability insurance policies, as well as losses those policies do not cover.

Under a **maintenance of underlying insurance condition**, the insured must carry certain basic amounts of liability on the underlying homeowners, auto, and watercraft policies. The underlying policies are listed on the Declarations Page of the personal umbrella policy. If the required amounts are not maintained, the umbrella policy acts as though the underlying coverage remains in force. The insurer pays only that amount it would have been required to pay if the underlying limit had been kept in force.

Losses covered by the umbrella policy but not the underlying insurance are subject to a self-insured retention or deductible (usually $1,000). For instance, underlying liability policies typically exclude claims for slander, libel, and defamation of character. However, coverage is provided under the umbrella policies.

✓ ***For Example:*** Bob has a homeowners policy with liability limits of $100,000 and a personal umbrella policy for $1 million with an SIR of $1,000. Bob's pet pit bull severely mauls a neighbor's child, and the court awards the neighbor $250,000. In this case, Bob's homeowners policy will pay $100,000 and the umbrella will pay $150,000. The SIR does not apply because there was underlying coverage.

Now suppose that Bob's homeowners policy has lapsed and the court awards damages of $250,000. If there is no underlying coverage, Bob would be personally liable for $100,000 of the loss plus the $1,000 SIR. The umbrella policy would pay the remaining $149,000. Bob cannot look to his umbrella liability insurer to pay the entire loss because it is liable only to the extent it would have been if Bob had complied with the maintenance of insurance provision.

Finally, suppose that the same insurance exists, but this time a judgment is made against Bob for $250,000 in damages because of slander. Because his homeowners insurance does not cover defamation, whether it is in force at the time of the slander is not an issue. However, the personal umbrella does provide coverage for slander and will pay $249,000; Bob must pay only the $1,000 SIR.

## Exclusions

Certain exclusions typically apply to personal umbrellas: workers' compensation; fellow employees; care, custody, or control; nuclear energy; intentional acts; aircraft; large watercraft (the definition varies by policy); business pursuits; professional liability; and directors' and officers' liability.

## Quick Quiz 6.3

1. An umbrella policy generally provides which coverages?

   A. ____________________
   B. ____________________
   C. ____________________

2. Some of the specific liability provisions a commercial umbrella liability policy contains include

   A. ____________________
   B. ____________________
   C. ____________________
   D. ____________________

3. Some of the specific liability provisions a personal umbrella liability policy contains include

   A. ____________________
   B. ____________________
   C. ____________________
   D. ____________________

### Answers

1. *General liability, automobile liability, and other separate basic liability contracts.*
2. *Products liability, blanket contractual liability, incidental malpractice, nonowned aircraft, nonowned watercraft, and employees' liability are all covered by a commercial umbrella liability policy.*
3. *Ownership of a private home, boat, auto, and sport and recreational vehicles.*

# Unit Test Six

1. The duties of professionals to perform services arise out of each of the following EXCEPT
   A. contractual obligations
   B. tort obligations
   C. duty to avoid causing harm
   D. duty to avoid blame

2. Medical malpractice insurance policies may be issued to each of the following types of professionals EXCEPT
   A. nurses
   B. optometrists
   C. veterinarians
   D. physical therapists

3. Errors and omissions claims may be brought against insurance agents by
   A. their clients
   B. third parties injured by their clients
   C. other agents
   D. professional associations

4. The primary cause of insurance agents' errors and omissions losses is failure to
   A. explain coverage limitations
   B. recommend needed coverage
   C. provide coverage
   D. advise of cancellation

5. Which of the following is NOT a method used to set the limits of liability in a professional liability policy?
   A. Single, aggregate limit
   B. Per-claim and aggregate limit
   C. Combined single limit
   D. Per-claim limit with no aggregate

6. All of the following are examples of the types of exclusions found in professional liability insurance policies EXCEPT
   A. uninsurable exposures
   B. contractual liability
   C. compensatory damages
   D. exposures covered under other policies

7. What is the purpose of a consent-to-settle clause in a professional liability policy?
   A. To allow the insurance company to settle claims regardless of the insured's desire
   B. To prevent the insured from negotiating a settlement on his own
   C. To protect the professional's reputation by allowing his input in the settlement process
   D. To protect a claimant by making it necessary that he participate in all settlement negotiations

8. A corporate director or officer possesses certain fiduciary duties. Which of the following is NOT an example of a fiduciary duty?
   A. Duty of loyalty
   B. Duty of reasonable care
   C. Duty of disclosure
   D. Duty of supervision

9. Which of the following is a type of suit brought by shareholders of a corporation against its officers or directors?
   A. Nonderivative
   B. Derivative
   C. Nondisclosure
   D. Disclosure

10. A typical directors' and officers' liability policy covers each of the following EXCEPT
    A. the directors and officers for their personal liability when not reimbursed by the corporation
    B. the corporation for suits brought against it by officers and directors
    C. the corporation for amounts it reimburses officers and directors in the event of a claim
    D. the directors and officers for wrongful acts they may commit in the scope of their duties

11. Each of the following is a law that creates an employment practices liability exposure EXCEPT the
    A. Civil Rights Act of 1964
    B. Age Discrimination Act of 1967
    C. Americans with Disabilities Act of 1992
    D. Privacy and Nondisclosure Act of 1997

12. Which of the following policies did NOT cover employment-related practices before specific policies were designed to treat those exposures?
    A. General liability
    B. Workers' compensation
    C. Umbrella
    D. Directors' and officers' liability

13. One of the distinguishing features of an EPLI policy compared to the professional liability policies is that it
    A. is a claims-made policy
    B. covers wrongful acts
    C. includes a coinsurance clause
    D. includes an aggregate limit

14. The reason to purchase an umbrella liability policy is to
    A. provide higher limits of liability
    B. expand coverage beyond primary policies
    C. provide coverage when primary limits are exhausted
    D. accomplish all of the above

15. The maximum limit of liability an umbrella policy contains is
    A. $1 million
    B. $10 million
    C. $100 million
    D. There is no maximum.

16. Umbrella policies typically contain exclusions for each of the following situations EXCEPT
    A. blanket contractual
    B. bodily injury
    C. incidental malpractice
    D. employees' liability

17. An umbrella policy provision that requires the insured to participate in a portion of a loss not covered by primary insurance is a
    A. coinsurance clause
    B. participation clause
    C. deductible
    D. self-insured retention

18. An insured purchases a $1 million umbrella policy with a $1,000 self-insured retention (SIR) and agrees to maintain the following underlying limits

| | |
|---|---|
| Auto liability | $100,000/$300,000/$50,000 |
| Personal liability | $300,000 |

Following a serious automobile accident, the insured is sued and injuries are awarded to the claimant in the amount of $200,000. What amount will the umbrella pay if it turns out the insured carried only $50,000/$100,000/$50,000 auto liability limits?

A. $50,000
B. $99,000
C. $100,000
D. The insurer will pay nothing because the insured violated the maintenance of the policy's underlying provision.

19. An insured purchases a $1 million umbrella policy with a $1,000 self-insured retention (SIR) and agrees to maintain the following underlying limits

| | |
|---|---|
| Auto liability | $100,000/$300,000/$50,000 |
| Personal liability | $300,000 |

Following a serious automobile accident, the insured is sued and injuries are awarded to the claimant in the amount of $200,000. How much must the insured pay for this loss?

A. $50,000
B. $100,000
C. $200,000
D. Nothing

# Unit Test Six Answers & Rationale

1. **D.** The duties of professionals arise out of tort and contractual obligations. In addition, it is the responsibility of professionals to do no harm.

2. **D.** Medical malpractice policies may be issued to physicians, surgeons, dentists, nurses, opticians, optometrists, chiropractors, veterinarians, and pharmacists.

3. **A.** Errors and omissions claims are brought against insurance agents by either their customers or the insurance companies with whom the agents contract.

4. **C.** Failure to place coverage promptly or to place requested coverage is the number one cause of E&O claims against agents by their clients.

5. **C.** Combined single limits are used in automobile and general liability insurance, but not professional liability.

6. **C.** Compensatory damages are given to claimants to offset the impact of such things as pain and suffering. Professional liability policies pay damages including both compensatory and special damages.

7. **C.** Although not used as often as in the past, a consent to settle clause allows a professional, particularly a physician, to review a settlement offer before it is made to a claimant. This is done to protect the medical professional's reputation.

8. **D.** The fiduciary duties of corporate directors and officers are the duty to exercise reasonable care, the duty of loyalty to the corporation and the stockholders, the duty to disclose material facts and ERISA duties.

9. **B.** Tort actions against officers and directors are based on negligence and intentional interference and result in derivative suits brought by shareholders and nonderivative suits brought by outsiders such as competitors.

10. **B.** A D&O policy protects corporate officers and directors. Typically, no coverage is provided for the entity itself, apart from its obligation to reimburse the officers and directors.

11. **D.** There is no such law as the Privacy and Non-disclosure Act of 1997.

12. **C.** General liability, workers' compensation, and D&O policies all were used to provide potential coverage, or at least defense, for employment-related claims before to the emergence of separate EPLI policies. These policies now contain exclusions for these losses.

13. **C.** Unlike other liability policies, EPLI includes a participation or coinsurance clause to encourage the insured to control loss.

14. **D.** Umbrella policies provide higher limits on primary coverages, broaden the coverage the underlying policies offer, and drop down to provide primary insurance in some cases.

15. **D.** Umbrella policies are available in a variety of limits with no maximum.

16. **B.** Bodily injury and property damage are two of the most basic types of coverage umbrella policies provide.

17. **D.** A self-insured retention is used in an umbrella policy when the umbrella does not exclude coverage, but no underlying or primary insurance exists.

18. **C**. When the insured does not maintain underlying limits as stated in the umbrella policy, the umbrella carrier pays as though those limits were in effect. Therefore, it does not affect the amount of coverage under the umbrella; it merely means the insured must make up the difference between what was required and what actually is provided.

19. **A**. When the insured does not maintain underlying limits as stated in the umbrella policy, the umbrella carrier pays as though those limits were in effect. Therefore, it does not affect the amount of coverage under the umbrella; it merely means the insured must make up the difference between what was required and what actually is provided.

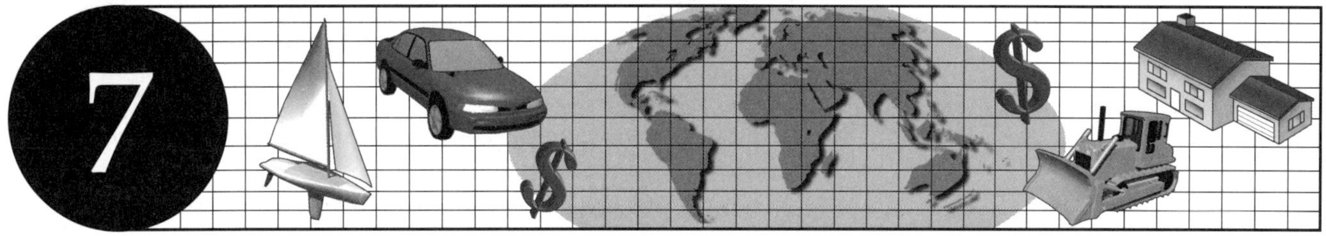

# Workers' Compensation

## INTRODUCTION

Workers' compensation is a system of benefits mandated by law for most workers who suffer job-related injuries or diseases. These benefits are paid regardless of fault and the amount of benefits is limited by law. Almost every employee hired and injured in a particular state is covered by that state's workers' compensation laws. A workers' compensation insurance policy is one means an employer can use to meet the requirements of workers' compensation laws. However, the employer's obligation and the limits of compensation differ in each state. Finally, a number of states have workers' compensation laws that allow workers' compensation insurance to be purchased from a state-run insurer only.

Workers' compensation is an exclusive remedy insurance program. This means that an injured employee can seek remedy for his loss only from the workers' compensation policy. He may not file suit against the employer even if the employer was negligent in causing the loss. However, if the employer fails to carry workers' compensation, the employee may seek restitution through the courts, and the employer has no insurance protection.

This unit discusses the development of workers' compensation, from its common-law beginnings to its current status. It is important to note that while coverage varies by state, it generally provides broad coverage for employees' occupational disease and injury.

## UNIT OBJECTIVES

When you have completed this unit, you should be able to:

- identify the common-law requirements and defenses for employers with regard to their employees;
- explain the historical development of workers' compensation laws;
- describe the different methods used to provide workers' compensation coverage for an employer;
- describe the benefits provided under a workers' compensation statute;

- describe the major coverage parts of the workers' compensation and employers' liability policy; and
- identify federal statutes designed to protect employees engaged in certain categories of employment.

# Workers' Compensation

## Common Law Provisions

Before the enactment of state workers' compensation laws in the early 20th century, common-law doctrines (legal precedents set through judicial rulings or court decisions as opposed to laws passed by a legislature) prevailed in the relationship between employer and employee.

### Common Law

Under common-law, an employer had obligations to:

- provide a reasonably safe place to work;
- provide reasonably safe tools;
- provide reasonably sane and sober fellow employees;
- set up safety rules and enforce them; and
- warn every worker of any dangers inherent in the work that the worker could not be expected to know about.

### Employer Defenses Against Liability

Before workers' compensation laws, if an employee was injured on the job, the only recourse that employee had was to file a lawsuit against the employer charging that its negligence caused the injury. The employer, however, had three defenses against liability, which made it very difficult for the employee to win the lawsuit and recover from the employer for the work-related injury (or disease). The three defenses available to the employer were:

- **contributory negligence**, which states that if the employee in any way contributed to his injury or disease, the employer was not liable for any damages;
- **fellow servant rule**, which states that if a fellow employee caused the injury, the injured worker could not recover from the employer but must seek to recover damages from the fellow employee; and
- **assumption of risk doctrine**, which states that the employee, by accepting the job, assumed the normal risks associated with that job because the wages compensated for that risk. In addition, if the person performing the job found it to be more dangerous or unsafe than anticipated but continued to do the job, his assumption of risk was apparent.

✓ ***Take Note:*** Before the enactment of workers' compensation statutes, it was difficult for an employee to receive any kind of compensation for workplace injuries. In fact, the more dangerous the job, and therefore the more likely an injury, the better able an employer was to assert assumption of risk as a defense to a lawsuit.

**Test Topic Alert!**

Before workers' compensation laws, an employer had three common-law defenses:

- contributory negligence;
- assumption of risk; and
- fellow servant rule.

## Statutory Workers' Compensation Laws

Wisconsin passed the first state constitutionally acceptable law in 1911. Workers' compensation laws, now found in all states and territories, provide for the compensation of employees who have sustained injuries, illness, or death arising out of and occurring in the course of their employment. The laws also make workers' compensation the exclusive remedy when an employee is injured. In other words, the employee cannot sue the employer for injuries. The amount of compensation is fixed by law.

The intent of workers' compensation laws is to provide a just and fair means of compensating employees who are injured on the job. Their purpose is to eliminate the expense and delay that accompany a lawsuit. Instead, when an employee suffers a work-related injury or disease, benefits are determined by law. In most cases, no dispute occurs between the employer and employee.

The compensation, which takes the form of a specified monetary benefit, is paid without any consideration of fault or negligence on the part of either the employer or employee. In exchange for this right of compensation, the employee gives up the right to sue the employer for perhaps a larger (or possibly a smaller) but uncertain benefit. In cases where a dispute exists between employer and employee, the state's Industrial Commission acts as arbitrator.

## Workers' Compensation Coverage

Workers' compensation provides an employee with insurance for accidental injuries, occupational disease, or death. In general, the law provides benefits to an employee, whether or not the employee or employer was negligent, as a type of no fault insurance.

## Coverage Territory

Benefits are provided if the injury, disease, or death arises out of and in the course of employment. Where coverage applies depends on where the employee works.

- If an employee has a fixed place of employment, benefits will be provided for injury, disease, or death while at that location.
- If an employee has no fixed location, such as a salesperson, the employee may be covered from the time he leaves home until he returns.
- Benefits may be available to an employee while he is not working if the activity is construed as promoting the employer's goodwill and interest.

The courts have distinguished between work-related injury or illness and recreational injury or illness.

✓ ***For Example:*** Thomas is employed by a construction company. While working on a new building, he falls from a ladder and breaks his leg. Because this injury occurred while Thomas was performing his job, the company's workers' compensation carrier covers the medical bills and any lost wages that arise from this incident. Two years later, Thomas is playing in a volleyball game at his employer's annual picnic. He breaks his leg again while diving for the ball. This time, the injury arose outside the course of his employment; therefore, the carrier does not cover the loss.

In addition, the scope of employment is very important.

✓ ***For Example:*** Cindy is a clerk in a florist shop. Her duties include delivering floral arrangements in the shop's van. On her return trip after making a delivery, Cindy stops for lunch. She slips on a puddle of water in the restaurant and injures her back. This incident is covered by her employer's workers' compensation carrier because it occurred within the scope of her employment: eating lunch would be a usual activity of her work day. A year later, Cindy completes a delivery and drives to her dry cleaner to pick up her laundry. She slips on a wet sidewalk and breaks her leg. This incident occurred beyond the scope of her employment: she was running a personal errand that was of no benefit to her employer. Therefore, the carrier does not cover her loss.

Finally, workers' compensation is primary over other available insurance coverage.

## Liability

Under workers' compensation laws, an employer is assured that its liability is limited to the benefits specified in the state law, provided the company has complied with the provisions of the law. However, the employer may be liable if the injury or disease does not fall under the workers' compensation laws.

The employee cannot sue a negligent fellow employee or the employer, but an employee can collect under workers' compensation, then sue a negligent third party, such as the manufacturer of a machine that caused the employee's injury. If the employee collects from the negligent third party, the employer or the insurer is entitled to reimbursement for any benefits it paid to the injured worker.

## Types of Workers' Compensation Laws

Although workers' compensation laws vary from state to state, they fall into one of two categories: compulsory or elective.

### *Compulsory Laws*

In states with compulsory laws, every employer must provide the benefits and amounts stipulated in the laws or face penalties for noncompliance. These penalties include:

- paying the benefits;
- paying stipulated fines and penalties; or
- having officials close down the business as a public nuisance.

### *Elective Laws*

Only Texas has elective workers' compensation laws. In Texas, an employer can decide whether to provide workers' compensation benefits. If an employer does not provide the benefits and an employee is injured, the employee can sue. In such a case, the employer cannot use the common law-defense of contributory negligence, fellow servant rule or assumption of risk. Due to the restrictions on defense, most employers voluntarily provide some form of coverage for their employees.

The Federal government has also played a part in protecting workers not covered by state workers' compensation laws. For instance, it enacted the **Federal Longshoremen's and Harbor Workers' Compensation Act (LHWCA)** to cover injuries sustained by certain maritime employees such as longshoremen and harbor workers. The **Federal Employees' Compensation Act** provides benefits to injured civilians who are employed by the federal government. Because the federal government administers these systems and provides the benefits, no private insurers are involved.

## Methods of Insuring

Two basic methods of providing insurance comply with a state's workers' compensation laws—monopolistic and competitive. In a **monopolistic state**, insurance must be purchased from a state-run insurer. The five monopolistic states are North Dakota, Ohio, Washington, West Virginia, and Wyoming. Nevada, formerly a monopolistic method state, became a competitive method state on July 1, 1999.

A state that uses the **competitive workers' compensation method** can provide coverage through:

- an insurance policy from a private carrier;
- a state-administered fund (as a competitor to private carriers);
- an assigned risk or rejected risk plan; or
- self-insurance, though the employer must be able to demonstrate:
  - a financial ability to cover the losses;
  - a formal program to fund and handle the benefits; and
  - procedures to handle loss.

### Self-Insurance

**Self-insurance** is simply the retention of risk. An employer that is self-insured sets aside funds to meet projected losses and absorbs the difference between the actual and calculated probable losses.

In general, a company may not self-insure unless it has proven to the state that it has the financial resources and processes necessary to cover the types of losses to which it is subject. If it cannot demonstrate this ability, the state will require it to obtain insurance through an insurer.

**Test Topic Alert!**

If an employer is self-insured for workers' compensation, the employer's insurance plan must meet state qualifications and obtain state approval every year.

### Assigned Risk Plans

An **assigned risk** or **rejected risk plan** is a risk-pooling arrangement for employers that cannot obtain workers' compensation insurance through private insurers or for those that simply prefer to purchase the insurance through this arrangement. Because workers' compensation is required by law, it is important that there be an insurer of last resort so that employers can comply with the law even if private carriers are unwilling to insure them.

✓ ***Take Note:*** Because workers' compensation coverage is required by statute in almost every state, it is important that there be a mechanism to provide coverage for all employers to comply with the law. Similar to automobile insurance, the compulsory nature of workers' compensation laws creates a need for a residual or an involuntary market mechanism, such as an assigned risk plan.

### Covered Employment

The laws dictating which employees are covered by workers' compensation law vary widely from state to state. In some states, nearly every employee must be covered. In other states, the law exempts employers that have small numbers of employees (e.g., three or less). Other possible exceptions are corporate officers who are the sole shareholders, domestic employees who work a limited number of hours, volunteers, and agricultural workers. When benefits are not required by law, an employer still may provide them on a voluntary or an elective basis.

### Benefits

Benefits provided under workers' compensation as mandated by law. They include the following:

### *Medical Expenses*

Coverage is provided for doctor, hospital, surgical, and similar expenses necessary to cure or relieve the effects of an injury or a disease.

### *Rehabilitation Benefits*

Rehabilitation benefits are provided for vocational training, transportation, and other necessary expenses.

### *Indemnity for Loss of Income*

Loss of income benefits are available after a three-day to seven-day waiting period, but generally retroactive benefits are available to cover the waiting period if a disability extends beyond a certain period of time. Indemnity benefits are based on a percentage of an employee's salary up to some dollar limit per week for:

- temporary partial disability (TPD);
- permanent partial disability (PPD);
- temporary total disability (TTD; or
- permanent total disability (PTD).

A **temporary partial disability** usually results in a restriction of duties, but does not cause a great deal of lost time because the injury is relatively minor. Compensation is limited to the difference between preloss wages and postloss wages for the recovery period.

**Permanent partial disabilities** include loss of a limb, sight, or hearing. Although these injuries do not result in an inability to work, they never go away. Therefore, in addition to any lost wages, the law allows a scheduled benefit based on the extent of the injury.

✓ ***For Example:*** Loss of a finger on the right hand of a right-handed person, results in a payment higher than loss of a finger on the left hand.

**Temporary total disability** is the inability to work at all for a short period of time. Lost wages are paid in this case.

**Permanent total disability** is a severe injury or disease that means the employee never can work again in that particular employment. This employee is compensated for the estimated loss of wages for his or her anticipated working years.

The type of benefits awarded depends on the injury sustained.

- Scheduled dollar awards are provided for permanent injuries, dismemberment, or permanent total disability.

- Death benefits include burial expense and survivors' benefits. These benefits usually are a weekly sum based on a percentage of the employee's salary.

**Occupational Diseases**

Coverage for occupational diseases is limited to those that arise out of and in the course of employment.

✓ ***For Example:*** Catching a cold from a co-worker is not considered an occupational disease because it is not peculiar to the employment. Exposure to harmful chemicals on the job that results in cancer, however, would be compensable as an occupational disease.

Benefits received under workers' compensation are usually exempt from income taxes.

**Second Injury Fund**

All states have second injury funds to encourage employers to hire disabled employees. The purpose of the second injury fund is to provide a source of funds for persons who have been injured and otherwise might be unemployable. After an employee has been injured, subsequent employers may be reluctant to hire that person. The employers are concerned about having to pay increased workers' compensation premiums or increased costs because of a second injury, perhaps resulting in total disability. To ease this reluctance, the fund pays some of the costs for a second injury.

✓ ***For Example:*** An employee who loses sight in one eye in a work-related accident with one employer may be hired by a second employer. If a similar accident causes loss of sight in the remaining eye, the second injury results in a permanent total injury, despite the fact that the injury itself was only partial.

## Quick Quiz 7.1

1. Under common law, an employer was required to provide employees with

   A. ____________________
   B. ____________________
   C. ____________________
   D. ____________________
   E. ____________________

2. Under common law, an employer could use which defenses if an employee filed suit?

   A. ____________________
   B. ____________________
   C. ____________________

3. The two types of workers' compensation laws are ________________ and ________________.

4. In a competitive state, an employer can comply with the state workers' compensation laws in what ways?

   A. ____________________
   B. ____________________
   C. ____________________
   D. ____________________

**Answers**

1. *Safe place to work, safe tools and equipment, reasonably competent (sane and sober) fellow employees, safety rules and enforcement, notification of dangers*
2. *Assumption of risk, fellow employee, contributory negligence*
3. *Compulsory, elective*
4. *Private carrier, competitive state fund, assigned or rejected risk plan, self-insurance*

## Workers' Compensation and Employers' Liability Policy

The **Workers' Compensation and Employers' Liability** policy is designed to cover:

- payments required by a state's workers' compensation law; and
- the liability risk for occupationally incurred injuries and diseases.

The policy is designed to accommodate the varied state workers' compensation laws. Physically, the policy consists of an information page, a standard provisions form, and necessary endorsements. The policy's coverage is split into three parts:

**Part I—Workers' Compensation** This part covers an employer's legal obligations under workers' compensation law. The policy adapts to the laws of the state as listed on the declarations page or information page. This coverage is considered the exclusive or sole remedy for recovery by an employee for injuries and diseases arising out of and in the course his or her employment.

**Part II—Employers' Liability** This part covers an employer's legal liability, determined by negligence, for injury to an employee in a situation not covered under workers' compensation or an action taken by a third party. Liability under this part might arise from the following:

- Accidents or diseases not compensable under workers' compensation and for which the employee may sue the employer. Sometimes this arises out of a legal doctrine called **dual capacity**. In some states, the law recognizes that at times, an employer stands in a two-fold capacity—one as an employer and another as a building owner, landlord or manufacturer. In those states, the employee may retain the right to sue the employer in tort.
- Loss of consortium—that is, the legal right of the injured employee's spouse to sue the employer for loss of the employee's companionship.
- A third-party-over case, which involves an employee who sues a third party, of a machine that the employee was using when the injury occurred. In the third-party-over case, the manufacturer (third party) in turn may sue the employer because the manufacturer believes the employer was negligent, perhaps in maintaining or using the machine, in supervising the employee's activities or in training the employee.

✓ ***Take Note:*** Because workers' compensation benefits are considered the sole remedy for employees, the Coverage Part II provides applies only to claims brought against employers by third parties or by employees who are not subject to the workers' compensation laws. This may be due to an exemption under the law, such as the one for small employers, agricultural workers or domestic employees. Coverage also applies to dual capacity claims.

### *Part III—Insurance in Other States*

This part provides insurance to cover benefits to an employee if an obligation for workers' compensation arises in a state other than the state(s) where the employer normally does business. Such states may be identified on the Declarations Page, or coverage may be indicated as blanket on the Declarations Page. Coverage does not apply in states the insured had operations in when the policy commenced unless they are listed on the policy.

## Other Provisions: Duties of Insured Employer in Case of Loss

The insured's duties in the event of a loss include:

- providing medical services as required by workers' compensation law;
- providing information to the insurer about the injury;
- notifying the insurer promptly of all notices, demands, and legal papers; and
- cooperating with the insurer in the investigation, settlement, or defense of a claim.

## Premium

The premium is based on the amount of payroll multiplied by the rates for various occupational classifications shown in the insurer's rate manual. Another basis is estimated exposures, subject to final audit at the end of the policy term. For a larger business, however, the premium audit may take place once a month. Premium factors include the classification of the business, its size, and its workers' compensation claim experience. The rates also vary greatly by employment classification.

✓ ***For Example:*** Clerical office workers may carry a rate of $1 for every $100 of payroll, while roofers may have a rate of $30 per $100. The total premium for workers' compensation is the rate applied to the estimated payroll for each classification, less any applicable premium discounts or credits.

In addition, larger employers have an experience modification applied to their premiums. If their loss experience is better than the average in their classifications, the experience modification is a credit. If it is worse than average, it is a debit and increases the overall premium.

**Test Topic Alert!** Premiums for workers' compensation insurance are based on the amount of payroll and the rates established for various occupational classifications.

**Conditions** The insurance company has the right to inspect the insured's premises, but is not obligated to do so. **Transfer of Insured's Rights and Duties and Assignment** applies to workers' compensation.

**Cancellation** The insured can cancel workers' compensation insurance with written notice to the insurer. The insurer can cancel it with 10 days' written notice to the insured. Once again, some states have placed time restrictions on such cancellations, nonrenewals or increases in premium. State laws determine whether additional restrictions apply.

**Exclusions** The following exclusions apply to workers' compensation:

- serious and willful misconduct by the insured;
- employment of a person hired in violation of the law;
- failure to comply with a health or safety regulation; and
- discharge or discrimination against an employee in violation of workers' compensation laws.

Additional exclusions apply to employer's liability coverage under Part II:

- liability assumed under contract (covered under the general liability policy);
- punitive damages awarded because a worker was employed in violation of the law;
- injury to a worker while employed in violation of the law with the insured's knowledge;
- damages arising out of the discharge, demotion, coercion, harassment, or humiliation of or discrimination against any employee in violation of the law (discussed and covered under employment practices liability insurance);

- injury to someone whose work is subject to a federal compensation law (such as longshore and harbor workers, offshore employees, coal miners, and captains and crew members of vessels);
- fines or penalties imposed by law; and
- damages payable under the Migrant and Seasonal Agricultural Worker Protection Act and other federal laws that deal with violations of law or regulations.

## Federal Workers' Compensation Laws

Persons in certain employments are not covered by the provisions of any state workers' compensation law. Instead, they receive their benefits under federal law.

### Federal Employers' Liability Act

Congress passed the **Federal Employers' Liability Act (FELA)** in 1908 to protect employees of interstate railroads. This occurred before the passage of state workers' compensation laws. The act provides broader protection to railroad employees than that available under state laws. Injured workers retain the right to sue their employers for negligence, and the employers cannot use certain common-law defenses. This law stands because railroad employees and their labor unions have not been willing to accept statutory workers' compensation benefits in lieu of the more favorable provisions of the federal act.

### United States Longshore and Harbor Workers' Compensation Act

Employees engaged in maritime activities, including loading, unloading, building, or repairing vessels, are covered by this federal statute. The benefits provided to injured workers are significantly better than those available under state law. When an employer has exposures under the act, an endorsement may be added to the workers' compensation policy to comply with the federal law. Coverage also is available under a separate policy.

### The Merchant Marine Act (Jones Act)

The **Jones Act** covers masters and members of the crews of ocean-going vessels. The law permits an injured seaman to sue his employer for damages and to have a jury trial. The injured worker is entitled to transportation, wages, maintenance and cure, which is roughly equivalent to workers' compensation benefits, but no maximums exist for wage loss. Insurance may be provided under a workers' compensation policy using a maritime coverage endorsement to the employers' liability coverage. If an employer does not wish to have employee suits brought against it, it voluntarily may provide benefits under the workers' compensation policy by using a voluntary compensation maritime endorsement.

### Contractors

Principals and contractors who engage subcontractors are responsible for workers' compensation benefits to the subcontractors' employees if the subcontractors have not provided such benefits. Therefore, contractors and principals should be sure to obtain certificates of workers' compensation insurance from subcontractors proving that the subcontractors have coverage. If the subcontractors do not have workers' compensation coverage, premiums will be assessed against the principals or contractors for the amount of payment made to the subcontractors.

**Test Topic Alert!**

A certificate of workers' compensation insurance is a standard form used to prove that an employee is covered by workers' compensation insurance.

In many states, the use of health insurance as an alternative for workers' compensation is prohibited. Only a few positions or individuals may be exempt from workers' compensation requirements. State statutes determine these classes.

✓ ***For Example:*** In some states, a business owner may elect to exclude himself from coverage, but his employees and subcontractors must be covered by a workers' compensation an policy. To accommodate this distinction, the definition of a subcontractor and an independent contractor differ in many workers' compensation laws.

✓ ***Take Note:*** The determination of employment status by a government body, such as the Internal Revenue Service (IRS), does not necessarily distinguish employees from independent contractors for insurance purposes, but it can help in the determination. To determine whether a person is an independent contractor or an employee, an insurance company may ask the following questions:

- Who provides the tools and other items required to perform the activity?
- Who determines when, where and how the work should be performed?
- Are separate licenses and insurance policies in place?
- How are required taxes collected and paid to governmental entities?
- Is a certificate of insurance on file for the person?

If the entity that retained the person takes responsibility for some of these duties, the IRS and the insurance company probably will view that entity as the person's employer. However, if the person assumes most of these duties, he or she probably will be considered an independent contractor.

## Quick Quiz 7.2

1. Each of the following benefits are provided under a workers' compensation law EXCEPT

   A. rehabilitation
   B. medical
   C. health insurance
   D. loss of income (disability)

2. Four types of indemnity benefits are provided for workers' compensation injuries. They are

   A. ____________________ disability
   B. ____________________ disability
   C. ____________________ disability
   D. ____________________ disability

3. A __________ __________ __________ is used in all states to encourage employers to hire people who may have disabilities that occurred while those people were employed by other firms or organizations.

4. The three coverages a standard workers' compensation policy provides are

   A. ____________________
   B. ____________________
   C. ____________________

5. A federal law that protects the captain of a ship and the members of its crew for injuries sustained in their employment is the

   A. Merchant Marine Act
   B. United States Longshoremen's and Harbor Workers' Compensation Act
   C. Federal Employers' Liability Act
   D. Federal Contractors' Compensation Act

## *Answers*

*1.* ***C****. The benefits included in workers' compensation statues are medical, loss of income (disability), rehabilitation and death (burial).*

*2. temporary partial, temporary total, permanent partial, permanent total*

*3. second injury fund*

*4. Workers' compensation, Employer's Liability, Other States*

*5.* ***A****. The Merchant Marine Act, commonly known as the Jones Act, applies to the master and members of the crew of ocean-going vessels.*

# Unit Test Seven

1. Which of the following does workers' compensation coverage provide?
   A. Health insurance
   B. Unemployment compensation
   C. No fault insurance
   D. Auto insurance

2. What is the primary purpose of workers' compensation coverage?
   A. To provide compensation to employees for injuries arising out of and in the course of their employment
   B. To provide benefits to employees temporarily laid off
   C. To provide accident insurance for employees both on and off the job
   D. To improve employees' working conditions

3. Which of the following established the first statutory workers' compensation laws?
   A. Social Security Administration
   B. State government
   C. Insurance industry
   D. National Conference of Commissioners on Uniform State Laws

4. Which of the following statements regarding workers' compensation coverage is CORRECT?
   A. Workers' compensation laws prescribe the nature and amount of benefits to be paid for injuries or death.
   B. In addition to receiving the benefits payable under workers' compensation, an employee has the right to sue his employer.
   C. An injured employee must sue his employer for damages.
   D. Workers' compensation laws are intended to prevent unsafe workplaces.

5. Workers' compensation insurance covers each of the following EXCEPT an employee who
   A. is injured by a coworker
   B. injures himself on the job to his own negligence
   C. is injured on the job regardless of fault
   D. is injured intentionally by an employer

6. A druggist sends an employee to deliver medicine to a customer's home. The wind blows down a tree in the customer's yard and injures the delivery person. The delivery person's injuries would be covered by
   A. workers' compensation
   B. the customer's homeowners policy
   C. the pharmacist's liability policy
   D. the customer's umbrella policy

7. An injured employee receives payment under workers' compensation insurance from the
   A. employer
   B. insurer
   C. Division of Workers' Compensation
   D. State Department of Employment

8. Which of the following statements about workers' compensation insurance is CORRECT?
   A. All benefits are unlimited.
   B. Benefits are payable up to the policy limit.
   C. Benefits are payable as required by statute.
   D. An employee may select the benefit he desires.

9. In a state with a compulsory workers' compensation law, all of the following statements are correct if any employer fails to carry workers' compensation insurance EXCEPT
   A. the employer still may have to pay benefits
   B. the employer may have to pay a fine
   C. workers' compensation officials may close the business down
   D. the employer need not worry because no law imposes any penalties for failure to secure coverage

10. An employee is NOT be eligible for benefits if the employee
    A. falls on the factory steps when entering the workplace
    B. sustains an injury caused by a third party while on the job
    C. sustains an injury while working in the plant on an overtime basis
    D. breaks a leg during a company picnic

11. Which of the following statements is CORRECT under a workers' compensation law?
    A. An employee can sue his employer.
    B. An employer has certain defenses, such as assumption of the risk.
    C. Workers' compensation is an employee's exclusive remedy.
    D. An employer may not recover damages from a third party who injures a worker.

12. How can a general contractor meet its social responsibility concerning workers' compensation insurance?
    A. By requiring certificates of insurance from all subcontractors
    B. By paying a sum equal to 10% of its annual premium to a second injury fund
    C. By paying uncovered losses itself
    D. By delegating its social responsibility

13. Workers' compensation pays under which of the following circumstances?
    A. Only when an employer is negligent
    B. Only when another employee is negligent
    C. Without regard to fault
    D. Only when an employee is at fault

14. Workers' compensation disability applies under which of the following circumstances?
    A. When an employee cannot work because he was injured on the job
    B. Only when an employee is totally disabled
    C. Only when an employee is partially disabled
    D. Only when an employer is at fault

15. Benefits under workers' compensation for injuries to employees who have prior impairments are paid partially by the
    A. employer's health insurance
    B. insurance commissioner
    C. second injury fund
    D. Americans with Disabilities Act

16. To be a qualified self-insurer for workers' compensation benefits, an employer must perform each of the following EXCEPT
    A. prove financial ability to provide required benefits
    B. establish a formal program for funding reserves
    C. establish specific procedures to handle loss
    D. provide evidence of workers' compensation insurance

17. All of the following losses are covered by workers' compensation EXCEPT
    A. death
    B. unemployment
    C. temporary total disability
    D. partial disability

18. Which defense may an employer assert in an elective state when it has not purchased workers' compensation coverage?

    A. Assumption of risk
    B. Contributory negligence
    C. Fellow servant
    D. The employer may not assert a common law defense when it has elected not to purchase coverage.

19. Under common law, each of the following was required of an employer EXCEPT

    A. safe place to work
    B. reasonably safe tools
    C. a safe place for recreation
    D. safety rules

20. When an employee is injured outside of his home state, how are workers' compensation benefits determined?

    A. The employee may elect to receive benefits from both the home state and the state in which the injury occurred.
    B. The employee must chose between the statutory benefits of the home state and the state in which the injury occurred.
    C. The court decides which state's benefits apply to the loss.
    D. The insurance carrier determines which state's benefits to pay based on the lower amount.

# Unit Test Seven Answers & Rationale

1. **C.** Workers' compensation coverage pays for injuries to workers without regard to fault on the employer's part.

2. **A.** Workers' compensation coverage pays for injuries to workers without regard to fault on the employer's part.

3. **B.** The state of Wisconsin was the first to pass a successful workers' compensation statute.

4. **A.** Workers' compensation statutes specify the type of benefits and the dollar amounts to be paid.

5. **D.** The workers' compensation policy excludes losses caused by the insured's serious or willful misconduct.

6. **A.** Because the customer is not legally responsible for the injuries, no coverage would apply under the homeowners or umbrella policy. Workers' compensation would be available because it pays for work-related injuries without regard to fault.

7. **B.** The workers' compensation insurer makes required payments on behalf of the employer.

8. **C.** A workers' compensation policy sets no specific limit for benefits. The policy simply states that it pays statutory limits.

9. **D.** Although they vary by state, the penalties for failure to comply with the law in a compulsory state include fines, imprisonment, closing the business and allowance for the employee to file suit against the employer.

10. **D.** Workers' compensation benefits are payable for accidents and occupational diseases only. An injury during nonwork hours is not compensable.

11. **C.** Workers' compensation benefits are considered the sole or exclusive remedy for injuries or diseases arising out of and in the course of employment.

12. **A.** Unless a general contractor obtains certificates of insurance from subcontractors, the amount paid to a subcontractor will be treated as payroll and charged to the general contractor's workers' compensation policy.

13. **C.** Workers' compensation is not a fault-based system. It pays for occupational disease and injuries without regard to fault on the part of employer or employee.

14. **A.** Workers' compensation disability benefits apply in cases of both partial and total disability.

15. **C.** Every state has a second injury fund that provides a source of funds for persons who have been injured in other work-related incidents and who otherwise might be considered unemployable.

16. **D.** Although it varies by state, to become a qualified self-insurer, an employer must demonstrate financial ability to pay benefits, have a formal program to fund loss and maintain a method by which it handles claims.

17. **B.** Workers' compensation benefits include medical, disability (temporary partial, temporary total, permanent partial, permanent total), rehabilitation, and death benefits.

18. **D.** An employer's defenses applied only before the enactment of statutory workers' compensation benefits.

19. **C**. Under common law, an employer was required to furnish workers with a safe place to work, reasonably competent fellow employees, safe tools, safety rules, and enforcement and to warn employers of hidden and inherent dangers.

20. **B**. In most cases, an employee may elect to have benefits paid at the statutory limit of the state in which the injury takes place if that person does not have a permanent state of residence.

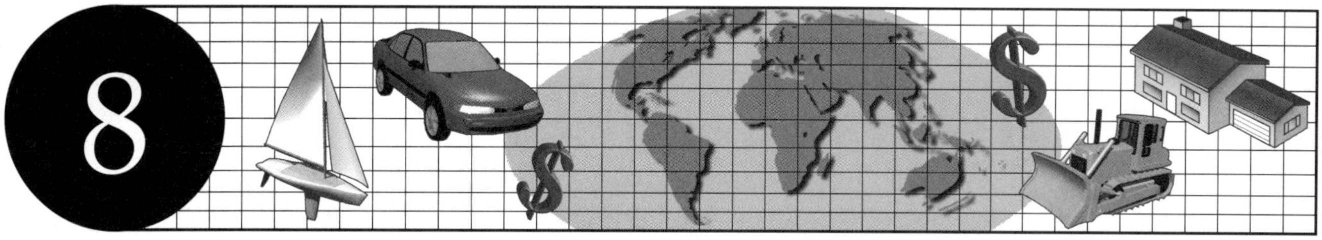


# Crime Insurance

## INTRODUCTION

Insurance for losses due to crime has become more important than ever for businesses and other types of organizations. As the nation's crime rate continues to rise and the seriousness of those crimes escalates and extends to all aspects of modern life, the need to include crime insurance in a comprehensive risk management program increases. Crime losses can impact a business from one of two sources: crimes committed by employees and crimes committed by others. Theft coverage often is included in a commercial property insurance policy, but the policy limits the type of property to which coverage applies. Employee-caused losses nearly always are excluded under property insurance policies. This creates a potential gap in coverage that commercial crime insurance policies fill.

This unit presents information that focuses on the various coverage forms developed for use with the Commercial Package Policy (CPP). Some policies were also developed for use on a monoline basis. The Crime forms incorporate the Crime General Provisions Form, and both discovery and loss-sustained versions are offered. The selected forms then are attached to a crime declarations page and a general crime provisions and exclusions form. The forms can be included in a CPP or issued on a monoline basis.

Although a number of states still use the Crime Forms developed by the Insurance Standards Office in 1986, a growing number of states have adopted ISO's newer crime forms published in 2000 and 2002. These are encapsulated in the Commercial Crime Coverage Form, which effectively replaces the older forms. The coverage forms now come in discovery and loss sustained versions. The forms were developed for use with the CPP and on a monoline basis. When used with the CPP, they incorporate the Crime General Provisions Form and eliminate the need for that separate form. These changes will be discussed in this unit.

## UNIT OBJECTIVES

When you have completed this unit, you should be able to:

- define the terms important to the study of crime insurance policies;
- describe the general provisions of and typical exclusions crime insurance policies contain;
- describe the coverage the major crime policies provide and exclude; and
- identify and describe the general conditions crime insurance policies provide.

# Commercial Crime Insurance

## Coverage Forms

ISO recently restructured the Crime Program forms and endorsements, rules, and rating plans. This restructuring was intended to simplify the use of these forms and endorsements. It introduced a number of separate policies and forms to meet the coverage needs of commercial and government entities. It also included coverage for fidelity losses.

The Crime Program now consists of:

- basic coverage forms;
- monoline policies;
- optional crime and fidelity insurance agreements;
- common crime and fidelity endorsements;
- fidelity amendatory endorsements; and
- crime amendatory endorsements.

## Definitions

The **Commercial Crime Coverage Form (CR 00 20 07)** defines the following terms, among others. These are the most significant.

**Banking Premises** The portion of a building occupied by a bank or other safe depository.

**Client** Any entity for which the insured performs services under a written agreement or contract.

**Custodian** The insured and any partner or employee while that person has care and custody of insured property inside the premises. This term does not include a janitor or watchperson.

**Employee** Any natural person who is:

- in the insured's service, or for 30 days after such service ended, who is compensated directly by salary, wages, or commissions, and whose performance of services is controlled by the insured;
- hired on a temporary basis to substitute for a permanent employee who is on leave, or to meet seasonal or short-term work requirements;
- leased to the insured to perform duties related to the insured's business, but not on a temporary basis;
- a trustee, officer, employee, administrator, or manager of an employee benefit plan insured under the policy;
- a director or trustee while handling funds or other property of any employee benefit plan insured under the policy;
- a former employee, director, partner, member, manager, representative, or trustee hired to serve as a consultant for the insured; or
- a guest student or intern.

(Do not confuse these definitions for *employee* with those used for workers' compensation, which were addressed in Unit 7.)

**Employee Benefit Plan** Any welfare or pension benefit plan named in the Declaration of Coverage that is subject to the Employee Retirement Income Security Act of 1974 (ERISA).

**Manager** A person who acts in a directorial capacity for a limited liability company.

**Member** The owner of a limited liability company who may also serve as a manager (see above.)

**Messenger** The insured, a relative of the insured, the insured's partners or employees, while having custody of property outside the premises.

**Watchperson** Any person the insured hires to have care or custody of property inside the premises, but who has no other duties.

**Money** This term includes:

- currency, coins, and bank notes in current use and having a face value; and
- traveler's checks, registered checks, and money orders held for sale to the public.

**Securities** Items such as negotiable and nonnegotiable instruments or contracts representing money or other property. Examples of securities are:

- tokens, tickets, revenue stamps, and other stamps in current use; and
- evidences of debt issued in connection with credit or charge cards not issued by the insured.

**Property Other Than Money and Securities** Any tangible property, other than money and securities, that has intrinsic value unless the coverage form specifically excluded it. Included would be such things as merchandise on shelves and office equipment.

**Burglary** The forcible entry in to or exit out of an insured's premises with the intent to carry off property belonging to the insured. Visible signs of forcible entry or exit must be present. The forcible entry may be made by tools, explosives, electricity, chemicals, or physical damage to the premises.

**Test Topic Alert!** Burglary involves visible signs of forced entry or exit.

**Robbery** The unlawful taking of property from the care or custody of a person by one who has:

- used or threatened bodily harm; or
- committed an unlawful act witnessed by the person.

**Test Topic Alert!** Robbery involves the forcible taking of property from a person by using violence, fear, or threat of violence.

**Safe Burglary** The unlawful taking of property from within a locked safe or vault by a person who enters the safe or vault unlawfully and leaves visible marks on the outside. It also includes the removal of a safe from the premises.

**Theft** The unlawful taking of money, securities, or other property with the intent of permanently depriving the insured of it.

**Premises** The interior of that portion of any building the insured occupies when conducting business. In effect, this is the inside of the perimeter wall.

**Test Topic Alert!** Theft is any act of stealing and includes robbery, burglary, and larceny.

**Occurrence** All loss, whether caused by one or more persons or whether by a single act or series of related acts.

✓ ***Take Note:*** State penal codes vary in the way they define larceny, burglary, and robbery. In general, however, larceny (or theft) is the intentional removal of property from the owner without the owner's consent. Burglary involves entering an unoccupied building or structure with the intent to commit a crime within it, unless the premises are open to the public or the person is permitted to enter. Robbery is the intentional removal of property from another's possession or vicinity against his will by using force or fear. In the context of an insurance policy, the policy terms dictate the definitions of these terms because they are established by contract between the insurer and the insured.

**Quick Quiz 8.1** Match the term on the left with the definition on the right that best describes it:

| | |
|---|---|
| 1. Theft | A. Natural person employed by an organization |
| 2. Premises | B. Unlawful taking of money |
| 3. Messenger | C. Currency, coins, and bank notes in current use |
| 4. Robbery | D. Forcible entry into or exit out of premises |
| 5. Employee | E. Interior portion of a building occupied by an insured |
| 6. Custodian | F. All loss, whether caused by one or more persons |
| 7. Money | G. Forcible removal of property by use or threat of bodily harm |
| 8. Securities | H. Negotiable and nonnegotiable financial instruments |
| 9. Burglary | I. Person with custody of property outside the insured premises |
| 10. Occurrence | J. Person with custody of property inside the insured premises |

***Answers*** *1. **B.** 2. **E.** 3. **I.** 4. **G.** 5. **A.** 6. **J.** 7. **C.** 8. **H.** 9. **D.** 10 **F.***

## Crime General Provisions

Some of the general provisions found in crime forms are similar to those in commercial property insurance, such as provisions for policy period, policy territory, and maintenance of books and records by the insured, as well as other insurance provisions (crime coverage is excess to other policies) and subrogation clauses. The provisions more specific to crime insurance include the following.

- *Insured's duties in the event of a loss*—A crime insurance policy contains a provision that the insured notify the police in the event of a loss that involves a violation of the law. This provision may be absent when the policy applies to suspected employee theft. The insured must provide a sworn proof of loss within 120 days and cooperate with the investigation and settlement of the claim.
- *Merger and consolidation*—A crime policy ordinarily extends coverage to new locations and new employees when the insured acquires or merges with another firm for the first 90 days after the acquisition or merger.

- *Discovery period*—Unlike other policies, a crime insurance policy applies to losses the insured discovers within 12 months of the policy's expiration date; however, this extended period terminates upon the effective date of any other insurance purchased to replace the policy.
- *Other insurance*—This insurance does not apply to any loss recoverable under another policy, unless that policy's limit is insufficient to cover the entire amount of the loss, in which case this insurance will apply to that portion of the loss up to the limits of liability.
- *Valuation clause*—Due to the nature of the property covered by crime insurance, the valuation clauses used in property insurance are not well suited to a crime policy. Therefore, specific valuation clauses cover items such as money, which is valued at its face value, and securities, which are valued at their market value as of the close of business on the day the loss is discovered. Losses to other types of property usually are paid on an actual cash value basis, unless the lost or damaged property is actually repaired or replaced as soon as reasonably possible.

## Crime General Exclusions

Crime coverage does not apply to:

- loss resulting from acts the insured or the insured's partners or members commit;
- loss resulting from acts of managers, directors, employees, trustees, or representatives, unless specifically covered in the Insuring Agreement;
- loss due to governmental authority's seizure or destruction of property;
- indirect losses, such as expenses incurred to establish the amount of a loss;
- legal expenses related to any legal action;
- nuclear hazards; and
- war or similar action.

## Crime Coverage Forms

As previously noted, the ISO published new crime forms in 2000 and 2002. A number of states, however, still use the forms that ISO developed in 1986. It is expected that insurers in these states will eventually adopt the newer forms. For purposes of this discussion, we will present the details of the most recent forms, with explanations of the earlier forms where appropriate. The newer forms, or *Insuring Agreements*, are encapsulated in the Commercial Crime Coverage Form, and effectively replace the older forms.

Some of the more common crime Insuring Agreements are presented below, with their predecessors in parentheses:

- Employee Theft (Employee Dishonesty Coverage Form A)
- Forgery or Alteration (Forgery or Alteration Form B)
- Inside the Premises—Theft of Money and Securities, CR 00 04 10 (Theft, Disappearance, and Destruction Coverage Form C)
- Inside the Premises—Robbery or Safe Burglary of Other Property, CR 00 05 10 (Robbery and Safe Burglary Coverage Form D)
- Outside the Premises, CR 00 06 10 (Premises Burglary Coverage Form E)
- Computer Fraud, CR 00 07 10 (Computer Fraud Form F): Coverage applies to loss of money and securities or property other than money and securities resulting from computer fraud. Computer fraud is the theft of property following and directly related to the use of any computer to cause a fraudulent transfer from inside the banking premises to a person other than a messenger or place outside the premises
- Kidnap, Ransom, and Extortion Policy, CR 00 08 10 (Extortion Form G): Coverage applies to loss of property surrendered as a ransom payment resulting directly from the abduction of an insured person, and for loss of property extorted from the insured under threat of bodily harm, damage to the insured premises, or introduction of a virus to the insured's computer system, or other such contamination or pollution of products. Coverage also applies to expenses incurred as a result of the threat of kidnap or extortion. There is no coverage for a loss that results from the surrender of money or property before a reasonable effort is made to report the situation to the local police, the FBI, or an associate, nor is there coverage for loss resulting from any dishonest or criminal act committed by an employee or other authorized representative
- Premises Theft and Robbery Outside The Premises Coverage (Property Other Than Money and Securities) Form H, CR 00 09 10: Coverage applies to loss of covered property that results from theft or attempted theft inside the premises, loss from damage to the premises or its exterior resulting from the theft or attempted theft, loss of covered property by actual or attempted robbery of a messenger outside the premises, or loss of covered property resulting directly from an outside robbery while the property is in the care or custody of an armored vehicle company
- Safe Depository Liability Form M, CR 00 14 10 (Safe Depository Direct Loss Form N, CR 00 15 10): These two coverages may be issued to any firm other than a financial institution. Form M requires that the insured be legally liable for the loss, while Form N covers direct damage. Both cover loss of a customer's property while in a safe-deposit

box, vault, or while being deposited or removed from a safe or vault on the premises
- Money Orders and Counterfeit Paper Currency, CR 00 19 06 (Money Orders and Counterfeit Paper Coverage Form R)

The first five insuring agreements are the most common and will be discussed in greater detail.

## Employee Theft (Employee Dishonest Coverage Form A)

Employee theft insurance provides coverage in the event of an employee's theft that results in the loss of money, securities, or other property.

### Schedule and Blanket Coverage (Schedule Fidelity Bond, Blanket Fidelity Bond)

Employee dishonesty insurance can be written either on a schedule basis or as blanket coverage. Under schedule coverage, either the employee positions to be covered are identified by title on the Declarations Page or the names of the persons to be covered are identified, with a dollar limit shown for each position or person. Under blanket coverage, all employees are covered; however, specific employees or positions can be excluded.

The two major differences between schedule and blanket coverage are (1) whether the dishonest employee must be identified specifically and (2) the way the limit of insurance applies.

#### *Employee Identification*

With respect to identification of employees, schedule coverage requires that the dishonest employee be identified by name on the Declarations Page. Under blanket coverage, the dishonest act may be committed by any employee of the business. The perpetrator must be identified as the person who committed the dishonest act either when the employee admits to the act or when a court of appropriate jurisdiction determines the employee's guilt.

#### *Insurance Units*

The second difference between the two types of coverage involves application of the limits of insurance. Under blanket coverage, the most the insurer pays for any one occurrence is the limit shown on the Declarations Page, regardless of the number of persons involved. However, under schedule coverage, if two or more specified persons or positions commit a dishonest act, the limit of insurance applies to each person's participation.

**Test Topic Alert!** A commercial blanket bond's policy limit applies for each loss. A blanket position bond's policy limit applies separately to each employee in that position.

### Coverage

The insurer pays for (1) loss of covered property and (2) loss because of damage to covered property resulting directly from the covered cause of loss.

Covered property includes money, securities, and property other than money and securities. The covered cause of loss is employee theft.

This coverage form pays for loss caused by any employee while temporarily outside the coverage territory specified in the policy, but only for a period not to exceed 90 days.

**Deductible**

The insurer pays only the amount of the loss that exceeds the deductible shown on the Declarations Page for any one occurrence. The insured must notify the insurer as soon as possible of any loss insured against, or the possibility of a such a loss, even though it falls entirely within the deductible amount. Coverage then is cancelled automatically for the employee(s) causing the loss.

**Additional Exclusions and Conditions**

The insurer does not pay for losses caused by employee theft, forgery, or alteration of negotiable instruments (such as checks, drafts, and promissory notes) when the loss is:

- caused by an employee for whom similar prior insurance has been cancelled and not reinstated since the last cancellation and results in inventory shortages that can be determined only by comparing an actual inventory of property, particularly merchandise, to the amount that should be on the shelves based on account records (as in the case of mysterious disappearance);
- results from trading; or
- results from fraudulent use of a warehouse receipt or document connected to it.

Employee theft insurance is cancelled for any employee:

- immediately upon discovery by the insured or any partners, officers, or directors (not in collusion with the employee) of any dishonest act committed by that employee whether before or after becoming employed by the insured; and
- on the date specified in a notice mailed to the insured, which must be at least 30 days after the date of mailing.

## Forgery or Alteration (Forgery or Alteration Form B)

This coverage protects the insured against forgery or alteration of checks, drafts, promissory notes, and similar instruments the insured issues. The coverage does not apply to incoming checks or other items the insured receives.

## Inside the Premises—Theft of Money and Securities (Theft, Disappearance, and Destruction Coverage Form C)

### Coverage

The insurer pays for loss resulting directly from the theft, disappearance, or destruction of covered property. This form specifically covers the loss of money and securities not covered under Crime Form D, Robbery and Safe Burglary. This form has two sections: Sections 1 and 2.

#### *Section 1: Inside the Premises*

In this section, covered property includes money and securities inside the premises or the premises of a bank. Coverage extensions require the insurer to pay for loss of or damage to a locked safe, vault, cash register, cash box, or cash drawer located in the premises, as well as for damage to the premises or its exterior resulting directly from an actual or attempted theft or unlawful entry.

#### *Section 2: Outside the Premises*

Covered property includes money and securities outside the premises in a messenger's care or custody. Coverage is extended so that the insurer also pays for loss of covered property that results from theft, disappearance, or destruction while outside the premises in an armored motor vehicle company's care and custody. However, this coverage extension applies only to the amount of loss the insured cannot recover from the armored motor vehicle company or its insurer.

### Additional Exclusions and Conditions

In addition to containing the general provisions (discussed at the end of this section), this coverage form makes several additional exclusions for:

- loss from accounting or mathematical errors or omissions;
- loss from dishonest or criminal act of any of the insured's employees, managers, directors, trustees, or authorized representatives commits either acting alone or in collusion with other persons or while performing services for the insured;
- loss resulting from the giving or surrendering of property in any exchange or purchase;
- loss from damage to the premises resulting from fire, however caused (Note: the contract pays for money and securities loss due to fire, or damage to a safe or vault);
- loss of property contained in any money-operated device, such as a vending machine, unless the amount of money deposited in it is recorded by a continuous recording instrument;
- loss from damage to the premises or its exterior or to containers of covered property by vandalism or malicious mischief;
- loss resulting from the insured, or anyone acting on the insured's express or implied authority, being induced by any dishonest act to part voluntarily with title to or possession of any property; and

- loss of property after it has been transferred or surrendered to a person or place outside the premises or banking premises:
  - on the basis of unauthorized instructions; or
  - as a result of a threat to do bodily harm to any person or damage to any property, such as holding someone from the business for ransom (Note: this exclusion does not apply to loss of covered property while outside the premises or banking premises in a messenger's care and custody if the insured had no knowledge of any threat at the time the conveyance began).

The insured has a duty in the event of loss to notify the police if it has reason to believe that any loss of covered property or loss because of damage to covered property involves a violation of law.

## Inside the Premises—Robbery or Safe Burglary of Other Property (Robbery and Safe Burglary—Property Other than Money and Securities—Coverage Form D)

**Coverage** The insurer pays for loss of covered property or loss due to damage to covered property, but not money or securities, resulting directly from the following types of losses inside the premises:

***Section 1: Inside the Premises***

- Robbery of a custodian
  - Covered property is property other than money and securities inside the premises in a custodian's care and custody.
  - Covered cause of loss is an actual or attempted robbery.
  - Coverage extension: the insurer pays for loss from damage to the premises or its exterior resulting directly from the covered cause of loss.
- Safe burglary.
  - Covered property is property other than money and securities inside the premises in a safe or vault.
  - Covered cause of loss is an actual or attempted safe burglary.
  - Coverage extension: the insurer pays for loss from damage to (1) the premises or its exterior or (2) a locked safe or vault located inside the premises resulting directly from the covered cause of loss.

**Test Topic Alert!** A custodian is an individual who has custody of the property on the insured's premises.

### *Section 2: Outside the Premises*

- Robbery of a messenger
  - Covered property is property other than money and securities outside the premises in a messenger's care and custody.
  - Covered cause of loss is an actual or attempted robbery.
  - Coverage extension: the coverage extension for the conveyance of property by an armored motor vehicle, as described under the Theft, Disappearance, and Destruction Coverage Form, also applies to this form.

**Test Topic Alert!**

A messenger is the insured or an employee of the insured entrusted with property away from the premises.

## Additional Exclusions and Conditions

Robbery and Safe Burglary Coverage Form D includes five additional exclusions for:

- loss resulting from any dishonest or criminal act committed by any of the insured's employees, managers, directors, trustees, or authorized representatives, acting either alone or in collusion with other persons or while performing services for the insured;
- loss resulting from fire, however caused, except loss from damage to a safe or vault;
- loss of or damage to motor vehicles, trailers, or equipment and accessories attached to them;
- loss from damage to any property by vandalism or malicious mischief; and
- loss of property after it has been transferred or surrendered to a person or place outside the premises or banking premises:
  - on the basis of unauthorized instructions; or
  - as a result of a threat to do bodily harm to any person or damage to any property, such as holding someone from the business for ransom (Note: this exclusion does not apply to loss of covered property while outside the premises or banking premises in a messenger's care and custody if the insured had no knowledge of any threat at the time the conveyance began).

Additional conditions under this coverage form include the following:

- The insured has a duty to notify police if he suspects a violation of law.
- A special limit of insurance covers certain specified property. The insurer pays only up to $5,000 for any one occurrence for loss of covered property or loss because of damage to covered property. This limit applies to the following property:
  - precious metals, precious or semiprecious stones, pearls, furs, or completed or partially completed articles made of or containing such materials that constitute the principal value of such articles; or

  - manuscripts, drawings, or records of any kind or the cost of reconstructing them or reproducing any information they contain.
- Outside the premises: the insurer pays for loss to covered property outside the premises, including money and securities, while in a messenger's care or custody. Coverage also applies to theft, disappearance, or destruction of property while in an armored motor vehicle company's care and custody, but only for the amount of the loss the insured cannot recover from the armored motor vehicle company or its insurer. Coverage also applies to loss resulting from the robbery of a messenger.

## Premises Burglary Coverage Form E

### Coverage

The insurer pays for loss of covered property and loss due to damage of covered property resulting directly from the covered causes of loss. Covered property is property other than money and securities inside the premises. Covered causes of loss include (1) actual or attempted robbery of a watchperson and (2) actual or attempted burglary.

Premises Burglary Coverage Form E includes a coverage extension to pay for loss from damage to the premises or their exterior resulting directly from an actual or attempted burglary or an actual or attempted robbery of a watchperson.

### Limit of Insurance

The insurer pays up to the limit of insurance shown on the Declarations Page. If a loss covered by this form occurs, coverage is suspended until the premises are restored to the same condition of security that existed before the loss. However, if the insured maintains at least one watchperson while the premises are closed for business, this restriction after a loss does not apply and coverage remains in effect.

### Additional Exclusions and Conditions

The additional exclusions and conditions for Premises Burglary Coverage Form E are the same as those under Robbery and Safe Burglary Form D.

✓ ***Take Note:*** The need for various crime insurance policies is created by limitations in property policy forms. Employee theft and dishonesty losses are excluded in all forms. Property coverage for money and securities is limited at best. However, the theft coverage most property policies provide apply to robbery and burglary that results in loss to property other than money and securities and therefore may eliminate the need for some crime forms such as Robbery and Safe Burglary Coverage Form D or Premises Burglary Coverage Form E.

# General Conditions

The following general conditions are common to all crime insuring agreements.

## Coverage Extensions

Unless stated otherwise in the specific coverage form, the insurer's liability under any coverage extension is part of, not in addition to, the limit of insurance that applies to the coverage form or coverage section.

For instance, the theft, disappearance, and destruction coverage form indicates that as an extension of coverage, the insurer pays for safes and vaults damaged as a result of an attempted theft or unlawful entry. If an insured has a $15,000 limit of insurance and suffers an $8,000 money loss and an additional $3,000 in damage to a safe, the insurer pays the $3,000, and the insured receives $11,000. On the other hand, if the money loss is $15,000 and there is an additional $3,000 in damage to the safe, the $3,000 damage is not covered because it exceeds limit of insurance.

## Discovery Period for Loss

The insurer pays only for covered loss discovered no later than one year from the end of the policy period.

The **Commercial Crime Policy Discovery Form (CR 00 22 07)** modifies the time during which the insured may discover and report a loss. That form allows for payment for a loss that the insured discovers:

- within 60 days from the date of the policy's termination or cancellation; and
- with respect to an employee benefit plan, no later than one year from the date on which such plan was terminated or cancelled. (An employee benefit plan is a welfare or pension benefit plan noted in the Declarations that is subject to the Employee Retirement Income Security Act of 1974, or ERISA.)

Furthermore, the extended period to discover loss ends immediately upon the effective date of other insurance coverage that replaces any part of the existing coverage.

The **Commercial Crime Policy Loss Sustained Form (CR 00 23 07)** is similar to the Discovery Form, but for the following extended discovery period: payment is allowed for a loss that the insured discovers within one year—not 60 days—from the date of the policy's termination or cancellation.

## Duties in the Event of Loss

After the insured discovers a loss or a situation that may result in the loss of or damage to covered property under a particular coverage form, the insured must:

- notify the insurer as soon as possible;
- notify the police if the loss may have resulted from an unlawful act, unless the loss resulted from employee theft, forgery, or alteration of negotiable instruments;
- submit to examination under oath and give the insurer a signed statement of the insured's answers;
- give the insurer a detailed, sworn proof of loss within 120 days; and
- cooperate with the insurer in the investigation and settlement of any claim.

**Joint Insured** The number of insureds determines the relationship to the insurer:

If more than one insured is named in the Declarations, the first named insured acts for itself and for every other insured for all purposes of the insurance. If the first named insured ceases to be covered, the next named insured becomes the first named insured. An employee of any insured is considered an employee of all insureds.

**Legal Action against the Insurer** The insured may not bring any legal action against the insurer involving a loss unless:

- the insured has complied with all the terms of the insurance;
- at least 90 days have expired since the insured filed proof of loss; and
- the action is brought within two years from the date the loss is discovered.

**Loss Sustained during Prior Insurance** Under certain circumstances, an insurer pays for a loss that occurs under a previous policy. Such circumstances occur when an insured has other insurance, cancels that policy, and purchases a new policy. If the insured later learns that a loss occurred during the previous policy, but that the discovery period for that policy has expired, the insurer under the new policy pays for the loss provided the:

- new insurance became effective at the time of cancellation or termination of the prior insurance; and
- loss would have been covered by the new insurance had it been in effect when the acts or events causing the loss occurred.

The amount of insurance is limited to the lesser of the amount recoverable under the:

- new insurance as of its effective date; or
- prior insurance, had it remained in effect.

The insurer will not pay more for a loss sustained by more than one insured than it would pay for a loss sustained by only one insured.

**Records** The insured must keep records of all covered property so the insurer can verify the amount of any loss.

The **Commercial Crime Policy Discovery Form (CR 00 22 07)** and **Loss Sustained Form (CR 00 23 07)** give the insurer (and insurance rating or advisory organizations) the right to:

- conduct inspections and surveys at any time;
- issue reports to the insured about the conditions found during such inspections; and
- recommend changes.

These inspections concern only the insurability of the risk and the premiums to be charged. They are not intended to determine or ensure that the conditions are safe or in compliance with the law, regulations, codes, or standards.

Both forms also allow the insurer to audit the insured's books and records as they relate to the policy at any time during its term and for the three years following its termination or cancellation.

## Recoveries

After the insurer settles a loss, any recoveries from a third party, less the cost of obtaining them, are distributed as follows:

- to the insured, until the insured is reimbursed for any loss that the insured sustained that exceeds the limit of insurance and the deductible amount, if any;
- then to the insurer, until the insurer is reimbursed for the settlement made with the insured; and
- then to the insured again, until the insured is reimbursed for that part of the loss equal to the deductible amount, if any.

## Coverage Territory

This insurance covers only acts committed or events occurring within the United States, US territories and possessions, Puerto Rico, and Canada.

## Transfer of the Insured's Rights of Recovery Against Others

Subrogation, as presented in Unit 3, applies to these coverage forms. In paying the insured for a loss that was the fault of another party, the insurer obtains the right to recover the money it paid for the loss from the other party.

## Valuation and Settlement

Subject to the applicable limit of insurance provisions, the insurer pays for:

- loss of money for not more than its face value;
- loss of securities for not more than their value at the close of business on the day the loss was discovered; and
- loss of property, loss from damage to property (other than money and securities) or loss from damage to the premises for not more than:
  - the actual cash value of the property on the day the loss was discovered;
  - the cost of repairing the property or premises; or
  - the cost of replacing the property with property of like kind and quality.

Repairs or replacement must be made as soon as is reasonably possible after the loss. The insurer chooses the settlement method. If agreement cannot be reached, the matter is subject to arbitration.

# Commercial Crime Coverage Form (Loss Sustained Form): CR 00 21 07

The **Commercial Crime Coverage Form** consolidates the coverage described in the earlier, multiple forms (Forms A, B, C, etc.), resulting in a more streamlined approach to coverage. As noted above, this form also includes 20 new and revised definitions that expand the scope of the earlier crime insurance forms.

## Insuring Agreements

This form contains seven insuring agreements. The insured may choose all or any of them, depending on the need for coverage. (The applicable exclusions are noted.)

- Employee Theft
- Forgery or Alteration
- Inside the Premises—Theft of Money and Securities
- Inside the Premises—Robbery and Safe Burglary of Other Property
- Outside the Premises
- Computer Fraud
- Money Orders and Counterfeit Paper Currency

### Insuring Agreement A.1: Employee Theft

The insured pays for losses concerning money, securities, and other property stolen by an employee who acts alone or with other persons.

***Exclusions***

- Losses caused by employees who were covered under a policy that had been cancelled and not reinstated
- Inventory shortages
- Losses resulting from trading
- Losses resulting from fraudulent warehouse receipts or related documents

### Insuring Agreement A.2: Forgery or Alteration

The insurer pays for losses due to forgery or alterations of checks, draft, promissory notes, or other promises to pay money. These instruments are covered if they are drawn by the insured or someone acting as the insured's agent.

If the insured is sued for refusing to pay a forged check, draft, promissory note or other promise to pay money, the insurer may agree to cover the insured's legal costs of defense. This coverage is in addition to coverage limits.

**Insuring Agreement A.3: Inside the Premises—Theft of Money and Securities**

The insurer pays for losses resulting from the theft, disappearance, or destruction of money or securities inside the insured's premises.

If the premises or its exterior are damaged during the theft or attempted theft or money and securities, the insurer will cover the cost of repair or replacement. The insurer will also pay for loss or damage done to a locked safe, vault, cash register, cash box, or drawer inside the premises during a theft or attempted theft.

***Exclusions***

- Losses caused by accounting or arithmetical errors
- Losses resulting from the exchange or purchase of property
- Loss caused by fire, unless the loss involves money and securities or damage to a safe or vault
- Property lost from a money-operated device, unless a continuous recording instrument records the amount of money deposited in it
- Loss or damage to motor vehicles, trailers, semi-trailers, or equipment and attachments
- Property lost or damaged when transferred out of the premises or banking premises due to unauthorized instructions, threat of physical harm, or threat of property damage (although the loss will be covered by Insuring Agreement A.5 if the property was money, securities, or other property in a messenger's care while the insured had no knowledge of the threat when the transfer began or had knowledge of a threat, but the loss didn't result from the threat)
- Losses due to vandalism of the premises; safe; vault; cash register, box, or drawer; or other property
- Loss resulting from the insured's—or any authorized person's—voluntary transferring title or possession of property due to another's dishonesty

**Insuring Agreement A.4: Inside the Premises—Robbery or Safe Burglary of Other Property**

The insurer will pay for loss or damage to property other than money or securities that are within the premises, when such loss or damage results from the actual or attempted robbery of a custodian. It will also pay when the loss or damage occurs inside the premises due to an actual or attempted burglary of a safe.

If the premises or its exterior are damaged during the robbery of a custodian, the burglary of a safe, or the attempt to commit either, the insurer will cover the cost of repair or replacement to the premises. The insurer will also pay for loss or damage done to a locked safe or vault inside the premises during an actual or attempted robbery of a custodian or burglary of a safe.

#### *Exclusions*

These are the same as those for Insuring Agreement A.3.

**Insuring Agreement A.5: Outside the Premises**

The insurer will pay for loss of money and securities from theft, disappearance, or destruction while outside the premises and in the custody of a messenger or an armored motor vehicle. Payment is also made for money and securities lost due to an actual or attempted robbery of the messenger or armored motor vehicle.

#### *Exclusions*

These are the same as those for Insuring Agreement A.3.

**Insuring Agreement A.6: Computer Fraud**

The insurer will pay for loss or damage to money, securities, and other property that results from the use of a computer to fraudulently transfer them out of the premises, bank or other safe depository to a person or place beyond the premises, bank or safe depository.

#### *Exclusions*

- Losses resulting from the exchange or purchase of property
- Losses resulting from fraudulent directions to pay or transfer funds
- Inventory shortages
- Loss resulting from the insured's—or any authorized person's—voluntary transferring title or possession of property due to another's dishonesty

**Insuring Agreement A.7: Funds Transfer Fraud**

The insurer will pay for loss of funds resulting from a fraudulent instruction directing a financial institution to transfer, pay, or deliver funds from the insured's transfer account.

**Insuring Agreement A.8: Money Orders and Counterfeit Paper Currency**

The insurer pays for the loss if the insured, during the course of business and in good faith, accepts money orders that are not paid or counterfeit money.

#### *Exclusion*

Loss resulting from the use of a computer to fraudulently transfer money, securities, and other property.

## General Exclusions

The following exclusions are in addition to the usual exclusions of the general crime coverage form as noted above. Unless specifically covered by an Insuring Agreement, there is no coverage for losses resulting from:

- theft or other dishonest act committed by the insured, partners, or members;
- theft or other dishonest act committed by the insured's employees, managers, directors, trustees, or authorized representatives, unless covered by Insuring Agreement A.1;
- property that is seized or destroyed by order of the government;
- lost income, payment of damages for legal liability, and payment of expenses incurred in determining the existence or amount of the loss resulting from a covered act or occurrence;
- legal expenses, unless covered by Insuring Agreement A.2;
- nuclear reaction, radiation, contamination, or related incident; or
- war, warlike action, insurrection, revolution, or related incident.

## Quick Quiz 8.2

Identify the type of property covered under each of the following crime forms

Money and securities (MS)
Property other than money and securities (OMS)
Both (B)

1. _____ Employee theft
2. _____ Forgery or alteration
3. _____ Theft, disappearance, or destruction
4. _____ Robbery and safe burglary
5. _____ Premises burglary
6. _____ Computer fraud
7. _____ Extortion
8. _____ Premises theft and robbery
9. _____ Safe depository

***Answers*** *1.* ***B*** *2.* ***MS*** *3.* ***MS*** *4.* ***OMS*** *5.* ***OMS*** *6.* ***B*** *7.* ***B*** *8.* ***OMS*** *9.* ***B***

# Unit Test Eight

1. A fidelity bond covers
   A. loss of receipts caused by a dishonest employee
   B. mysterious disappearance of the insured's accounting books
   C. dishonesty of anyone who causes a loss to the insured
   D. theft of money by a customer of the insured

2. In crime insurance, the definition of theft includes which of the following?
   A. Burglary
   B. Robbery
   C. Larceny
   D. All of the above

3. Under Premises Burglary Coverage Form E, loss of insured property caused by burglars is covered EXCEPT
   A. when the premises are not open for business
   B. when the burglars only broke out of the premises
   C. when explosives were used to break in
   D. when the stolen property consists only of securities

4. Which of the following statements is CORRECT?
   A. Under Inside the Premises—Robbery and Safe Burglary Coverage, loss is not covered unless visible signs of forcible entry have been established.
   B. Robbery and safe burglary coverage protects the insured against loss resulting from an employee who knew the combination of the safe and stole from it.
   C. The insurance definition of theft means any type of crime.
   D. The employee dishonesty coverage form includes embezzlement by a partner in the firm.

5. Which of the following forms provides the broadest protection for money and securities?
   A. Robbery or Safe Burglary Coverage
   B. Employee Theft
   C. Theft of Money and Securities
   D. Forgery or Alteration

6. Which of the following possible causes of loss to money is excluded under Employee Theft Coverage?
   A. Fire damage to cash
   B. Mysterious disappearance
   C. Dishonesty of the insured
   D. Misplacement of a bank deposit

7. The owner of a small warehouse is insured under a premises burglary coverage form. Which of the following losses is covered under this contract?
   A. Theft of cash from within a cash drawer
   B. Merchandise stolen when the premises were open for business
   C. Loss caused by a dishonest act of the insured's partner
   D. Inventory stolen by an unknown person while the warehouse was closed

8. Which of the following losses does the Premises Burglary Coverage Form insure?

   A. Loss of merchandise due to shrinkage
   B. Loss of merchandise from within the insured premises due to burglary
   C. Loss of merchandise due to shoplifting
   D. Loss of merchandise due to employee theft

9. Under a Premises Burglary Coverage Form, loss to which of the following is covered?

   A. Merchandise
   B. Money
   C. Bank drafts
   D. Promissory notes

10. Robbery or Safe Burglary Coverage covers loss of insured property under each of the following circumstances EXCEPT by

    A. robbery or attempted robbery within the premises
    B. kidnapping of a messenger
    C. theft of money from a custodian inside the premises
    D. theft of merchandise from within a locked safe

11. The insuring agreements found in Robbery or Safe Burglary Coverage include all of the following EXCEPT

    A. robbery of a messenger outside the premises
    B. robbery of a custodian inside the premises
    C. safe burglary
    D. robbery of a watchperson

12. Robbery or Safe Burglary Coverage excludes all of the following EXCEPT loss

    A. caused by a trustee of the insured
    B. resulting from fire
    C. based on unauthorized instructions
    D. to premises damaged by burglars

13. A person who has custody of property inside the insured's premises is called a

    A. watchperson
    B. custodian
    C. messenger
    D. janitor

14. Some provisions of crime insurance policies are specific to those forms and typically not found in other insurance policies. Among the unique provisions of a crime policy is (are)

    A. effective and expiration dates
    B. limits of liability
    C. discovery period
    D. valuation clause

15. Computer Fraud coverage applies to loss of

    A. money
    B. money and securities
    C. money, securities, and other property
    D. property other than money and securities

16. Extortion coverage applies to loss of

    A. money
    B. money and securities
    C. money, securities, and other property
    D. property other than money and securities

17. Premises Theft and Robbery Outside Premises coverage applies to loss of

    A. money
    B. money and securities
    C. money, securities, and other property
    D. property other than money and securities

18. An insured hotel encourages guests to place valuable property in the hotel's safe-deposit boxes. To protect itself against loss to guest property, the hotel should purchase

    A. Broad Form Property of Others
    B. Safe Depository Liability
    C. Bailee's Customers' Policy
    D. Building and Personal Property Coverage Form

19. When an insured wishes to purchase protection against employee dishonesty, it secures the coverage on

    A. blanket basis
    B. schedule of positions
    C. schedule of named employees
    D. any of the above

# Unit Test Eight Answers & Rationale

1. **A.** Historically, loss of money or other property by employees has been covered under a fidelity bond. Coverage now is provided under a crime policy's employee dishonesty section.

2. **D.** *Theft* is a broad term defined in crime insurance policies as any act of stealing. Burglary, robbery, and larceny have very specific meanings.

3. **D.** Premises Burglary Coverage Form E defines covered property as property other than money and securities.

4. **A.** Employee dishonesty is covered only under a separate coverage form.

5. **B.** Because disappearance and destruction are not defined in the theft form, they can be all-inclusive terms ranging from inadvertently putting money in a paper shredder to fire damage to cash.

6. **C.** Dishonesty of the insured is excluded in all crime forms.

7. **D.** Premises burglary coverage provides no protection when the business is open.

8. **B.** By definition, burglary requires the wrongful or criminal entry into the premises and forcible exit from the premises as well. Shoplifting and shrinkage do not meet those tests.

9. **A.** The Premises Burglary Form specifically excludes money and securities.

10. **C.** The form covers only the theft of property other than money and securities while inside the premises.

11. **D.** Coverage applies only to losses of property with a custodian or messenger, not a watchperson.

12. **D.** Damage caused by burglars is a covered cause of loss under the Robbery and Safe Burglary Coverage Form.

13. **B.** A messenger is someone with custody of property off premises. A watchperson has custody of property on premises, but has no other duties. The term *custodian* excludes both a janitor and a watchperson.

14. **C.** The discovery period that allows an insured to report losses up to 12 months after the policy expires is a unique provision of a crime policy. It is comparable to tail coverage under liability contracts, but has differences.

15. **C.** The form applies to money, securities, and other property.

16. **C.** The form applies to money, securities, and other property.

17. **D.** Coverage applies only to property other than money and securities.

18. **B.** Although limited coverage is available for property of others in the insured's care, custody, or control under property policies, the Safe Depository Liability Policy is designed specifically for this purpose.

19. **D.** Employee dishonesty coverage is provided using either a schedule or blanket approach. When scheduling, individual employees may be named or only the various positions the employer wishes to cover.

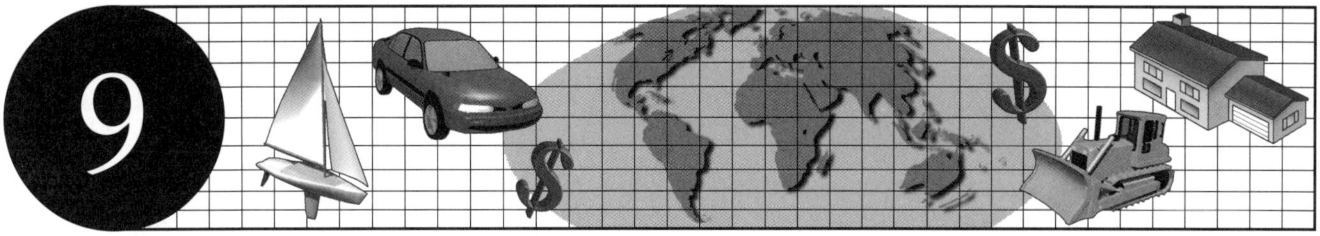

# Surety Bonds

## INTRODUCTION

Surety bonds guarantee that specific obligations will be fulfilled. An obligation may involve meeting a contractual commitment, paying a debt or performing certain duties. Typically, a bond is written for a certain amount and if the party whose obligation is bonded fails to meet it, the bond amount is paid to the person or organization that required it, up to the full amount of the bond.

Suretyship dates back many thousands of years. Simple arrangements were made when one person's promise to do something was not enough to provide adequate security. For instance, a creditor may have been unwilling to loan money if he was not confident that the amount would be repaid. In bygone days, the guarantor of the other person's promise may have been a friend or relative who would pledge personal property or other assets if the borrower defaulted on his obligation.

Corporate suretyship began in the 1800s. Organizations undertook the obligations individuals and family members previously provided and the surety field was formed. This required the issuance of surety contracts backed by corporate assets. Business interests, courts, government bodies, and public agencies now require surety bonds routinely as a means of reducing or transferring the risks of transactions or proceedings.

## UNIT OBJECTIVES

When you have completed this unit, you should be able to:

- identify the parties to a surety bond;
- distinguish between surety bonds and insurance; and
- describe the major types of surety bonds and their purposes.

# Surety Bonds

A **bond** is an agreement by one party (the **surety** or guarantor), to answer to a third person (the **obligee** or beneficiary), for the debt or default of a responsible party called the **principal** (or obligor). Stated simply, the surety guarantees the principal's conduct, and if that conduct falls short, the surety is responsible to the obligee.

✓ ***Take Note:*** A bond is a three-party contract involving the surety, principal, and obligee. By comparison, insurance is a two-party contract between the insured and insurer. Unlike in a traditional insurance contract, the third party has some control over the bond contract as well as an insurable interest.

**Fidelity bonds** protect an employer for losses their employees cause. These types of bonds were previously discussed.

**Test Topic Alert!**

A fidelity bond, not a surety bond, is purchased to protect an employer from the actions of dishonest employees.

A **surety bond** provides monetary compensation if the bonded party fails to perform a certain act, such as a contract. It is commonly issued (1) in connection with a court action, (2) to someone seeking a license or permit, and (3) to a construction contractor. The surety bond guarantees that the principal is honest and has both the financial capacity and the work expertise to carry out the obligation for which he is bonded. Historically, the surety was an individual and still can be. It is more common today is for the surety to be a casualty insurance company. The obligee is the person who contracts for work to be completed or to whom the courts seek to provide financial protection.

A surety bond serves as a guarantee of performance. The surety merely lends its name and credit to guarantee an obligation between two parties.

## Parties to a Surety Agreement

There are three parties to a surety agreement:

### *Principal*

Also known as the **obligor**, the principal is the responsible party who has agreed to perform a service, such as a contractor.

### *Obligee*

The obligee is the insured—that is, the party who benefits from the bond. In construction, the obligee is the project owner.

### *Surety*

This is the guarantor or insurance company that guarantees that the obligor will fulfill all undertakings, covenants, terms, conditions, and agreements of a contract. In construction, the surety guarantees that the obligor will complete the project and pay for all labor and materials.

✓ ***Take Note:*** The penalty for failing to fulfil the terms, conditions, and agreements of a contract is the forfeiture of the bond's face amount.

**Test Topic Alert!**

A surety bond serves as a guarantee of performance. Once a surety bond is issued, it cannot be cancelled and does not expire until the contract has been performed.

## Differences between Bonds and Insurance

Most surety bonds are issued by insurance companies, although some companies specialize in bonds. Suretyship and insurance share some characteristics, such as indemnity, risk transfer, and contract law, but in many respects they are quite different.

A major contrast between insurance and surety is that the surety agreement involves three parties, whereas insurance has only two contracting parties. (The third party in a liability situation is not a party to the contract.) In addition, insurance contemplates that losses will occur, and the price of the insurance reflects that anticipation. Surety, on the other hand, if properly underwritten, involves no losses. Thus, the price of a surety bond is merely an administrative fee and does not have sufficient premium to pay losses.

Another major difference is that unlike insurance, the surety may pursue subrogation against its insured. If a default occurs under a surety bond, the surety may (and probably will) institute legal action against the person or firm bonded to recoup any losses. This is in stark contrast to a first-party insurance policy designed to pay claims.

## Underwriting

The surety, in determining whether to issue a bond for a principal, bases its decision on the principal's:

- ability to perform the prescribed work (technical ability);
- financial strength or ability to complete the project (financial ability); and
- character and reputation (in some cases, the principal's spouse also is investigated).

✓ ***Take Note:*** In surety bonds, the underwriting criteria often are called the three Cs:

- **C**apacity
- **C**ollateral
- **C**haracter

**Bond Terms** A bond gives both the surety and principal certain protection and legal remedies.

- Subrogation is well established and should the surety have to pay, it usually looks to recover the payment from the principal.
- Once the bond is issued, the surety cannot cancel it.
- An indemnity agreement often is executed that requires the principal to pledge assets, such as a letter of credit, to the surety in exchange for the issuance of the bond. If a default occurs, the surety first goes to the letter of credit or other pledged collateral for reimbursement.

## Quick Quiz 9.1

1. The obligation that is the subject of a surety bond might be

   A. paying a debt
   B. performing certain duties
   C. meeting contractual obligations
   D. all of the above

2. Which of the following statements is true about a bonded contractor who defaults on a construction performance agreement?

   A. The obligee can hire another contractor and be paid by the surety.
   B. The principal has no obligation to pay expenses or damages.
   C. The surety may cancel the bond and owe nothing to the obligee.
   D. The surety may seek reimbursement for any losses from the principal.

3. The three parties to a surety agreement are

   A. ____________________
   B. ____________________
   C. ____________________

4. The three criteria used for underwriting surety are

   A. ____________________
   B. ____________________
   C. ____________________

## *Answers*

*1. **D.** There are many reasons why a principal may approach a surety and request a guarantee, including: in connection with court actions; for guarantee of a payment of debt; for performing certain duties, such as those in connection with licenses, permits, or contracts; or for performance of other contractual duties.*

2. **A**. *If a principal fails to complete bonded work, the person to whom the obligation is owed may hire another contractor to complete the job. The guarantee provided to the principal by the surety is that it will pay for this additional contract.*
3. *Obligee, principal, surety*
4. *Character, capacity, collateral*

# Types of Bonds

The many types of surety bonds available generally can be classified as contract bonds, judicial or court bonds, and miscellaneous bonds.

## Contract Bonds

**Contract bonds** are issued to guarantee performance of the terms and provisions of written contracts. The principals on these instruments are usually construction contractors, although the work of other types of firms may be bonded. Government entities typically require contract bonds for construction of roads, bridges, and other infrastructure items. For building construction, the obligee is usually a private firm or an individual, as opposed to a public entity. Some of the more common contract bonds are described below.

### Bid Bonds

Sometimes contracts are awarded to the firms that enter the lowest bids. This is almost always true with government contracts. A **bid bond** guarantees two things: first, that the firm will enter into a contract if chosen and second, that it will secure a performance bond for the work.

### Performance Bonds

A **performance bond** guarantees to the owner (obligee) that the contractor (principal) will complete the contract as drawn. If the contractor fails to do so, the surety may hire another contractor to complete the work. In this case, the surety pays those expenses. If the original contractor fails to complete the work on time, the surety pays any losses that result from the delay in completion.

### Payment Bonds

A **payment bond** also is known as a **labor and material bond**. It guarantees that the principal will complete and deliver the work free of any liens or encumbrances. The bond assures the owner that if the contractor does not pay the bills for subcontracted labor or materials, the property will be turned over to the owner free of any financial attachments.

### Completion Bonds

When a contractor borrows funds to finance a construction project, the lender may require a guarantee that the project will be carried out and that the contractor will be paid for the work. A **completion bond** guarantees that the lender (obligee) will be paid for any loans from the proceeds of the contracted work.

### Supply Bonds

A **supply bond** guarantees that a supplier will faithfully furnish the supplies, materials, products, or equipment required under a contract. The bond frequently is written to ensure that a business dependent on a steady supply of materials, components, or finished goods is furnished with these items. Manufacturers and others who provide finished goods are particularly vulnerable to these types of losses and may require supply bonds.

✓ ***For Example:*** One of the most common types of contract bonds is used when a homeowner contracts for construction of a swimming pool. It is not uncommon to have the contractor complete only a portion of the work, leaving the homeowner with a partially completed job and the loss of any advance payments. If the work is bonded, the homeowner is guaranteed that the job will be completed by either the original contractor or another hired by the contractor or the surety.

## Judicial Bonds

Under our legal system, certain types of privileges are available only when a bond or another form of security has been furnished. **Judicial bonds** fall into two broad categories—**court** (or **litigation**) and **fiduciary**.

## Litigation Bonds

### Bail Bonds

Most people are familiar with **bail bonds**, the most common form of litigation bond. When someone is arrested, he may be held in jail awaiting trial unless a bail bond has been furnished to the court. When issued, a bail bond guarantees that the person will appear in court at the designated time and place. The court (federal, state, or municipal) is the obligee. If the person fails to appear, the bond amount is paid to the court as penalty. Bail bonds usually require collateral to protect the sureties. Generally, the issuance of bail bonds is left to firms that specialize in them.

### Court Bonds

The other major type of litigation bond is a **court bond**. Courts cannot afford to operate on the assumption that those who initiate legal action can pay court costs. This is particularly true when a party loses a suit. Plaintiffs often are required to furnish court bonds to pursue legal action. A court bond guarantees that the plaintiff will pay court costs and damages to the defendant if the plaintiff loses the case. If the losing party appeals the case, an **appeal bond** guarantees that the judgment will be paid if affirmed and that any court costs for the appeal also will be paid.

### *Attachment Bonds*

In certain cases, a party to a legal action may obtain a court order that requires another party to turn over certain assets in satisfaction of a judgment. The court will not issue such an order until an **attachment bond** has been issued. The bond guarantees that if the action to attach the property was wrongful, any damages the other party suffers will be paid.

If the party whose property has been attached wishes to vacate the attachment, he must furnish a **release of attachment bond**. This bond guarantees that if the party is found to owe an obligation to another party, the first party will turn over the assets, but is not encumbered in the meantime.

### *Injunction Bonds*

A plaintiff also may seek an injunction against another party. However, a court requires that an **injunction bond** be furnished before it issues the injunction. This bond, similar to an attachment bond, guarantees that damages will be paid to a defendant if it is decided that the injunction should not have been issued.

### Fiduciary Bonds

A fiduciary is someone who holds property in trust for another. A fiduciary bond guarantees that the fiduciary will perform his or her duties faithfully and act in the best interest of the person he or she represents. A fiduciary bond often is required to protect the interest of a person who has a legal interest in the property being held in trust.

### *Administrator and Executor Bonds*

An **administrator and executor bond** may be issued when someone has been appointed to handle the affairs of a deceased person. An executor named in a will is obligated legally to carry out the provisions of that document. A court appoints an administrator when a person dies without a will.

Guardians may need to be bonded because they often are appointed by courts to handle the affairs of persons who are not capable of doing so themselves, such as minors or those who are mentally incompetent. Fiduciary bonds also may be issued to receivers in bankruptcy cases or to trustees. Receivers and trustees may have to make decisions about how to use assets and pay debts.

## Miscellaneous Bonds

Many local, state and federal laws require that a bond be furnished before someone can obtain a license or permit. A wide variety of **license and permit bonds** exist, but they can be classified into two broad categories. The first is bonds designed to guarantee that laws and regulations of particular business

FIGURE 9.1 Fidelity and Surety Bonds

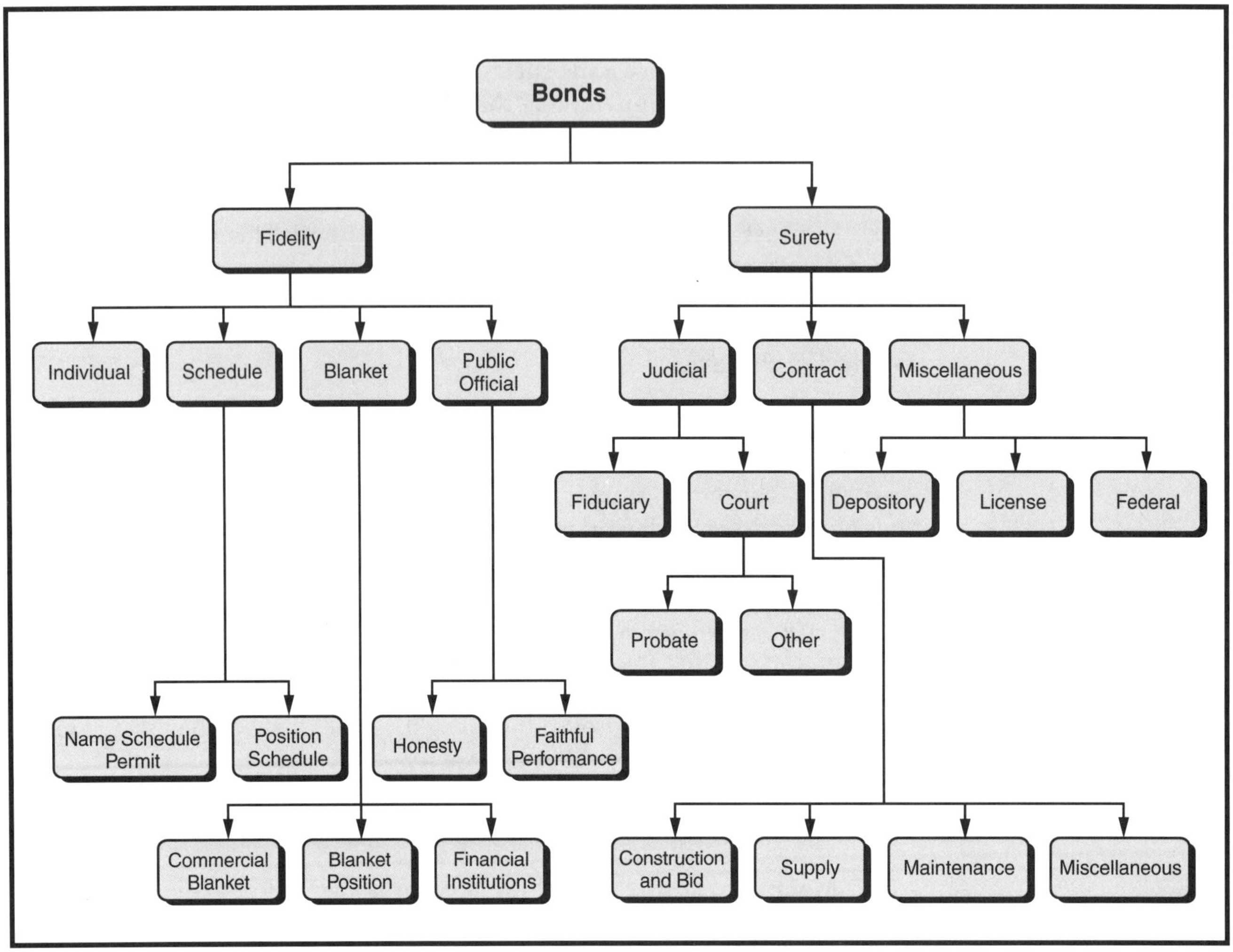


activities are carried out. Such bonds cover funeral directors, private detectives, real estate brokers and insurance brokers. The second category is bonds that guarantee that certain taxes are paid, such as for the sale of gasoline, liquor and tobacco products.

## Public Official Bonds

**Public official bonds** guarantee that elected officials will perform the duties and obligations of their offices faithfully. If they misuse public funds or otherwise cause harm to the public, the sureties pay. This bond is often a condition preceding the acceptance of public office.

## Lost Instrument Bonds

**Lost instrument bonds,** also known as **securities bonds**, guarantee that if instruments are lost, stolen, or destroyed, the owners of the securities will be indemnified. If an instrument is found later, the bond calls for the owner to reimburse the surety.

**Motor vehicle bonds** may be issued when individuals must provide proof of financial responsibility for accidents. The bonds also are required for car dealers to guarantee that they will turn over motor vehicle registration fees collected as part of the sale of vehicles.

When an entity has become a **self-insurer for workers' compensation**, it often must furnish a bond to the state to ensure that it will make benefit payments to injured employees.

The chart in Figure 9.1 represents a schematic of fidelity and surety bonds that have been discussed in this text.

# Unit Test Nine

1. Which of the following statements regarding suretyship is CORRECT?
   A. It is the same as insurance.
   B. Each contract of suretyship has three partners.
   C. It grew out of marine insurance.
   D. It is an exclusion under the CGL policy.

2. Which of the following statements regarding a surety bond is CORRECT?
   A. The principal is the surety bond's beneficiary.
   B. Because the bond always involves three parties, it is called third-party insurance.
   C. The person whose work is being bonded is the obligee.
   D. The surety acts as a guarantor of the principal's obligations.

3. Which of the following statements regarding surety underwriting is CORRECT?
   A. The two major classifications of surety bonds are fidelity and litigation.
   B. The surety, in theory, should sustain no losses.
   C. The principal's financial status is not important.
   D. The principal will not be asked to reimburse the surety for losses.

4. Which of the following statements regarding surety bonds is CORRECT?
   A. It would defeat the purpose of the bond requirements if the surety had the right to cancel.
   B. The surety reserves the right to collect from the obligee in case it suffers a loss by the principal.
   C. The obligee has no recourse against the surety in the event of default.
   D. If the bond is canceled midterm, all premium is refunded to the principal.

5. The face amount of a bond is called the
   A. face value
   B. limit of liability
   C. penalty
   D. stated amount

6. Which of the following is NOT a consideration of an underwriter in evaluating an application for a surety bond?
   A. Applicant's financial strength
   B. Principal's character and reputation
   C. Past works of a similar nature the applicant has completed
   D. Obligee's financial status

7. A bail bond is an example of which of the following types of bonds?
   A. Contract
   B. Performance
   C. Judicial
   D. Fiduciary

8. A performance bond guarantees that a contractor will
   A. enter into a contract if awarded
   B. complete the work described in the contract
   C. make payments to subcontractors
   D. pay a lender all amounts owed as a result of the contract

9. A supply bond guarantees that a supplier will
   A. be awarded a contract if it is the low bidder
   B. furnish materials and supplies at cost
   C. furnish supplies, materials, products, or equipment faithfully
   D. advance ship items before the user requires them

10. Which of the following types of bonds guarantees that if the action to attach property in a legal dispute was wrongful, any damages the other party suffered will be paid?
    A. Attachment
    B. Release of attachment
    C. Court
    D. Appeal

11. Which of the following people may NOT obtain a fiduciary bond?
    A. Executor of an estate
    B. Guardian of a minor child
    C. Trustee in a bankruptcy proceeding
    D. Beneficiary of a life insurance policy

12. A public official bond guarantees that the elected official will
    A. not embezzle public funds
    B. not commit perjury
    C. maximize the return on investment of public funds
    D. not seek a second term

# Unit Test Nine Answers & Rationale

1. **B.** Surety bonds involve a principal, an obligee and a surety, unlike insurance arrangements which involve only two parties.

2. **D.** Surety bonds are nothing more than financial guarantees that the principals will do something.

3. **B.** If surety underwriting is performed properly, almost no chance of loss to the surety exists because the principal must provide some kind of security to the surety in exchange for the bond. In addition, the surety may proceed directly against the principal in the event of default.

4. **A.** Once a bond has been issued, the surety may not cancel it. If a surety could suspect default and cancel a bond, it would render the bond useless.

5. **C.** The face amount of a bond is called the penalty because it is that amount the surety must pay in the event of default.

6. **D.** Only the principal's characteristics are relevant to surety underwriting.

7. **C.** Judicial or court bonds are a common type of surety arrangement. A bail bond guarantees that a person will appear in court at the time and place designated.

8. **B.** A performance bond, a type of contract bond, guarantees that a contractor will carry out the work specified in the contract.

9. **C.** A supply bond, a special type of contract bond, guarantees that a supplier will faithfully furnish the supplies, materials, products, or equipment required under a contract.

10. **A.** In certain cases, a party to a legal action may obtain a court order that requires another party to turn over certain assets in satisfaction of a judgment. The court will not issue such an order until an attachment bond has been executed.

11. **D.** A fiduciary bond guarantees that the fiduciary will perform his duties faithfully and act in the best interest of the person the fiduciary represents.

12. **A.** Public official bonds guarantee that elected officials will perform the duties and obligations of their offices faithfully. If they misuse public funds or otherwise harm the public, the sureties pay.

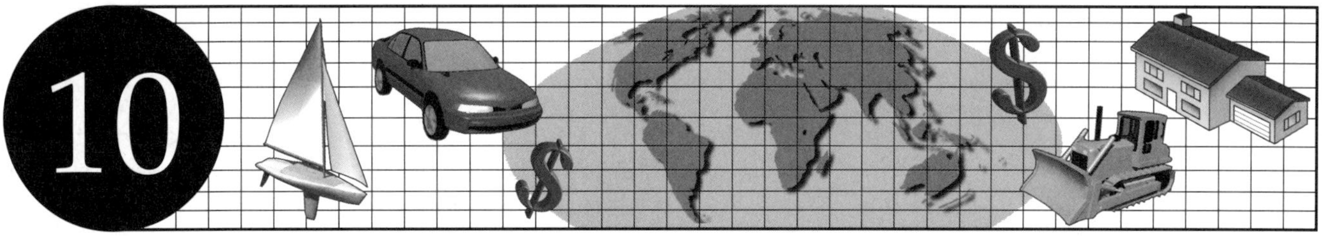


# Personal Automobile Insurance

## INTRODUCTION

Insurance for automobiles represents one of the largest segments of the property and casualty industry. By far, the most significant portion of automobile insurance premiums is generated by personal insurance policies. Although the premiums earned are large, so are the losses insurers must pay. Automobile accidents account for more than 50,000 deaths each year and millions of dollars in property damage. Many states have enacted laws making automobile insurance a legal necessity to operate a motor vehicle. Still, the number of uninsured drivers continues to rise, particularly in urban areas, and the cost of auto insurance remains a source of concern to consumers, insurers, regulators and lawmakers.

## UNIT OBJECTIVES

When you have completed this unit, you should be able to:

- describe the various methods used to compensate auto accident victims;
- determine who is eligible to purchase a Personal Auto Policy (PAP);
- list and describe the coverages the PAP provides;
- describe the PAP's limitations and exclusions; and
- identify major endorsements that can be used to tailor the PAP's coverage.

This unit generally discusses the personal automobile policy forms published by the Insurance Services Office in 1998 and adopted by most states. Note that some states have not yet adopted these forms and still use older ISO forms. Check with your state's test publisher to see which edition of these forms is covered on the state licensing exam.

You can determine which test publisher administers the exam by visiting the publishers' websites. For Promissor, Inc., go to www.promissor.com or call 1-888-204-6231. For Experior, go to www.experioronline.com or call 1-800-786-3926. Access the exam content outlines to see which edition of the ISO forms is on the exam (expressed as a year). If you do not see your state listed on the Promissor or Experior sites, your state does not retain either company and instead administers its own exams. Contact your state's insurance department for more information about the exam.

## Compensation of Auto Accident Victims

Under the current legal system, victims of automobile accidents are entitled to compensation from those who cause the accidents as a result of negligence. The many systems in place designed to provide that compensation vary by state. Some of the approaches used to compensate accident victims are:

- the tort system (civil litigation);
- financial responsibility laws;
- compulsory insurance laws;
- unsatisfied judgment funds;
- uninsured/underinsured motorists coverage; and
- no fault laws.

### Tort System

Under the **tort system**, which is based on fault, anyone whose negligent operation of a motor vehicle results in injuries or damages to others may be held legally responsible for his or her actions. Damages usually are apportioned based on each party's degree of fault. The tort system has come under attack due to its perceived high cost and lengthy delays in adjudicating claims of accident victims.

### Financial Responsibility Laws

Every state has a **financial responsibility law** that requires proof of financial responsibility when a person has been involved in an automobile accident, has been convicted of a serious offense (such as drunk driving), or has failed to pay a judgment from an earlier accident. Failure to provide proof of financial responsibility may result in loss of license or vehicle registration, or both.

### Compulsory Insurance Laws

In an attempt to address the shortcomings in the financial responsibility laws, many states have enacted compulsory auto insurance laws. These laws require a person to demonstrate that liability insurance is in force before an accident and usually are tied to vehicle registration, driver licensing, or some other event.

## Unsatisfied Judgment Funds

Some states with compulsory insurance laws also have established **unsatisfied judgment funds**. These funds are used to pay accident victims who cannot recover the full amount of their damages from the negligent parties. The funds, which limit the amounts that may be obtained from them, are financed in a variety of ways, including assessment of insurance companies, penalties on drivers convicted of moving violations, and fees charged to all drivers in the state.

## Uninsured/Underinsured Motorists Coverage

Recognizing that all other methods of eliminating the uninsured driver population were less than perfect, insurers began to include **uninsured motorists coverage** in all auto policies. This coverage is designed to reimburse the insureds for amounts due from negligent drivers who do not carry insurance. Initially, coverage was for bodily injury only, but included general damages such as pain and suffering if the other driver was legally responsible for the accident.

Coverage was later expanded to include **underinsured drivers**—that is, those who were insured, but carried limits of liability too low to cover the damages sustained by the injured party.

## No Fault Laws

Another way to compensate victims of automobile accidents is through no fault automobile insurance. Under the **no fault system**, the primary source of recovery for injuries sustained in an auto accident is the driver's or passenger's own automobile policy. Unlike the tort system, no fault laws require no determination of fault or negligence. In fact, a distinguishing feature of the no fault system is that it limits or eliminates the right to sue the other party in tort for injuries or damages that result from an auto accident.

Many states have adopted no fault laws in an attempt to reduce the amount of litigation arising out of motor vehicle accidents and thus the cost of auto insurance. To date, no state has adopted a pure no fault statute. In every case, there remains a limited right to sue once a threshold has been reached. Some states impose a monetary threshold, such as $5,000, and a claim below that amount is collected from the party's own insurer. In other states, the threshold is verbal, meaning the trigger for a tort action is something like serious bodily injury or loss of sight or a limb. Once the threshold has been reached, the person who has been injured or suffered property damage may initiate legal action against the negligent party.

# Overview of the Personal Automobile Policy (PAP)

The **Personal Auto Policy (PAP)** has, like other property and casualty products, gone through an evolutionary process designed to respond to changes in the law, driver and vehicle safety, and consumer demands. The discussion in this manual is limited to the policy developed by ISO, although it is important to understand that the predominant insurers of personal autos may use their own proprietary forms. Although no standard personal auto policy exists, the format, coverages, and policy terms are quite similar from carrier to carrier.

## Policy Format (PP 00 01 06 98)

The PAP comprises six major parts: four relate to the coverages the policy provides, a fifth part specifies the insured's duties, and the final part contains general provisions. Specifically, these six parts are:

- **Part A—Liability to Others Coverage**. This part covers bodily injury and property damage to others when the occurrence (accident or loss) is due to the insured's negligence.
- **Part B—Medical Payments Coverage**. This part covers necessary medical and funeral expenses for the insured, his family members, and others in the insured auto.
- **Part C—Uninsured/Underinsured Motorists Coverage**. UM/UIM coverage insures the policyowner and others occupying the insured's auto when the occurrence is the fault of someone else who is not insured or does not have adequate insurance. These coverages normally are written together.
- **Part D—Coverage for Damage to the Insured's Auto**. This part covers auto losses resulting from collision, from other than collision (comprehensive) and consequential transportation expenses (in case of theft or other causes of loss.) Part D does not cover personal property in the auto; it insures only the auto and parts of the auto.
- **Part E—Duties after an Accident or a Loss**. This part outlines the insured's duties and obligations when an accident or a loss occurs.
- **Part F—General Provisions**. This section of the PAP includes general policy provisions (e.g., policy period and termination).

## Miscellaneous Policy and Underwriting Considerations

Many factors affect the premium calculated for the policy.

**Basis of Coverage**

Coverage is stated as being on an accident basis; however, it is interpreted to include damage from repeated exposures. Thus, coverage actually is on an occurrence basis.

**Inception of Coverage**

The policy becomes effective at 12:01 am on the first day of coverage and expires at 12:01 am on the expiration date.

**Premium Determination**

In calculating the premiums for any insurance policy, the insurance company considers the amount of risk involved based on such factors as:

- territory of garaging, such as the principal place (county, city, zip code) where the auto is garaged and where the car is kept (such as in a garage);
- use of the auto, such as for pleasure, commuting to and from work, and business (in general, the more miles driven, the higher the risk and the higher the premium);
- driver's age, sex, marital status, and driving records;
- limits of insurance; the higher the limits, the greater the premium (but the lower the cost per thousand because the premium does not increase proportionately); and
- merit rating (companies may give discounts for insureds who have good driving records or students who earn good grades).

**Limits of Liability**

Limits are per person, per occurrence for both bodily injury and property damage.

## Eligibility

To be eligible for coverage under a PAP, an auto must be owned or leased by an individual or by a married couple who are residents of the same household. Autos owned jointly by other persons who are not related and residents of the same household may be insured with a special endorsement.

The types of automobiles eligible for coverage under the PAP include a:

- four-wheel, private passenger auto; or
- pickup or van, provided it does not exceed 10,000 pounds gross vehicle weight and is not used to deliver persons or property for a fee.

Further, a private passenger-type auto is deemed to be owned and eligible for coverage if it is leased under a written agreement and the lease is for a continuous period of at least six months.

## Definitions

The following terms appear in the personal auto policy.

The **named insured** is the individual named on the Declarations Page, as well as their spouse if that spouse resides in the same household.

The **insured** is the person or organization described under the person insured section in each of the coverage parts (e.g., Liability to Others, and Uninsured Motorist).

A **family member (relative)** is someone (1) related to the named insured or spouse by blood, marriage, or adoption and (2) who also resides in the named insured's household.

The **covered auto (owned automobile)** the 1998 PAP protects is any:

- automobile listed on the Declarations Page;
- newly acquired auto that the insured acquires during the policy period. (see the section entitled "Additional Conditions for a Newly Acquired" Auto);
- any trailer the insured owns (it does not have to be listed on the Declarations Page to have coverage for liability); or
- temporary substitute auto for any other vehicle described in this definition.

A **temporary substitute automobile** is an auto or a trailer used, with the owner's permission, as a substitute vehicle for the insured's covered auto while the covered vehicle is out of normal service because of breakdown, repair, servicing, loss, or destruction.

**Test Topic Alert!**

A temporary substitute automobile is used with permission as a substitute for an owned auto when the owned auto is out of service because of mechanical breakdown or while undergoing repairs.

A **nonowned automobile** is any auto, pickup, van, or trailer (other than the covered auto) the insured uses occasionally, such as the incidental use of a friend's or neighbor's car. Consequently, that PAP covers insured persons while they operate a nonowned auto.

**Test Topic Alert!**

A nonowned automobile is not used regularly by the insured, such as a rental car or a car borrowed from a friend.

**Occupying** means in the auto, on the auto, or getting in, on, out of, or off the auto.

**Business** includes trade, profession, or occupation.

## Additional Conditions for a Newly Acquired Auto

A **newly acquired auto** includes a private passenger auto, pickup, or van with no other insurance coverage that has a gross vehicle weight of less than 10,0000 lbs. and is not used for the delivery or transportation of goods unless such use is incidental to the business of installing, maintaining, or repairing furnishings or equipment, or is used for farming or ranching.

For any coverage except Coverage for Damage to Your Auto, a newly acquired auto will have the broadest coverage provided for any vehicle shown in the Declarations. Coverage begins on the date the insured becomes the owner. However, if the newly acquired auto is in addition to any vehicle shown on the Declarations, it must be insured within 14 days after the insured become the owner.

If a newly acquired auto replaces a vehicle shown in the Declarations, coverage is provided without the insured having to apply for it.

For Coverage for Damage to Your Auto, Collision Coverage begins on the date the insured becomes the owner. However, the insured must request the auto be insured within 14 days of becoming the owner, if Collision Coverage applies to at least one auto already listed on the Declarations Page. If Collision Coverage does not apply to at least one auto, the insured must ask to insure the newly acquired vehicle within four days of ownership. If the insured complies with the four-day notice, and a loss occurs before this notice, a $500 deductible will apply.

The requirements for Collision Coverage that apply to a newly acquired auto also exist for Other Than Collision Coverage under Coverage for Damage to Your Auto.

# Personal Automobile Policy

## Part A—Liability Coverage

### Insuring Agreement

The **Insuring Agreement** states that the insurer pays, on behalf of the insured, damages for **bodily injury (BI)** or **property damage (PD)** for which any covered person becomes legally responsible because of an auto accident, including any prejudgment interest awarded against the insured. Although the policy says *auto accident*, we have seen that this is interpreted to include an occurrence.

The insurer settles or defends any claim as it deems appropriate, and the insurer pays in addition to the policy's limits of liability. However, the insurer's obligation to pay damages or defense costs ends when the limit of liability has been exhausted.

## Supplementary Payments

As with other liability policies, certain **supplementary payments** are made on behalf of an insured in addition to the limits of liability.

Supplementary payments include:

- expenses the insurer incurs in determining claims, including interest on judgments and other costs taxed against the insured;
- premiums for appeal bonds and bonds to redeem attachment in any suit the insurer defends;
- up to $250 for bail bonds, including related traffic law violations, required because of an accident (the accident must result in bodily injury or property damage covered under this policy);
- interest accruing after a judgment is entered in any suit the insurer defends; and
- up to $200 a day for loss of earnings by the insured only because of attendance at hearings or trials and other reasonable expenses, if incurred at the insurer's request.

## Persons Insured

Part A insures the:

- named insured for the ownership, maintenance, or use of any auto or trailer;
- any person who uses the covered auto with the named insured's permission; and
- any family member who resides in the named insured's household (this includes small children (whether or not licensed) and students who live away from home, but still depend on the insured).

In addition, with respect to the covered auto, the PAP also covers any person or organization that becomes liable because of acts or omissions of a person using a covered auto. That is, insurance extends to anyone who is vicariously liable because of the negligence of a person who uses the auto with the named insured's permission.

✓ ***For Example:*** Mrs. Brown, while using her car in her employment, has an accident for which she is responsible. Her employer might be sued for damages under vicarious liability along with Mrs. Brown. As a result, Mrs. Brown's policy covers both Mrs. Brown and her employer.

✓ ***For Example:*** Eight-year-old Paul gets into his mother's car, starts it, and drives down the street, where he collides with another automobile. Coverage is extended to Paul, even though he is not a licensed driver. He is, however, a relative of the named insured residing in the named insured's household.

With respect to an auto other than a covered auto, an *insured person* includes any other person or organization legally responsible for the acts or omissions of the named insured or a family member as long as that person or organization does not own the auto. Again, this means the PAP provides vicarious liability coverage for persons other than the owner of the auto.

The number of insureds involved in a situation does not increase the limits of coverage. The policy's full limits of liability are available just once per occurrence, but the number of occurrences in a policy period is unlimited.

## Exclusions

The PAP's liability section does not provide coverage under the following circumstances.

### *No Permission*

The PAP provides no coverage for a person using a vehicle without reasonable belief that he is entitled to do so. The exception is a family member who lives in the same household using the insured's covered auto which is owned by the named insured.

### *Livery*

The PAP provides no coverage if the insured is paid a fee for transporting people or property. However, if the insured accepts a small amount of money as part of a car pool (or similar situation), the insured is covered. This is considered to be a sharing of expenses rather than livery. Livery includes a taxi or a limousine service.

### *Intentional Injury or Damage*

Coverage is for accidental injury or damage only.

### *Nuclear Energy Liability Coverage*

If a person is insured under a nuclear energy liability policy, the PAP provides no coverage.

### *Employees*

The PAP does not cover an employee of any insured person who sustains bodily injury in the course of employment. This exclusion does not apply to a domestic employee unless workers' compensation benefits are required or available.

### *Automobile Business*

The PAP does not cover an owned automobile while it is used by another person who is employed or otherwise engaged in the business of selling, repairing, servicing, storing, or parking automobiles.

✓ ***For Example:*** If a service station employee has an accident while road testing a customer's car, the customer's PAP does not provide coverage for any liability. Neither is there coverage if an insured drives a nonowned auto in the auto business. (Automobile businesses must carry their own garage liability policies to cover their liability for the operation of customers' cars.)

✓ ***Take Note:*** Coverage is provided if an insured or a family member is in the auto business and uses the covered auto in the auto business (for instance, to deliver parts.) Thus, if the named insured drives his or her own covered car to deliver parts to a customer, liability coverage applies.

### *Business Pursuits*

Maintenance or use (but not ownership) of any vehicle while employed or otherwise engaged in any business (trade, profession, or occupation) is excluded from coverage. This exclusion does not apply to maintenance or use of private passenger autos, pickups, or vans the insured owns.

✓ ***Take Note:*** The general intent is to eliminate coverage for commercial vehicles used regularly in business. Business use of private passenger-type vehicles, however, is covered. Therefore, coverage extends to an insurance agent driving to visit a client.

### *War*

The PAP does not provide coverage for liability, damage, or destruction resulting from war, insurrection, or riots.

### *Property Owned by or in the Care, Custody, or Control of the Insured*

The PAP provides no liability coverage for damage to or destruction of property that is:

- owned by the insured (so no coverage applies if the insured runs over his own property);
- transported by the insured;
- rented to the insured; or
- in the care, custody, or control of the insured.

However, coverage does extend to damage to a residence or a garage that the insured does not own.

✓ ***For Example:*** An apartment building tenant who inadvertently runs into the garage door is covered under the PAP. However, if an insured damages a residence or garage he or she owns with the covered auto, the PAP does not provide coverage.

### Certain Vehicles

The insurer does not provide liability coverage for ownership, maintenance, or use of the following vehicles:

- a motorized vehicle of fewer than four wheels that is designed for use off public roads;
- a vehicle other than the covered auto owned by or furnished or available for regular use by the named insured, such as a company-furnished car for a salesperson;
- a vehicle other than the covered auto owned by or furnished or available for the regular use of any family member, such as an auto a child owns that is not listed in the Declarations Page (except the insured is covered while using such vehicle); or
- a vehicle inside a facility designed for racing, for the purpose of competing in, practicing, or preparing for a race or contest of speed.

### Out-of-State Coverage

If the auto is used in another state (other than where it is principally garaged) where coverage limits required by a financial responsibility law are higher than the limits of the insured's PAP, the insurer interprets the policy to provide the higher limits required by the law. Similarly, if the insured is driving in another state where a compulsory insurance or similar law requires a nonresident using a vehicle in that state to maintain insurance, the PAP provides at least the required minimum amounts and types of coverage required by law.

### Other Insurance

If two or more policies cover one vehicle, each insurance company pays the portion that its policy limit bears to the total of all applicable limits (pro rata liability). However, for any vehicle the insured does not own (temporary substitute or other than the covered auto), the PAP pays that amount exceeding any other collectible insurance.

✓ ***For Example:*** Assume a loss of $100,000:

| | Company A | Company B | Total |
|---|---|---|---|
| Limits of liability | $100,000 | $200,000 | $300,000 |
| % of total coverage | 33⅓% | 66⅔% | 100% |
| Amount of loss paid | $ 33,333 | $ 66,667 | $100,000 |

## Quick Quiz 10.1

1. The various methods used to compensate automobile accident victims are

   A. ____________________
   B. ____________________
   C. ____________________
   D. ____________________
   E. ____________________
   F. ____________________

2. The four major coverage parts of the Personal Auto Policy are

   A. ____________________
   B. ____________________
   C. ____________________
   D. ____________________

3. Which of the following is a covered auto under the Personal Auto Policy?

   A. Vehicle shown in the declarations
   B. Temporary substitute autos
   C. Owned trailers
   D. All of the above

4. Supplementary payments under the Personal Auto Policy include all of the following EXCEPT

   A. defense costs
   B. cost of appeal bonds
   C. furnishing bail bonds
   D. loss of earnings

## *Answers*

*1.* *tort system, financial responsibility laws, compulsory insurance, unsatisfied judgment funds, uninsured motorists/underinsured motorists laws, no fault laws*

*2.* *Liability, Medical Payments, Uninsured Motorists, Damage to the Insured's Auto*

*3.* ***D.*** *The definition of covered auto includes automobiles listed in the Declarations, owned trailers, newly acquired replacement and additional vehicles under certain circumstances, and temporary substitute autos.*

*4.* ***C.*** *Supplementary payments under the auto policy include the cost of bail bonds in connection with vehicle accidents, but the insurer is not obligated to obtain or furnish those bonds.*

## Part B—Medical Payments Coverage

**Insuring Agreement** The insurer pays reasonable expenses for necessary medical and funeral services incurred within three years from the date of an accident without regard to fault.

Covered persons in Part B include the insured and any family member while they occupy the insured vehicle or any nonowned auto. In addition, the insured and family members are covered if struck as pedestrians by a motor vehicle designed for use on public roads or a trailer of any type. Also covered are other persons while they occupy the insured auto.

**Exclusions** The exclusions for Part A apply to Part B. In addition, Part B provides no coverage for bodily injury sustained while occupying any motorized vehicle with fewer than four wheels.

✓ ***Take Note:*** Also not covered is bodily injury sustained while using the insured vehicle as a residence or premises.

Many states have adopted a no-stacking rule that prevents the insured or injured person from collecting medical payments from more than one policy.

**Other Insurance** Any amounts payable under this coverage are reduced by amounts paid for medical expenses under Part A liability or Part C uninsured motorists. In other words, Part B medical payments coverage is excess to other coverages that might apply under the PAP.

✓ ***Take Note:*** If other auto medical insurance applies, this policy's share is proportionate to all limits of liability (pro rata).

When an insured occupies a non-owned vehicle, this policy is excess over any other auto medical insurance.

## Part C—Uninsured Motorists (UM) and Underinsured Motorists Coverage (UIM)

**Insuring Agreement** Part C of the PAP pays those bodily injury damages that a covered person is legally entitled to recover from the owner or operator of an uninsured motor vehicle. The intent is to provide coverage under this policy for what an injured person could have collected for bodily injury if the other person had been carrying insurance.

**Test Topic Alert!** Uninsured and underinsured motorists coverage pays the insured for losses resulting from bodily injury only when caused by another vehicle that is not insured or is inadequately insured.

## Definitions

The following terms are specifically defined for purposes of UM and UIM coverage.

### *Insured*

This term refers to:

- the named insured and any family member (resident relative) while:
  - driving or riding in an owned auto insured under this policy;
  - driving or riding in a nonowned auto; or
  - traveling as a pedestrian; or
- any other person while occupying an auto insured under the PAP.

## Uninsured Motorists (UM)

An uninsured motorist is a person operating an uninsured motor vehicle.

An uninsured motor vehicle is a motor vehicle or trailer of any type which holds no bodily injury bond or automobile policy at the time of the accident, or, to which a bodily injury liability bond or policy applies at the time of the accident, but its limit for bodily injury liability is less than specified by the financial responsibility law of the state where the auto is principally garaged, or the bonding or insuring company denies coverage or becomes insolvent.

An uninsured motor vehicle is also a hit-and-run vehicle whose operator or owner cannot be identified which hits the insured or any family member, or hits a vehicle that the insured or any family member is occupying.

An uninsured motor vehicle is not one that is owned or available for use by the insured or a family member, owned by a self-insurer or by any government agency, designed for use off public roads, operated on rails, or being used as a residence.

## Exclusions

Generally, the exclusions are similar to those in other parts of the PAP. In addition, several exclusions are unique to Part C:

- No coverage is provided if the injured person settles with the negligent party without the insurer's consent.
- Coverage does not apply to benefit an insurer or a self-insurer under a workers' compensation or disability benefits law.
- Coverage does not apply for punitive or exemplary damages.

## Limits of Insurance

Some states require that if a person carries liability insurance, he must carry uninsured motorists coverage to some specified minimum limits—for instance, up to the limits of liability in Part A. To eliminate Uninsured Motorists coverage, the insured must sign a declination of coverage. No one will be entitled to payment for the same elements under this coverage and Part A, Part B, or the Underinsured Motorists Coverage provided in this policy.

**Arbitration**

If the insured and insurance company, under Uninsured Motorists coverage, do not agree on (1) whether the covered person is legally entitled to recover damages or (2) the amount of damages, either party may make a written demand for arbitration. Disputes concerning coverage, however, may not be arbitrated.

**Other Insurance**

If other insurance applies, the insurer under this policy is liable on a pro rata basis. Any insurance provided on an auto the insured does not own will be excess coverage over any other applicable insurance.

**Underinsured Motorists**

The coverage under underinsured motorists (UIM) is similar to but slightly different from uninsured motorists coverage. UIM coverage may be required by state statutes as part of the uninsured motorists coverage.

The limits under underinsured motorists coverage can be up to those of uninsured motorists coverage (if higher than the minimum required). Thus, if an insured is injured because of another driver's negligence, he can collect from the negligent party's insurer to the limits of liability the negligent driver has on his policy, then from his own insurer to the limits of liability under this endorsement.

✓ ***For Example:*** Sam's underinsured motorists limit is $100,000/$300,000, and Sally's liability limit is $25,000/$50,000. They are involved in an accident where Sally is at fault. Sam sues Sally in a court of law and is awarded $150,000 in damages. The UIM takes the maximum amount of insurance available less what is recoverable to obtain the amount the UIM will pay:

| | |
|---|---|
| Sam's UIM | $100,000 |
| Sally's Liability | $ 25,000 |
| Sam's UIM pays | $ 75,000 |

If Sally's liability limit were $50,000, Sam's policy would pay only an additional $50,000 to bring the total to $100,000. The at-fault driver would pay any award exceeding the total amount of insurance.

**Uninsured Motorists Property Damage (UMPD)**

Some states also require insurers to offer coverage for **uninsured motorists property damage (UMPD)**. UMPD functions in one of two ways. If a vehicle is insured for collision losses, UMPD functions as a waiver of the collision deductible. If a vehicle is not insured for collision, UMPD pays up to $3,500 of the actual cash value of the damage to the insured vehicle.

**Personal Injury Protection (PIP)**

**Personal Injury Protection (PIP)** is used in states that have adopted a form of no-fault auto insurance. It provides first-party protection by covering the insured for bodily injury from any occurrence without regard to fault. This means that a person injured in an auto accident, whether as a driver, passenger, or pedestrian, receives protection under his own auto policy, or that policy in effect on the vehicle he occupied.

A person involved in an accident looks to the insured motor vehicle for reimbursement for medical expenses, lost wages, and loss of service. Pain and suffering are not covered. Many states have a threshold whereby if a person is injured seriously, he can sue the negligent driver for damages.

✓ ***Take Note:*** Check your state law study manual to note any state laws concerning no fault.

**Exceptions**

Two major exceptions involve out-of-state use of an insured vehicle and car pooling (or sharing). When an insured vehicle is used in a state other than the state in which it is principally garaged, an insured under PIP usually is limited to the named insured, a relative who resides in the named insured's household and any permissive user. Thus, if a friend is a passenger in the vehicle, he or she must look to another source for recovery.

When members of a car pool reimburse the owner for gas, parking, and maintenance, each injured person would seek to have his own insurance policy pay any medical bills. The involved vehicle's policy then becomes secondary, or excess.

## Part D—Coverage for Damage to Your Auto

**Insuring Agreement**

Part D provides two major types of coverage—**Other than Collision (Comprehensive) Coverage and Collision Coverage.** If these coverages are shown on the Declarations Page, the insurer pays for direct accidental loss to the covered auto and any nonowned auto and its equipment minus any deductible shown in the declarations.

**Test Topic Alert!**

Part D on a Personal Auto Policy covers damage to the insured auto and provides comprehensive coverage and collision coverage. This is the only part of the PAP in which the insured may see a deductible.

For nonowned autos, the insurer provides the broadest coverage applicable to any covered auto shown on the Declarations Page. Under Part D, a nonowned auto includes a private passenger auto not owned or available for regular use by the insured or a family member. A nonowned auto does not include a temporary substitute when the regularly insured auto is unavailable, because it is insured as a covered auto. Autos the insured does not own (temporary substitute and nonowned autos) are covered on an excess basis.

**Other Than Collision (Comprehensive)**

Other Than Collision Coverage protects against almost all accidental damage, with the exception of coverage provided under collision.

Coverage includes:

- fire;
- theft;
- explosion;
- earthquake;
- windstorm;
- missiles;
- falling objects;
- hail, water;
- flood;
- vandalism and malicious mischief;
- riot and civil commotion;
- glass breakage; and
- contact with birds or animals.

Wear and tear, mechanical breakdown and road damage to tires are not covered.

✓ ***Take Note:*** While glass breakage is addressed under comprehensive coverage, if a collision causes the breakage, the insured may elect to have it included in the collision coverage to avoid paying two deductibles.

**Transportation Expenses**

The insurer will pay, up to a maximum of $600, temporary **transportation expenses** incurred by the insured in a loss to a covered auto. These expenses will be paid up to $20 a day. If the loss is caused by other than collision, transportation expense applies only if Other Than Collision Coverage is provided for that auto. If the loss is caused by collision, transportation expense applies only if Collision Coverage is provided for that auto.

The same expenses and limits will apply if the insured becomes legally responsible for loss to a non-owned auto, if the loss is caused by collision or other than collision, and the covered auto has the required coverage.

If the loss is due to the total theft of the insured's covered auto or non-covered auto, expenses are paid beginning 48 hours after the theft and ending when the auto is returned to use or is paid for. Other than theft, expenses are paid when the auto is withdrawn from use for more than 24 hours, and payment is limited to a reasonable time to repair or replace the auto.

**Collision**

Collision Coverage protects against damage done to the covered or non-owned auto by (1) impact with another vehicle, (2) impact with an object, or (3) upset (rolling the car over). Damage caused by hitting birds or animals is covered under comprehensive.

**Deductibles/ Loss of Use**

Both comprehensive and collision coverage generally have a deductible of $100, $250, or more.

No loss of use coverage is provided with comprehensive or collision coverage. In other words, the policy contains no provision for a rental car or other transportation expenses unless the insured has comprehensive coverage and the car is stolen (in which case, limited coverage for transportation expenses is allowed, as previously noted). The insured might be able to recover for auto rental expenses from a negligent third party if the accident was that person's fault.

✓ ***Take Note:*** Coverage for rental vehicles is available by endorsement with an additional premium.

### Towing and Labor

Coverage for towing and labor is available by endorsement with an additional premium. When a car is disabled, such coverage pays for labor at the site of the disablement (such as jump starts and tire changes) and for towing charges.

### Limits of Liability

Under Part D of the PAP, recovery is on an actual cash value basis. The company pays the lesser of the:

- actual cash value (ACV) of the damaged or stolen property (based on either the ACV formula already discussed or by fair market value); or
- amount necessary to repair or replace the property with like kind and quality.

However, the insurer limits payment for a non-owned trailer to $500, and for equipment designed solely for the reproduction of sound installed in a location other than what is used by the auto manufacturer, to $1,000.

The insurer may pay for the loss in money or may repair or replace any damaged property. If a stolen vehicle is returned, the insurer pays for damage resulting from the theft.

### Exclusions

Some of the Part D exclusions are the same as were discussed for Part A. These include:

- war;
- automobile business;
- nuclear energy liability coverage;
- other insurance; and
- use without permission.

In addition, Part D excludes damages from wear and tear, freezing, mechanical breakdown, electrical breakdown, or road damage to tires unless these damages result from total theft of the auto.

Also excluded from coverage is special equipment, including loss to:

- equipment designed for reproducing sound, including radios and stereos, tape decks, and compact disc players, unless such equipment is permanently installed where the auto manufacturer intended and are designed to be operated from the auto's electrical system;
- equipment that receives or transmits audio, visual or data signals, including citizens band radios, telephones, two-way mobile radios, scanning monitor receivers, television monitor receivers, video cassette recorders, audio cassette recorders, or personal computers (this exclusion does not apply to any equipment that is necessary for the operation of the auto or the autos's operating systems);
- any custom furnishings or equipment in a pickup or van; and
- radar detection equipment.

✓ ***Take Note:*** Trailers are not covered automatically for Part D physical damage, as they are for Part A liability. If the insured desires physical damage coverage for a trailer, it must be added specifically as an endorsement to the policy.

**Other Insurance and Stacking** If the insured carries more than one policy on the covered auto, each policy pays its proportionate share of the loss (pro rata distribution). Coverage on autos the insured does not own is excess over any other insurance. Many states have **anti-stacking rules** that allow the insured to collect no more than the actual cash value of the damage to the auto.

This insurance does not benefit directly or indirectly any carrier or other bailee for hire. Thus, if a parking lot attendant damages an auto, the PAP pays the insured for damages, but looks to the parking lot operator for recovery.

**Test Topic Alert!** The policy covering the auto is always the primary payor, and the policy covering the driver is secondary.

## Part E—Duties after Accident or Loss

The insurer must be notified of how, when, and where an accident or a loss happens, including names and addresses of witnesses and any injured persons.

A person seeking recovery for damages must:

- cooperate with the insurer;
- submit, as often as reasonably required, to physical examinations and to examination under oath;
- authorize the insurer to obtain medical reports and other pertinent records; and

- submit a proof of loss when the insurer requires it;
- promptly send copies of any notices or legal papers in connection with the loss.

Under Uninsured Motorists Coverage, the insured must notify police promptly if a hit-and-run driver is involved.

Under Damage to Your Auto Coverage, the insured must:

- protect the auto and its equipment from further loss (the insurer pays reasonable expenses to do this);
- notify police promptly if the vehicle is stolen; and
- permit the insurer to inspect and appraise the damaged property before its repair or disposal.

## Part F—General Provisions

### Policy Period and Territory

PAP coverage applies only to losses, accidents, or occurrences that take place during the policy period and within the United States, its territories and possessions, Puerto Rico, or Canada, or while being transported between ports in any of those places.

✓ ***Take Note:*** Usually, the PAP provides no coverage for vehicles operated in Mexico. Coverage must be purchased from Mexican insurers. (However, some insurers provide coverage for vehicles from the US operating within a certain distance inside the Mexican border, such as 100 miles.) Check individual state law concerning this issue. Many states require some limited insurance for physical damage in Mexico.

### Two or More Auto Policies (Anti-Stacking Clauses)

If two policies issued to the insured apply to the same accident, the maximum limit of liability under all policies will not exceed the highest limit under any one policy. This policy provision is intended to prevent the stacking of more than one policy.

✓ ***For Example:*** If an insured purchased two separate auto policies from the insurer and somehow both applied to a single accident, this provision would limit recovery to the highest limit available under any one policy.

This is most often an issue involving uninsured motorists claims. Antistacking clauses have come under much judicial scrutiny in recent years, and their ultimate fate likely will be decided by the courts.

### Action Against the Company

An insured agrees not to sue the insurance company to provide coverage until:

- he has complied fully with all terms of the policy; and
- the obligation to pay has been determined by judgment after trial or the insurer agrees in writing that the insured has an obligation to pay.

**Bankruptcy** The insured's bankruptcy or insolvency does not relieve the insurance company of its obligation.

**Fraud** The PAP provides no coverage for an insured who has made fraudulent statements or engaged in fraudulent conduct.

**Right to Recover Payment (Subrogation)** The insurer has **subrogation rights** under all coverages of the PAP except under Coverage D against a person using a covered auto with a reasonable belief that he is entitled to do so. The insured must reimburse or hold in trust for the insurer any recovered damages the insured collects after the insurer has made payment.

**Changes** A written endorsement by the insurer that forms part of the policy is the only way to change the policy. Premiums are computed from the effective date of the change.

If the insurer changes its PAP form generally to provide more coverage, without additional premium, or if a statute requires a change in coverage, any PAP policy already issued automatically provides the additional coverage. (This is known as the **liberalization clause**.)

**Transfer of the Insured's Interest in the PAP (Assignment)** The PAP may not be assigned without the insurer's consent. However, if a named insured dies, coverage will be provided for the surviving spouse if a resident of the same household at the time of death, or the legal representative of the deceased person in order to maintain or use a covered auto. This coverage is only provided until the end of the policy period.

**Termination** The following conditions apply to the termination of a policy by the insured or the insurer.

### *Cancellation During the Policy Period*

During the policy period, the insured can cancel the policy by returning it or giving advance written notice. If the insurer cancels the policy, it must provide 10 days written notice when the cancellation is made:

- for nonpayment of premium; or
- during the first 60 days of a new policy for almost any underwriting reason.

The insurer must give 20 days written notice when (1) the policy has been in effect for 60 days or (2) it is a renewal or continuation policy and cancellation occurs because:

- the driver's license of the insured, someone who lives with the insured, or someone who normally drives the insured's auto is revoked or suspended during the policy period or since the last anniversary of the effective date; or

- the policy was obtained through material misrepresentation.

### *Nonrenewal*

If the insurer decides not to renew the insured's policy, it notifies the insured at least 20 days before the end of the policy period.

✓ ***Take Note:*** Many states have specific laws concerning cancellations, nonrenewals, increases in premium and reduction in coverage. Check your state *Guide to Property and Casualty Insurance Law* for further information.

## Automatic Termination

The insured renews the policy by paying the premium. Therefore if the insured does not pay the premium, the policy is automatically terminated.

If the policyowner obtains other insurance on an auto covered under this policy, any similar insurance this policy provides terminates as to that auto on the effective date of the other insurance.

## Other Termination Provisions

If a state has specific laws requiring a longer notice period, special forms or procedures, or modified reasons for termination, the PAP provisions are adjusted automatically to meet those requirements.

✓ ***Take Note:*** Refunds are computed according to the insurer's terms.

## Quick Quiz 10.2

1. Medical payments coverage applies to each of the following EXCEPT the

   A. vehicle's driver
   B. insured's employees
   C. vehicle's occupants
   D. insured and family members while pedestrians struck by an auto

2. Uninsured motorists coverage may include all of the following EXCEPT

   A. uninsured motorists property damage (UMPD)
   B. underinsured motorists (UM) coverage
   C. personal injury protection (PIP)
   D. nonowned auto coverage

3. Causes of loss included in other than collision coverage include

   A. earthquake
   B. flood
   C. fire
   D. all of the above

4. The exclusions under Part D—Damage to Your Auto include

   A. mechanical breakdown
   B. towing and labor
   C. glass breakage
   D. upset or overturn of the vehicle

***Answers***

1. ***B.*** *Employees of the insured have coverage by workers compensation laws as their sole remedy for work-related injuries.*
2. ***C.*** *UM coverage includes UMPD by endorsement, underinsured motorists coverage by statute, and coverage while the insured and family members occupy non-owned autos. PIP is the benefit provided in no-fault states. It is first-party coverage and would apply to injuries suffered by the insured and family members without regard to fault.*
3. ***D.*** *The other than collision coverage of the PAP is very broad, excluding only wear and tear, mechanical breakdown, and road damage to tires.*
4. ***A.*** *The other than collision coverage of the PAP is very broad, excluding only wear and tear, mechanical breakdown, and road damage to tires.*

# Endorsements to the Personal Auto Policy

**Miscellaneous-Type Vehicle Endorsement**

This endorsement allows the PAP to cover motorcycles, motorhomes, all-terrain vehicles (ATVs), dune buggies, and other types of vehicles that otherwise are excluded by the policy. This endorsement contains a passenger hazard exclusion that the underwriter may require in situations involving motorcycles and off-road vehicles.

**Named Nonowner Coverage**

In some cases, a person does not have an owned vehicle, but still drives automobiles.

✓ ***For Example:*** Someone residing in an urban area using public transportation or someone furnished with a company vehicle. In this case, the person has no covered auto to insure, but still needs coverage when he or she drives the borrowed or rented autos.

The named nonowner endorsement provides liability, medical payments, and uninsured motorists coverage in these situations.

**Extended Nonowned Coverage for Named Individuals**

This endorsement provides coverage by effectively eliminating several PAP exclusions or limitations. First, it allows coverage for a nonowned vehicle furnished or available for the insured's regular use. This may be the company-furnished car. Second, the endorsement provides excess auto liability for business use of a commercial-type vehicle that the named insured does not own, such as one an employer owns. Third, the endorsement could be used to provide excess liability coverage for public or livery use of a nonowned auto, such as a taxicab. Finally, this endorsement also covers suits by co-workers arising out of automobile accidents in the course of employment.

### Snowmobile Endorsement

A homeowners policy provides only limited liability coverage for snowmobiles. Owned snowmobiles are covered while used on an insured location, but not off premises. Use of nonowned snowmobiles is covered completely. Therefore, coverage on owned snowmobiles probably is arranged best by attaching the snowmobile endorsement to the PAP.

✓ ***Take Note:*** This endorsement applies to the named insured's and family members' use of any snowmobile and may include liability, medical payments, uninsured motorists, collision and other than collision coverages.

### Towing and Labor Costs

When added to the PAP, this endorsement provides a selected amount of insurance ($25, $50, or $75) for the cost of towing or roadside service. Coverage also applies to the insured's use of a nonowned automobile.

### Electronic Equipment and Tapes

The PAP excludes various types of electronic equipment, tapes, recordings, and other media. This endorsement provides coverage at ACV for the equipment and up to $200 for the media. However, several restrictions on the coverage apply and the insured should weigh the cost of the endorsement against the amount of loss exposure.

### Coverage for Damage to Your Auto—Maximum Limit of Liability (Stated Amount)

Some people own vehicles for which determining the value at the time of a loss might be difficult. This endorsement allows the insured and insurer to establish the value at the beginning of the policy period. The stated amount is inserted in the endorsement, along with a description of the vehicle.

✓ ***Take Note:*** Many people think the stated amount is the minimum amount the insurer pays in the event of a loss. Note the actual name of the endorsement. The stated amount endorsement calls for payment in the event of a loss for the lesser of (1) the amount stated in the endorsement, (2) the property's actual cash value, or (3) the amount necessary to repair or replace the property with like kind and quality.

# Unit Test Ten

1. An insured, while operating his automobile, negligently struck a light pole, damaging the pole and interrupting electrical power to a grocery store, which caused perishable food to spoil. The insured's property damage liability coverage pays for each of the following losses EXCEPT the damage to the
   A. store
   B. light pole
   C. spoiled food
   D. automobile

2. Mr. Adams has an automobile policy with bodily injury limits of $15,000/$30,000, property damage limits of $10,000, and a $100 deductible for collision. He negligently runs into Ms. Smith's car. Ms. Smith is awarded $30,000 for her injuries and $6,000 for the damage to her car. Mr. Adams's car is damaged to the extent of $750. The total payment made under Mr. Adam's policy is
   A. $21,650
   B. $21,750
   C. $36,650
   D. $36,750

3. Mr. Adams has an auto liability policy with $25,000/$50,000/$10,000 limits. An accident covered by the policy occurs in which Mr. Bates and Mr. Charles are injured. They are awarded damages of $30,000 and $15,000, respectively. How much does Mr. Adams's insurance pay?
   A. $25,000
   B. $40,000
   C. $45,000
   D. $50,000

4. Mr. Adams carries a personal auto policy with BI limits of $15,000/$30,000. His wife is driving his insured vehicle and negligently injures Mr. Bates. Mr. Bates is awarded $27,000 from Mrs. Adams as driver and $3,000 from Mr. Adams as owner. The company incurred $4,000 in expenses handling the case for Mr. and Mrs. Adams. What total payment does Mr. Adams's policy make?
   A. $15,000
   B. $19,000
   C. $30,000
   D. $34,000

5. Which of the following statements regarding liability coverage under the PAP is NOT true?
   A. An automobile loaned to the insured while hers is being repaired is covered automatically.
   B. A newly acquired automobile that replaces an owned automobile is covered automatically.
   C. A newly acquired additional auto is covered for 30 days.
   D. A rented trailer the insured uses on a regular basis is covered automatically.

6. Mr. Brown has a PAP with BI limits of $25,000/$50,000 and a PD limit of $10,000. While driving his car, Mr. Brown collides with a truck, injuring Mr. Jones and Mrs. Smith, who are riding in the truck. The accident also kills a horse, which belongs to Mr. Jones and is being carried in the truck. A court awards damages of $40,000 to Mr. Jones; $10,000 to Mrs. Smith; $1,000 to Mr. Jones for the loss of his horse; and $500 for damage to Mr. Jones's truck. How much does Mr. Brown's policy pay?

   A. $25,000 to Mr. Jones for injuries; $10,000 to Mrs. Smith for injuries; $1,500 to Mr. Jones for damage to his truck and death of his horse; plus attorney fees and court costs
   B. $40,000 to Mr. Jones for injuries; $10,000 to Mrs. Smith for injuries; $1,500 to Mr. Jones for loss of his horse and damage to his truck
   C. $50,000 to Mr. Jones and Mrs. Smith for injuries; $1,000 to Mr. Jones for the horse; and $500 to Mr. Jones for damage to his truck
   D. $25,000 to Mr. Jones for his injuries; $10,000 to Mrs. Smith for her injuries; nothing for the horse; and $500 to Mr. Jones for damage to his truck

7. When an insured is driving a nonowned automobile on which there is other valid insurance, coverage under the insured's policy is what type of insurance?

   A. Invalid
   B. Excess
   C. Primary
   D. Contributory

8. Which of the following is NOT an exclusion common to a personal automobile policy?

   A. Bodily injury caused accidentally by the named insured
   B. Bodily injury caused by owned automobiles used as public or livery conveyance
   C. Bodily injury to an employee of the insured
   D. Bodily injury caused by a person using the vehicle without a reasonable belief that he or she is entitled to do so

9. Which of the following judgments would be paid under the bodily injury coverage for a PAP?

   A. Claim against the insured, the owner of a small manufacturing plant, by an employee injured in a car the insured drove
   B. Claim by a woman pedestrian injured by the insured while driving to work
   C. Claim by a driver of the insured's vehicle for injuries when using the vehicle without permission
   D. Claim by another driver injured while the insured used the vehicle as an airport taxi

10. The definition of a family member in the personal auto policy includes all of the following EXCEPT a

   A. person related to the insured by marriage
   B. spouse living in the insured's household
   C. person related to the insured by adoption
   D. resident relative

11. The supplementary payments section of the PAP covers all of the following EXCEPT
    A. up to $200 per day for loss of earnings
    B. all reasonable expenses the insurer incurs in defending a suit against the insured
    C. premiums on appeal, release of attachment, and bail bonds
    D. interest that accrues before the settlement of a suit under the policy

12. Which one of the following statements concerning the PAP's liability insuring agreement is NOT true?
    A. The insurer's obligation to defend suits ends when the limit of liability is exhausted.
    B. Bodily injury or property damage must arise out of the automobile's ownership, maintenance, or use.
    C. The insurer must defend any suit alleging bodily injury or property damage except those that are groundless, false, or fraudulent.
    D. The insurer pays post-judgment interest awarded against the insured.

13. Liability arising from which of the following is NOT excluded under the PAP?
    A. Use of a vehicle without permission
    B. Property the insured owns
    C. Ownership of an automobile
    D. Use of the vehicle to transport people for a fee

14. A PAP insurer pays up to the policy limits for bodily injury and property damage under which of the following circumstances?
    A. A third party suffers bodily injury and damage to his vehicle when involved in an accident with the insured
    B. The insured incurs sums for which she is legally liable as a result of an auto accident
    C. The insured is involved in an accident with an uninsured motor vehicle
    D. A third party is injured in an accident that is not the insured's fault

15. All of the following are eligible for a personal auto policy EXCEPT
    A. a husband and wife living together
    B. two brothers living next door to each other and jointly owning an automobile
    C. a single, 19-year-old man living in an apartment
    D. a divorced woman living with her mother

16. A supermarket is out of business for 2 days after an automobile hit the pole that carried electricity to it, causing it to fall on the building. Which of the following is covered under the driver's auto policy?
    A. Revenue the supermarket's owner lost
    B. Spoilage of refrigerated products in the market
    C. Damage to the supermarket building
    D. Damage to the vehicle

17. Which of the following is NOT an insured driver under the personal auto policy?
    A. Named insured's child, who resides in another town and uses the vehicle without permission
    B. Named insured's child, who is temporarily away at college
    C. Named insured's 10-year-old child while backing the car out of the driveway without permission
    D. Named insured's uncle, who resides in the household

18. Which of the following is the purpose of unsatisfied judgment funds?
    A. To allow an injured claimant to seek public funds for injuries and avoid court action
    B. To allow an injured claimant to seek reimbursement from his own insurer when the other party has inadequate insurance
    C. To prevent an injured person from rejecting an offer to settle within the other party's limits of liability
    D. To allow an injured claimant access to funds when he cannot recover the full amount of his damages from the negligent party

19. The threshold in no fault insurance may be stated as a
    A. specific dollar amount
    B. percentage of the damages
    C. percentage of the limits of liability
    D. single limit

20. In calculating premiums for personal automobile insurance, an insurance company may use which of the following factors?
    A. Vehicle operator's driving experience
    B. Auto usage
    C. Insured's territory or garaging address
    D. All of the above

# Unit Test Ten Answers & Rationale

1. **D.** Property damage liability insurance covers direct damage as well as loss of use of property that is caused by the insured's negligence. Damage to property the insured owns is not covered.

2. **A.** The amount of coverage for Ms. Smith's injuries is limited to $15,000. The damage to Ms. Smith's car ($6,000) is covered in full. The damage to Mr. Adams's vehicle is covered minus the $100 deductible. Thus, the total payment is $21,650.

3. **B.** Mr. Bates is entitled to the $25,000-per-person policy limit. Mr. Charles is paid in full, $15,000, for a total payment under the policy of $40,000.

4. **B.** The policy limits are the maximum amounts payable, regardless of the number of insureds under the policy. Therefore, Mr. and Mrs. Adams have only $15,000 in coverage for this accident. The company pays the $4,000 in addition to the damages, for a total payment of $19,000.

5. **D.** Coverage under the PAP includes trailers the insured owns, but not trailers the insured uses but does not own.

6. **A.** The horse is Mr. Jones's property and therefore covered under Mr. Brown's PAP policy.

7. **B.** The PAP states that the policy is primary as to any owned autos and excess when the insured uses a nonowned auto.

8. **A.** The PAP contains no exclusion for accidental bodily injury; that is one of the coverage's prime purposes.

9. **B.** Injuries to employees are specifically excluded. Neither is coverage provided for use of a covered auto as a public or livery conveyance or use of a vehicle without permission (relatives in the insured's household excepted.)

10. **B.** A spouse who is a resident of the household is included in the definition of a named insured, not of a family member.

11. **D.** Prejudgment interest is included in damages; thus, it is not part of supplementary payments.

12. **C.** The PAP's insuring agreement provides a defense for suits that are groundless, false, or fraudulent.

13. **C.** Insuring ownership of an automobile is the personal auto policy's primary purpose.

14. **B.** To trigger coverage under the PAP, the insured must be legally liable. Under uninsured motorists coverage, the other party must be legally liable before the insured can collect from his or her own insurer.

15. **B.** Eligibility for a PAP is limited to an individual or a married couple. Others who own automobiles jointly must be named specifically as insureds for coverage to apply.

16. **D.** The supermarket's losses are indirect

17. **A.** Although actual permission is not required under the PAP (only a reasonable belief that one is entitled to use the auto), the person in question is not an insured because he or she is not a resistant relative.

18. **D.** Unsatisfied judgment funds are a method to compensate automobile accident victims who cannot recover the full amount of their damages from the responsible parties.

19. **A.** Thresholds in no fault insurance are expressed in terms of dollar amounts or in words, such as *serious injury.*

20. **D.** In rating automobile insurance, an insurer may consider territory; vehicle use; the driver's age, sex, marital status, and driving record; coverage limits; and merit rating.

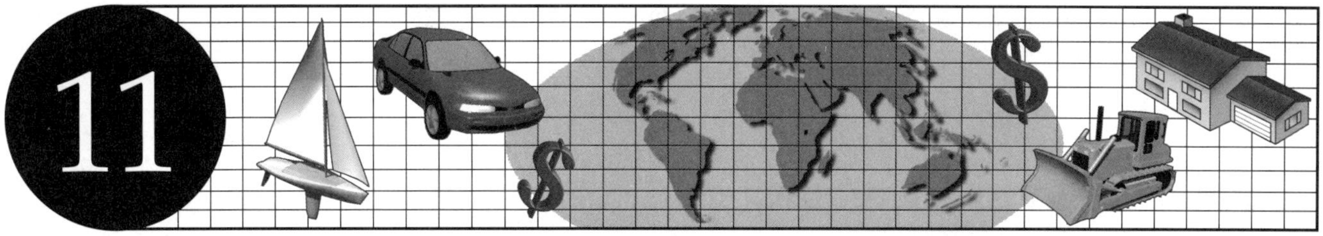


# Commercial Automobile and Garage Liability Insurance

## INTRODUCTION

Businesses are subject to many of the same automobile exposures as individuals. Use of owned vehicles, as well as those rented or borrowed, subject a business to liability arising out of that use. A business may become liable for an employee's use of automobiles the employer owns or for use of employee-owned vehicles in the employer's business. A firm may want to insure the vehicles for loss due to collision, theft, or other perils. In many cases, the coverage a commercial policy provides is the same or very similar to that of the personal auto policy.

The business auto policy (BAP), developed in 1978 by the Insurance Services Office (ISO), offers a flexible way to arrange the various policy coverages for a business entity. BAP provisions are examined in this unit, followed by a discussion of another commercial automobile policy, the garage policy.

## UNIT OBJECTIVES

When you have completed this unit, you should be able to:

- identify the various commercial automobile coverage forms;
- understand how covered auto symbols define coverage under the BAP;
- determine who is insured under the BAP's liability section;
- describe the coverages and exclusions applicable to the BAP's liability section;
- describe the coverages and exclusions applicable to the BAP's physical damage section;
- explain the various endorsements available under the BAP;
- describe the coverage provided under the garage policy; and
- describe how the coverage provided under the garage policy differs from that under the business auto policy.

# Commercial Auto Coverages

Automobiles owned or operated by individuals, unincorporated associations, joint ventures, governmental entities, partnerships, or corporations, or autos that are not eligible for personal automobile policies because of auto type, can be insured under a commercial package policy by using a business auto coverage form. The coverages available under the business auto policy (BAP) are very similar to those presented under the personal auto policy. Because of this similarity, the description of coverages presented here will be brief. Coverages that are part of the BAP include only liability and physical damage coverage. Medical payments coverage, uninsured motorists coverage, underinsured motorists coverage, or personal injury protection must be added to the basic policy by endorsement.

Business auto coverage can be included as part of a **commercial package policy (CPP)** or written as a monoline policy.

## Commercial Auto Coverage Forms

When issued as part of a CPP, common policy declarations and common policy conditions are combined with the commercial auto coverage forms, consisting of:

- one or more commercial auto declarations forms;
- one or more commercial auto coverage forms; and
- any endorsements that apply.

Various coverage forms have been developed for different types of commercial automobile exposures. A policy may include one or more of the following:

- Business auto coverage form
- Business auto physical damage form
- Garage coverage form
- Truckers coverage form

## The Business Auto Policy (BAP) (CA 00 01 10)

A **business auto policy (BAP)** may be used to insure both individually owned vehicles and those registered to the business. This is a common practice because business owners prefer to insure all their vehicles under a single policy for convenience. Premium considerations often apply as well because insuring private passenger automobiles under a business policy may be less expensive than purchasing a personal auto policy for that purpose.

✓ ***Take Note:*** Despite its name, a business auto policy can be used to insure personal vehicles in addition to business vehicles.

The business auto policy is divided into five major sections:

- Section I—Covered autos
- Section II—Liability coverage
- Section III—Physical damage coverage
- Section IV—Business auto conditions
- Section V—Definitions

Two additional coverages, medical payments and uninsured motorists, must be added by endorsement.

✓ ***Take Note:*** Unlike the personal auto policy, the business auto policy includes only liability and physical damage coverage sections. Medical payments and uninsured motorists coverages must be added to the policy by endorsement. This is because some business clients do not wish to provide these coverages on vehicles used in business and operated only by employees.

## Section I—Covered Autos

The BAP uses a system of nine covered auto symbols to denote the vehicles to which each of the policy's coverages applies:

- Symbol 1—Any auto
- Symbol 2—Owned autos only
- Symbol 3—Owned private passenger autos
- Symbol 4—Owned autos other than private passenger autos
- Symbol 5—Owned autos subject to no fault benefits
- Symbol 6—Owned autos subject to compulsory uninsured motorists law
- Symbol 7—Specifically described autos only
- Symbol 8—Hired autos (leased, hired, rented, or borrowed)
- Symbol 9—Nonowned autos (owned by employees or partners of the insured)

Coverage can be customized to meet an insured's needs by selecting the appropriate symbols. Symbol 1 affords the broadest coverage, because it applies literally to any auto, whether owned, nonowned, or hired. However, it can only be used for liability coverage. Symbol 7 provides the most restrictive coverage because it applies only to autos listed in the policy and no others. Symbols 3 and 4 differentiate between private passenger autos and commercial vehicles. Symbols 5 and 6 are used only in states that have no fault laws or laws that require inclusion of uninsured motorists coverage. Symbol 8 applies to autos the insured leases, hires, rents, or borrows, but not to autos the insured's employees own. Symbol 9 includes all autos the insured does not own, lease, hire, or borrow used in connection with the business, including those vehicles owned by employees or members of their households.

Covered auto symbols also determine how coverage applies to vehicles the insured acquires after the policy effective date. Newly acquired autos are covered automatically until the end of the policy period if Symbol 1, 2, 3, 4, 5, or 6 is used. If Symbol 7 is used, a newly acquired auto is covered for 30 days only if it replaces an auto already scheduled on the policy or if all owned vehicles are insured for that coverage.

For liability coverage, *covered autos* also include small trailers the insured owns, nonowned trailers of any size and mobile equipment that is being transported by a covered auto. An auto serving as a temporary substitute for a covered auto that is being repaired or serviced or that has been lost or destroyed also is covered.

## Quick Quiz 11.1

Indicate whether the following statements are True or False.

_____ 1. Symbol 1 may be used only for liability coverage under the BAP.

_____ 2. Symbols 8 and 9 must be included whenever Symbol 1 is used.

_____ 3. When Symbol 7 is used in the BAP, automatic coverage applies to newly acquired vehicles within the first 30 days of ownership only if the company already insures all owned vehicles for that coverage and the new vehicle replaces one of those.

_____ 4. Symbol 5 is used whenever a business needs to provide uninsured motorists coverage for a vehicle.

_____ 5. Symbol 2 provides the broadest coverage for owned vehicles under the BAP.

_____ 6. Symbol 9 covers vehicles owned by the insured's employees.

_____ 7. Symbol 8 covers all nonowned autos except employee vehicles.

_____ 8. Symbols 8 and 9 may not be used for physical damage coverage under the BAP.

### Answers

1. ***True***. *The only coverage that Symbol 1 may be used for is liability.*
2. ***False***. *Symbols 8 and 9 are unnecessary when using Symbol 1, since Symbol 1 applies to any auto.*
3. ***True***. *When Symbol 7 is used, automatic coverage for newly acquired vehicles is limited to 30 days and only applies if the company insures all vehicles for that coverage and the new vehicle replaces one covered by the policy.*

4. ***False***. *Symbol 5 applies to vehicles requiring no fault coverage.*
5. ***True***. *Symbol 2 applies to any owned auto of the insured.*
6. ***True***. *Symbol 9 provides coverage for employee's vehicles (non-owned auto coverage).*
7. ***True***. *Symbol 8 is used to provide coverage for hired, borrowed, rented, or leased automobiles belonging to anyone other than the insured's employees.*
8. ***False***. *Symbol 8 and Symbol 9 may be used for any coverage under the BAP.*

## Section II—Liability Coverage

Section II coverage provides for:

- bodily injury or property damage resulting from ownership, maintenance, or use of a covered auto; and
- expenses to defend, investigate, and settle claims.

The insurer only pays if:

- it has a legal obligation to pay;
- the obligation arises from bodily injury or property damage;
- an accident as defined in the policy has occurred; and
- a covered auto was involved.

Limits of liability may be combined for bodily injury and property damage, or a policy could be issued with **split limits**. The minimum amount of coverage is the financial responsibility limit of the state in which the vehicle is principally garaged.

### *Who Is an Insured?*

Insureds include the following:

- Named insured for any covered auto
- Anyone else while using, with the insured's permission, a covered auto the insured owns, hires, or borrows
- Anyone else who otherwise is not excluded and who is liable for the conduct of an insured, but only to the extent of that liability

### *Coverage Extensions*

In addition to the limit of insurance, the following supplementary payments are provided:

- all expenses the insurer incurs;
- up to $2,000 for bail bonds;

- cost of bonds to release attachment in any suit the insurer defends;
- costs taxed against the insured in any suit the insurer defends; and
- all interest that accrues after entry of the judgment in any suit the insurer defends.

When the covered auto is used in a state other than the one in which it is principally garaged, the following out-of-state coverage extensions apply.

- Increased limits of coverage to meet the limits specified by a compulsory or financial responsibility law of the state where the auto is being used
- Minimum amounts and types of other coverages, such as no fault, required by the state where the auto is being used.

### *Exclusions*

Exclusions for liability coverage include damages from:

- expected or intended injury;
- contractual liability;
- workers' compensation;
- employee indemnification and employers' liability;
- fellow employee;
- care, custody, or control;
- handling of property before the property is moved from the place where it was accepted or after it is moved from where it was placed;
- movement of property by mechanical device;
- operations;
- completed operations;
- pollution; and
- war.

✓ ***Take Note:*** Some of the BAP's exclusions, such as handling of property and movement by a mechanical device, are intended to complement the coverage provided under the commercial general liability (CGL) policy discussed in Unit 5. In other words, the movement of property before loading onto a vehicle and movement by devices such as conveyor belts represent exposures covered under the CGL, not the BAP. When properly coordinated, the BAP and CGL work together to provide coverage needed by a typical insured without duplicating coverage or creating gaps.

## Section III—Physical Damage Coverage

In addition to collision coverage, an insured has two choices regarding coverage for damage other than collision. Explanations of these choices—comprehensive and specified cause of loss—follow.

- **Comprehensive coverage**. Comprehensive coverage pays for loss to a covered auto or its equipment for any cause, except collision and overturn (or upset). Glass breakage, hitting a bird or an animal, falling objects, and missiles are covered under comprehensive if the policy provides that coverage. These perils are mentioned specifically to make it clear that insurance is provided under comprehensive rather than collision coverage because confusion on that point could occur. If a collision causes glass breakage, the policy provides coverage under collision to avoid payment of two deductibles.

- **Specified cause of loss**. This coverage pays for specified causes, including:
  - fire, lightning or explosion;
  - theft;
  - windstorm, hail or earthquake;
  - flood;
  - mischief or vandalism; and
  - the sinking, burning, collision or derailment of any conveyance transporting the covered auto.

### *Collision and Overturn*

A covered auto or its equipment is insured against damage from collision with another object or from overturn. Towing coverage is available only for private passenger autos.

Various deductibles are available for each of the physical damage coverages.

### *Coverage Extension*

A coverage extension is provided for transportation expenses the insured incurs of theft of a covered private passenger auto. The BAP allows up to $20 per day, with a maximum of $600. The insured must have comprehensive coverage and coverage begins 48 hours after the theft.

### *Exclusions*

No physical damage coverage is allowed for damages from:

- nuclear explosion, radiation, or hazard;
- war or military action;
- racing or demolition contests or stunting; or
- wear and tear, freezing, mechanical or electrical breakdown or blowouts, punctures, or other road damage to tires.

In addition, the BAP does not cover loss to:

- tape decks or other sound-reproducing equipment unless permanently installed in a covered auto; or
- tapes, records, or other sound-reproducing devices designed for use with sound-reproducing equipment.

## Section IV—Business Auto Conditions

Section IV states the conditions applicable to the policy in addition to the common conditions. This coverage form contains five loss conditions and eight general conditions. Some of the BAP's important policy conditions include the requirement that the insured file a police report in the event of a theft, submit to an appraisal process if a claim is disputed, and cooperate with the insurer in defending any claim.

✓ ***Take Note:*** The BAP provides primary insurance for owned automobiles, as well as excess over any other applicable insurance for nonowned autos. This is where the phrase *the insurance follows the car* originates because the policy on the vehicle pays first and the driver's policy provides excess protection. This section uses the term *first-named insured* to clarify who must pay premiums and receive notices when many insureds are listed.

## Section V—Definitions

Some of the important definitions contained in the business auto policy follow.

- An **accident** includes a continuous or repeated exposure to the same conditions, resulting in bodily injury or property damage.
- **Auto** means a land motor vehicle, trailer, or semitrailer designed for travel on public roads, but the term does not include mobile equipment. For liability insurance, the term includes mobile equipment only while a covered auto is carrying or towing it.
- **Bodily injury** means bodily injury, sickness or disease any person sustains and includes death resulting from any of these.
- **Property damage** means damage to or loss of use of tangible property.

The definitions of mobile equipment and insured contract are the same as under the CGL policy and therefore are not repeated here.

## Business Auto Endorsements

### *Medical Payments and Uninsured Motorists*

As mentioned earlier, unlike the personal auto policy, the BAP does not include medical payments and uninsured motorists coverages. These important options can be added by endorsement. **Medical payments coverage** is written with a limit per person and per accident, and it applies to the driver and others in the vehicle who are injured as a result of a covered accident.

**Uninsured motorists (UM) coverage** provides payment for bodily injury to the driver and vehicle occupants that results from an accident with an uninsured vehicle. This coverage is only available if the uninsured driver is legally responsible for the accident. In addition, UM coverage in some states includes **underinsured motorists (UIM) coverage**, so an accident involving another vehicle that is insured but at a lower limit than the insured carries also may be paid.

An optional coverage, **uninsured motorists property damage (UMPD)**, is also available in some states. This coverage is not as important if all the vehicles are insured for collision because it serves only to waive the collision deductible. However, in the event a vehicle is not insured for collision,

FIGURE 11.1 Business Auto Policy

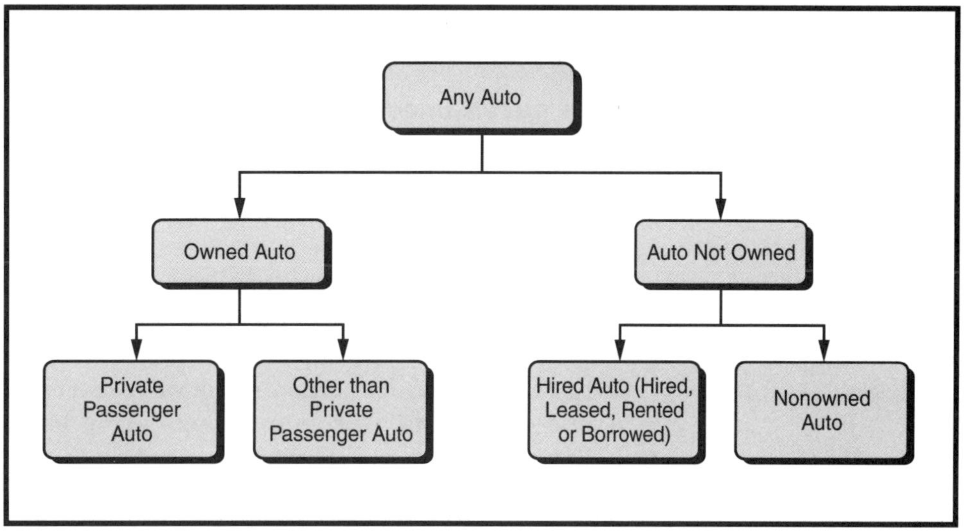


UMPD provides up to $3,500 for damage to the insured's vehicle if the other driver is not insured.

**Test Topic Alert!**

Unlike the personal auto policy (PAP), the business auto policy (BAP) does not include medical payments and uninsured motorists coverages. These coverages can be added by endorsement.

The reason these important coverages are not included automatically under the BAP, as they are in the personal auto policy, is that many businesses do not wish to provide the coverage for their commercial vehicles.

✓ ***For Example:*** Fast Freight Company is a package delivery service. The only persons who use its delivery vans are employees. Jeff, a driver for Fast Freight, is injured in a traffic accident. His exclusive remedy is workers' compensation. Therefore, neither medical payments nor uninsured motorists coverage provides him with any benefits. Because this situation can arise easily with the use of a commercial auto such as a delivery van, Fast Freight can save a substantial amount of money by not carrying these coverages on its vehicles. Under the laws of many states, however, uninsured motorists coverage must be included on all policies that provide liability insurance. To delete the UM coverage, Fast Freight would have to sign a waiver and keep it on file.

Several other endorsements are available under the business auto policy that are important to consider for commercial clients.

**Drive Other Car Endorsement.** **Drive other car (DOC) coverage** is needed whenever all the named insured's vehicles are covered under the BAP and they carry no personal auto coverage. This endorsement extends coverage to the nonbusiness exposures of the individuals named in the endorsement. If a corporate executive is furnished with a company car and does not carry a personal auto policy because he has no other vehicles in the household, DOC coverage is necessary in the event that individual rents or borrows a vehicle. This arises out of the fact that the business is protected by the BAP, but the individual is neither a named insured nor an insured under the policy.

**Individual Named Insured Endorsement.** An **individual named insured endorsement** added to the BAP duplicates the coverage a personal auto policy provides. This endorsement is important whenever the BAP also ensures the business owner's personally registered private passenger vehicles.

**Employees as Additional Insureds.** Although the BAP covers employees while they drive autos the business owns, the employees are not insured for the use of their own autos in the course of business. An employee's personal auto policy provides some protection, but a claim may exceed the employee's limits. This endorsement extends the employer's business auto policy to protect employees as insureds.

**Rental Reimbursement Coverage.** This endorsement covers expenses incurred to rent another auto because of a loss to a covered auto shown in the policy. Coverage begins 24 hours following a physical damage loss and continues until the vehicle is repaired using due diligence.

**Deductible Liability Insurance.** This endorsement is used to establish deductibles for bodily injury, property damage, or both. The insurance may be an underwriting requirement, or the insured may choose it to reduce premiums.

**Truckers Coverage Form.** A special policy for trucking operations is available. The coverages are the same as those provided under the business auto policy, with two exceptions. First, coverage is available for trailers owned by others and in the insured's possession. Second, the insured's trailers may be covered when they are in the possession of others. These trailer interchange agreements are common in the trucking industry.

## Quick Quiz 11.2

1. The insured under the BAP includes all of the following EXCEPT

   A. permissive user of a covered auto
   B. anyone liable for the insured's conduct
   C. an employee of the insured
   D. the named insured

2. Supplementary payments or extensions of coverage of the business auto policy include all of the following EXCEPT

   A. expenses the insurer incurs in investigating and defending claims
   B. bail bonds, up to a total of $2,000
   C. prejudgment interest
   D. increased limits to comply with state laws when vehicles are operated out of state

3. Liability coverage applies under the BAP whenever

   A. the insured is legally obligated to pay
   B. bodily injury or property damage arises out of an accident
   C. the loss involves a covered auto
   D. all of the above

4. Which of the following situations is covered under the BAP's physical damage section?

   A. The insured drives over a nail and punctures a tire.
   B. A rock flies out of the vehicle in front of the insured, breaking the insured's windshield.
   C. The handheld CD player is stolen from the insured's vehicle.
   D. The insured's vehicle must be repaired when the radiator begins to leak.

***Answers***

1. **C.** *Employees may be included as insureds under the BAP only by endorsement.*

2. **C.** *Only postjudgment interest is included in the supplementary payments portion of the auto policy. Prejudgment interest is subject to the limits of liability.*

3. **D.** *The conditions for coverage to apply under the BAP are that the insured be legally obligated, that the obligation arises out of bodily injury or property damage, that there has been an accident as defined in the policy, and that the accident involved use of a covered auto.*

4. **B.** *The physical damage section of the BAP excludes road damage to tires, electronic devices not permanently installed in the vehicle, and mechanical breakdown.*

## The Garage Policy (CA 00 05 10)

Companies in the business of selling, servicing, storing, or parking autos have unique insurance needs. To meet the special needs of garages, the Insurance Services Office (ISO) developed a special **Garage Program** and the **Garage Coverage Form (CA 00 05 10)**. The garage policy combines a business auto policy (BAP), a commercial general liability policy (CGL), and garagekeepers insurance, a special type of bailee coverage, into a single policy.

Like the BAP, the garage policy is a commercial auto form. It provides liability coverage for bodily injury arising out of the ownership, maintenance, or use of an automobile. It also provides physical damage protection for covered vehicles, including vehicles held for sale.

The garage policy, like the CGL policy, provides liability coverage for bodily injury and property damage arising from the garage's commercial premises and operations. Included in the basic premium for the policy are the following legal liability hazard clauses:

- premises and operations;
- products and completed operations; and
- automobile liability.

✓ ***Take Note:*** The garage policy's premises and operations and the products and completed operations coverages are essentially the same as the separate coverage parts available in a CGL policy.

In addition, the contract may be used to provide physical damage coverage on owned and hired automobiles, including the inventory of automobiles held for sale by automobile dealers.

✓ ***Take Note:*** One important difference exists between a garage policy and a CGL policy: the CGL policy's standard care, custody, or control exclusion causes problems for the garage class of business because it excludes damage to automobiles caused by the insured's customers that are in the insured's care.

The garage policy contains garagekeepers coverage, a specialized coverage for bodily injury or property damage arising out of the garage business operations. This special form of bailee liability insurance covers customers' automobiles while they are in a garage's care and requires a separate premium.

## Perils

Garagekeepers insurance protects garage operators against direct damage or legal liability for damage to vehicles in the insured's care, custody, or control. For each of its locations, the insured may select from three physical damage coverage options:

- **Comprehensive Coverage:** loss to a customer's auto from any cause except collision with another object;

- **Specified Causes of Loss Coverage:** damage from fire, lightning, explosion, theft, mischief, or vandalism; or
- **Collision Coverage:** damage caused by the customer's auto colliding with another object or overturning.

The garage policy covers legal liability for property damage, which applies only if the garage is legally liable for damage. If the insured needs or wants additional coverage, the policy can be amended by checking the appropriate box in the **Auto Dealers' Supplementary Schedule (CA DS 00 07 10)**, which is attached to the garage policy. There are two direct coverage options item:

- **primary basis**, in which the garagekeepers coverage becomes primary (or pays first) with respect to a customer's automobile, regardless of the garage's liability; and
- **excess basis**, in which the garagekeepers coverage responds regardless of liability, on an excess basis (or over any other collectible insurance).

There is a premium charge for each selection.

## The Garage Policy: Auto Dealer's Supplementary Schedule

The garage policy, like the Business Auto Policy, uses coverage symbols to denote covered autos. The 11 coverage symbols and their descriptions appear on the first page of the Garage Coverage Form.

Like the BAP, the type of coverage afforded for autos is determined by the use of covered auto designation symbols. The appropriate symbols must be included in Item Two of the declarations page of the garage policy or on the Garage Coverage Form—Auto Dealer's Supplementary Schedule (CA DS 00 07 10).

### Section I—Covered Autos

*Part A*

Numerical symbols describe the autos that may be covered.

| Symbol | |
|---|---|
| 21 | Any auto |
| 22 | Owned autos only (for liability coverage, includes trailers the insured does not own while attached to owned power units) |
| 23 | Owned private passenger autos only (including private passenger autos the insured acquires after the policy begins) |
| 24 | Owned autos other than private passenger autos |
| 25 | Owned autos subject to no fault rules |
| 26 | Owned autos subject to a compulsory uninsured motorists law |

| | |
|---|---|
| 27 | Specifically described autos |
| 28 | Hired autos only (those the insured leases, hires, rents or borrows, but not from any of the insured's employees or partners or from members of the insured's household) |
| 29 | Nonowned autos used in the insured's garage business (including autos owned by the insured's employees or partners or by members of his or her household while used in the insured's garage business) |
| 30 | Autos left with the insured for service, repair, storage or safekeeping (including autos owned by the insured's employees or members of his or her household who pay for the services performed) |
| 31 | Dealers' autos and autos nondealers or trailer dealers hold for sale (only physical damage coverage). |

***Part B***

For Symbols 21, 22, 24, 25, and 26, coverage is provided for autos the insured acquires of the type described for the remainder of the policy period.

Under Symbol 27, newly acquired autos are covered if:

- all autos the insured owns already are covered or if it replaces an auto the insured previously owned that had that coverage; and
- the insured notifies the insurer within 30 days of his desire to cover the newly acquired auto.

## Section II—Liability Coverage

***Garage Operations: Other than Covered Auto (Customers Autos)***

This insurance covers:

- all sums an insured must pay legally as damages because of bodily injury or property damage caused by an accident resulting from garage operations other than the ownership, maintenance, or use of covered autos; and
- the right and duty to defend any suit asking for these damages (the duty to defend or settle ends when the applicable liability coverage limit of insurance has been exhausted by payment of judgments or settlements).

***Garage Operations: Covered Autos (Business's Autos)***

This insurance covers:

- all sums an insured must pay legally as damages because of bodily injury or property damage caused by an accident resulting from garage operations involving the ownership, maintenance, or use of covered autos;

- all sums an insured must pay legally as a covered pollution cost or an expense caused by an accident resulting from garage operations involving the ownership, maintenance, or use of covered autos;
- only if the same accident causes either bodily injury or property damage to which this insurance applies; and
- the right and duty to defend any suit until liability coverage limits are exhausted.

Also considered covered autos for liability purposes are certain trailers and temporary substitute autos, such as:

- trailers with a load capacity of 2,000 lbs. or less designed primarily for travel on public roads; and
- any nonowned auto while used with its owner's permission as a temporary substitute for a covered auto that is out of service due to breakdown, repair, servicing, loss, or destruction.

### *Coverage Extensions*

**A. Supplementary Payments.** In addition to the limit of insurance, coverage includes:

- up to $2,000 for the cost of bail bonds, including bonds for related traffic law violations, required because of an accident the insurer covers (the insurer does not have to furnish these bonds);
- the cost of bonds to release attachments in any suit the insurer defends, but only for bond amounts within the limit of insurance (**attachment** is a statutory legal remedy whereby one party may prevent removal of property belonging to another party, pending determination of a court action.);
- all reasonable expenses the insured incurs for court appearances, depositions, and other legal proceedings, including actual loss of earnings up to $250 a day because of time off work;
- all costs taxed against the insured in any suit; and
- all interest on the full amount of any judgment that accrues after entry of the judgment (the insurer's duty to pay interest ends when it has paid, offered to pay or deposited in court the part of the judgment that is within its limit of insurance).

**B. Out-of-State Coverage Extensions.** The extensions for vehicles garaged out of state:

- increase the limit of insurance for liability coverage to meet the limits specified by a state's compulsory or financial responsibility law (this extension does not apply to the limit or limits specified by any law governing motor carriers of passengers or property); and
- provide the minimum amounts and types of other coverages, such as no fault coverage, required of out-of-state vehicles by the jurisdiction where the covered auto is being used.

### *Exclusions*

Excluded from coverage are the following.

**Expected or Intended Injury.** Except bodily injury resulting from the use of reasonable force to protect persons or property.

**Contractual Liability.** Except liability for damages assumed in a contract or an agreement that is an insured contract or that the insured would have in the absence of the contractual agreement.

**Workers' Compensation.** Any obligation under state disability benefits or unemployment compensation law.

**Employee Indemnification and Employer's Liability.** Bodily injury to an employee arising out of or in the course of employment or damages suffered by an employee's spouse, child, parent, brother, or sister as a consequence of injury to an employee.

**Fellow Employee.** Bodily injury to any fellow employee of the insured arising out of and in the course of the fellow employee's employment. (Covered under workers' compensation.)

**Care, Custody, or Control.** Property damage to or covered pollution cost or expense involving (1) property the insured owns, rents, or occupies; (2) property loaned to the insured; (3) property the insured holds for sale, or transports; or (4) property in the insured's care, custody, or control. This exclusion does not apply to liability assumed under a sidetrack agreement.

**Leased Autos.** A covered auto the insured rents to one of its customers when the customer leaves his auto with the insured for service or repair.

**Pollution Exclusion—Garage Operations other than Covered Auto.** Bodily injury, property damage or loss, cost, or expense arising out of the actual, alleged or threatened discharge, dispersal, seepage, migration, release, or escape of pollutants.

**Pollution Exclusion: Garage Operations—Covered Auto.** Bodily injury or property damage arising out of the actual, alleged, or threatened discharge, dispersal, seepage, migration, release, or escape of pollutants.

**Other Exclusions.** Race cars, watercraft or aircraft, defective products or work the insured performed, loss of use (does not apply if the loss of use was caused by sudden and accidental damage to or destruction of insured's products or work insured performed after the products have been put to their intended use), product recalls, losses due to war and warlike acts, and liquor liability (similar to commercial liability policy).

### *Limits of Insurance*

An aggregate limit of insurance applies to garage operations other than covered autos and also to the following endorsements, if provided:

- Personal injury liability coverage
- Advertising injury liability coverage
- Host liquor liability coverage
- Fire legal liability coverage
- Incidental medical malpractice liability coverage
- Nonowned watercraft coverage
- Broad form products coverage

No aggregate limit applies on covered autos the business owns.

✓ ***Take Note:*** Nearly all of the garage policy provisions are found in the commercial general liability form, the business auto policy, or both. The unique exposures of firms engaged in the automobile business, such as damage to customers' vehicles, make a separate policy necessary to avoid any coverage conflicts that might arise by simply combining the two standard forms.

### *Deductible*

A $100 deductible is assessed for damages in any accident resulting from property damage to an auto as a result of work the insured performed on that auto.

When the Garage Program was developed, ISO intended to cover two broad categories: dealers and service operations:

- **Dealers** are franchised and non-franchised operations that sell various motor vehicles.
- **Service operations** include repair shops, service stations, storage garages, and public parking places, franchised and non-franchised trailer dealers, and tow truck operators.

However, as garages and service stations began to offer a variety of services related more to the personal needs of the motorist than to auto repair and maintenance (such as convenience stores that dispense fuel but also sell food and sundries), insurers began to question whether these risks unrelated to auto repair and maintenance were covered under the Garage Program.

ISO determined that the Garage Coverage Form was not intended to cover this type of auto service risk exposure. In mid-2001, ISO revised the Garage Program so that it no longer applies to non-dealer auto service risks. Currently, the garage policy covers only auto dealerships defined as individuals or organizations in the business of selling autos, trucks, motorcycles, or other vehicles.

ISO's **Commercial General Liability (CGL) Program** can provide coverage for auto service risks. Underwriting guidelines, general rules, and other information are available in the CGL sections of the *Commercial Lines Manual* from ISO. This class of business must now be covered by

- A combination of the CGL, BAP, and a Garagekeepers Coverage (CA 99 37) endorsement; or
- ISO's new Auto Service Risks Program.

Introduced in mid-2001, the Auto Service Risks Program has its own policy forms, rules, and loss costs. The forms do not replace basic commercial or liability coverage forms, but provide additional coverages and enhancements to the underlying coverage forms. The forms are designed to wrap around an existing commercial package policy (CPP).

## Quick Quiz 11.3

1. The garage policy combines__________ __________ __________ and __________ ________ coverages for insureds who are automobile dealers.

2. Garagekeepers insurance includes options of coverage for damage to customer's vehicles based on

   A. ____________________
   B. ____________________
   C. ____________________

3. The special covered auto symbols a garage policy uses to provide coverage for customers vehicles in the insured's care, custody, or control and for dealers autos are Symbol _____ and Symbol _____, respectively.

4. True or False? An aggregate limit applies to coverage under the garage policy.

## Answers

1. *commercial general liability, business auto*
2. *Legal liability, direct primary, direct excess*
3. *30, 31*
4. ***True**. The garage policy contains an aggregate on the general liability portion of coverage, but not on the business auto coverages.*

**Section III—Garagekeepers Coverage**

Details of this coverage were provided above.

**Section IV—Physical Damage Coverage**

This section covers physical damage to autos the business owns.

**Section V—Garage Conditions**

Conditions are similar to those in the CGL and business auto policies.

**Section VI—Definitions**

Definitions are similar to those in the CGL and business auto policies.

# Unit Test Eleven

1. Which of the following is the same between a personal auto policy and a business auto policy?
   A. Number of units each policy covers
   B. Types of vehicles each policy covers
   C. Coverage for no fault benefits
   D. Use of covered auto symbols

2. All of the following are examples of a commercial auto form EXCEPT
   A. Garage coverage
   B. Truckers coverage
   C. Business auto coverage
   D. Personal auto coverage

3. Which of the following coverages is not included automatically under a business auto policy?
   A. Liability
   B. Physical damage
   C. Uninsured motorists
   D. Defense costs

4. Which of the following covered auto symbols provides the broadest protection under the business auto policy?
   A. Symbol 1
   B. Symbol 2
   C. Symbol 3
   D. Symbol 4

5. Which of the following covered auto symbols provides the most restrictive coverage for the insured's vehicles under the business auto policy?
   A. Symbol 6
   B. Symbol 7
   C. Symbol 8
   D. Symbol 9

6. To provide coverage for the vehicles employees own and use in the insured's business, the business auto policy should include Symbol
   A. 6
   B. 7
   C. 8
   D. 9

7. Why are Symbols 8 and 9 unnecessary when providing coverage using Symbol 1 under the business auto policy?
   A. They are not available when Symbol 1 is used.
   B. Symbol 1 includes coverage for these vehicles as "any auto."
   C. Symbols 7, 8, and 9 provide the same coverage.
   D. They are incompatible.

8. Which of the following symbols is available to an insured who must provide compulsory no fault benefits?
   A. Symbol 3
   B. Symbol 4
   C. Symbol 5
   D. Symbol 6

9. Which of the following symbols is available to an insured with vehicles subject to compulsory uninsured motorists coverage?
   A. Symbol 3
   B. Symbol 4
   C. Symbol 5
   D. Symbol 6

10. When Symbol 7 is provided, which of the following statements regarding newly acquired autos is CORRECT?
    A. They are covered automatically until the end of the policy term.
    B. They are covered only if they replace covered autos.
    C. They are covered only for 10 days.
    D. They are not covered at all until they are reported to the insurer.

11. Which of the following is NOT a requirement for coverage to apply under a business auto policy's liability section?
    A. Legal obligation to pay damages
    B. Bodily injury or property damage
    C. Court award of damages
    D. Occurrence as defined in the policy

12. Which of the following is included as an insured under a business auto policy?
    A. Employee of the insured who operates a vehicle on company business
    B. Partner of the insured when using his or her own automobile
    C. Permissive user of a covered auto
    D. Corporate officer who uses his or her own vehicle on company business

13. Which of the following is NOT a supplementary payment under a business auto policy?
    A. Cost to the insured to render first aid at an accident scene
    B. Cost of bonds to release attachments
    C. Expenses the insurer incurs
    D. Interest that accrues after entry of a judgment

14. Which of the following statements is CORRECT when a vehicle is used outside the state in which it is principally garaged?
    A. No coverage applies because the vehicle is outside the coverage territory.
    B. The same coverage applies to any losses that would be available in the home state.
    C. The coverage complies automatically with the laws of the state where the vehicle is operated.
    D. The coverage provides excess insurance over any coverage available to the insured in that state.

15. All of the following are examples of exclusions in the business auto policy EXCEPT
    A. care, custody, or control
    B. workers' compensation
    C. completed operations
    D. use of the vehicle as a public or livery conveyance

16. Which of the following is NOT a specified cause of loss under the business auto policy's physical damage portion?
    A. Theft
    B. Flood
    C. Vandalism
    D. Collision

17. If, while driving on a country road, an insured strikes a deer, which of the following statements is CORRECT?
    A. The damage to the vehicle is covered under specified causes of loss.
    B. The damage to the vehicle is covered under collision coverage.
    C. The damage to the deer is covered under comprehensive coverage.
    D. The damage to the vehicle is covered under comprehensive coverage.

18. When an insured vehicle is stolen, the policyholder may obtain coverage for transportation expenses subject to which of the following limits?
    A. $20 per day; $500 maximum
    B. $20 per day; $600 maximum
    C. $15 per day; $150 maximum
    D. $20 per day; $300 maximum

19. The deductible or waiting period that applies to the transportation expense coverage under the business auto policy is
    A. $100
    B. $250
    C. 24 hours
    D. 48 hours

20. For which of the following reasons might some commercial insureds NOT wish to include medical payments and uninsured motorists coverage in their business auto policies?
    A. They are unconcerned about injuries to the passengers in their vehicles.
    B. Because some employees only drive certain vehicles, they are covered by workers' compensation.
    C. They do not feel a social responsibility to the passengers in commercial vehicles.
    D. They are covered for injuries to passengers under the bodily injury portions of their coverage.

21. Which of the following is an important endorsement to the business auto policy when the insured will have all vehicles registered to the corporation and insured under the BAP, including their personal vehicles?
    A. Individual Named Insured
    B. Drive Other Car
    C. Family Auto Endorsement
    D. Coverage for Other Autos

22. The reason for buying a garage policy is to provide
    A. liability coverage for owners of auto repair facilities who cannot get coverage elsewhere
    B. coverage for buildings and other structures occupied as garages and service stations
    C. a combination of automobile and general liability coverage for garage-type operations
    D. coverage for the automobiles auto dealers and others in the automobile business own

23. Each of the following options is available to insure damage to customers' vehicles in an insured's care, custody, or control EXCEPT
    A. direct primary
    B. legal liability
    C. direct excess
    D. direct legal

24. Which one of the following symbols provides the broadest liability protection under the garage policy?
    A. Symbol 21
    B. Symbol 22
    C. Symbol 23
    D. Symbol 24

# Unit Test Eleven Answers & Rationale

1. **C.** Personal auto policies usually cover private passenger automobiles in small numbers. Usage can be for pleasure, business, or travel to and from school or work. Like its commercial counterparts, the PAP provides no fault benefits when required or desired.

2. **D.** The commercial auto forms consist of the business auto policy, the garage form and the truckers form.

3. **C.** Unlike they are in the PAP, uninsured motorists and medical payments are not included automatically under the business auto policy because many policyholders do not want or need the coverage.

4. **A.** Symbol 1 (any auto) provides the broadest covered available under the BAP.

5. **B.** Symbol 7 (specifically described autos) provides the most limited coverage for the insured's autos under the BAP because of the limitations that apply to newly acquired automobiles.

6. **D.** Symbol 9 covers nonowned automobiles that the insured's employees own and use in the insured's business.

7. **B.** Symbol 1 applies to any auto and therefore covers autos that the insured owns or nonowned autos that employees borrow, lease, rent, use, or own.

8. **C.** Symbol 5 covers owned autos subject to compulsory no fault benefits.

9. **D.** Symbol 6 covers for owned autos subject to a compulsory uninsured motorists law.

10. **B.** If Symbol 7 is used, coverage applies to newly acquired autos for 30 days, but only if they are replacement vehicles and the company already insures all owned vehicles for that coverage. If these requirements are not met, no automatic coverage applies.

11. **C.** Although liability may be decided by a judge or jury, it often is established by a claims adjuster based on the facts of a case.

12. **C.** The BAP includes as insureds the named insured, permissive users and anyone liable (and vicariously liable) for an insured's conduct. Employees, partners, and officers may be included only by endorsement.

13. **A.** Cost to render first aid at the scene of an accident is not a coverage the BAP provides.

14. **C.** Under the BAP's coverage extensions, increased limits required to meet the minimum financial responsibility or compulsory insurance laws of another state or other required coverages, such as no fault, are provided automatically when a vehicle is operated out of the state in which it is principally garaged.

15. **D.** Use of a vehicle as a public or livery conveyance is excluded only under the personal auto policy. It would defeat the purpose of a business auto policy, which can be used to insure taxis, limousines and other types of livery risks

16. **D.** The specified causes of loss under the BAP are fire, lightning, explosion, theft, windstorm, hail, earthquake, flood, mischief, vandalism and the sinking, burning, collision, or derailment of any conveyance transporting a covered auto, but not collision of the auto itself.

17. **D.** Hitting a bird or an animal is included specifically under the BAP's comprehensive coverage.

18. **B.** The BAP's transportation expense coverage extension covers necessary expenses the insured incurs, up to $20 per day, with a maximum of $600 when a covered auto is stolen.

19. **D.** The deductible or waiting period before transportation expense is payable under the BAP is 48 hours.

20. **B.** When the only occupants of an insured's vehicles are employees, workers' compensation is their sole remedy for injuries suffered in automobile accidents. Therefore, the insured may not wish to provide medical payments or uninsured motorists coverage for commercial vehicles.

21. **B.** When all the vehicles the named insured uses are registered to the business and insured under a BAP, the insured and others in the household must be included in a Drive Other Car endorsement to extend coverage to their nonbusiness use of automobiles they do not own.

22. **C.** Because of limitations and exclusions in both CGL and business auto policies for insureds in the automobile business, the garage policy combines the liability and auto coverage those types of businesses need.

23. **D.** An insured who wishes to purchase coverage for damage to customers' automobiles in his care, custody, or control may do so on a direct primary, direct excess, or legal liability basis.

24. **A.** The broadest coverage available under the garage policy is Symbol 21, any auto.

Part Three

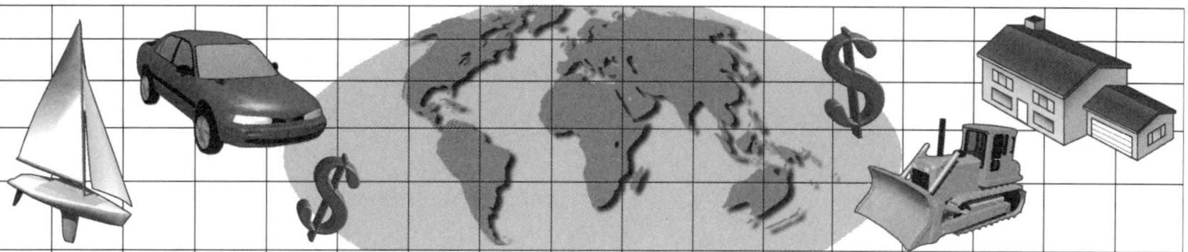

# Principles of Property Insurance

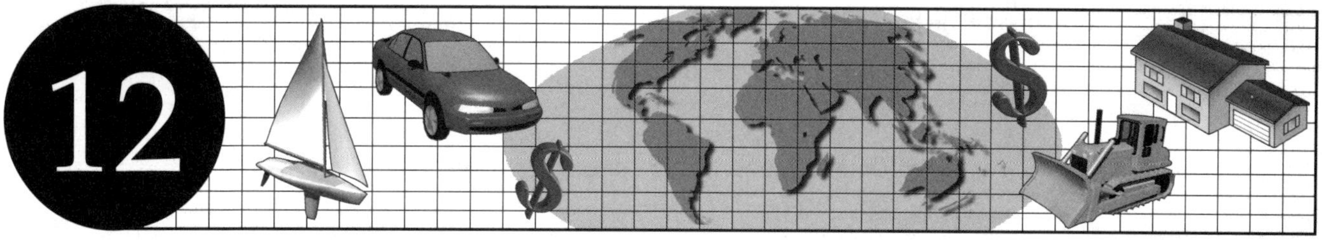


# Homeowners Policies

## INTRODUCTION

Following the passage of multiple-line legislation, the homeowners policy was introduced to provide a package or bundle of coverages that owners of residential property typically need. This was meant to be a single, indivisible contract that provides the coverage every homeowner requires. Policies for tenants of rented buildings and condominium unit owners followed, each designed for the unique exposures they presented.

A homeowners policy is relatively inflexible, meaning the coverages and limits have been predetermined and may be changed only by endorsement to the policy. Despite this inflexibility, homeowners policies offer policyholders:

- broader protection;
- single policy document;
- lower cost;
- one agent and insurance company; and
- single expiration date.

It is important to understand that the homeowners policy and the dwelling policy (discussed in a later unit) fill different needs in the insurance marketplace and thus still exist side by side.

## UNIT OBJECTIVES

When you have completed this unit, you should be able to:

- identify the types of policies available under the homeowners program;
- compare the policies in terms of covered property, covered causes of loss and loss settlement provisions;
- determine who is an insured under a homeowners policy;
- determine whether coverage would apply to a specific situation under Section I—Property—of the homeowners policy;

- describe endorsements to Section I of the homeowners policy;
- determine whether coverage would apply to a specific situation under Section II—Liability—of the Homeowners Policy;
- describe endorsements to Section II of the homeowners policy; and
- identify the method of providing coverage for owners of mobile homes.

This unit generally discusses the homeowners policy forms published by the Insurance Services Office in 2000 and adopted by most states. Note that some states have not yet adopted these forms and still use older ISO forms. Check with your state's test publisher to see which edition of these forms is tested on the state licensing exam.

You can determine which test publisher administers the exam by visiting the publisher websites. For Promissor, Inc., go to www.promissor.com or call 1-888-204-6231. For Experior, go to www.experioronline.com or call 1-800-786-3926. Access the exam content outlines to see which edition of the ISO forms is on the exam (expressed as a year). If you do not see your state listed on the Promissor or Experior sites, your state does not retain either company and instead administers its own exams. Contact your state's insurance department for more information about the exam.

## Homeowners Coverage

One of the challenges the insurance industry faces is keeping its products current to meet the consumers' needs. The homeowners program, originally developed in the 1950s, has undergone extensive change over the past half-century. New coverages have been added, obsolete or seldom-used forms have been eliminated, and the policy language has evolved to respond to changes in society.

Currently, five different forms are available for homeowners and one each for tenants and condominium owners. To be eligible for coverage under one of the homeowners policy forms, a dwelling must be (1) occupied by the owner (owner-occupied) and (2) a one-, two-, three- or four-family building. The five forms are:

- HO-1 Basic Form (HO 00 01 04; withdrawn from use in many states);
- HO-2 Broad Form (HO 00 02 05);
- HO-3 Special Form (HO 00 03 05);
- HO-5 Comprehensive Form (HO 00 05 05); and
- HO-8 Modified Form for Special Risks (HO 00 08 05; based on value or construction).

The **HO-1 Basic Form** is not purchased with enough regularity to support its continued use. Therefore, it has been withdrawn from use in many states and replaced by HO-8. An **HO-5 Comprehensive Form (HO 00 05 05)** has been reinstated to replace an endorsement added to the HO-3 that duplicated the coverage this separate form provided. As its name implies, this form covers both the dwelling and the insured's personal property.

The forms for coverage for tenants and condominium owners are:

- HO-4 Tenant's or Renter's (HO 00 04 05); and
- HO-6 Condominium Owner's (HO 00 06 05; also includes townhome owners).

Homeowners policies have two major coverage sections. Section I contains the property insurance and in many ways is similar to the coverages of the dwelling program. Section II of the homeowners program provides personal liability and medical payments to others coverages. Unlike the dwelling policies, however, a homeowners policy is an indivisible package of coverage, so all policies contain both sections. The pricing of a homeowners policy is determined largely by the limit selected for Coverage A Dwelling. In fact, the insured is not asked to determine limits for other coverages under the policy because they are percentages of the Coverage A (or Coverage C) limit.

### *Coverage Parts for HO-1, HO-2, HO-3, HO-5, HO-8*

*Section I—Property Coverage Form*

| | HO-1 and HO-8 | HO-2, HO-3 and HO-5 |
|---|---|---|
| Coverage A—Dwelling | Declared Value | Declared Value |
| Coverage B—Other Structures/Appurtenant Structures | 10% of Coverage A | 10% of Coverage A |
| Coverage C—Personal Property | 50% of Coverage A | 50% of Coverage A |
| Coverage D—Loss of Use | 10% of Coverage A | 30% of Coverage A |

*Section II—Liability Coverage*

| | |
|---|---|
| Coverage E—Personal Liability | Minimum all forms $100,000 |
| Coverage F—Medical Payments | Minimum all forms $1,000 |

### Coverage Parts for Tenant and Condominium Owners Forms

*Section I—Property Coverage Form*

| | HO-4 Tenant | HO-6 Condo |
|---|---|---|
| Coverage A—Dwelling | Not Covered | Declared Value |
| Coverage B—Other Structures | Not Covered | Part of Coverage A |
| Coverage C—Personal Property | $6,000 minimum (varies by state) | $10,000 minimum (varies by state) |
| Coverage D—Loss of Use | 30% of Coverage C | 50% of Coverage C |

*Section II—Liability Coverage*

| | |
|---|---|
| Coverage E—Personal Liability | Same as for Other Forms |
| Coverage F—Medical Payments | Same as for Other Forms |

### Covered Causes of Loss and Settlement for Tenant and Condominium Policies

| | HO-4 Tenant | HO-6 Condo |
|---|---|---|
| **Buildings** Coverage A & B | Not Applicable | Broad Form-Limited |
| **Personal Property** Coverage C | Declared Value Broad Form-ACV | Declared Value Broad Form-ACV |

## Policy Provisions and Requirements

**Eligibility** Eligibility for coverage under each form depends on the type of dwelling, its use, and its age.

- HO-1, HO-2, HO-3:
  - Owner-occupied, one-, two-, three- or four-family dwellings
  - Intended owner-occupant of a dwelling in the course of construction
  - One co-owner when each distinct portion of a two-, three- or four-family dwelling is occupied by co-owners
  - Purchaser-occupant when the seller retains title under an installment contract
  - Occupant of a dwelling under a life estate arrangement
- HO-4: Renters of a single-family home, a condominium, an apartment, or a mobile home.

- HO-5:
  - Owner-occupied, one-, two-, three-, or four-family dwellings
  - That part of any other building where the insured resides
  - Vacant land owned by or rented to the insured (other than farm land)
  - Land owned by or rented to the insured on which a one-, two-, three- or four-family dwelling is being built for the insured's residence
  - Individual or family cemetery or burial vaults of the insured
- HO-6: Owners of condominium or cooperative units.
- HO-8: For owners of dwellings who do not wish, or find it difficult to insure, their older properties on a replacement cost basis because replacement cost would far exceed the market value. In addition, the form can be used for homes of unusual construction that may be difficult to value. Losses are settled on an actual cash value basis, and coverages are similar, but in some cases more restrictive than, an HO-1 Basic Form. Additional restrictions apply on theft coverage and property away from the premises.

## Risks Not Eligible

Certain risks are not eligible for coverage by any of the forms, though coverage can be obtained through other means.

- Farms—A farmowners policy can be used.
- Mobile homes—These can be covered by endorsement to a homeowners policy, by mobile homeowners policy or by dwelling form.
- Buildings that are not owner-occupied—These can be covered by another policy designed to fit the use to which the owner puts the property.

## Definitions

The following terms arise in the context of these policies.

**Bodily injury** means bodily harm, sickness, or disease, including death that results from these and care or loss of services.

**Business** includes a trade, a profession, or an occupation, with the exception of volunteer activities or home day-care services that are rendered to a relative of an insured or are non-paid.

**Occurrence** means an accident, including repeated or continuous exposure to harmful conditions, that results in bodily injury or property damage.

**Property damage** means physical injury to or loss of use or destruction of tangible property.

**Residence employee** means an employee of an insured whose duties are related to the maintenance or use of the residence premises. If off-premises, duties cannot be related to the business of the insured.

**Residence premises** means the single-family dwelling, other structures or grounds insured or the part of any other building where the insured resides and that is shown in the Declarations. It also includes a two-, three-, or four-family dwelling when the insured resides in at least one of the family units if that dwelling is shown in the Declarations. (This definition is modified in the HO-6.)

**Persons Insured/Insured**

For **Section I—Property**, the insured is the person named on the Declarations Page and:

- a spouse if he resides in the same household; and
- other persons younger than age 21 and in the insured's care, or students enrolled in school full-time who are under the age of 24 and related to the insured.

For **Section II—Liability**, an insured also includes:

- any animal owned by the insured or other persons as described above;
- watercraft, as described in the policy, owned by the insured or other persons as described above; and
- any person legally responsible for this animal or watercraft, but not someone who has custody in the course of business, such as a veterinarian, or without the owner's consent, such as a thief.

**Insured Location**

The **insured location** is specifically defined on the Declarations Page and can be any of the following:

- Residence premises as defined
- Other premises described in the declarations and used by the insured as a residence
- Premises acquired by the named insured or a spouse during the policy term and used by the insured as a residence
- Nonowned premises at which an insured temporarily resides or occasionally rents to an insured for other-than-business use
- Vacant land, other than farmland the insured owns or rents
- Land the insured owns or rents on which a one-, two-, three-, or four-family dwelling is being built as a residence for the insured
- The insured's individual or family cemetery plots or burial vaults

## Quick Quiz 12.1

Match the homeowners form with the eligibility:

A. HO-1, HO-2, HO-3, HO-5
B. HO-4
C. HO-6
D. HO-8

_____ 1. Coverage for an owner-occupied one-, two-, three-, or four-family dwelling

_____ 2. Coverage for renters of single-family homes, apartments, condominiums, or mobile homes

_____ 3. Coverage for owners of dwellings who find it difficult to insure their properties on a replacement cost basis

_____ 4. Coverage for owners of condominium or cooperative units

***Answers*** *1. **A.*** *2. **B.*** *3. **D.*** *4. **C.***

# Section I—Property

In a homeowners policy, Section I defines the limits payable to the insured for covered loss of property. This coverage is referred to as Coverage A: Dwelling, Coverage B: Other Structures, Coverage C: Personal Property, and Coverage D: Loss of Use.

## Coverage A: Dwelling

A **covered structure** is any:

- dwelling on the residence premises, including structures attached to the dwelling (such as an attached garage); or
- materials and supplies located on or next to the premises that are intended for use in the construction, alteration, or repair of the building.

The homeowners policy specifically excludes land, including the land on which the dwelling is located. A dwelling under construction is not considered vacant.

All forms exclude glass coverage to the residence premises if the dwelling has been vacant for 60 consecutive days immediately before the loss, but the forms cover glass breakage otherwise.

## Coverage B: Other Structures

A covered structure is any structure set apart from the dwelling by clear space, such as detached garages, fences, swimming pools, or storage sheds. Structures connected to the dwelling by only a fence, utility wire, or similar connection are considered unattached.

Excluded from coverage are land, buildings used in whole or in part for business purposes, and buildings rented to anyone other than a tenant, except if used only for private garage purposes.

✓ ***Take Note:*** The restriction on coverage for detached structures used in whole or in part for business purposes is a problem for many people. Special home-based business policies have been developed to deal with these unique exposures.

## Coverage C: Personal Property

**Covered personal property** includes personal property:

- the insured owns or uses which is located anywhere in the world;
- of others at the insured's request while it is on the portion of the residence premises the insured occupies;
- of a guest or residence employee when it is located in any residence the insured occupies; and
- usually located in a secondary residence limited to 10 percent of Coverage C, or $1,000, whichever is greater.

Personal property not covered includes:

- articles described and insured separately elsewhere in this or another policy;
- animals, birds, and fish;
- motor vehicles and all other motorized land conveyances, including equipment or accessories while in or on the vehicle, such as:
  - automobiles;
  - motorcycles;
  - ATVs;
  - go carts;
  - golf carts (liability is covered in Section II when the golf cart is used to play golf on a golf course); and
  - owned snowmobiles;

- electric apparatus and accessories designed to be operated by power from the electrical system of the motor vehicle;

✓ ***Take Note:*** This exclusion does not apply to vehicles or land conveyances used to service the premises or designed to assist the handicapped if they are not subject to motor vehicle registration.

- aircraft and parts, except model or hobby aircraft;
- hovercraft and parts;
- property of roomers, boarders, or other tenants unrelated to the insured;
- property in an apartment the insured rents to others (except as provided under Additional Coverages);
- property rented or held for rental to others away from the residence premises;
- business data, though the cost of blank recording, storage media, and prerecorded computer programs is covered;
- credit cards or fund transfer cards, except as provided under Additional Coverages; and
- water or steam

Special loss limits, maximums and aggregates of certain property apply (they do not increase the Coverage C limit):

- $200 on money, bullion, bank notes, etc.;
- $1,500 on securities, deeds, valuable papers, manuscripts, tickets, personal records, and stamps;
- $1,500 on watercraft, including trailers, motors, and equipment;
- $1,500 on trailers other than those used with watercraft;
- $1,500 on furs, watches, jewelry, and precious and semiprecious stones (theft only);
- $2,500 on firearms and related equipment (theft only);
- $2,500 on silverware, goldware (both solid and plated), and pewterware (theft only);
- $2,500 on business property on the residence premises;
- $500 on business property away from the residence premises, used primarily for business purposes;
- $1,500 on electronic apparatus and accessories, while in or upon a motor vehicle if the apparatus is equipped to be operated by power from the motor vehicle's electrical system, e.g., antennas, tapes, discs; and
- $1,500 on electronic apparatus and accessories used primarily for business while away from the residence premises and not in or upon a motor vehicle.

Special provisions for theft coverage are as follows:

- Theft coverage is included on all forms and applies to Coverages A, B and C.
- Theft is defined as loss of property from a known place under circumstances in which a probability of theft exists. Mysterious disappearance is not included in the definition of theft.
- Two theft exclusions exist:
  - General:
    (1) theft the insured commits;
    (2) theft from buildings under construction, including materials for use in construction; and
    (3) theft from any part of a residence rented to someone else.
  - Property away from premises:
    (1) in other owned or rented living quarters unless the insured is residing there temporarily;
    (2) watercraft and related furnishings or equipment; and
    (3) trailers, semitrailers and campers.
- The insured must notify the police and insurance company for coverage to apply.

✓ ***Take Note:*** Property of an insured student is covered while the student resides away from home if the student has been at the residence at any time during the 60 days immediately before the loss.

## Coverage D: Loss of Use

**Coverage D** provides protection when the residence cannot be used because of an insured loss. For that part of the residence premises where the insured resides, the following may be applied at the insured's choice:

- the necessary increase in additional living expense the insured incurred in order to continue his normal standard of living following a loss by an insured peril;
- coverage for prohibited use if the insured cannot use the dwelling for two weeks because of a loss to a neighboring premises by a peril insured against in this policy; or
- the fair rental value of that part of the premises where the insured resides. For that part of the premises rented or held for rental to others, the fair rental value may be applied, less noncontinuing expenses.

The coverage period is limited to the shortest time required to repair or replace the insured property.

# Section I—Additional Coverages

## Extensions

All homeowners policies provide the following extensions of coverage.

**Debris Removal** The cost to remove debris after a loss, including ash, dust, or particles from a volcanic eruption that has caused direct loss to a building or property. The insurer also pays up to $1,000 to remove a tree from the residence premises, provided it damaged a covered structure, but only for perils of windstorm, hail, or weight of ice, snow or sleet if it is the insured's tree or for any of the broad form perils if the tree belongs to a neighbor, if the neighbor's tree damages a covered structure or blocks a driveway or ramp on the residence premises. Coverage is limited to $1,000 regardless of the number of felled trees, with no more than $500 paid for the removal of any one tree.

**Reasonable Repairs** The reasonable cost of necessary repairs made solely to protect property from further damage.

**Trees, Shrubs, and Other Plants on Residence Premises** 5% of the limit on Coverage A, subject to a maximum of $500 for any one tree, shrub, or plant. This applies only to the limited specified perils of fire, lightning, explosion, riot or civil commotion, aircraft, vehicles not owned or operated by a resident of the premises, vandalism or malicious mischief, or theft.

**Fire Department Service Charge** Up to $500 for liability assumed for fire department charges to save or protect covered property from a peril insured against, if the fire department is from another community. No deductible applies, and this is additional insurance.

**Building Additions and Alterations** HO-4 covers the insured's interest in additions, alterations, fixtures, improvements, or installments to the insured's residence premises as an extension of Coverage C, but not to exceed 10% of Coverage C.

**Credit Card, Electronic Fund Transfer Card or Access Device, Forgery, and Counterfeit Money** Covered to a maximum of $500 if the card is stolen or used without authorization, or the insured accepts counterfeit money unknowingly. This does not cover use of a credit card or fund transfer card by residents of the insured's household or a person entrusted with such a card, nor does it cover business use or insured dishonesty.

**Property Removed** Covers loss to property while being removed from a premises endangered by a peril insured against for up to 30 days.

**Loss Assessment** Up to $1,000 for any loss assessment charged against the named insured because of loss to property owned collectively by a corporation or an association.

**Collapse** Limited coverage provided if the loss is caused by:

- perils insured against in Coverage C;
- hidden decay;
- hidden insects or vermin;
- weight of contents, equipment, animals, or people;
- weight of rain on a roof; and
- use of defective materials or construction methods.

**Landlord's Furnishings** Up to $2,500 is provided under this extension for Perils Insured Against, other than theft of appliances, carpeting, and other household furnishings.

**Ordinance or Law** Additional coverage that provides 10% of Coverage A as an additional amount of insurance for the increased costs of repair or reconstruction due to zoning laws or building ordinances that require upgrades in the event of a loss.

**Grave Markers** The insurer will pay up to $5,000 for grave markers, including mausoleums, on or away from the residence premises.

## Exclusions to Section I

The general exclusions applicable to the property coverage under the homeowners forms include the following.

**Ordinance or Law** Coverage does not apply to the enforcement of any law or ordinance that regulates the construction, repair, or demolition of a building or another structure unless that coverage is provided specifically elsewhere in the policy.

**Earth Movement** Excluded are earthquakes, including the land shock waves or earth movement caused by a volcanic eruption, landslide, mine subsidence, mudflow, and earth sinking, rising, or shifting. Coverage is provided if a fire or explosion follows, but only for the damage the ensuing loss causes.

**Water Damage** Coverage does not apply to loss due to flood, surface water, waves, tidal water, overflow of a body of water, or the spray from any of these situations, whether or not wind-driven. Coverage also does not apply to water that backs up through sewers or drains or that overflows from a sump, nor to water below the surface of the ground that seeps or leaks through buildings or other structures.

**Power Failure** A utility failure off the residence premises is not covered unless an insured peril results on the residence premises, and then coverage only applies to that ensuing loss.

**Neglect** The insured must use reasonable means to protect covered property from further damage. Failure to do so results in denial of the claim.

**War** Excluded from Section I.

**Nuclear Hazard** Excluded from Section I.

**Intentional Loss** Any loss arising out of an act an insured commits with intent to cause a loss.

**Governmental Action** Any loss resulting from the destruction, confiscation, or seizure of property by a governmental or public authority.

## Conditions to Section I

When a loss has occurred, the insured has certain duties to the insurer. The insurer can exercise numerous options in settling the claim.

- The insured's duties after a loss include:
  - reporting claims;
  - obtaining police reports for theft losses;
  - preparing inventories;
  - displaying damaged property; and
  - submitting to examination under oath.
- Settlement for a loss to a pair or set is based on the difference between the value of the pair or set before the loss and the value after the loss.
- Glass replacement is settled based on replacement with safety glazing materials.
- Appraisal is required if a dispute occurs as to the amount of a loss.
- Other insurance provisions require settlement on a pro rata basis if two or more policies apply to the same loss.
- A suit against the insurer may be commenced only after compliance with all policy conditions and within one year of the loss.
- An insurer has the option of repairing or replacing damaged or destroyed property if it gives the policyholder notice within 30 days of the claim.
- Loss payments are to be made within 60 days of receiving proof of loss.
- The policy does not allow abandonment of property to the insurer.
- A mortgage or loss payable clause provides certain rights to lienholders of property, including the right to make premium payments and receive claim payments even if the insured causes a loss intentionally.
- A no-benefit-to-bailee provision means that an individual or organization that has insured property in care, custody, or control is not an insured under this policy.
- Recovered property, at the insured's option, can be turned over to the insured, in which case the insurer adjusts the settlement made previously with the insured.

- There is no coverage if an insured has concealed or misrepresented a fact or engaged in fraudulent actions.

## Deductibles

Each of the forms contains a standard deductible clause of $250. Other deductibles are available.

The deductible is applied once against any loss Coverages A, B, or C covers and applies per occurrence.

**Test Topic Alert!** The standard $250 homeowners deductible applies to all losses except Coverage D.

## Valuation-Recovery Considerations/Loss Settlement

Replacement cost applies to all buildings (except those covered by HO-8), and will be paid up to the lesser of the:

- policy limit;
- replacement cost of that part of the building damaged on the same premises; or
- necessary amount actually spent to repair or replace the property.

**Test Topic Alert!** If an insured fails to carry coverage of at least 80% of replacement cost, he is responsible for part of the loss. This insurance-to-value provision is calculated by using this formula:

$$\frac{\text{Policy limit}}{\text{Replacement cost } 80\%} \times \text{loss } (-\text{ deductible}) = \text{amount covered}$$

Failure to carry insurance of at least 80% of the replacement cost value (insurance-to-value clause) results in the payment of the greater of the:

- actual cash value; or
- result from dividing the amount of insurance on the building by calculating 80% of the replacement cost of the building, then multiplying that amount by calculating the actual cost to repair or replace the damaged part of the building, then subtracting the deductible.

✓ ***For Example:*** If a home's replacement cost at the time of a loss is $100,000, the insured must carry a limit of at least $80,000 to receive a replacement cost settlement. If the limit is $75,000, the company pays either the quotient of $75,000 divided by 80,000 for the replacement cost of the loss or the actual cash value, whichever is greater.

✓ ***Take Note:*** Unlike the coinsurance provision common to commercial property insurance policies, the insurance-to-value provision of the homeowners policy seeks to reward those policyholders who carry adequate insurance with a replacement cost settlement. If, however, the amount of insurance carried is insufficient, the insured still receives at least the actual cash value of the loss or an amount between ACV and replacement cost.

Personal property and other items are settled on an actual cash value basis.

## Endorsements to Section I

Endorsements to the property portion of the homeowners policy include the following.

**Special Personal Property Coverage (HO-15)** This is perhaps the most important of the homeowners policy endorsements in those states that have not (re-)adopted the HO-5 form. The HO-15 endorsement may be attached to an HO-3 policy only, and when added converts the Coverage C causes of loss from broad to special form. This endorsement eliminated the need for the HO-5 form, which provided the same coverage.

**Personal Property Replacement Cost** Without endorsement, losses to personal property are settled on an actual cash value basis. This endorsement changes the valuation basis for Coverage C to replacement cost, with few exceptions.

**Other Structures—Increased Limits** This endorsement allows an increase in the Coverage B limit beyond the 10% provided automatically.

**Increased Limit on Personal Property in Other Residences** The 10% limitation on Coverage C property usually located at a secondary residence may be increased using this endorsement. The endorsement could be important to a policyholder with children away at college.

**Coverage C Increased Special Limits of Liability** The special loss limits that apply to certain categories of property, such as jewelry, firearms, and securities, can be increased using this endorsement.

**Scheduled Personal Property** Broader coverage for personal jewelry, furs, cameras, musical instruments, silverware, fine art, golf equipment, and stamp or coin collections may be provided by attaching an endorsement instead of writing a separate personal articles floater policy. Articles must be described and insured on a full value basis.

✓ ***Take Note:*** When coverage is provided for valuable articles using the scheduled personal property endorsement to the homeowners policy, an additional covered cause of loss is mysterious disappearance. This can be an important coverage when the insured is uncertain as to whether an item was stolen.

**Increased Limit on Business Property** If the insured maintains a home office, the $2,500 special loss limit for business property may be inadequate. This endorsement allows an increase in the limit, but does not apply to property pertaining to a business conducted on the residence premises or to property in storage or held as a sample for sale or delivery after a sale.

**Ordinance or Law—Increased Amount of Coverage** If the amount provided under Additional Coverage is insufficient, the insured may purchase additional amounts of coverage under this endorsement.

**Earthquake** If coverage is desired for earthquake, this endorsement should be attached to the homeowners policy.

**Water Back-Up and Sump Overflow** Unendorsed homeowners policies exclude coverage for water that backs up through sewers and drains or that overflows from a sump. This important coverage can be purchased with this endorsement. Coverage is limited to $5,000. A separate $250 deductible applies to losses.

## Quick Quiz 12.2

1. Coverage A, Dwelling of the Homeowners Policy, includes coverage for

   A. ____________________
   B. ____________________

2. Coverage B, Other Structures of the Homeowners Policy, eliminates coverage for

   A. ____________________
   B. ____________________

3. Coverage C, Personal Property of the Homeowners Policy, includes coverage for personal property

   A. ____________________
   B. ____________________
   C. ____________________
   D. ____________________

4. The special limits of the homeowners policy provide coverage in what amount for the following types of property?

   $__________ Money, bullion, bank notes, and the like
   $__________ Securities, deeds, valuable papers, manuscripts, and tickets
   $__________ Watercraft, including their trailers
   $__________ Trailers, other than those used with watercraft
   $__________ Jewelry, watches, and furs for loss due to theft
   $__________ Firearms for loss due to theft
   $__________ Silverware, goldware, and pewterware for loss due to theft
   $__________ Business property on the residence premises
   $__________ Business property off-premises
   $__________ Electronic devices used in a vehicle

**Answers**

1. *dwelling, attached structures*
2. *usage in whole or in part for business; rental to one other than a tenant of the dwelling except solely as a private garage*
3. *owned by the insured; used by the insured; owned by others while on the residence premises; owned by a guest or residence employee while on any residence occupied by the insured; usually located at a secondary residence (10% limitation).*
4. *$200; $1,500; $1,500; $1,500; $1,500; $2,500; $2,500; $2,500; $500; $1,500*

# Section II—Liability Coverages

In a homeowners policy, Section II defines the liability coverages payable to someone other than the insured. These coverages are known as Coverage E: Personal Liability Limit and Coverage F: Medical Payments to Others.

Section II coverages are the same in all forms. These coverages are substantially the same as those provided in the Personal Liability supplement to the dwelling program.

## Coverage E: Personal Liability

The insurer agrees to pay on the insured's behalf all sums up to the limit of liability that the insured becomes legally obligated to pay as damages because of bodily injury or property damage. The insurer also agrees to defend the insured in a lawsuit, even if the suit is fraudulent. The insurer may investigate and settle any claim it deems appropriate. The cost of defense is in addition to the limit of liability.

## Coverage F: Medical Payments to Others

The insurer agrees to pay all reasonable medical expenses incurred within three years from the date of an accident to or for each person who sustains bodily injury to which the insurance applies, when such person is:

- on the insured premises with the insured's permission; or
- off the insured premises, if such bodily injury:
  - arises out of a condition in the insured premises or the ways immediately adjoining;
  - is caused by the insured's activities;
  - is caused by an animal owned by or in the care of any insured; or
  - is caused by any residence employee in the course of employment by the insured.

Coverage does not apply to the insured or regular residents of the insured's household. Coverage is paid without regard to fault or negligence. Therefore, it is a type of no-fault coverage.

# Section II—Additional Coverages

Coverage may also extend to property damage suffered by others, legal expenses, and first aid expenses for other parties to an accident.

**Damage to Property of Others** Physical damage to property of others up to $1,000 per occurrence. This applies (1) even if the insured is not legally liable or (2) the property is in the insured's care, custody, or control. Coverage does not apply to damage caused intentionally by an insured who is at least 13 years old.

**Claim Expenses** No limit on legal and other costs the insurer incurs. The insurer pays only a maximum of $250 per day reimbursement to the insured for loss of earnings while assisting in the investigation or defense of a claim or suit.

**First Aid Expenses** No limit for first aid expenses incurred at the time of an accident for persons other than the insured.

**Loss Assessment** Coverage provided for certain loss assessments up to $1,000.

## Section II—Exclusions

Coverages E and F do not apply to any motor vehicle liability if the vehicle is registered for use on public road, or if such registration is required by law.

Coverages E and F also do not apply if the motor vehicle is:

- operated in any organized race or speed contest;
- rented to others;
- used to carry persons or cargo for a charge; or
- used for any business except for a motorized golf cart while on a golfing facility.

**Motor Vehicle Liability**

Even if the above exclusions do not apply, coverage for motor vehicle liability is generally excluded unless the motor vehicle is:

- in dead storage on an insured location;
- used solely to service an insured's residence;
- designed to assist a handicapped person, and at the time of the occurrence, is either being used to do so, or parked on an insured location;
- designed for recreational use off public roads and not owned by an insured, or owned by an insured on the insured location; or
- a motorized golf cart owned by the insured, designed to carry up to four persons and not built to exceed 25 miles per hour, which is within the boundaries of a golfing facility or in a residential community where motorized golf carts can legally travel.

**Watercraft Liability**

Coverages E and F also do not apply to any watercraft liability if the watercraft is being operated in a race, rented to others, used to carry cargo for a charge, or used for any business purpose.

Even if the above exclusions do not apply, there is still no coverage for watercraft liability unless at the time of the occurrence the watercraft is:

- stored;
- a sailing vessel less than 26 feet in length, or more than 26 feet and not owned by or rented to an insured;
- not a sailing vessel, and powered by an engine of 50 horsepower or less and not owned by an insured, or
- powered by an inboard or inboard-outdrive engine of more than 50 horsepower and not owned by or rented to an insured, or
- powered by one or more outboard engines of 25 horsepower or less, or more than 25 horsepower and not owned by an insured, or
- more than 25 horsepower and owned by an insured who acquired it during the policy period.

If the watercraft is more than 25 horsepower and acquired by an insured before the policy period, and if the insured declares it at policy inception and intends to insure it within 45 days, the coverages apply for the policy period.

✓ ***Take Note:*** This confusing exclusion is meant to eliminate coverage for many types of watercraft, and yet there are many types covered by operation. The following types of powerplants and vessels are covered:

| Type of Engine/Vessel | Specifications | Relationship to Insured |
|---|---|---|
| Inboard or inboard-outboard motor | ≤ 50 HP<br>≥ 50 HP | Rented or borrowed<br>Borrowed |
| Outboard motor | ≤ 25 HP<br>≥ 25 HP | Owned, rented, or borrowed<br>Rented, borrowed, or newly acquired |
| Sailboat | ≤ 26′ Long<br>≥ 26′ Long | Owned, rented, or borrowed<br>Borrowed |
| Any Type | In storage | Owned, rented, or borrowed |

In other words, the policy does not cover owned inboards, but coverage applies to small owned outboards, short owned sailboats and anything while stored.

Aircraft and hovercraft liability is excluded.

### Section II—Exclusions for Coverage E

With respect to Coverage E liability only, the policy excludes:

- contractual liability under any oral or written contract or agreement. (however, the exclusion is modified so that the policy covers written contracts that relate to the ownership, maintenance, or use of an insured location or where the insured assumes the liability of others before an occurrence);
- loss assessments charged against the insured as a member of an association, a corporation or a community of property owners;
- bodily injury subject to workers' compensation law or a similar law;
- property damage to property the insured owns, occupies, rents or to property in the insured's care, custody, or control. However, the exclusion is again modified so that the policy covers property damage caused by fire, smoke, or explosion, even if occupied by or in the care, custody or control of the insured (known as **fire legal liability**);
- loss from nuclear hazards; and
- bodily injury to the insured.

**Section II—Exclusions for Coverage F**

With respect only to Coverage F, Medical Payments, there is no coverage for bodily injury to any:

- person subject to a workers' compensation law or similar law;
- insured;
- person other than a residence employee residing on the insured premises (such as a boarder); or
- residence employee if bodily injury occurs off the insured's location and does not arise out of or in the course of the residence employee's employment by the insured.

## Conditions to Section II

With respect to Coverage E and F, the policy includes the following conditions to any claim for bodily injury or property damage.

- The limit of liability applies per occurrence and does not increase regardless of the number of persons the policy insures.
- The severability of insurance means that the policy applies to each insured as though a separate policy were issued, but does not increase the limit of liability.
- An insured's duties after a loss include giving notice of claims and forwarding any suits or demands.
- The insured must cooperate in the defense and settlement of any claim.
- Other insurance is considered primary, and this policy is excess, except in the case of a policy designed specifically to provide excess coverage above this policy.

### Quick Quiz 12.3

1. Under Coverage E, Personal Liability of the Homeowners Policy, the insurer agrees to pay all sums the insured is legally obligated to pay as damages for __________ __________ or __________ __________.

2. Coverage F, Medical Payments to Others, applies to reasonable medical expenses incurred within __________ years of an accident.

3. Additional Coverages under Section II of the homeowners policy provides coverage for up to __________ for damage to property of others.

4. Coverage is provided under Section II of the homeowners policy for assessments against the insured under certain circumstances. The limit provided is __________.

5. A sailboat is covered for liability under a homeowners policy if it is less than __________ feet in length.

**Answers**

1. *bodily injury; property damage*
2. *three (3)*
3. *$1,000*
4. *$1,000*
5. *26*

## Endorsements to Section II

Endorsements available under Section II apply to the following.

**Personal Injury** This endorsement changes the definition of bodily injury to include false arrest, detention, or imprisonment; malicious prosecution, libel, slander, or defamation of character; and invasion of privacy, wrongful eviction, and wrongful entry.

**Business Pursuits** This endorsement extends coverage under Section II to any of the insured's business pursuits listed in the endorsement. The endorsement does not apply to businesses the insured owns or controls, to professional liability; or to injuries to fellow employees.

**Additional Residence Rented to Others** This endorsement extends liability and medical payments coverage to a one-family to four-family residence the insured owns and rents to others. The locations must be listed in the endorsement.

✓ ***Take Note:*** This endorsement eliminates the need to add the personal liability supplement to a dwelling policy issued to cover the residential structure the insured owns and rents to others.

## Endorsements to Section I and Section II

Some endorsements to the homeowners policy affect both Section I and Section II. Some of the more common endorsements include the following.

**Permitted Incidental Occupancies—Residence Premises** This endorsement deletes or modifies the exclusions pertaining to a business under both the policy's property and liability sections. The business must be described in the endorsement and conducted by the insured on the residence premises. The endorsement eliminates the exclusion for other structures used in whole or in part for business, deletes the $2,500 limitation for business property under Coverage C and eliminates the exclusion for business pursuits under the policy's liability section.

**Structures Rented to Others** Coverage B excludes coverage for structures that are rented to anyone other than a resident of the household. This endorsement deletes that exclusion and also adds coverage under the liability section for property rented to others. This can be an important endorsement for someone with a garage or another outbuilding that has been put to use for a home business.

**Home Day-Care Coverage** This coverage deletes the exclusion under Coverage B for business use, eliminates the $2,500 restriction on business property under Coverage C and extends the coverage under Section II to apply to day care operations. The endorsement also changes the limit for Coverage E liability from an occurrence limit to an annual aggregate. Requests for this endorsement receive a great deal of underwriting scrutiny.

# Basic Types of Construction

Fire has the greatest potential to inflict a total property loss. When insurance underwriters are evaluating a potential fire loss, they assess four property features COPE:

- **C**onstruction
- **O**ccupancy
- **P**rotection
- **E**xternal exposures

The construction of the building is determined by the types of materials used in the building and roof of the insured structure. Construction materials are also found in the building's interior finish and insulation. Other construction factors that an underwriter considers include the number of fire divisions in the building, the adequacy of electrical circuits for the occupancy, the number of stories, the building's age, and the type of heating system.

Most underwriters recognize six construction classifications or types:

- Class #1–frame
- Class #2–joisted masonry
- Class #3–noncombustible
- Class #4–masonry noncombustible
- Class #5–modified fire resistive
- Class #6–fire resistive

**Class 1–Frame** Frame structures have outside support walls, roof, and floors constructed of wood or other combustible materials. The exterior walls may be covered with stucco or brick veneer and the interior walls are typically lath and plaster.

**Class 2–Joisted Masonry** Joisted masonry structures have outside support walls made of noncombustible masonry materials (concrete, brick, hollow concrete block, stone, or tile) and a roof and floor made of combustible materials (e.g., wood).

**Class 4–Masonry Noncombustible** Masonry noncombustible structures have exterior walls made of masonry materials, such as adobe, concrete, stone, tile, or gypsum block. The floors and the roof are constructed of noncombustible or slow burning materials.

**Class 5–Modified Fire Resistive** Modified fire resistive buildings have exterior walls, floors, and roof constructed of masonry or fire resistant material, with a fire resistant rating of one hour or more, but less than two hours.

**Class 6–Fire Resistive** Fire resistive buildings are constructed of fire resistive materials to reduce the severity of a potential fire. Lower fire insurance rates apply to fire resistive construction.

## Mobile Home Insurance

Mobile homeowners insurance was written historically on a monoline form (coverage on the property only) similar to the dwelling policy form written on other houses. With the advent of package policy forms in the 1950s, the policy was changed to a multi-line form resembling the regular homeowners package policy form discussed previously. Monoline mobile homeowners policies had one important distinction in that any structure attached to the mobile home had to be added by endorsement.

The coverages available under the multiline mobile homeowners form are very similar to those presented in the homeowners policy section. Because of this similarity, the description of coverages presented here will be brief. Coverage for a mobile home may be provided by Endorsement HO 12 45 10 to a homeowners policy (HO-2 or HO-3). Also, a mobile home tenant may be covered by a tenant homeowners form (HO-4). The endorsements available for a homeowners policy also are available for the mobile homeowners form, along with many others unique to a mobile home.

## Coverage

The mobile homeowners form may be written on an open perils basis and the coverage on the building (the mobile home) is settled on the basis of replacement cost. Additional items of property attached to the mobile home are covered on an ACV basis.

**Test Topic Alert!** The mobile homeowners form covers damage from earthquakes.

The mobile homeowners form differs from the homeowners policy in some respects, while following it in others.

### Distinctions in Coverage

- Mobile home coverage Section A applies to the building (mobile home), attached structures, utility tanks, and permanently installed items, such as appliances, dressers and cabinets, floor coverings, and similar property if installed on a permanent basis.
- Mobile home coverage Section B for other structures is similar to the homeowners form.
- Mobile home coverage Section C for personal property generally is written with a limit equal to 40% of Coverage A rather than the 50% specified for homeowners coverage.
- Mobile home coverage Section D, loss of use, is 20% of Coverage A.
- The pair and set clause is expanded to include panels as a series of pieces or panels.
- Removal coverage is expanded to provide up to $500 for reasonable expenses incurred in moving the mobile home when threatened by a covered peril.
- The ordinance or law additional coverage (to cover increased costs of repair or reconstruction due to zoning laws or building ordinances that require upgrades after a loss) does not apply to mobile home policies.

### Endorsements

#### *Transportation/Permission to Move Endorsement (Transportation Trip Endorsement)*

The coverage is 30 days for collision, upset, stranding, or sinking while being moved to a new location.

#### *Mobile Home Actual Cash Value Settlement*

Rather than insure to 80% of replacement cost, an option exists to insure the building on an ACV basis.

#### *Property Removed Increased Limit*

This endorsement increases the $500 automatic limit in increments of $250, up to a maximum of $2,500.

### *Ordinance or Law*

This endorsement provides coverage similar to that under the homeowners program. Part of the coverage may be used for expenses incurred in removing debris.

## Premium Credits

The following will lower the insurance premium for the owner of the mobile home.

- Reduce Coverage C (personal property) limits to 30% of Coverage A
- Insurer-approved alarm, fire system, or both
- Automatic sprinkler system
- Two versions of tie-down (secure mobile home): Tie-down credit is based on the fact that mobile homes are, by their nature, more susceptible to losses due to windstorms. Credit is given whenever the mobile home is more securely attached to land.

# Unit Test Twelve

1. A house has an actual cash value of $40,000 and a replacement cost of $60,000. To receive a replacement cost settlement in the event of a loss, what is the minimum amount of insurance that must be carried?
   A. $32,000
   B. $40,000
   C. $48,000
   D. $60,000

2. Which of the following kinds of property is NOT excluded under the homeowners policy?
   A. Property specifically insured elsewhere
   B. Property of a relative living with the insured
   C. Motorized vehicles
   D. Animals, birds, and fish

3. Which homeowners form provides open perils coverage for both the dwelling and its contents?
   A. HO-3
   B. HO-5
   C. HO-4
   D. HO-8

4. Which of the following is NOT automatically included in homeowners coverage?
   A. Personal property
   B. Personal liability
   C. Additional living expense
   D. Personal injury

5. Which homeowners form provides open perils coverage for the dwelling and broad perils coverage for its contents?
   A. HO-1
   B. HO-2
   C. HO-3
   D. HO-8

6. Which of the following does NOT provide broad form coverage on personal property?
   A. HO-1
   B. HO-2
   C. HO-4
   D. HO-6

7. Under an HO-3 policy, if the insured meets the 80% insurance-to-value requirement, replacement cost coverage applies to all of the following EXCEPT
   A. buildings
   B. personal property
   C. storage sheds
   D. patio covers

8. Homeowners policy Coverage A applies to which of the following?
   A. Other structures
   B. The dwelling
   C. Loss of use
   D. Personal property

9. If a dog chews up the insured's fur coat, which of the following homeowners policies provides coverage?
   A. HO-2
   B. HO-3
   C. HO-5
   D. None of the above

10. In a homeowners policy, how much is the insured's personal property covered for when it is permanently located in a secondary residence?
   A. 10%
   B. 25%
   C. 50%
   D. 100%

11. Under Section I of a homeowners policy, if there is a loss to an article that is part of a pair or set, the insurance company pays
    A. the total value of the pair or set
    B. the total value of the pair or set after confiscating the remaining item
    C. a fair proportion of the total value of the pair or set
    D. only the value of the item lost

12. If, shortly after the inception date of a homeowners policy, the insured builds an addition to his home, which of the following statements is CORRECT?
    A. The materials used are covered, but not the addition.
    B. The addition is covered as part of the described dwelling.
    C. The policy continues in force, but covers only the original part of the dwelling.
    D. There is no coverage for remodeling under a homeowners policy.

13. Homeowners policies contain special limits on each of the following items of property EXCEPT
    A. theft of money, securities, and valuable papers
    B. theft of jewelry, watches, and furs
    C. fire damage to guns and firearms
    D. theft of silverware or goldware

14. An insured buys a house for $52,000. It is estimated that if the house were destroyed totally by fire, it would cost $47,000 to rebuild. Because of condition and age, the actual cash value of the house is $39,000. What is the proper amount of insurance the owner should purchase under a homeowners policy?
    A. $39,000
    B. $41,600
    C. $47,000
    D. $52,000

15. Under homeowners policies, what percentage of Coverage A applies to personal property?
    A. 40
    B. 50
    C. 70
    D. 75

16. An example of coverage provided under HO-2 that is NOT covered under HO-1 is
    A. falling objects
    B. theft
    C. windstorm
    D. vandalism

17. The standard deductible under any homeowners policy is
    A. $100
    B. $250
    C. $500
    D. $750

18. Under an HO-2 policy, the amount of insurance that applies to other structures is
    A. 10%
    B. 20%
    C. 40%
    D. 50%

19. All of the following are eligible for a homeowners policy EXCEPT an owner of a
    A. mobile home
    B. two-family dwelling
    C. condominium
    D. dwelling under construction

20. Under the homeowners program, which of the following is included as an insured?
    A. Spouse of the named insured who lives in an apartment several blocks away
    B. A 19-year-old exchange student who resides temporarily with the insured
    C. Child of the insured who lives in an apartment on the other side of town
    D. 35-year-old invalid who is cared for by the named insured

21. An insured location under the homeowners program includes all of the following EXCEPT

    A. vacant land
    B. land on which a new home is being constructed
    C. premises acquired during the policy term
    D. premises owned but not declared on the inception date of the policy

22. Which Homeowners form provides broad form coverage for both the dwelling and its contents?

    A. HO-1
    B. HO-2
    C. HO-3
    D. HO-8

23. If an HO-2 broad form policy is issued with a limit of $50,000 on the dwelling, the standard amount of personal property coverage is

    A. $20,000
    B. $25,000
    C. $30,000
    D. $50,000

# Unit Test Twelve Answers & Rationale

1. **C.** The homeowners policy requires that to obtain a replacement cost settlement for a loss, the insured must carry an amount of insurance on Coverage A equal to at least 80% of the full replacement value. 80% of $60,000 is $48,000.

2. **B.** The property of any resident relative is covered under Coverage C of the homeowners policy.

3. **B.** The HO-3 policy provides open perils coverage on Coverages A and B. However, the HO-5 policy also provides open perils coverage on Coverage C.

4. **D.** Personal injury coverage can be added to the homeowners policy only by endorsement.

5. **C.** The HO-3 policy provides open perils coverage on Coverages A and B. However, the HO-5 policy also provides open perils coverage on Coverage C.

6. **A.** The basic HO-1 policy provides limited named perils coverage for all property items the policy covers.

7. **B.** Replacement cost coverage under the homeowners program is included only for real property items, buildings, and attached structures. Replacement cost on personal property (Coverage C) is included by endorsement only.

8. **B.** Coverage A of the Homeowners policy covers dwellings and attached structures.

9. **D.** Homeowners policies exclude damage to personal property by domestic animals.

10. **A.** All homeowners policies provide worldwide coverage for personal property. The only limitation is 10% of Coverage C applicable to personal property located permanently in a secondary residence.

11. **C.** The insurer's obligation for loss to a pair or set is limited to the difference between the value of the set before the loss and the value of items that remain following the loss.

12. **B.** Coverage A of the homeowners policy includes coverage for the dwelling on the residence premises, including structures attached to the dwelling, such as an attached garage.

13. **C.** The only limitation on firearms under the homeowners policy is a special limit of $2,000 for theft of guns and other items. No such limitation exists for fire losses.

14. **C.** A home's market value is irrelevant to the insurable amount for homeowners policy purposes. In this case, the full cost to repair or replace the home is $47,000 and should be the amount of insurance purchased.

15. **B.** Although not a contractual requirement, the homeowners policy includes a limit on Coverage C equal to 50% of the Coverage A limit unless it has been increased by endorsement.

16. **A.** The HO-1 policy includes the named perils of fire, lightning, windstorm, hail, explosion, riot, civil commotion, aircraft, vehicles, smoke, vandalism, malicious mischief, theft, breakage of glass, and volcanic eruption.

17. **B.** The standard deductible included in the homeowners program is $250. This amount may be increased and a rate credit applied.

18. **A.** Under HO-1, HO-2, HO-3, HO-5, and HO-8, the amount that applies to Coverage B, Other Structures, equals 10% of the limit for Coverage A.

19. **A.** Eligibility for a Homeowners policy is limited to an owner-occupied one-family or two-family dwelling, the intended owner-occupant of a dwelling under construction, one co-owner

occupant of a two-family dwelling, a person occupying and purchasing a home under a sales contract and a person occupying a dwelling under a life estate.

20. **B.** Persons insured under homeowners policies include the named insured and a spouse if he resides in the household, resident relatives, and anyone younger than age 21 in the insured's care.

21. **D.** Insured locations under the homeowners program include the residence premises, other premises the insured uses as a residence if declared in the policy, new premises acquired during the policy period, nonowned premises where the insured is residing temporarily, vacant land, land on which a residence is being constructed and cemetery or burial plots.

22. **B.** The HO-2 broad form provides broad named perils coverage for Coverages A, B, and C.

23. **B.** The policy includes 50% of the Coverage A limit for Coverage C automatically unless increased by endorsement.

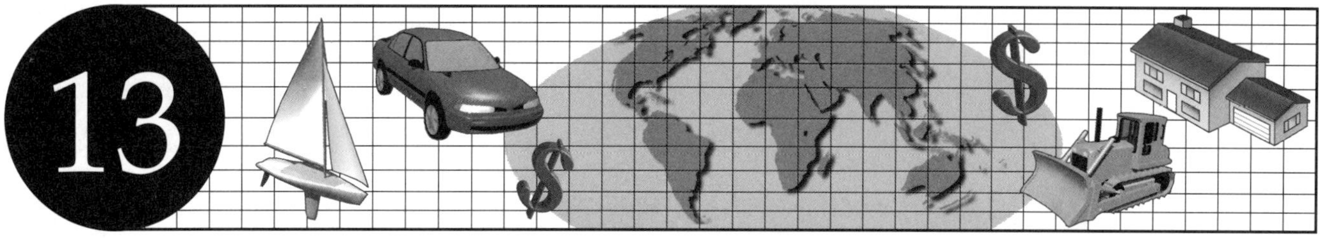


# Dwelling Policies

## INTRODUCTION

During the early 1950s, most states passed legislation permitting insurance companies writing specified lines to write all lines, or multi-lines insurance. As a result, a single insurer might be authorized to write fire and marine insurance, as well as casualty and surety insurance. For financial as well as regulatory reasons, life and health insurance lines were kept separate.

Until this change in the law, personal buyers of insurance were forced to obtain several policies to treat their exposures to loss. Purchasing one policy for the dwelling structure, one for the dwelling contents, and a separate one for liability was commonplace. Following multiple-line legislation, the homeowners policy began packaging coverages in a single contract to provide for most of a homeowner's, tenant's or, later, condominium unit owner's insurance needs.

These package policies were discussed in the previous unit. The dwelling fire policy available from ISO fills a significant need in the marketplace for owners of residential property who otherwise do not qualify for homeowners policies.

## UNIT OBJECTIVES

When you have completed this unit, you should be able to:

- state the purpose of the dwelling program and its special characteristics;
- identify the coverages provided under the basic, broad, and special dwelling forms; and
- describe the endorsements available under the dwelling program and how they may be used to tailor coverage for an insured.

# Dwelling Coverage

When homeowners insurance is unavailable, an individual may wish to buy a **dwelling policy**, as in the following situations:

- a residential structure is owned by one person and rented to others (tenant-occupied);
- the dwelling involves certain risks that may not be acceptable to the insurer for homeowners coverage, such as age or value; and
- the dwelling is disclosed as a seasonal dwelling on the application.

The most common use of a dwelling form is to provide coverage for a single-family residential structure that the owner does not occupy, but rents to others. Because this is the most common situation, the dwelling policy does not provide theft or liability coverage. The reason for these limitations is simple: if property is stolen from a rented dwelling, it does not belong to the insured, but to the tenant. Liability insurance usually is extended from the insured's homeowners policy using an endorsement. If there is a need to provide either theft or liability coverage under the dwelling program, both coverages are available as endorsements to the basic policy.

**Test Topic Alert!** Theft is not a covered peril in a dwelling policy.

## Eligible Property

Properties eligible for dwelling coverage include:

- dwellings (except farm dwellings) that are:
  - designed for not more than four families or four apartments; or
  - occupied by not more than five roomers or boarders;
- mobile homes, but only those on permanent foundations;
- private outbuildings used in connection with an insured property;
- household and personal property in the above risks; and
- vacant buildings.

## Coverage Forms

### Dwelling Forms

The **dwelling fire (DF) program**, first developed in the early 1970s, used the standard fire policy with the attachment of a separate dwelling form. In 1977, a new form was developed—the **dwelling policy (DP)**, a simplified or plain language policy. Unlike the DF program, the DP is a complete policy, not an attachment to the standard fire policy. Three versions of the DP form are available: **DP-1 Basic** (DP 00 01 12), **DP-2 Broad** (DP 00 02 12), and **DP-3 Special** (DP 00 03 12).

**FIGURE 13.1 Outline of Dwelling Policies**

| | Basic Form DP-1 | Broad Form DP-2 | Special Form DP-3 |
|---|---|---|---|
| ***Coverage:*** | | | |
| A—Dwelling | X | X | X |
| B—Other Structures | X | X | X |
| C—Personal Property | X | X | X |
| D—Rental Value | X | X | X |
| E—Living Expense | By endorsement | X | X |
| ***Perils Insured Against:*** | Fire<br>Lightning<br>Internal explosion<br><br>*Optional*<br>Extended Coverage Endorsement (ECE) includes:<br>Windstorm or Hail<br>Explosion<br>Riot or Civil Commotion<br>Aircraft<br>Vehicles<br>Smoke<br>Volcanic Eruption<br>Vandalism and Malicious Mischief (VMM) includes:<br>Vandalism | Fire<br>Lightning<br>ECE–see DP-1<br>VMM–see DP-1<br>Damage by burglars<br>Falling objects<br>Weight of ice, snow, sleet<br>Discharge/overflow of water/steam<br>Tearing apart, cracking, burning, bulging of steam or water system<br>Freezing of plumbing, heating, air conditioning, or sprinkler systems<br>Artificially generated electric current<br>Volcanic eruption | *Dwelling and Other Structures*<br>Risks of direct physical loss<br><br>*Personal Property*<br>Broad Form Perils Only |

The Basic and Broad forms of coverage are specified or named perils. DP-3, the Special form, is an open perils policy.

## Coverages Provided

Coverages A, B, C, and D are available on all DP forms. Coverage E may be added by endorsement to DP-1. The coverages are available in any combination, making the dwelling program very flexible. Coverages D and E may be purchased only if other property coverage is included in the policy. Coverage is indicated by a limit shown on the Declarations Page.

### Coverage A: Dwelling

**Coverage A: Dwelling** applies to the dwelling building shown in the Declarations, to attached structures and to service-related equipment, and outdoor equipment, located on the premises. Coverage also is provided for materials and supplies located on or adjacent to the described location that are to be used in the construction, repair, or alteration of the dwelling or other structures. The insured may select any limit under Coverage A. This coverage does not apply to land, including land on which the dwelling is located.

### Coverage B: Other Structures

**Coverage B: Other Structures** applies to real property located on the described location and separated from the dwelling by clear space. Structures that are attached to the dwelling only by a fence, utility line, or similar connection are considered other structures and should be included in Coverage B. A detached garage, storage shed, or pump house all are considered other structures. This coverage does not apply to land, including land on which the dwelling is located. Up to 10% of Coverage A is included automatically for other structures in all DP forms, so insureds with minimal exposures may not need to purchase it as a separate item of insurance. Under the DP-1, this 10% coverage extension does not increase the amount of insurance available, while under DP-2 and DP-3 it serves as an additional amount of insurance.

### Coverage C: Personal Property

**Coverage C: Personal Property** applies to personal property located at the described location that is usual to the occupancy of a dwelling. The property may be owned or used by the insured or family members. At the insured's request, personal property items belonging to guests or domestic employees may also be covered. Personal property moved to a new location intended to be a principal residence is covered automatically for up to 30 days, subject to policy expiration. If the insured is a tenant, improvements, alterations, and additions to the property are an extension of coverage for up to 10% of Coverage C. In DP-1, this does not increase the amount of insurance. Once again, for DP-2 and DP-3 this is an additional amount of insurance.

The insurer does not cover accounts, bank notes, bills, coins, and other types of documentation and valuables (see Coverage C, Personal Property), animals, aircraft, motor vehicles and their equipment and accessories, watercraft, data, credit cards, or fund transfer cards.

### Coverage D: Fair Rental Value; Coverage E: Additional Living Expense

Coverages D and E are indirect property coverages and apply only in the event there is a covered loss to other property items insured under the policy.

**Coverage D: Fair Rental Value** pays the fair rental value of the portion of the described location that is rented or held for rental to others at the time of the loss. Fair rental value refers to the market rental value less any expenses that would not continue in the event of a loss, such as utilities. Payment is for the shortest time required to repair or replace the part of the location rented.

**Coverage E: Additional Living Expense** pays those expenses the insured incurs when the property is unfit for its normal use following a covered loss. Additional living expenses refers to the increased expenses that must be incurred for the occupants to maintain their normal lifestyles and standards of living. Payment will be for the shortest time required to repair or replace the property, or for the insured to settle elsewhere.

✓ ***For Example:*** The cost to relocate to a hotel while fire damage is being repaired is covered as an additional living expense because it represents an extraordinary expense to the insured, over and above the normal rent or mortgage payment.

Under the basic form, the insured may apply up to 10% of the Coverage A limit for fair rental value. Payment is limited to 1⁄12 of the total amount per month, and it does not increase the limit of liability. Under the Broad and Special forms, up to 10% of Coverage A may be applied to either or both fair rental value and additional living expense. It functions as an additional amount of insurance.

✓ ***Take Note:*** The additional coverages the dwelling policy provides, such as 10% for other structures, 10% for tenant's improvements and betterments, 10% for fair rental value, and 10% for an ordinance or law requiring the construction demolition or remodeling of an insured property are included as Additional Coverage under forms DP-2 and DP-3. Under the Basic form DP-1, these amounts are included in the limits of liability and thus do not provide additional coverage.

## Quick Quiz 13.1

1. All of the following types of property are eligible for a dwelling policy EXCEPT

   A. dwellings designed for four families
   B. mobile homes on permanent foundations
   C. farm dwellings
   D. vacant buildings

2. Dwelling Policy DP-1 (Basic form) automatically includes all of the following coverages EXCEPT

   A. Coverage A: Dwelling
   B. Coverage C: Personal Property
   C. Coverage D: Fair Rental Value
   D. Coverage E: Additional Living Expense

3. Which of the following statements regarding the Dwelling Policy DP-3 Special form is CORRECT?

   A. Other Structures are included for coverage equal to 10% of Coverage A.
   B. The policy is issued on an open perils basis.
   C. Collapse of the building is included for coverage for limited named perils.
   D. All of the above are correct.

### Answers

1. **C.** *Farms are not eligible for either dwelling or homeowners policies. They must be separately insured under the farm program.*

2. **D.** *Additional living expense can be added to the DP-1 only by endorsement.*

3. **D.** *Each of the listed features is contained in the Special form DP-3.*

## Other Coverages

Other extensions of coverage that do not increase the amount of insurance are:

- debris removal;
- personal property located anywhere in the world (up to 10% of Coverage C);
- rental value, so that the insured may use up to 10% of the Coverage A limit of liability for loss of fair rental value (20% in DP-2 and DP-3 with additional living expense also included)
- cost of reasonable and temporary repairs;
- property removed from an endangering peril (5 days in DP-1; 30 days in DP-2 and DP-3);
- collapse of the building or any part due to any of the Broad form perils or hidden decay, hidden insect or vermin damage, the weight of contents or rain that collects on the roof, or use of defective building materials or methods if the collapse occurs during the course of construction, repair, or remodeling (DP-2 and DP-3); and
- breakage of glass or safety glazing material, but not if the dwelling has been vacant for more than 30 consecutive days before the loss (DP-2 and DP-3).

All DP forms include an additional amount of coverage of $500 for fire department service charges incurred to save or protect property from loss by a covered peril. No deductible applies. This coverage does not apply if the insured property is located in a city, municipality or fire protection district.

Both the broad and special forms provide additional amounts of insurance for lawns, trees, shrubs, and plants. The coverage is for the limited specified

**FIGURE 13.2 Limits in the Dwelling Program**

| | DP-1 | DP-2 | DP-3 |
|---|---|---|---|
| Coverage A: Real Property | Declared Value | Declared Value | Declared Value |
| Coverage A: Other Structures | 10% Within Limits | 10% Outside Limits | 10% Outside Limits |
| Coverage C: Personal Property | Declared Value | Declared Value | Declared Value |
| Coverage D: Rental Value | 10% Within Limits | 10% Outside Limits | 10% Outside Limits |

perils of fire, lightning, explosion, riot or civil commotion, aircraft, vehicles not owned or operated by a resident of the described location, and vandalism or malicious mischief. Coverage is limited to 5% of Coverage A, subject to a sublimit of $500 applicable to any one tree, shrub or plant.

## Endorsements

As noted earlier, the dwelling program is designed for individuals who do not qualify for homeowners policies and, as such, is not intended to be as comprehensive in scope as the homeowners program. Therefore, some coverage must be purchased separately.

### Theft

Coverage for **theft** of personal property may be added to any of the DP forms using one of two endorsements. Broad theft coverage is available only if the insured is an owner-occupant of the dwelling. Coverage is included for theft, including attempted theft, and for vandalism and malicious mischief as a result of a theft or an attempted theft. **Vandalism and malicious mischief (VMM) coverage** does not apply if the dwelling has been vacant for more than 30 consecutive days before the loss. Coverage is available for both on- and off-premises exposures.

The **limited theft coverage** endorsement may be added to a dwelling policy when the insured is not an owner-occupant. The causes of loss are the same as they are under the broad theft endorsement, but coverage is provided for on-premises exposures only.

Both endorsements contain a list of property that is limited to a specific dollar amount in the event of loss. Both also contain an extensive list of property that is not included for coverage under the terms of the endorsements.

## Personal Liability

The personal liability supplement to the dwelling program is available for those instances when the owner cannot attach coverage to a homeowners policy. When included in the dwelling policy, coverage is essentially the same as Section II of a homeowners policy, discussed in the preceding unit.

**Test Topic Alert!**

A dwelling policy provides no coverage for personal liability. Personal liability can be covered under the insured's homeowners policy, or the coverage can be added by endorsement.

## Dwelling Under Construction

This endorsement covers a dwelling or structure while it is under construction, if the dwelling or structure is under Coverage A. The premium is determined from an average amount of insurance during construction.

The limit of liability as noted in the declarations for Coverage A is provisional, and the actual amount of insurance on a specific date is a percentage of the provisional amount. This percentage is based on the proportion that the property's actual value bears to its value when it is completed.

The insured must notify the insurer when construction is completed and allow the insurer to inspect the dwelling for the purpose of adjusting the premium. The building may be occupied as a dwelling under Coverage A for 30 days after construction is completed.

## General Exclusions

Loss caused directly or indirectly by the following are excluded:

- Ordinance or law, although DP-2 and DP-3 have some limited coverage for such events
- Earth movement, meaning earthquake, volcanic eruption, and other shifting; if fire or explosion occurs, the ensuing loss is covered
- Water damage
- Power failure
- Neglect, meaning failure to use reasonable means to save and preserve property
- War
- Nuclear hazard
- Intentional loss

Lawns, plants, shrubs, or trees outside of buildings are also excluded.

# Unit Test Thirteen

1. Which of the following is NOT a situation that warrants the use of a dwelling policy?
   A. The insured does not wish to purchase a homeowners policy due to cost.
   B. A residential structure is not owner-occupied, but is rented by a tenant.
   C. The dwelling involves unacceptable risks that may not qualify for homeowners coverage.
   D. The dwelling is seasonal and occupied only during certain times of the year.

2. All of the following are eligible for dwelling policies EXCEPT a
   A. mobile home
   B. vacant building
   C. farm dwelling
   D. four-family dwelling

3. Which of the following dwelling forms are issued on a special causes of loss basis?
   A. DP-1
   B. DP-2
   C. DP-3
   D. All of the above

4. Which of the following statements regarding vandalism coverage under the dwelling program is CORRECT?
   A. It is included automatically in DP-1 and DP-2.
   B. It can be added by endorsement to DP-3.
   C. It is available by endorsement to DP-1 and DP-2.
   D. It is provided automatically in DP-3.

5. Which of the following statements regarding Coverage E of the dwelling program is CORRECT?
   A. It provides liability coverage under all the forms.
   B. It is available as an endorsement to DP-1.
   C. It is available by endorsement only to DP-2 and DP-3.
   D. Coverage E is not available in the dwelling program.

6. When coverage is provided using the DP-1 form, the amount of coverage provided automatically for other structures is what percentage of the limit for Coverage A?
   A. 10%
   B. 20%
   C. 30%
   D. There is no automatic coverage.

7. When coverage is provided under the DP-3 policy, which of the following statements regarding other structures coverage is CORRECT?
   A. It is included within the limit for Coverage A.
   B. It is provided in addition to the limit for Coverage A.
   C. It is not provided except by endorsement.
   D. It is provided only when Coverage B is selected.

8. All of the following are considered other structures under a dwelling policy EXCEPT a(n)
   A. detached garage
   B. free-standing storage shed
   C. pump house
   D. attached patio cover

9. A DP-3 form covers personal property for what limit?
   A. The limit the insured selects
   B. 50% of Coverage C
   C. 50% of Coverage A
   D. 10% of Coverage A

10. Coverage D under the dwelling program provides coverage for
    A. additional living expense
    B. loss of use
    C. fair rental value
    D. extra expense

11. Which of the following statements regarding coverage for fair rental value under the DP-1 form is CORRECT?
    A. It is an additional 10% of Coverage A.
    B. It is limited to 1⁄12 of the total amount of coverage per month.
    C. It includes coverage for additional living expenses.
    D. It is included as Coverage E under the dwelling program.

12. Worldwide coverage for personal property under the dwelling program is limited to
    A. 10% of Coverage A
    B. 10% of Coverage C
    C. 50% of Coverage A
    D. Coverage is unlimited.

13. Removal coverage under the DP-3 form is included for how many days?
    A. 5
    B. 10
    C. 30
    D. 45

14. Which of the following statements regarding coverage for trees, shrubs and plants under the dwelling program is CORRECT?
    A. The dwelling program provides no coverage for these items.
    B. They are limited to 10% of Coverage A.
    C. They are included without limit.
    D. They are limited to a maximum of 5% of Coverage A.

15. The additional coverage that may be required under a dwelling policy but is not included automatically is
    A. personal liability
    B. other structures
    C. fair rental value
    D. internal explosion

# Unit Test Thirteen Answers & Rationale

1. **A.** Dwelling policies insure residential structures that do not qualify for homeowners policies because of occupancy or other risk characteristics.

2. **C.** Farm dwellings are not eligible for either dwelling or homeowners policies and must be insured using the farm program.

3. **C.** Both DP-1 and DP-2 are named peril forms. DP-3 is issued on a special causes of loss basis.

4. **D.** Because the DP-3 is an open or special perils form and vandalism is not excluded, it provides coverage automatically for this peril.

5. **B.** Coverage E of the dwelling program is additional living expense coverage. It is included automatically in DP-2 and DP-3, but must be added by endorsement to DP-1.

6. **A.** DP-1 covers other structures in the amount of 10% of the limit for Coverage A. This is not an additional amount of insurance.

7. **B.** Under DP-3, the 10% limit included for other structures increases the total limit available under the policy.

8. **D.** An attached patio coverage is included under Coverage A of a dwelling policy. Only detached structures are included under Coverage B.

9. **A.** No specific limit applies to Coverage C of the dwelling policy. It may be any amount the insured selects.

10. **C.** Coverage D of the dwelling program applies to the property's fair rental value, an indirect loss coverage.

11. **B.** Coverage for fair rental value, Coverage D of the dwelling policy, is limited to $\frac{1}{12}$ of the total limit available. This amount is meant to represent the monthly amount of the covered property's rental value.

12. **B.** A coverage extension of the dwelling policy allows for coverage of personal property while located anywhere in the world. The limit on such losses is 10% of Coverage C.

13. **C.** Removal coverage under DP-1 is limited to 5 days, while DP-2 and DP-3 provide 30 days' coverage for property removed from an endangering peril.

14. **D.** The maximum amount of coverage for lawns, trees, shrubs, and plants under the dwelling program is 5% of Coverage A, subject to a maximum of $500 for any one item.

15. **A.** Because many insureds who purchase dwelling policies also have homeowners coverage, the liability for secondary or rented structures usually is provided by an endorsement to a homeowners policy and therefore is not needed under a dwelling policy.

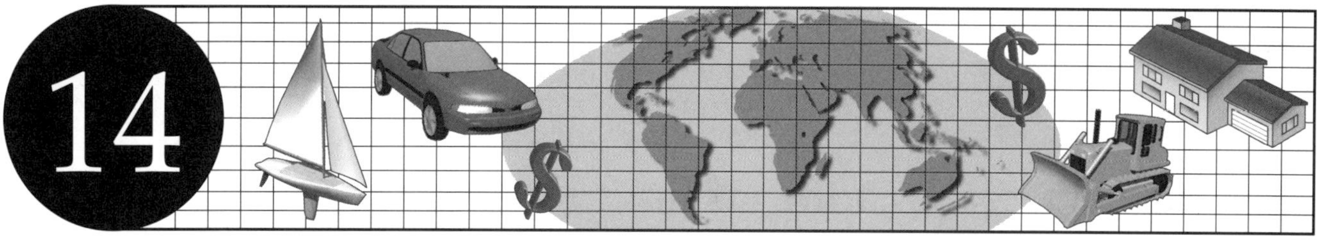


# Marine Insurance and Commercial Floaters

## INTRODUCTION

Marine insurance is an extension of land-based property insurance. Ocean marine coverage was designed to protect ships and their cargo. Inland marine insurance evolved out of ocean marine and was created to insure shipments carried by railroads, trucks and aircraft. Marine insurance is not limited, however, to ocean-going or even transportation risks. Modern marine insurance policies cover any type of property that is being transported, has the potential to be transported or is designed to move property or information from place to place.

The coverages provided under marine policies are highly specialized, unique and, to a great degree, unregulated. Therefore, the marine insurance underwriter has more discretion over pricing and coverage determination. Various exclusions and limitations under commercial property insurance policies apply to property in the course of transit between locations. For this reason, marine insurance policies, both ocean and inland, were developed. The regulated portion of marine insurance is referred to as *filed* because the state insurance department approves the rates and forms companies use. This unit deals with the filed forms of inland marine coverage the Insurance Services Office (ISO) offers.

## UNIT OBJECTIVES

When you have completed this unit, you should be able to:

- describe the coverage an ocean marine insurance policy provides;
- give details of the coverage an ocean marine cargo policy provides;
- discuss the need for inland marine insurance and describe the policies that fall into that insurance category;
- describe the policies available for coverage of personal property under inland marine insurance; and
- discuss coverage for personal watercraft under marine policies.

# Commercial Ocean Marine Insurance

Despite technological advances in marine transportation, ocean disasters remain an ever-present hazard for those engaged in foreign trade. Four major classes of ocean marine insurance provide coverage against four types of losses:

**Hull Insurance**

- Protects a vessel's owner against loss to the ship itself
- Written on an open perils basis
- Contains a special provision called the **running down clause** that provides a form of property damage liability coverage for collision damage to other ships

**Cargo Insurance**

- Written separately from the insurance on the ship
- Protects the cargo's owner from financial losses that result from the cargo's destruction or loss

**Test Topic Alert!**

A commercial ocean marine policy covers **jettison**, which is the throwing of cargo overboard to save the vessel and its crew.

**Freight Insurance**

- Special form of business income insurance
- In the event the vessel is lost or destroyed, this coverage indemnifies the shipowner for the loss of any income that would have been earned upon completion of the voyage.

**Protection and Indemnity (P&I) Insurance**

- Liability insurance that protects the shipowner from the consequences of his agents' negligent acts
- Provides workers' compensation insurance for the vessel's crew members

The policies remain largely unchanged since the early days at Lloyd's coffeehouse, and the contract language has been tested in the courts.

## The Marine Hull Form

The **marine hull form** covers the perils of the seas, including the hostile actions of Men-of-War (fighting ships), pirates, rovers and thieves, fire, lightning, earthquakes, enemies, jettison, barratry, and other perils. **Jettison** is a voluntary act of destruction in which cargo is cast overboard to save the ship or crew. In **barratry**, the master or mariners steal the ship and its cargo, willfully sink or desert the ship, or imperil the vessel by disobeying instructions.

**Free of Capture and Seizure Clause**

When something is **free** in marine insurance, it means that the policy excludes coverage for that particular cause of loss. The **Free of Capture and**

**Seizure Clause** excludes war in all of its aspects. A separate war risk policy may be purchased to cover the perils of war.

### Strike, Riot, and Civil Commotion Clause

The **Strike, Riot, and Civil Commotion Clause** excludes loss or damage caused by acts of strikers, rioters, or persons engaged in civil commotion. It is sometimes deleted if the underwriter is willing to assume the risk.

### Additional Perils Covered

Also covered can be damage caused directly by:

- accidents in loading, discharging, or handling cargo;
- accidents while entering, leaving, or sitting in dry-dock, graving docks, ways, gridirons, or pontoons;
- explosions aboard ship or elsewhere; and
- breakdown of motor generators or other electrical machinery.

### Test Topic Alert!

A **lay-up endorsement** covers watercraft at a reduced premium when the vessel is in storage.

### Deliberate Damage

**Deliberate damage** is covered if caused by government authorities to prevent or mitigate a pollution hazard.

### The Insuring Agreement

The Insuring Agreement includes collision liability and loss during pilotage and towage. Additional coverages are disbursement, manager commissions, profits or excess or increased value of hull and machinery, and freight (including chartered freight or anticipated freight) insured for time in an amount not exceeding in the aggregate 25% of the agreed value, where agreed value is the coverage on the vessel.

### The Deductible Condition

All heavy weather damage or damage caused by contact with floating ice that occurs during a single sea passage between two successive ports is treated as though due to one accident. Therefore, one deductible is applied.

### Exclusions

Commercial ocean marine insurance does not cover the following:

- Capture, seizure, arrest, restraint, or detainment
- Any taking of the vessel by requisition or otherwise, whether in time of peace or war
- Damage or destruction from any mine, bomb, or torpedo not carried as cargo aboard the vessel
- Strikes, lockouts, civil commotions, riots, and martial law
- Malicious acts or vandalism unless committed by the vessel's master or mariners.

# The Ocean Marine Open Cargo Policy

## The Insuring Agreement

Because they date back to 17th century England, ocean marine policies read in a very erudite and poetic manner. The insuring agreement says the policy pays for losses

> "...touching the adventures and perils the underwriters are contended to bear and take upon themselves, they are of the seas, fire, assailing thieves, jettison, and barratry of the Master and Mariners, and like perils."

Unlike the open perils policy, which covers risks of direct physical loss, except as excluded in the form, the ocean marine policy is still technically a named perils policy, because the phrase referring to *like perils* means the coverage applies only to perils very similar to those listed.

## Inchmaree Clause (Additional Perils)

The **Inchmaree Clause** (also called the **Additional Perils clause**) covers bursting boilers, breaking propellor shafts, or damage resulting from any latent defect in the machinery, hull, or appurtenances. The policy also applies to loss due to faults or errors in navigation by the master, mariners, mates, engineers or pilots. The Inchmaree Clause was added to hull policies to counteract an 1887 decision of the British House of Lords, which found that a loss aboard the *Inchmaree* (a vessel) was not covered because it was not of the same nature as the perils of the sea.

✓ ***Take Note:*** The coverage the Inchmaree Clause provides, which includes negligence of the vessel's master and crew members, was important when the Exxon *Valdez* ran aground in 1989 and caused a major oil spill in Alaskan waters. The loss apparently was caused when the ship's captain turned control of the vessel over to an inexperienced junior officer.

## Marine Extensions

The insurance attaches from the time the goods leave the warehouse at the place named in the policy until the goods are delivered to the final warehouse at the destination named.

**Definition of Conveyances**

A means of conveying goods from a point of origin to a destination can take many forms:

- by metal self-propelled vessels and connecting conveyances, but excluding barges and sailing vessels with or without auxiliary power, except as connecting conveyances;
- by aircraft and connecting conveyances; and
- by first class or registered mail; by ordinary registered or government parcel post; and by air or otherwise.

## Quick Quiz 14.1

1. What are the four major classes of ocean marine insurance?

______________________________
______________________________
______________________________
______________________________

2. The Inchmaree Clause of the Ocean Cargo policy provides coverage for what additional causes of loss?

______________________________
______________________________
______________________________
______________________________
______________________________

### *Answers*

1. *hull, cargo, freight, protection and indemnity*
2. *boiler explosion, fault or error of the master, mariners, mates, engineers or pilots*

## Aviation Insurance

Similar to marine insurance, **aviation insurance** covers physical damage to the fuselage (hull) or parts of an aircraft. It also covers liability for personal injury or damage to property that results from the operation of the aircraft.

**Aircraft Hull Insurance** Synonymous with aviation insurance, **aircraft hull insurance** indemnifies the policyholder for damage to or the loss of the aircraft hull, or fuselage.

**Aircraft Liability Insurance** A policy may provide coverage for liability arising from operation of an aircraft. Coverage extends to an insured or other person who operates the insured's aircraft. Benefits are paid for personal injury or property damage arising out of the ownership, maintenance, use, operation, loading, or unloading of the aircraft.

## Inland Marine Insurance

One of the earliest forms of insurance coverages was ocean marine, which covered ships and their cargo on the ocean. This contract covered physical damage as well as liability and tended to be very broad in coverage, what generally is referred to as **open perils**. **Inland marine insurance** developed out of ocean marine insurance to cover property being shipped by land or inland waterways. (Contrast this to fire insurance, which covers property at a specific location.) Because of this concept, the term *floater* is used and applies only to inland marine insurance. For purposes of this text, floaters may be interpreted to mean inland marine insurance policies.

### Nationwide Marine Definition

In 1976, a **Nationwide Marine Definition** was developed that makes no distinction between ocean marine and inland marine, grouping marine insurances together as marine, inland marine, and transportation policies. The principal effect of this definition is to explain inland marine insurance because the definition of ocean marine coverages is generally understood. Inland marine insurance usually is based on transit exposures, but it includes many situations where transit exposure is either negligible or absent. These exceptions have resulted from historical development.

**Test Topic Alert!**

Marine forms cover property in transit. The nationwide marine definition includes property that is imported, exported or shipped to a domestic destination.

Inland marine contracts usually are divided into several categories:

- domestic goods in transit;
- property held by bailees;
- mobile equipment;
- property of certain dealers;
- commercial and personal property floaters;
- means of transportation and communication; and
- difference in conditions policies.

The ISO has developed 13 filed forms for inland marine coverages that are designed to be included in the Commercial Package Policy (CPP):

- accounts receivable (CM 00 66 09);
- camera and musical instrument dealers (CM 00 21 09);
- commercial articles (CM 00 20 09);

- commercial fine arts (CM 00 42 09);
- equipment dealers (CM 00 22 09);
- film coverage (CM 00 45 09);
- floor plan merchandise (CM 00 52 09);
- jeweler's block (CM 00 59 09);
- mail coverage (CM 00 60 09);
- physician's and surgeon's equipment (CM 00 26 09);
- signs (CM 00 28 09);
- theatrical property (CM 00 29 09); and
- valuable papers and records (CM 00 67 09).

## Domestic Goods in Transit

Usually, at least three parties are involved with respect to domestic goods in transit. Because of this, some uncertainty may exist as to who must bear a loss: the shipper (the one sending the goods), the consignee (the one to whom the goods are being sent), or the people actually involved in handling or moving the goods.

### Transit Insurance

**Transit insurance** covers the owners of domestic goods in transit. Often, these policies offer very broad coverage for loss or damage to the property, with many of the policies written on an open perils basis. The coverage may be on an annual basis or for specific cargo during a specific trip, or it may apply only to parcel post or registered mail. Some specific forms include a motor truck cargo-owner's goods on owner's trucks for a firm that transports its own cargo and a transportation floater for a firm that ships goods via a trucking company, a railroad or an airline.

### Cargo Liability Insurance

**Cargo liability policies** cover the carriers of domestic goods in transit. These policies usually provide coverage on a named perils basis and provide coverage only if the insured carrier is liable for loss or damage to the property.

One form that could be used is the **motor truck cargo liability broad form**. However, the term *broad form* has a different meaning here than it does in general property coverage. In marine insurance, the term generally means open perils. This form insures against the direct loss of or damage to property of others that the carrier transports (care, custody or control), but only if the insured carrier is liable for that loss or damage.

## Property Held by Bailees

Some businesses, known as bailees, have a large amount of customer property in their custody. A **bailee** is someone who has care, custody, or control of another's property.

Bailees have custody of others' property for a fee and therefore have a higher degree of responsibility to care for that property while it is in their custody. The customers expect their property to be returned intact or to be paid for any loss or damage to the property, regardless of whether the business was at fault. Businesses such as laundries, dry cleaners, warehouses, parking garages, and storage facilities find it advantageous to provide insurance for the benefit of their customers, even if the bailees are not legally liable. The bailee's policy also covers their own legal liability for damage to customer property when they are negligent. The policy provides coverage under both circumstances, so this type of policy is called a **dual interest policy**.

✓ ***For Example:*** When Bob drives downtown to run errands, he enters a large parking garage with a gated entrance, parks his car and takes the keys with him. He then goes to a dry cleaner to leave some shirts for laundering. When Bob transfers temporary possession and control of the shirts to the dry cleaner, he creates a bailment. For a while, he cannot possess or use the shirts, and the dry cleaner assumes responsibility for their care. When he completes his errands, he returns to the parking garage. There he pays the cashier and drives his car out of the lot. No bailment was created with respect to the car because, by retaining the keys, Bob did not transfer temporary possession or control of the car to the garage. He did not intend to transfer possession or control of it to the garage and could drive it away at any time (after paying the parking fee). The garage also did not accept responsibility for his car.

### Bailee's Customers Insurance

**Bailee's customer policies** are purchased by laundries, dry cleaners and other businesses that have customer property in their care, custody, or control. The policies usually are written on a named perils basis. The insurance covers loss of customer goods regardless of legal liability on the part of the bailee.

These policies usually permit a bailee, such as a dry cleaner, to settle small losses without submitting each small claim to the insurer individually. Such losses are limited, often to $500 per occurrence.

### Furrier's Customers Insurance

Furrier's customer policies differ from bailee's customers insurance in several aspects. First, coverage usually is on an open perils basis. Second, the policies generally require a customer to state a property value on the receipt he or she is given. The policies then limit coverage to the stated amount. Coverage applies only if such a receipt was given with a stated value.

## Use of Floaters for Mobile Equipment and Property

A person or business that has custody or control of property, such as mobile articles, machinery or mobile equipment that is not held for sale, on consignment, or in the course of manufacture, and that intends to use the property for the purpose for which it was manufactured can purchase an **equipment floater**. This kind of property historically has not been covered under property insurance, which primarily covers property at a specified location and only on a limited basis off the premises. Equipment floaters were developed to cover this kind of mobile exposure.

Equipment floaters usually are nonstandard, or manuscripted, policies. The perils to be covered, such as fire, lightning, explosion, and theft, as well as the deductibles and the limits of liability, all are subject to negotiation between the insured and the insurer. Consequently, policies are tailored to meet the insureds' specific needs and circumstances.

### Contractor's Equipment Floaters

Contractors involved in constructing buildings and highways, for instance, may own equipment valued in the hundreds of thousands of dollars, ranging from small hand tools to large pieces of machinery. A contractor can negotiate with an insurer to cover specifically identified equipment as listed in the policy (this method usually is used for large and expensive equipment), equipment at a specific location only or property on a blanket basis (this method is generally used for small, less expensive hand tools). The contractor also may obtain a combination of specified and blanket coverage.

Contractor's equipment floaters often are used to provide the property portion of coverage for vehicles covered for liability insurance under a commercial general liability policy as mobile equipment.

### Other Floaters

Many other types of floaters cover property that may be moved readily from place to place. These include farm equipment floaters, pattern and die floaters, and rented equipment floaters.

## Property of Certain Dealers

Most inland marine policies are designed to cover items that are mobile in nature and not merchandise kept on the insured's premises. However, several policies have been developed to insure certain kinds of merchandise, even though it may be kept on the owner's premises. These kinds of merchandise typically are:

- individual items of high value, even though the items may be small in size;
- property that generally is on the owner's premises, but sometimes may be off the premises because it is loaned, sold on approval or out on consignment; and
- property subject to a broad range of perils.

Coverage on dealer's policies generally is on an open perils basis. Exclusions apply to events that may result in catastrophic loss or events that the insurer considers uninsurable risks.

### Jeweler's Block Policy

Property covered under the **jeweler's block policy** is described in general terms, but includes property customarily found in a jewelry store or in the jewelry department of a department store. Because jewelers often have custody of customers' property for repair, the jeweler's block policy includes coverage similar to the bailee's customers coverage discussed earlier.

This policy excludes property worn by the insured, corporate officers, members of the firm, employees, family members, or relatives. The policy also excludes jewelry worn by a model or another jewelry dealer.

### Furrier's Block Policy

This policy is designed to cover the stock of furs, fur garments, garments trimmed with fur, and accessories that are the insured's property or have been sold but not yet delivered. This policy is similar to the jeweler's block policy.

### Other Policies

Many other types of dealer policies are available, including camera dealer's, musical instrument dealer's, and equipment dealer's policies.

### Fine Art Floaters

**Fine art floaters** can be written to cover art objects such as pictures, statuaries, bronzes and antiques, rare manuscripts and books, antique furniture, and art glass windows. Coverage is generally provided on an open perils basis. Fine art floaters usually are **agreed valued policies**, meaning the insured and insurer agree on a property value and list it in the policy. The insurer pays this amount in case of loss or damage.

These types of policies may be written for fine art dealers or for individuals who own expensive fine art objects. Special provisions exclude damage caused by repair, restoration, or retouching. Breakage of glass and similar fragile items is excluded unless loss is caused by one of the named perils.

## Means of Transportation and Communication

A means of transportation and communication policy covers property at a fixed location that is used in transportation or communication, such as bridges, tunnels, docks, television and radio towers, and power transmission lines.

✓ ***Take Note:*** Although the property such policies cover does not move, vehicles, boats, and data move through or on them, making them suitable subjects for transportation insurance. The technical description of this under the nationwide marine definition is "instrumentalities of transportation or communication."

## Quick Quiz 14.2

1. The ISO commercial lines program provides how many inland marine coverage forms?

   A. 5
   B. 7
   C. 10
   D. 13

2. An owner of goods who uses common carriers for shipping orders may protect the goods while in transit by purchasing which of the following types of policies?

   A. Motor truck cargo
   B. Transit
   C. Bailee's customers
   D. Scheduled personal property

3. Customized bailee forms provide coverage for

   A. legal liability
   B. errors and omissions
   C. expense reimbursement
   D. customer property

### *Answers*

*1.* ***D.*** *13*

*2.* ***B.*** *The transit policy is issued for movement of an insured's property via common or contract carriers.*

*3.* ***D.*** *The policy issued to someone who wishes to insure the property of customers in their care, custody, or control is referred to as a bailee's customers policy.*

# Exclusions in Inland Marine Policies

The typical exclusions inland marine policies contain are:

- governmental action;
- nuclear hazard;
- war and warlike action;
- delay, loss of use, loss of market or other consequential loss, unless specifically added by endorsement;

- dishonest acts by the insured, the insured's employees, or representatives or anyone entrusted with the property (except a carrier for hire);
- alteration, falsification, concealment or destruction of records;
- bookkeeping, accounting, or billing errors;
- electrical or magnetic injury, disturbance, or erasure of electronic recordings;
- voluntary parting with any property if induced to do so by any fraudulent scheme, trick, device or false pretense; and
- unauthorized transfer of property to any person or place.

## Inland Marine Policy Conditions

Two categories of conditions apply under an inland marine policy: loss conditions and general conditions. The general conditions are similar to those discussed under property insurance. **Loss conditions** under an inland marine policy include:

- no abandonment of the property;
- appraisal;
- insured's duties to the insurer in the event of loss;
- insurance under two or more coverages;
- loss payment;
- other insurance (coverage applicable to the property);
- pair, set or parts;
- privilege to adjust with owner (particularly important in bailee's customers policies);
- recovery or salvage;
- reinstatement of limit where the limit of insurance is not reduced by payment of any loss, except a total loss, in which case the insurer deletes the item insured and refunds the unearned premium; and
- transfer of rights of recovery to the insurer.

The **general conditions** consist of:

- fraud, concealment or misrepresentation;
- legal action against the company;
- no benefit to bailee;
- policy period; and
- valuation, which may be the agreed value for fine art and antiques, the actual cash value for some items, such as contractor's equipment floaters, or the replacement cost.

**Quick Quiz 14.3**

1. What are three typical exclusions found in inland marine policies?

   A. ______________________
   B. ______________________
   C. ______________________

2. How does the reinstatement of limit provision operate in an inland marine policy?

   ______________________________________________________________
   ______________________________________________________________

3. How can an inland marine policy's valuation clause be altered for coverage on fine art, antiques and similar items?

   ______________________________________________________________
   ______________________________________________________________

***Answers***

1. *Typical exclusions in inland marine policies are governmental action; nuclear hazard; war and warlike action; delay; loss of use; loss of market and other consequential losses; employee dishonesty and dishonesty of the insured; alteration; falsification; concealment; or destruction of records; bookkeeping or accounting errors; electrical injury or disturbance; voluntary parting with property by way of scheme; trick; or device; and unauthorized transfer of property.*
2. *The limit under an inland marine policy is not reduced because of a loss, with the exception of a total loss to a scheduled item. In that case, the item is deleted from the policy and the unearned premium is returned to the insured.*
3. *Coverage may be issued on an agreed value basis for fine art, antiques, and other items whose replacement cost or actual cash value is difficult or impossible to determine.*

## Difference in Conditions Contract (DIC)

Because all property policies contain exclusions (such as for earthquake, flood and mysterious disappearance), an insured may be interested in covering these gaps. A **Difference in Conditions (DIC) contract** is designed to cover events commercial property policies otherwise exclude.

The DIC excludes coverages normally found in a commercial or personal property policy. It provides coverage for the difference between a very broad open perils policy and the insured's property coverage, typically provided by a building and personal property coverage form or a homeowners policy.

When a DIC is written to insure residential property, the coverage may be referred to as a **wrap around** since it broadens the coverage a homeowners or dwelling policy provides.

# Other Inland Marine Policies

**Installment Sales or Deferred Payments**

Inland marine policies also are available to cover property sold on an installment sales or deferred payment basis. Because a purchaser often does not obtain title to the property until he pays the final installment, the seller could suffer a financial loss if the property were damaged by fire, wind, or another peril. Policies are available to cover the seller's interest in the property upon which the purchaser makes payments.

**Specific Property Otherwise Excluded**

Because most commercial and personal property policies exclude specific property, inland marine policies also are available for:

- neon signs;
- automatic or mechanical electrical signs and street clocks;
- accounts receivable (to cover amounts a business might not be able to collect because its accounts receivable records were destroyed);
- valuable papers and records, such as blueprints, architectural plans, manuscripts, deeds, maps and similar documents; and
- historical documents.

✓ ***Take Note:*** Each of these is written as a separate coverage.

# Personal Property Coverage Forms

## Personal Articles Floater (Scheduled Items)

A **personal articles floater** is characterized by the following:

- Types of property insured include jewelry, furs, fine art, stamp or coin collections, silverware, musical instruments, cameras, golf equipment, and collectibles.

- Coverage may be written as a separate policy or an endorsement to the homeowners form.
- Coverage against risks of direct loss to property (open perils coverage).
- Worldwide coverage is provided, except for fine arts, which are covered only within the United States and Canada.
- Usually, no deductible applies.
- Loss settlement is for the lesser of:
  - actual cash value;
  - cost to repair;
  - cost to replace with a substantially identical article (of like kind and quality); or
  - amount of insurance.

**Test Topic Alert!** A personal articles (or personal property) floater can be purchased as a stand-alone policy or as an endorsement to a homeowners policy. The stand-alone policy usually has no deductible and provides worldwide coverage.

Exceptions to the usual settlement procedure apply to fine art and collectible coins and stamps:

- The settlement amount for fine art is based on an agreed value.
- Coins or stamps are covered on a blanket basis, where the loss settlement is cash market value, but the settlement amount does not exceed $1,000 on any unscheduled coin collection or $250 for any single item.

**Test Topic Alert!** The pair and set clause pays the difference between the value of the property before the loss and its value after the loss.

The personal articles floater includes:

- pair and set clause; and
- automatic coverage for newly acquired items of jewelry, furs, cameras, musical instruments, and fine art, but the limit is 25% of coverage of that class of property or $10,000 maximum. (Note that the maximum limit does not apply to fine art.) The purchase must be reported within 30 days (90 days for fine art), and the premium is charged pro rata from the date of acquisition.

**Exclusions** Exclusions included are those common to open perils property policies:

- wear and tear, gradual deterioration, or inherent vice;
- insects or vermin; and
- war or nuclear hazard.

**Fine Art Coverage**

Fine art coverage has specific exclusions for:

- loss due to any repairing, restoration, or retouching process; and
- breakage, unless caused by fire or an additional listed peril.

Fine art coverage sets specific limits:

- Insurance is on a valued basis, up to the agreed value printed in the schedule.
- A total loss of one item or part of a set results in the insurer paying the value of the entire set and the insured surrendering the remainder of the set to the insurer.
- Coverage continues while the insured property is on exhibition within the continental United States or Canada, but not at fairground, national or international expositions.

✓ ***Test Topic Alert!*** Fine art is insured on a valued basis.

**Postage Stamps and Coins Coverage**

Postage stamps or coins coverage has specific exclusions:

- fading, creasing, denting, scratching, tearing, dampness, extremes of temperature, shipping by other than registered mail; and
- other detailed but similar exclusions.

## Unscheduled Personal Property Floaters

Both of the following policies provide coverage on a worldwide basis and on an open perils basis.

**Personal effects policies** cover any and all personal effects, such as tourists and travelers usually carry or wear.

**Personal property policies** cover all personal property an insured owns, uses, or wears including household property.

## Watercraft

A boat owner faces risks similar to those of an automobile owner. One risk is damage to the owned boat. Another risk is causing injury to others through negligent use of the boat. Watercraft can be covered in a number of ways depending on their size and type. Such craft may be covered under a homeowners policy, a boatowners policy or a yacht policy. These policies insure pleasure craft rather than water taxis or other commercial watercraft.

## Homeowners Treatment of Boats

Under the ISO Homeowners 2000 edition, it was noted that watercraft, including their trailers, furnishings, equipment, and outboard motors, are covered up to $1,500 for physical damage, but not for theft away from the premises.

With respect to liability coverages, the homeowners policy excludes:

- inboard motors the insured owns;
- inboard-outboard motors the insured owns;
- inboard or inboard-outboard motors of more than 50 horsepower the insured rents;
- outboard motor boats of more than 25 horsepower owned by the insured; and
- sailing vessels of 26 feet or more in length, with or without auxiliary power, that the insured owns or rents.

An outboard motor boat of more than 25 horsepower may be covered if the insured:

- acquired it before the policy period; and
- declared it on the policy or reported it within 45 days of the policy's inception; or
- acquires it during the policy period, in which case the boat may be insured for the remainder of the period.

### Boatowners Policy

The **boatowners package policy** provides liability and physical damage coverage much like an auto policy. The general sections of coverage follow:

- Coverage A: Vessel
- Coverage B: Motor (Outboard)
- Coverage C: Trailer
- Coverage D: Miscellaneous Boat Equipment
- Coverage E: Liability
- Coverage F: Medical Payments

### Property Covered

The policy covers physical damage to any boat identified in the Declarations, including:

- permanently attached equipment;
- any motor noted in the declarations, with remote controls and batteries;

- any trailer for transporting the boat; and
- portable equipment and accessories for marine use, but not portable electronic equipment, photographic equipment, water sports equipment, or fishing gear.

The insurer also pays costs to protect the boat from further damage if the boat is involved in a mishap or to recover the boat in the event of sinking or stranding. However, this coverage exists only when the peril causing the loss is covered.

**Coverage** The insurer pays for physical damage resulting from direct and accidental loss to covered property—in other words, open perils coverage. In addition to the liability coverages, the insurer agrees to pay the defense costs of litigation, as is common in liability policies.

**Conditions** One of the policy conditions is that the insured warrants that the covered property will be used exclusively on rivers, streams or inland lakes of the continental United States or Canada.

**Exclusions** The following exclusions apply:

- wear and tear, inherent vice, latent defect, mechanical breakdown, faulty manufacturing, war, and nuclear hazard;
- damage caused by repair or restoration;
- damage the insured causes;
- carrying people for a fee;
- using property in an official race; and
- portable equipment or fishing gear.

## Yacht Policy

The yacht policy is similar to the boatowners policy in that it covers physical damage and liability. The policy sections are as follows:

- **Section I—Hull Insurance**—Open perils coverage on boats and equipment.
- **Section II—Protection and Indemnity Insurance**—Provides marine liability coverage.

The policy generally does not have specific territorial limits. Instead, cruising limits are defined by endorsement and may be worldwide. Premiums are charged based on these limits.

## Optional Coverages

The owner of the vessel may purchase additional coverage to cover a variety of situations in which the vessel may be placed.

- **Federal Longshoremen's and Harbor Workers' Compensation Insurance**—This insurance covers dockside workers attending the vessel.
- **Boat Trailer Insurance**—Provides open perils coverage for the trailer while it transports the boat within the 48 contiguous states.
- **Land Transportation Insurance**—Provides open perils coverage while the boat is being transported on land within 300 miles of home port.
- **Water-Skiing Clause**—Limits coverage while the vessel is engaged in sports like waterskiing. Participants are not covered under liability or medical expense, and other coverages have reduced limits.

# Unit Test Fourteen

1. If an insured has $64,000 of jewelry, furs, and silverware, the best way to cover these items is with a

   A. personal auto policy
   B. homeowners policy
   C. personal effects floater
   D. personal articles floater

2. A woman leaves a very expensive watch on her dressing table in her apartment when she departs on a business trip. When she returns, the watch is gone. This type of loss is referred to as open perils

   A. burglary
   B. robbery
   C. liability
   D. mysterious disappearance

3. Which of the following statements regarding inland marine policies is CORRECT?

   A. Instrumentalities of transportation and communication are insurable.
   B. The personal articles floater covers the ring the insured lost down the drain while doing dishes.
   C. Construction equipment may be insured while located at a job site.
   D. Buildings and personal property at fixed locations can be covered.

4. Which of the following statements regarding inland marine policies is CORRECT?

   A. The personal articles floater excludes coverage as a result of inherent vice.
   B. Standard policy forms are the rule in inland marine insurance.
   C. The exclusions are the same as they are under property insurance policies.
   D. Coverage is not as broad as it is under a commercial property policy.

5. Which of the following statements regarding inland marine policies is CORRECT?

   A. The personal property floater covers the loss of the insured's fur coat stolen out of a parked, unlocked automobile.
   B. Most inland marine policies are written on an open perils basis.
   C. Inland marine policies are not filed with the state regulatory authorities.
   D. A personal property floater covers loss due to a diamond becoming cloudy.

6. Which of the following statements is CORRECT?

   A. Insureds who purchase homeowners coverage may not buy personal property floaters.
   B. Personal jewelry and fur floaters cover all furs and jewelry the insured owns.
   C. Personal property floaters cover personal articles worldwide except for fine art.
   D. Personal property items are covered on a valued basis, meaning the scheduled amount is paid in the event of a loss.

7. All of the following statements are correct EXCEPT

   A. rates for inland marine insurance policies are not filed with the state insurance department
   B. in inland marine insurance, a transportation policy covers a trucker's legal liability for cargo in his custody
   C. inland marine policies usually are issued for personal lines customers only
   D. inland marine policies are more strictly regulated than commercial property policies

8. All of the following statements are correct EXCEPT the
   A. nationwide marine definition sets forth the types of property that marine policies may insure
   B. fine art policy is written on an agreed value basis
   C. jewelry floater policy is issued on an agreed value basis
   D. nationwide marine definition determines which vessels may be insured

9. Which of the following statements regarding the transportation floater is CORRECT?
   A. It usually covers merchandise shipped by various means of transportation.
   B. It covers the insured for liability when injury is sustained.
   C. It covers property located mainly at the insured's location.
   D. It covers only the interest of a shipper of goods, not the owner's interest.

10. All of the following statements regarding the bailee's customers policy are correct EXCEPT
    A. the insured often is permitted to adjust small claims
    B. the insured is protected for loss to customer goods in his custody or control
    C. a loss may be adjusted with the property owner
    D. the only time a loss is covered is if the insured is legally liable

11. All of the following statements regarding inland marine insurance are correct EXCEPT
    A. a personal articles floater is an open perils policy covering only the items scheduled in the policy
    B. a contractor's equipment floater protects the insured for damage to its own equipment
    C. an insured may decide to take cash for a loss rather than replace the property
    D. there are 13 forms of inland marine policies

12. The four major classes of marine insurance include all of the following EXCEPT
    A. cargo insurance
    B. hull insurance
    C. liability insurance
    D. freight insurance

13. In marine insurance the term *free* means which of the following?
    A. Coverage is provided without charge.
    B. Coverage is provided without a deductible.
    C. No coverage is available for certain causes of loss.
    D. Coverage is available only for items designated as *free* on the policy declarations.

14. All of the following are considered barratry of the master or mariner in marine insurance EXCEPT
    A. placing the vessel in peril by disobeying orders or instructions
    B. willfully sinking or deserting the ship
    C. stealing the ship or its cargo
    D. negligently running the ship aground

15. All of the following risks are excluded under a marine hull policy EXCEPT
    A. detainment of the vessel
    B. mines, bombs and torpedoes not on board vessel
    C. jettison of cargo
    D. strikes, riots, and civil commotions

16. The Inchmaree Clause of an ocean marine cargo policy covers which of the following?
    A. Barratry of the master or members
    B. Latent defect of machinery or hull
    C. Riots and civil commotion
    D. Capture, seizure, and arrest

17. The purpose of the running down clause in a hull insurance policy is to
    A. provide coverage for collisions with other ships
    B. protect the owner of the vessel against loss to the ship
    C. provide workers' compensation insurance for the vessel's crew members
    D. protect the owner of the vessel against destruction or loss to the vessel's cargo

# Unit Test Fourteen Answers & Rationale

1. **D.** Jewelry, furs, and silverware are provided limited theft coverage under homeowners policies. However, their high values could erode the limit for personal property in a homeowners loss. Therefore, they should be scheduled under a personal articles floater.

2. **D.** When it cannot be presumed that a theft has taken place and the insured is uncertain about the disposition of property, the loss is considered a mysterious disappearance.

3. **D.** Inland marine policies are designed for property that can be moved. Fixed-location property, on the other hand, is best insured under commercial property policies.

4. **A.** Inland marine coverage usually is written on nonstandard forms that provide broader coverage and fewer exclusions than commercial property forms. Inherent vice is a typical exclusion found in inland marine forms.

5. **B.** Most inland marine policies are written on an open perils basis, although named perils forms also are available. Both filed and nonfiled inland marine forms exist. The situation described in answer option A is not covered under an inland marine form. A diamond that becomes cloudy is considered a deterioration loss and therefore excluded by most inland marine forms.

6. **C.** Insureds frequently purchase inland marine coverage to supplement that provided by their homeowners policies. The only items covered under inland marine policies are those an insured schedules. Most property is covered on an actual cash value or a replacement basis, but fine arts and antiques often are provided with valued coverage. Coverage is worldwide, with the exception of fine arts, which is limited to the continental United States and Canada.

7. **D.** One of the reasons people use inland marine forms is that they are less strictly regulated than their commercial property counterparts.

8. **C.** A personal articles floater that covers jewelry pays the lesser of the actual cash value, the cost to repair, the cost of replacement with a substantially identical article of like kind and quality or the limit of insurance.

9. **A.** Transportation policies are designed for both the owners and shippers of goods to protect against loss of property in transit by various means, including air, rail and motor vehicle.

10. **D.** A bailee's customers policy is designed to protect against loss of a customer's property in the insured's care, custody, or control, without regard to whether the bailee is legally responsible for the loss.

11. **C.** Under an inland marine policy, the insurer always possesses the option of how to settle losses. At the insurance company's option, covered property may be repaired or replaced with like kind or quality, or a cash settlement may be offered to the insured.

12. **C.** Ocean marine insurance includes coverage for vessels (hull and machinery), cargo, protection and indemnity, and freight.

13. **C.** When something is warranted free, as in "free of capture and seizure" or other circumstance in a marine policy, it means that no coverage applies in that situation.

14. **D.** Barratry includes attempts to steal a ship and its cargo, willfully sinking or deserting a ship, and imperiling a vessel by disobeying orders or instructions.

15. **C**. Jettison of cargo to save the voyage is one of the most time-honored perils included in marine insurance policies.

16. **B**. The Inchmaree Clause in an ocean marine policy covers bursting of boilers, breakage of propellor shafts, latent defects of the hull, machinery or appurtenances, and loss due to fault or error in navigation by the master, mariners, mates, or engineers.

17. **A**. A hull policy's running down clause provides a form of property damage liability applicable to collision damage to other ships.

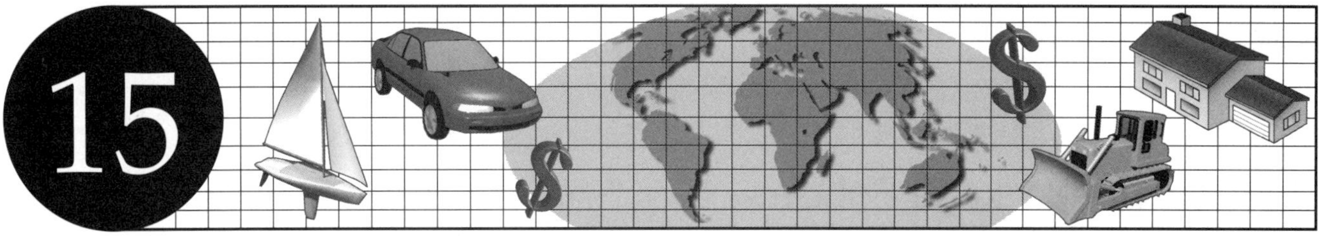


# Commercial Property Insurance

## INTRODUCTION

Property insurance is one of the oldest forms of coverage in the property-liability industry. Although property at one time was restricted to the peril of fire, over time property policies have evolved to include coverage for a variety of losses, such as windstorm, vandalism, theft, and earthquake. While still not all-encompassing, modern property insurance policies are considered to be multiperil policies, meaning that the form insures a number of causes of loss.

This unit presents a general overview of commercial property insurance and common property insurance policy provisions. In some cases, a policy also covers losses that are consequences of damage to real or personal property. This unit begins with a discussion of the development of property insurance and how it applies to the exposures of individuals and businesses. A review of the commercial package policy (CPP) follows, along with policies used to insure buildings in the course of construction and additional causes of loss, such as earthquake.

## UNIT OBJECTIVES

When you have completed this unit, you should be able to:

- describe the property covered in and property excluded from the building and personal property (BPP) coverage form, additional coverages, and coverage extensions;
- identify the perils insured under the basic, broad, and special cause of loss forms;
- describe the coverages the business income coverage form provides;
- describe the coverages the extra expense coverage form provides;
- explain the various endorsements available under commercial property insurance; and
- discuss the ways buildings, in the course of construction, may be insured using commercial property insurance forms.

## Commercial Package Policies

The most common way to provide property insurance for a larger business or organization is with a **Commercial Package Policy (CPP)**. This policy may include coverage for liability, automobiles, crime, and other major lines of insurance. A common Declarations Page is combined with separate insuring agreements for each type of coverage. This approach allows the insured to select the coverage needed and tailor it to the needs of the insured's business. A business owner can select from among the following types of coverage:

- commercial property, including direct and indirect loss coverage;
- commercial general liability;
- crime;
- inland marine;
- boiler and machinery;
- commercial auto; and
- farm.

To simplify the discussion of the CPP, each policy form and its coverages are presented in a separate unit in this text. Here, we will begin with an overview of the property forms, then discuss each in detail.

### Building and Personal Property Coverage Form (CP 00 10 04 02)

As its name implies, the **Buildings and Personal Property (BPP) coverage** form provides insurance protection for buildings and business personal property. The form describes:

- what property will and will not be covered;
- additional coverages provided;
- any coverage extensions;
- the limits of insurance;
- the deductible; and
- specific conditions.

The form provides coverage for three major types of property:

- **buildings and structures** described in the Declarations, including machinery and fixtures;
- **business personal property** at or within 100 feet of the insured location; and
- **property of others** in the insured's care, custody, or control, on or within 100 feet of the insured location.

The form does not describe the perils insured against. A separate cause of loss form (described below) must be attached.

## Property and Time Element Forms

This section provides detailed information on the building and personal property coverage form, the business income coverage form and the cause of loss form.

### *Building and Personal Property Coverage Form (CP 00 10 04)*

The **building and personal property coverage form** describes the property to be covered for direct physical loss or damage, located at the premises described in the Declarations. In addition, the loss must be caused by a peril included in the attached cause of loss form. Each building and location must be identified specifically.

## Covered Property

**Covered property** includes the building, business personal property, and personal property of others.

The covered building, described in the Declarations, includes:

- completed additions;
- fixtures, including outdoor fixtures such as light poles;
- permanently installed machinery and equipment, such as a hoist or crane; and
- personal property the insured owns that is used to maintain or service the building or structure or its premises, including:
  - fire extinguishing equipment;
  - outdoor furniture;
  - floor coverings; and
  - appliances used for refrigerating, ventilating, cooking, washing dishes, or laundering.

If they are not covered elsewhere, the form also includes coverage for additions under construction, alterations, and repairs to the building or structure and materials, equipment, supplies, and temporary structures on or within 100 feet of the described premises that are being used to make additions, alterations, or repairs to the building or structure.

Business personal property located in or on the building described in the declarations, or in the open (or in a vehicle) within 100 feet of the described premises, includes such items as:

- furniture and fixtures, such as desks and filing cabinets;
- machinery and equipment;
- stock, which includes merchandise for sale (such as the clothes and furniture for sale in a department store), raw materials and in-process or finished goods, plus supplies used in their packaging or shipping;
- all other personal property the insured owns and uses in his business;

- labor, materials, or services the insured furnishes or arranges on the personal property of others, such as the labor and material used to repair a customer's TV; and
- the value of improvements or additions, like a partition, that a tenant has made in a building he or she rents or leases but does not own.

Finally, coverage is provided for the personal property of others—for instance, the value of the TV set that a customer brings in for repair—as long as the property is:

- in the insured's care, custody, or control; or
- located in or on the building described in the Declarations.

If property is owned by someone other than the insured, the insurer pays the owner of the property (the customer), not the insured (the business owner).

## Property Not Covered

Some property that is not covered includes:

- accounts, bills, currency, deeds, evidences of debt, money, notes, or securities;
- animals, unless owned by others and boarded by the insured or owned by the insured and considered stock, such as animals in a pet store;
- automobiles held for sale;
- bridges, roadways, walks, patios, or other paved surfaces;
- contraband or other illegally transported property;
- cost of excavation;
- foundations of buildings below basement or surface level;
- land, water, crops, or lawns;
- personal property while airborne or waterborne;
- pilings, piers, wharves, docks, or bulkheads;
- property covered under any other policy in which it is described more specifically, except for the excess of the amount due (whether or not one can collect on it) from that other insurance;
- the cost to research, replace, or restore the information on valuable papers and records, including those that exist on electronic or magnetic media, except as provided in the coverage extensions;
- vehicles or self-propelled machines, including aircraft and watercraft, that are licensed for use on public roads or operated principally away from the described premises; and
- the following property while outside of buildings: grain, hay, straw or other crops, fences, radio or television antennas (including their lead-in wiring, masts or towers), signs (other than signs attached to buildings), trees, shrubs, or plants. Some coverage is provided under the coverage extensions.

## Additional Coverages

Additional coverages are available for the following activities.

### *Debris Removal*

Following a covered loss, the insurer pays for the expenses to remove the debris of covered property caused by or resulting from a covered cause of loss. The cost of debris removal is subject to a limit of 25% of the amount of the loss plus the extension for uncovered debris removal costs.

✓ ***For Example:*** If a direct loss of $100,000 occurs and the policy extension is $1,000, the most that the insurer will pay for debris removal is $25,000 (25% of $100,000) plus $1,000, for a total of $26,000.

The insurer will pay up to an additional $10,000 if the total of debris removal expense plus the amount paid for direct physical loss exceeds the limit of insurance for the covered property, or if the actual debris removal expense exceeds 25% of the deductible plus the amount paid for direct physical loss. The total payment will never exceed the Limit of Insurance on covered property, plus $10,000.

### *Preservation of Property*

If it is necessary to move covered property from the described premises to preserve it from loss or damage by a covered cause of loss, the insurer pays for any direct physical loss or damage to that property occurring:

- while the property is being moved or while temporarily stored at another location; and
- only if the loss or damage occurs within 30 days after the property is first moved.

### *Fire Department Service Charge*

When the fire department is called to save or protect covered property from a covered cause of loss, the insurer pays up to $1,000 for fire department service charges. No deductible applies to this additional coverage.

### *Pollutant Clean-Up and Removal*

If a covered loss results in the discharge, dispersal, seepage, migration, release, or escape of pollutants, the cost to clean up those pollutants is covered up to a maximum of $10,000 in each separate 12-month period if these expenses are reported within 180 days of the loss.

## Increased Cost of Construction

For buildings to which the Replacement Cost Optional Coverage applies, the insurer will pay the increased costs to comply with the enforcement of an ordinance or law to repair or replace damaged property. This coverage is limited to $10,000 or 5% of the Limit of Insurance on the property, whichever is less. This coverage is not subject to the Ordinance or Law exclusion.

## Electronic Data

The insurer will pay for the cost to replace or restore electronic data which was destroyed or corrupted by a covered cause of loss. Coverage is limited to specified causes of loss listed under Causes of Loss–Special Form and Broad Form for collapse, and include viruses or other harmful codes. The coverage is limited to $2,500 for any loss within one policy year, regardless of the number of occurrences.

## Coverage Extensions

The following coverage extensions apply if a coinsurance percentage of 80 percent or more is shown on the declarations page. Amounts arising from the following items are in addition to the limits of insurance shown on the Declarations Page. The coinsurance requirement does not apply.

### *Newly Acquired or Constructed Property*

Coverage can be applied to new buildings while being constructed on the premises described on the declarations page and to buildings that the insured acquires at locations other than the described premises. The limit for buildings is not more than $250,000 at each building.

Coverage can be applied to business personal property at any location that the insured acquires, not to exceed $100,000 at each building where such personal property may be located.

Coverage for newly acquired or constructed property and personal property ends at the earliest of:

- the policy's expiration;
- 30 days after the insured acquires or begins to construct the property; or
- the date the insured reports the values to the insurer.

A premium is charged from the time construction began or the property was acquired.

### *Personal Effects and Property of Others*

Coverage that applies to business personal property can be extended to apply to personal effects owned by the insured or the insured's officers, partners or employees (e.g., a fire at an office that destroys some employees' coats). This coverage also can be applied to personal property of others in the insured's care, custody, or control, such as customer computers in a store for repair.

Because the dollar amount of coverage is limited, this is appropriate when the exposure is relatively small. For larger dollar values, coverage should be provided under personal property of others.

The limit is $2,500 at each described premises. The insurer pays the property owner, not the insured business owner.

### *Valuable Papers and Records—Cost of Research*

Coverage that applies to business personal property can be extended to apply to the insured's cost to research, replace, or restore the information on lost or damaged valuable papers and records. This coverage includes information on electronic or magnetic media for which duplicates do not exist. The limit of coverage under this extension is $2,500 at each described premises, unless a higher limit is shown in the Declarations.

### *Property Off Premises*

Coverage may be extended to apply to covered property other than stock that is temporarily at a location the insured does not own, lease, or operate (e.g., office furniture taken to a shop for repair). This extension applies only if loss or damage is caused by a peril that would have been covered had it happened on the insured's premises. The extension does not apply to covered property in or on a vehicle, in the care, custody or control of the insured's salespeople or at any fair or exhibition. The limit under this extension is $10,000.

### *Outdoor Property*

Coverage may be extended to apply to the insured's outdoor fences, radio and television antennas, signs (other than signs attached to buildings), trees, shrubs, and plants, including debris removal expense. Coverage applies when the loss is caused by or results from:

- fire;
- lightning;
- explosion;
- riot or civil commotion; or
- aircraft.

The limit under this extension is $1,000, but not more than $250 for any one tree, shrub or plant.

## Non-Owned Detached Trailers

The insured may extend the Business Personal Property Insurance to apply to loss or damage to non-owned trailers if the trailer is used in the insured's business, is in the insured's care and custody, and the insured is contractually obligated to pay for its damage. This coverage is limited to $5,000, and is in excess of any other applicable insurance.

## Limits of Insurance

The most the insurer will pay for loss or damage for any one occurrence is the applicable limit of insurance shown in the declarations. For example, if the limit indicated is $100,000 and the loss is $125,000, the most the policy will pay is $100,000 less the appropriate deductible.

The most the insurer will pay for loss or damage to outdoor signs attached to buildings is $1,000 per sign in any one occurrence.

The limits applicable to the coverage extensions and the fire department service charge are in addition to the limits of insurance.

Payments under Preservation of Property coverage will not increase the applicable limit of insurance.

## Quick Quiz 15.1

1. What are the three major coverages available under the Building and Personal Property (BPP) form?

   A. ______________________________
   B. ______________________________
   C. ______________________________

2. What are the 6 additional coverages provided under the BPP form?

   A. ______________________________
   B. ______________________________
   C. ______________________________
   D. ______________________________

3. Five extensions of coverage are available under the BPP form; however, they apply only if

   ______________________________.

4. Under the extension of coverage for newly acquired or constructed property, coverage is provided for a maximum of __________ days. Building coverage is limited to __________% of the limit for buildings and a maximum of $__________. Personal property at newly acquired locations is limited to __________% of the limit for business personal property and a maximum of $__________.

5. The limit for property off premises under the extensions of coverage is $__________.

**Answers**

1. *Buildings, Business Personal Property, Personal Property of Others*
2. *Debris removal, Preservation of property, Fire department service charge, Pollutant cleanup and removal, Increased cost of construction, and Electronic data.*
3. *At least 80% or higher coinsurance is indicated in the Declarations*
4. *30 days; 25%; $250,000; 10%; $100,000*
5. *$10,000*

## Conditions

As discussed in Unit 12, the following general conditions also apply to the buildings and personal property coverage form:

- abandonment;
- appraisal;
- insured's duties to the insurer in the event of loss or damage;
- loss payment; and
- recovered property.

**Test Topic Alert!**

An appraisal condition (in the BPP form, as in homeowners policies) provides a means to settle disputes over the value of property lost or damaged.

In addition, the following conditions apply.

### *Vacancy*

If the building where loss or damage occurs has been vacant for more than 60 consecutive days before the loss or damage, the insurer either does not pay if some specified perils occur or reduces the loss payment if other perils occur. The insurer does not pay for any loss or damage caused by any of the following, even if the attached cause of loss form normally covers the loss:

- vandalism;
- sprinkler leakage, unless the insured has protected the system against freezing;
- building glass breakage;
- water damage;
- theft; or
- attempted theft.

For other losses, the insurer reduces by 15% the amount that it otherwise would have paid for the loss or damage.

✓ ***Take Note:*** The rationale for reducing loss payments by 15% in the event of vacancy is based on the fact that the hazard insured against is increased in this situation. A hazard is any condition that increases the likelihood of a loss or the severity (dollar amount) of a loss. A fire that starts in a vacant building is unlikely to be detected until it has caused extensive damage. The 15% reduction is warranted based on the increased hazard.

Also note that buildings under construction are not considered vacant.

### *Valuation*

The insurer determines the value of covered property in the event of loss or damage at actual cash value (ACV), as of the time of loss or damage, with the following exceptions:

- If the coinsurance clause requirements are met and the cost to repair or replace the damaged building is $2,500 or less, the insurer pays the cost of building repairs or replacement.
- Stock or inventory, sold but not yet delivered, is valued at selling price less discounts.
- Glass is covered at cost of replacement with safety glazing material if required by law.
- Valuable papers and records are covered at the cost of blank materials for reproducing the records and labor to transcribe or copy the records when a duplicate exists. The insurer does not pay for the recreation of lost data. The recovery of data may be covered under an electronic data processing (EDP) policy, a type of inland marine coverage.

### *Additional Conditions*

The following conditions apply in addition to the common policy conditions and the commercial property conditions:

- **Coinsurance**. If a coinsurance percentage is shown in the Declarations, the coinsurance settlement technique discussed previously applies to settlement of a loss.
- **Mortgage Holders**. The insurer pays for covered loss of or damage to buildings of each mortgage holder shown in the declarations in their order of precedence, as financial interests may appear at the time of loss. In other words, holders of first mortgages are paid before second mortgagees.

**Test Topic Alert!** The mortgage holders condition in the BPP form gives the mortgagee (the party loaning the funds to purchase the property) the right to pay the premiums and report losses if the insured mortgagor (the party who borrows the funds to purchase the property) fails to do so. The mortgagee gets paid on a loss even if the loss results from the insured's intentional act, including arson.

### *Optional Coverages*

If shown in the Declarations, the following optional coverages apply separately to each item.

**Agreed Value.** The coinsurance clause does not apply if the agreed value option has been attached to the contract. When the insured agrees to carry an amount of insurance equal to or greater than the agreed value, the coinsurance clause is waived in the event of a loss.

- If the expiration date for this optional coverage as shown in the declarations is not extended, the coinsurance clause is reinstated and the agreed value optional coverage expires.
- The optional coverage applies only to loss or damage that occurs on or after the effective date of the agreed value option and before the agreed value expiration date shown in the declarations or the policy expiration date, whichever occurs first.

**Inflation Guard Endorsement.** The inflation guard option can be added to increase policy limits to keep pace with increasing property values.

**Replacement Cost.** If noted on the Declarations Page, replacement cost (cost of new material at the time of loss) replaces actual cash value in the loss conditions of the buildings and personal property coverage form.

This optional coverage does not apply to:

- property of others;
- contents of a residence;
- manuscripts;
- works of art, antiques, or rare articles, including etchings, pictures, statuary, marbles, bronzes, or porcelains; or
- stock (inventory or merchandise for sale or raw materials), unless the replacement cost option is shown in the declarations.

The insurer pays on a replacement cost basis only if the:

- lost or damaged property actually is repaired or replaced; and
- the repair or replacement is made as soon as reasonably possible after the loss or damage.

The insurer does not pay more for loss or damage on a replacement cost basis than the lesser of the following:

- limit of insurance applicable to the lost or damaged property;
- cost to replace, on the same premises, the lost or damaged property with other property (1) of comparable material, quality, and quantity and (2) used for the same purpose; or

- amount that the insured actually spends to repair or replace the lost or damaged property.

The insurer settles the claim on an actual cash value basis, allowing the insured to make an additional claim for the replacement cost when the lost or damaged property is replaced. Such a decision to claim the additional amount must be made within six months (180 days) of the replacement. Sometimes a company grants an extension to this requirement under specific request.

## Quick Quiz 15.2

1. Under the BPP form, vacancy of an insured building beyond __________ days results in two coverage restrictions. First, coverage for some causes of loss is eliminated. Those causes are

   A. ____________________
   B. ____________________
   C. ____________________
   D. ____________________
   E. ____________________

   Second, all other losses payable under the BPP form are reduced by _____%.

2. The BPP form pays for loss based on the __________ __________ __________ of the property at the time of the loss. Exceptions to this valuation method are made for certain types of losses

   A. ____________________
   B. ____________________
   C. ____________________

3. The optional coverages available under the BPP form are

   A. ____________________
   B. ____________________
   C. ____________________

### Answers

1. *60 days; vandalism; sprinkler leakage; building glass breakage; water damage; theft or attempted theft; 15%*
2. *actual cash value; damage to buildings when the cost to repair or replace is less than $2,500; stock or inventory sold but not delivered (at selling price); glass (at cost to replace with safety glazing material)*
3. *agreed value; inflation guard; replacement cost*

# Business Income Coverage Form (CP 00 32 04)

Business income coverage is an important part of the insurance program for nearly all businesses. Business income coverage is disability insurance for the business. When the business cannot earn income due to a covered loss, business income coverage replaces the lost earnings.

Business income coverage includes expenses to avoid or minimize the suspension of business and to continue business operations at:

- the described premises;
- replacement premises; and
- temporary locations.

Such expenses as relocation expenses and costs to equip and operate the replacement or temporary locations are covered. Also covered are expenses to minimize the suspension of business if the insured cannot continue business operations. To the extent it reduces the amount of loss that otherwise would be payable under this coverage form, covered expenses also include the costs to:

- repair or replace any property and
- research, replace, or restore the lost information on damaged valuable papers and records.

## Coverage

During the **restoration period**, the insurer pays for the actual loss of business income the insured sustains due to the necessary suspension of operations.

The restoration period begins on the date the direct physical loss or damage occurred at the described premises and ends on the date when the property at the described premises should be repaired, rebuilt, or replaced with reasonable speed and similar quality. The policy's expiration date does not cut short the period of restoration.

Business income includes the following:

- net income (net profit or loss before income taxes) that would have been earned or incurred; plus
- continuing normal operation expenses, including payroll.

## Extra Expense Coverage Form

With the **Extra Expense Coverage Form**, the insurer pays for any necessary extra expenses the business incurs during a period of interruption that follows a direct physical loss to property by a covered cause of loss. The expenses must be of a type that would not have been incurred had the loss not taken place. This is also a time element coverage, because the loss is continuous in nature.

This type of coverage is purchased by a business that must continue to operate if a loss occurs, despite the costs of keeping the business running. Such a business is one that will lose customers to competitors if it does not remain open and one that is the only business of its kind in the area.

✓ ***For Example:*** Businesses that probably would buy extra expense coverage to enable them to continue operations despite a loss are a hospital, an electric company and a dry cleaner. A hospital may be the only medical facility in the area. An electric company could be the only source of such power for an entire city. Even a dry cleaner could benefit from this coverage in that it would remain open and serve customers who otherwise would go to a competitor.

### Additional Coverages

Payment under any of the additional coverages is within the limit of insurance shown on the Declarations Page. Thus, if payment is made for business income loss, payment for any of the following coverages can be made only to the extent that the limit of insurance amount listed on the Declarations Page exceeds the payment for business income loss:

### Extra Expense

The insurer pays the necessary expense the insured incurs during the period of restoration that would not have been incurred if no direct physical loss or damage to the property had been caused by or had resulted from a covered cause of loss.

While this form is designed primarily to cover loss of business income, it pays for extra expenses that reduce the length of business interruption as long as the expenses are within the limit of insurance.

The insurer pays for any extra expenses to avoid or minimize the suspension of business and to continue operations at the described premises, at replacement premises, and at temporary locations.

The insurer pays any extra expense to minimize the suspension of business if the insured cannot continue operations. The insurer also pays any extra expense to repair or replace any property or to research, replace or restore the lost information on damaged valuable papers and records to the extent that it reduces the amount of loss that otherwise would have been payable under this coverage form.

**Test Topic Alert!** Extra expenses include relocation expenses and costs to equip and operate the replacement or temporary locations.

### Civil Authority

The insurer pays for the actual loss of business income and the necessary extra expense caused by an action of civil authority (such as firemen or police) that prohibits access to the described premises due to direct physical loss of or damage to property other than at the described premises.

✓ ***For Example:*** A major fire breaks out in a nightclub. The art gallery next door sustains structural damage from the water the firefighters use to extinguish the blaze. In addition, much of the artwork is ruined. The owner is forced to close the gallery for repairs. The insurer will cover the business income lost while the gallery is closed for repairs as well as the expenses that the owner incurs in repairing the gallery.

The loss must be caused by or result from a loss that would have been covered had it occurred at the insured's premises. This coverage applies for a period of up to two consecutive weeks from the date of the civil authority's action.

### Alterations and New Buildings

The insurer pays for the actual loss of business income that the insured sustains due to direct physical loss or damage at the described premises. The loss or damage must be caused by or result from a covered cause of loss to:

- new buildings or structures, whether complete or under construction;
- alterations or additions to existing buildings or structures; and
- machinery, equipment, and supplies.

If such direct physical loss or damage delays the start of business operations, the period of restoration begins on the date operations would have begun if the direct physical loss or damage had not occurred.

### Extended Business Income

This additional coverage provides insurance while a business is starting back up after a loss. When resuming operations after a major loss, the business probably will not receive as much income as it would have received had no loss occurred.

This coverage helps make up the difference between what the business could have earned and what it actually did earn. The insurer pays for the actual loss of business income the insured incurs during the period that begins on the date the property actually is repaired, rebuilt or replaced and operations are resumed, and ends either in 30 days or when the business has achieved the level of income it would have had no loss occurred.

Loss of business income is an **indirect** or a **consequential loss**. The insurer pays for loss of business income (1) if the insured suffers a loss to property covered by the buildings and personal property coverage form and (2) if the loss is caused by a peril described in the cause of loss form attached to the policy. This type of coverage also is called **time element coverage** because it pays for loss of income that occurs over a period of time, as opposed to a direct loss that happens at a specific time. The amount of the loss is calculated based on the firm's past financial performance, estimated into the future.

The intent of business income coverage is to provide a firm with the same level of profit (or loss) that it would have earned had no loss occurred.

✓ ***Take Note:*** This type of insurance often is referred to, incorrectly, as profits insurance. A business need not be earning a profit to purchase and collect business income coverage. Even if a business is producing a net loss (so that expenses exceed income), it is still earning revenue. It is the lost earning stream that is the subject of business income coverage.

Included are expenses to avoid or minimize the suspension of business and to continue business operations at:

- the described premises;
- replacement premises; and
- temporary locations.

Such expenses as relocation expenses and costs to equip and operate the replacement or temporary locations are covered, as are expenses to minimize the suspension of business if the insured cannot continue business operations. To the extent it reduces the amount of loss that otherwise would be payable under this coverage form, covered expenses also include the costs to:

- repair or replace any property; and
- research, replace, or restore the lost information on damaged valuable papers and records.

### *Exclusions to the Business Income Coverage Form*

The only exclusions are those shown in the attached cause of loss form.

### *Limits of Insurance*

The most the insurance company pays for loss in any one occurrence is the applicable limit of insurance shown in the declarations.

## Loss Conditions

The general loss conditions, including appraisal and the insured's duties to the insurer in the event of loss, apply here as well. The business income coverage form imposes an additional loss condition upon the insured, which is to resume operations as quickly as possible. The following conditions also apply to business income coverage.

### *Loss Determination*

The amount of business income loss is determined based on:

- the business's net income before the direct physical loss or damage occurred;
- the business's likely net income if no loss or damage occurred;
- the operating expenses, including payroll expenses, necessary to resume operations with the same quality of service that existed just before the direct physical loss or damage occurred; and
- other relevant sources of information, including:
  - the insured's financial records and accounting procedures;
  - bills, invoices, and other vouchers; and
  - deeds, liens, or contracts.

The amount of extra expense loss is determined based on all expenses that exceed normal operating expenses that the business would have incurred during the period of restoration if no direct physical loss or damage had occurred. The insurer deducts from the total of such expenses:

- the proceeds from the sale of property bought for temporary use during the restoration period, such as temporary display cases;
- any extra expense that other insurance pays for, except for insurance that is written subject to the same plan, terms, conditions, and provisions; and
- all necessary expenses that reduce the business income loss that otherwise would have been incurred.

### *Loss Payment*

The insurer pays for a covered loss within 30 days after receiving the sworn statement of loss if the insured has complied with all of the policy terms and if both the insurer and the insured have reached an agreement on the amount of loss or have an appraisal award.

### *Proof of Loss*

The proof of loss is a formal statement the insured makes that describes the nature and extent of a loss. It gives the insurer information about the loss so it can determine the extent of its obligation to the insured following the loss.

### *Resumption of Operations*

The insurer reduces the amount of the insured's business income loss to the extent the insured can resume operations, even partially, by using damaged or undamaged property, including merchandise or stock. It reduces the extra expense loss to the extent the insured can return operations to normal and discontinue such extra expense.

## Additional Condition

If a coinsurance percentage is shown in the Declarations, the insurer does not pay the full amount of any loss unless the limit of insurance for business income is equal to or greater than the coinsurance percentage multiplied by the sum of:

- the net income (net profit or loss before income taxes); plus
- all operating expenses, including payroll expenses, that the insured's business operations would have incurred for the 12 months following the policy's effective date. Instead, the insurer determines the most it will pay by applying the coinsurance formula presented in an earlier unit.

✓ ***Take Note:*** The coinsurance percentage is applied to net income plus all normal operating expenses to determine the amount of insurance the policyholder must carry. However, the amount to be paid in the event of a loss is limited to net income plus all continuing expenses. While this may seem unfair, it is actually a way to ensure that policyholders have adequate insurance in the event of a loss, because it causes them to purchase a greater amount of insurance than they would have otherwise. Insureds often underestimate the amount of insurance required when a business is shut down.

## Optional Coverages

If shown in the declarations, the following optional coverages apply separately to each item.

### *Maximum Period of Indemnity*

The coinsurance provision is waived if the maximum period of indemnity optional coverage is selected. Under this coverage, the most the insurer pays for loss of business income is the lesser of the:

- amount of loss sustained during the 120 days immediately following the direct physical loss or damage; or
- limit of insurance shown in the Declarations.

### *Monthly Limit of Indemnity*

The coinsurance provision does not apply if the monthly limit of indemnity optional coverage is selected. Under this coverage, the most the insurer pays for loss of business income in each period of 30 consecutive days following a loss is the limit of insurance multiplied by the percentage shown in the declarations for this optional coverage.

✓ ***For Example:*** If the Declarations Page shows a limit of insurance of $140,000 and a percentage of 25%, the insurer pays 25% of $140,000 ($35,000) or the actual loss for each month of loss, whichever is less, until the limit of insurance is reached. This coverage imposes no time limit.

### *Agreed Value*

This optional coverage also suspends the policy's coinsurance provision. To activate the coverage, the insured must complete a business income report/worksheet that shows financial data for business operations over the 12-month period before the policy inception and estimated for the 12 months immediately following the inception of the coverage. The agreed value should be at least the coinsurance clause required amount, which is net income plus all operating expenses for the 12 months following the worksheet date multiplied by the coinsurance percentage.

## Loss Conditions

The loss conditions of appraisal and duties of the insured following a loss are the same as those that generally apply to property insurance. There is the additional duty to resume operations as quickly as possible.

### *Limits on Loss Payment*

If extra expense coverage is provided, the Declarations show a limit of insurance for extra expense and three percentages.

The amount of payment to the insured is limited to the lesser of the:

- limit of insurance;
- actual extra expenses; or
- result of multiplying one of the percentages shown on the declarations page by the limit of insurance.

The percentage used depends on the period of restoration as follows:

- if the restoration period is 30 days or less, the first percentage is used;
- if the restoration period exceeds 30 days but is less than 60 days, the second percentage is used; and
- if the restoration period exceeds 60 days, the third percentage is used.

✓ ***For Example:*** Assume the limit of insurance is $100,000 and the percentages shown on the Declarations Page are 40%, 80%, and 100%. The actual extra expenses incurred from a loss were $95,000, and the restoration period was 40 days. The settlement amount the insurer will pay is based on 80%, the second percentage shown on the declarations page because restoration was between 30 and 60 days. The amount the insured will receive then is 80% times $100,000 (note this is the limit of insurance, not the amount of the loss), or $80,000.

### *Loss Determination*

The amount of extra expense is determined based on all expenses that exceed the normal operating expenses that the business operations would have incurred during the restoration period if no direct physical loss or damage had occurred. The insurer then deducts from the total of such expenses:

- the sales (or salvage) value that remains of any property bought for temporary use during the restoration period, once operations are resumed; and
- all necessary expenses that reduce the extra expense otherwise incurred.

### *Loss Payment*

The insurer pays for any loss within 30 days after it receives the statement of loss if:

- the insured has complied with all of the policy terms; and
- an agreement is reached between the insurer and the insured on the amount of loss; or
- an appraisal award has been made.

### *Resumption of Operations*

The insurance company reduces the amount of extra expense loss to the extent the insured can return business operations to normal and discontinue such extra expense.

## Exclusions for Business Income and Extra Expense Coverages

The common property exclusions already described apply here also. Some special exclusions appear in the cause of loss forms that apply to the business income coverage form and the extra expense coverage form.

### *Special Exclusions*

The following provisions apply only to the business income coverage form or the extra expense coverage form:

- The insurer does not pay for any loss caused by or resulting from (1) damage or destruction of finished stock or (2) the time required to manufacture new merchandise. This exclusion does not apply to extra expense.
- The insurer does not pay for any loss caused by or resulting from direct physical loss or damage to radio or television antennas, including their lead-in wiring, masts, and towers.
- The insurer does not pay for any increase of loss caused by or resulting from:
  - delay in rebuilding, repairing, or replacing the property or resuming normal business operations, due to interference at the location of the rebuilding, repair, or replacement by strikers or other persons; or
  - suspension, lapse, or cancellation of any license, lease, or contract. But if the suspension, lapse, or cancellation is caused directly by the

suspension of business operations, the insurer covers such loss that affects the insured's business income during the restoration period.

- The insurer does not pay for any extra expense caused by or resulting from suspension, lapse, or cancellation of any license, lease or contract beyond the restoration period.
- The insurer does not pay for any other consequential loss.

## Quick Quiz 15.3

1. Which of the following defines business income?

   A. Net income plus continuing normal expenses, including payroll
   B. Net income plus continuing normal expenses, excluding payroll
   C. Net income minus continuing normal expenses, including payroll
   D. Net income minus continuing normal expenses, excluding payroll

2. Extra expenses to reduce a loss are paid under business income if they occur at any of the following locations EXCEPT

   A. a temporary location
   B. the described premises
   C. a newly acquired location
   D. a replacement location

3. The coverage provided under the business income coverage form that allows an extra amount of time for the insured to resume normal operations once the property has been repaired is called

   A. extended period of indemnity
   B. extended business income
   C. extension of coverage
   D. extended loss clause

4. Each of the following is an optional coverage under business income EXCEPT

   A. monthly limit of indemnity
   B. maximum period of indemnity
   C. extra expense
   D. agreed value

5. Which of the following situations is NOT covered by the business income coverage form?

   A. A fire damages the insured's building that requires a temporary relocation to another site.
   B. A strike by construction workers that delays the repair of the insured's building and results in an additional month of lost income.
   C. An adjacent building is damaged by fire that results in a 2-week loss of income when the insured's location is inaccessible.
   D. A replacement machine is ordered from Europe, and to expedite delivery, the insured incurs an additional $20,000 freight charge.

**Answers**

1. ***A.*** *The definition of business income is net income (net profit or net loss before income taxes) that would have been earned or incurred, plus continuing normal operating expenses including payroll.*
2. ***C.*** *Extra expenses incurred may include temporary or replacement locations, or costs at the insured's premises, but not newly acquired locations.*
3. ***B.*** *Extended business income coverage is automatically included in the form and applies up to 30 days coverage after the period of restoration for operations to return to a normal (pre-loss) level.*
4. ***C.*** *Extra expense coverage is included automatically in the business income coverage form.*
5. ***B.*** *The business income form excludes loss caused or resulting from delay in rebuilding, repairing, or replacing the property or resuming normal business operations, due to interference at the location of the rebuilding, repair or replacement by strikers or other persons.*

# Cause of Loss Forms

Three cause of loss forms apply:

- basic form;
- broad form; and
- special form.

Each form describes the covered perils, along with the exclusions and conditions. An insured may choose among the forms, but must select one to make the building and personal property coverage form complete.

**FIGURE 15.1 Coverages and Exclusions under Basic, Broad, and Special Forms**

| Basic Form | Broad Form | Special Form |
|---|---|---|
| ***Coverages***<br>• Fire<br>• Lightning<br>• Explosion<br>• Windstorm and Hail<br>• Smoke<br>• Aircraft or Vehicles<br>• Riot or Civil Commotion<br>• Vandalism (including Malicious Mischief)<br>• Sprinkler Leakage<br>• Sinkhole<br>• Volcanic Action | ***Coverages***<br>• Coverages found in the basic form plus:<br>– Falling Objects<br>– Weight of Snow, Ice, or Sleet<br>– Water Damage<br>– Glass Breakage | ***Coverages***<br>• The Special form is open perils coverage. |
| ***Exclusions***<br>• Ordinance or Law<br>• Earth Movement<br>• Governmental Action<br>• Nuclear Hazard<br>• Utility Services (off-premises)<br>• War and Military Action<br>• Water | ***Exclusions***<br>• Same as Basic Form | ***Exclusions***<br>• Same as Basic Form |

## Cause of Loss—Basic Form

The **basic cause of loss form** describes the perils covered if this document is attached to the buildings and personal property coverage form. Most of the perils have been described previously. Additional perils and modifications from the basic coverages already described are listed below:

- Fire
- Lightning
- Explosion
- Windstorm or hail
- Smoke
- Aircraft or vehicles (coverage requires physical contact and includes damages from objects falling from aircraft; this does not include loss or

damage caused by or resulting from vehicles the insured owns or operates)

- Riot or civil commotion
- Vandalism
- Sprinkler leakage (coverage includes leakage or discharge of any substance from an automatic sprinkler system, including collapse of a tank that is part of the system; the building or structure containing the automatic sprinkler system must be insured under this policy; as a result, this coverage generally applies only to the person who owns the building, not to a tenant who just insures his business personal property)
  - An automatic sprinkler system encompasses any automatic fire protective or extinguishing system, including items connected to it, such as:
    (1) sprinklers and discharge nozzles;
    (2) ducts, pipes, valves, and fittings;
    (3) tanks, their component parts and supports; and
    (4) pumps and private protection means.

✓ ***Take Note:*** The insurer pays the cost to repair or replace damaged parts of the automatic sprinkler system if the damage results in sprinkler leakage or is caused directly by freezing. In addition, the insurer pays the costs to tear out and replace any part of the building or structure to repair damage to the automatic sprinkler system that has resulted in sprinkler leakage.

- Sinkhole collapse (sinkhole collapse means loss or damage caused to property insured under the policy by the sudden sinking or collapse of land into underground empty spaces created by the action of water on limestone, sand, or similar rock formations; this cause of loss does not include the cost of filling sinkholes)
- Volcanic action—volcanic action means direct loss or damage to property insured under the policy resulting from the eruption of a volcano when the loss or damage is caused by:
  - an airborne volcanic blast or airborne shock waves;
  - ash, dust, or particulate matter; or
  - lava flow.

Earth movement due to volcanic tremor is not a covered peril.

All volcanic eruptions that occur within any 72-hour period constitute a single occurrence for purposes of the basic form. This cause of loss does not include the cost to remove ash, dust or particulate matter that does not cause direct physical loss or damage to the described property, but that just falls in the yard.

## Cause of Loss—Broad Form

The **broad form cause of loss** includes all the perils the basic form contains plus the following additional perils:

- Breakage of glass by any cause. This coverage does not apply to neon tubing attached to the building or structure. Coverage is limited to $100 for each plate, pane or panel and no more than $500 in any one occurrence
- Falling objects
- Weight of snow, ice, or sleet. This coverage does not include loss or damage to gutters, downspouts, or personal property outside the building
- Water damage. This coverage includes accidental discharge or leakage of water or steam as the direct result of the breaking or cracking of any part of a system or an appliance containing water or steam, other than an automatic sprinkler system. If the building or structure containing the system or appliance is covered under the policy, this generally applies to the building owner, not to the tenant who just insures his business personal property. The insurer also pays the cost to tear out and replace any part of the building or structure to repair damage to the system or appliance from which the water or steam escapes. The insurer does not pay for the following:
  - the cost of repairing or replacing the system or appliance from which the water or steam escapes;
  - loss or damage caused by or resulting from continuous or repeated seepage or leakage that occurs over a period of 14 days or more; or
  - for loss or damage caused by or resulting from freezing unless (1) the insured does his or her best to maintain heat in the building or structure or (2) the insured drains the equipment and shuts off the water supply if the heat is not maintained.

### Additional Coverage—Collapse

The insurer pays for loss or damage from direct physical loss involving collapse of a building or any part of a building caused by one or more of the following:

- any of the broad form causes of loss, including breakage of building glass;
- hidden decay;
- hidden insect or vermin damage;
- weight of animals, people, or personal property;
- weight of rain that collects on a roof; or
- use of defective material or methods in construction, remodeling, or renovation if the collapse occurs during the course of the construction, remodeling, or renovation.

Collapse does not include settling, cracking, shrinkage, bulging, or expansion.

This additional coverage does not increase the limits of insurance the policy provides.

**Exclusions** The form excludes the common property exclusions plus the special exclusions relating to business income described previously.

## Cause of Loss—Special Form

When the word *special* is shown in the Declarations, the **special cause of loss form** applies and insures against risks of direct physical loss unless the loss is:

- listed in the exclusions; or
- limited in another section under limitations.

**Exclusions** The common property exclusions apply to:

- building ordinance;
- earth movement;
- governmental action;
- nuclear hazard;
- power failure;
- war and military action, riot, and insurrection; and
- water damage.

In addition, the following exclusions apply to the special form, some of which also apply to the broad form and were presented previously. The insurer does not pay for loss or damage caused by or resulting from any:

- artificially generated electric current, including electric arcing, that disturbs electrical devices, appliances, or wires (but if loss or damage by fire results, the insurer pays for that resulting loss or damage);
- delay, loss of use, or loss of market;
- smoke, vapor, or gas from agricultural smudging or industrial operations;
- wear and tear;
- rust, corrosion, fungus, decay, deterioration, hidden, or latent property defect or any quality in property that causes it to damage or destroy itself;
- smog;
- release, discharge, or dispersal of contaminants or pollutants;
- settling, cracking, shrinking, or expansion;
- insects, birds, rodents, or other animals;
- mechanical breakdown, including rupture or bursting caused by centrifugal force;

- the following causes of loss to personal property:
  - dampness or dryness of atmosphere;
  - changes in or extremes of temperature; and
  - marring or scratching.

  (However, if loss or damage by certain specified causes of loss or building glass breakage results, the insurer pays for that resulting loss or damage);
- explosion of steam boilers, steam pipes, steam engines, or steam turbines owned or leased by the insured or operated under the insured's control;
- continuous or repeated seepage or leakage of water that occurs over a period of 14 days or more;
- water that leaks or flows from plumbing, heating, air conditioning, or other equipment (except fire protective systems) when the leakage is caused by or results from freezing unless the insured:
  - does his best to maintain heat in the building or structure; or
  - drains the equipment and shuts off the water supply if the heat is not maintained;
- dishonest or criminal acts by the insured, by his partners, employees, directors, trustees, or authorized representatives or by anyone to whom the insured entrusts the property for any purpose:
  - whether or not the person was acting alone or in collusion with others and whether or not the act occurred during the hours of employment.
  - This exclusion does not apply to acts of destruction (other than theft) by the insured's employees.
- the voluntary parting with any property by the insured or anyone else to whom the insured has entrusted the property if induced to do so by any fraudulent scheme, trick, device or false pretense;
- rain, snow, ice, or sleet damage to personal property in the open; or
- collapse, except as provided as an additional coverage for collapse.

The insurer does not pay for loss or damage caused by or resulting from any of the following perils:

- Weather conditions that contributed to or caused earth movement, nuclear hazard, failure of utility services away from the described premises, flooding, seepage, mudslides, and other water-related events, each of these being subject to its own exceptions
- Acts or decisions, including the failure to act or decide, of any person, group, organization or governmental body
- Damage to part or all of any property on or off the described premises that results from faulty, inadequate or defective:
  - planning, zoning, development, or surveying;
  - design, specification, workmanship, repair, construction, renovation, remodeling, grading, or compaction;
  - materials used in repair, construction, renovation, or remodeling; or
  - the maintenance of part or all of any property on or off the described premises.

However, if loss or damage by a peril that would be covered results, the insurer pays for that portion of the resulting loss or damage.

✓ ***For Example:*** If damage results because of faulty workmanship during the construction of an insured building, no coverage would apply for the faulty workmanship itself. However, if the faulty workmanship resulted in a fire, the fire damage would be covered under the special cause of loss form.

In addition, the special exclusions relating to business income and extra expense apply here.

**Limitations** For loss of or damage to glass that is part of a building or structure, the insurer does not pay more than $100 for each plate, pane, or panel. The insurer does not pay more than $500 for all loss of or damage to building glass that occurs at any one time. This limitation does not apply to loss or damage by the certain specified causes of loss, except vandalism.

The insurer does not pay for loss of or damage to the following types of property unless caused by the specified causes of loss or building glass breakage:

- valuable papers and records, such as books of account, manuscripts, abstracts, drawings, card index systems, film, tape, disc, drum, cell, or other data processing, recording or storage media and other records;
- animals, and then only if they are killed or their destruction is made necessary;
- machinery, tools, and equipment the insured owns or that are entrusted to the insured, unless held for sale; or
- fragile articles, such as glassware, statuary, marbles, chinaware, and porcelains, if broken. This restriction does not apply to:
  - glass that is part of a building or structure;
  - containers of property held for sale; or
  - photographic or scientific instrument lenses.

The following types of property are covered for loss or damage by theft only, up to the limits shown:

- $2,500 for furs, fur garments, and garments trimmed with fur;
- $2,500 for jewelry, watches, watch movements, jewels, pearls, precious and semiprecious stones, bullion, gold, silver, platinum, and other precious alloys and metals (but this limit does not apply to jewelry and watches worth $100 or less per item);
- $2,500 for patterns, dies, molds, and forms; and
- $250 for stamps, tickets, and letters of credit.

**Additional Coverage—Collapse** The coverage for direct physical loss involving collapse was presented under the broad form.

## Additional Coverage Extensions

A property in transit extension applies only to the insured's personal property to which the cause of loss form applies. Under this extension, the insured may extend the insurance to apply to personal property in transit other than property in the care, custody or control of the insured's salespeople. Property must be in or on a motor vehicle the insured owns, leases, or operates, and the vehicle must be between points in the coverage territory.

Loss or damage must be caused by or result from one of the following causes of loss:

- fire, lightning, explosion, windstorm, hail, riot or civil commotion, or vandalism;
- vehicle collision, upset, or overturn; or
- theft of an entire bale, case, or package by forced entry into a securely locked body or compartment of the vehicle, upon which marks of the forced entry must be visible.

The most the insurer pays for loss or damage under this extension is $1,000.

This coverage for property in transit is additional insurance. The coinsurance clause does not apply.

## Water Damage

If loss or damage caused by or resulting from a covered water damage loss occurs, the insurer also pays the cost to tear out and replace any part of the building or structure to repair damage to the system or appliance from which the water or steam escapes.

The insurer does not pay the cost of repairing or replacing the system or appliance itself, but it pays the cost to repair or replace damaged parts of fire extinguishing equipment if the damage results in sprinkler leakage or is caused directly by freezing.

## Definitions

Under the section on limitations, it was noted that coverage on glass was limited unless caused by certain specified causes of loss. An exclusion for loss also applied to certain types of property unless the loss resulted from the following specified causes of loss:

- fire;
- lightning;
- explosion;
- windstorm or hail;
- smoke;
- aircraft or vehicles;
- riot or civil commotion;
- vandalism;
- leakage from fire extinguishing equipment;
- sinkhole collapse;
- volcanic action;

- falling objects;
- weight of snow, ice, or sleet; or
- water damage.

## Endorsements to Commercial Property Forms

Many endorsements can be added to the commercial property portion of the commercial property policy (CPP) to customize coverage for an insured. Some of the more important endorsements follow.

### Manufacturer's Selling Price

When attached to the CPP form, the **Manufacturer's Selling Price** endorsement amends the valuation clause that applies to business personal property that has been sold but not delivered at its selling price, less any discounts or expenses the insured would not have incurred except for the loss.

### Additional Property Not Covered

To lower premiums, an insured may wish to exclude certain items of property from coverage. The **Additional Property Not Covered endorsement** allows the insured to schedule categories of property that will not be covered in the event of a loss, thus decreasing the insurance cost.

### Functional Building Valuation

A building may have a replacement cost that far exceeds its market value. The **Functional Building Valuation endorsement** allows for replacement of property with less costly building materials that perform the same function as the damaged or destroyed property. The endorsement also deletes the policy's coinsurance provision.

### Brands and Labels

When an insurance company pays a loss and retains the salvage property, it may wish to sell the damaged property to offset its loss. This might, however, harm the insured's reputation or relationship with its customers. When added to the policy, the **Brands and Labels endorsement** allows the insured, at its own expense, to stamp the merchandise as *salvage* or to remove the labels if that does not cause further damage to the product.

### Peak Season

If an insured has inventory that tends to increase in value at certain predictable times of the year, it may wish to purchase a **Peak Season endorsement**. This coverage automatically increases the limit for business personal property to a preselected amount during the time period listed on the endorsement. This is particularly important to retailers that stock up during holiday seasons.

### Building Ordinance Coverage

When a building suffers damage, three types of consequential losses may occur: the undamaged portion of the building may have to be torn down due to local building codes; there is a cost to demolish the undamaged structure; and there is additional cost to rebuild due to the passage of stricter building laws. These losses are excluded under the BPP form unless the building ordinance coverage endorsement has been attached to the policy. When provided, coverage applies to loss to the undamaged portion of the building, including demolition costs, and to the increased cost of construction necessary to meet current building laws.

**Value Reporting Form**

For a policyholder who owns property that fluctuates constantly in value, the value reporting form allows it to select an amount of insurance that represents the maximum amount of exposure the insured has during the policy year, but pays based only on the actual amount of exposure. A report of values is sent to the company on a regular basis, and at the end of the policy term, the average is computed and the final premium determined.

**Off-Premises Utility Services**

The off-premises utility services endorsement covers direct damage losses to insured property caused by an interruption of utility services that occurs away from the insured's premises. The services included are water, power, and communication.

**Earthquake Cause of Loss Form**

To provide coverage for earth movement, including volcanic eruption, the earthquake cause endorsement must be attached to the BPP form. The endorsement contains a separate deductible, expressed as a percentage of the limit applicable to the covered property. The deductible applies separately to each building (if more than one are insured), to buildings and personal property (if both are covered) or to personal property at different locations.

The earthquake cause of loss form includes a deductible, which applies every 168 hours (one week). Any losses that occur within 168 hours are treated as a single occurrence, and a single deductible applies.

✓ ***For Example:*** On Monday, an earthquake causes minor damage in the part of the city where Acme Company maintains its offices. On Thursday, an aftershock causes more damage, and on Sunday the city experiences yet another tremor. Acme can file a claim to recover damages it suffered during the earthquake, the aftershock and the tremor. Although the company suffered losses in three separate incidents, these incidents occurred within a 168-hour period. Therefore, the earthquake, aftershock and tremor are treated as a single occurrence. Acme pays a single deductible.

## Quick Quiz 15.4

1. What are the three major cause of loss forms used in commercial property insurance?

   A. ____________________
   B. ____________________
   C. ____________________

2. Which of the cause of loss forms is(are) issued using a named perils approach?

   ______________________________________________

   ______________________________________________

3. What four additional perils are included in the broad form but not included in the basic form?

   A. ____________________
   B. ____________________
   C. ____________________
   D. ____________________

4. When glass breakage is included as a covered cause of loss, limitations of $__________ per pane and $__________ per loss apply when the loss is due to certain perils.

5. Which of the following losses is not covered under the basic cause of loss form?

   A. Damage to an exterior building wall caused by spray painting of graffiti
   B. Damage to a building caused by a vehicle that runs into the structure
   C. Damage to a roof caused by a heavy snowfall
   D. Damage to personal property caused by a sprinkler that accidentally discharges in the insured's building

***Answers***

1. *basic, broad, special*
2. *basic, broad*
3. *breakage of glass; falling objects; weight of ice, snow, or sleet; water damage*
4. *$100; $500*
5. ***C.** Weight of ice, snow, or sleet is only a covered peril under the broad or special causes of loss forms.*

## Builder's Risk Coverage Form (CP 00 20 04 02)

A building under construction normally is covered under a specialized contract. Under the Insurance Service Office (ISO) simplified commercial lines program of January 1986, one form provides coverage on a completed value basis, although by endorsement it can be converted into a reporting form. The most recent update was issued in 2002.

For homeowners, a special endorsement is added to the policy that covers the building while under construction and the materials on site before they are made part of the structure. The policy usually is written on a reporting form basis. This allows the change of value as new material is delivered to the job location.

## Builder's Risk Coverage Form

The insurer pays for direct physical loss of or damage to covered property caused by or resulting from a covered cause of loss. The property must be at the premises described in the declarations.

### Covered Property

**Covered property** includes buildings under construction, as described in the Declarations.

### Covered Cause of Loss

**Covered losses** are defined in the attached cause of loss form, as shown on the Declarations Page.

### Loss Payment

The **loss payment condition** provides that the insurer must:

- pay the value of lost or damaged property;
- pay the cost of repairing or replacing lost or damaged property;
- take all or any part of the property at an agreed on or appraised value; or
- repair, rebuild, or replace the property with other property of like kind and quality.

### Coverage Termination

Coverage ceases at the earliest of the following:

- the policy expires or is cancelled;
- the purchaser accepts the property;
- the insured's interest in the property ceases;
- the insured abandons the construction;
- 90 days have passed since construction is completed; or
- building occupancy occurs in whole or in part, or the building is put to its intended use.

Coverage includes the foundation, fixtures, machinery, and equipment used to service the building, as well as temporary structures if they are not insured elsewhere.

## Terrorism Risk Insurance Act of 2002

Insurance professionals must know the purpose of the **Terrorism Risk Insurance Act (TRIA) of 2002** to properly advise policyholders of the new insurance coverage options.

The act established a temporary federal program to provide for public and private compensation for insured losses resulting from terrorist acts. The intent is to:

- protect consumers by addressing market disruptions and ensure the availability and affordability of property and casualty insurance for terrorism risk; and
- give time for the private insurance markets to stabilize, resume pricing of this insurance, and shore up reserves to absorb any future losses, while preserving states regulatory authority over insurance and consumer protection.

### Stipulations of the TRIA

Under the TRIA, all commercial property and casualty policies, with some exceptions noted below, must offer coverage for certified acts of terrorism. TRIA voids any existing terrorism exclusions.

A certified act of terrorism is an act that is certified by the Secretary of the Treasury, the Secretary of State and the Attorney General of the United States to be an act of terrorism pursuant to TRIA:

- The terrorist act must result in aggregate insured property and casualty losses in excess of $5 million.
- The act must be a violent one or an act that is dangerous to human life, property or infrastructure.
- The act must be committed by individuals acting on behalf of any foreign person or foreign interest with the intent to coerce citizens of the US or to influence government policy or conduct.

### Lines Excluded from TRIA

The TRIA applies to commercial lines property and casualty insurance only, including workers' compensation and surety insurance, but specifically excludes:

- life or health insurance; including group life;
- certain federally-backed insurance programs (such as flood or crop insurance);
- medical malpractice insurance;
- reinsurance; and
- financial guaranty insurance written by monoline insurance companies.

The TRIA currently does not apply to personal lines. TRIA impacts workers' compensation policies, but the mandatory terrorism coverage is not a change. Workers' compensation policies have never excluded terrorism or war.

**Government's Reimbursement for Losses**

The federal government is responsible for reimbursing 90% of each insurer's terrorism losses above the insurer's annual deductible, which is based on a percentage of its direct earned premium for TRIA property and casualty covered insurance lines in the previous year. The percentage of the deductible increases each year, starting at 1% in 2002, increasing to 7% in 2003, to 10% in 2004, and to 15% in 2005.

## Insurer's Liability Limit

If the aggregate insured property and casualty losses for certified acts of terrorism exceed $100 billion during any one year TRIA is in effect (it expires on December 31, 2005), the federal government is not obligated under the act to make any payments for any portions of any losses that exceed $100 billion annually. (For these purposes, 2002 and 2003 are treated as a single transition period.) Once the federal government reaches the $100 billion annual limit, insurers that have met their deductible will no longer be liable for payments to insureds for certified acts of terrorism. An insurer's liability for certified acts of terrorism is thus limited by TRIA.

Policyholders should be aware of the importance of the TRIA coverage cap. Even if a policyholder buys coverage for certified acts of terrorism, once the annual $100 billion cap is met, and the insurer has paid its deductible, that insurer will not be obligated to pay any additional or subsequent losses resulting from certified acts of terrorism. Considering that the cost of the September 11, 2001 terrorist attacks is estimated to be $40 billion, the TRIA provides a significant amount of insurance protection.

In the event of a certified act of terrorism, the Secretary of the Treasury is required by the TRIA to spread the risk of the loss among insurers and to recoup certain amounts paid under the Act from insurance carriers. Insurers can add a premium surcharge of no more than 3%, known as the **Terrorism Loss Risk-Spreading Premium**, to all commercial lines property and casualty policies to help spread the risk of loss. This special premium is charged in addition to premiums for the purchase of coverage for certified acts of terrorism.

**Policyholder Awareness**

Producers need to make commercial policyholders aware that the TRIA allows carriers to assess no more than a 3% risk-spreading premium surcharge to all policyholders, even those who reject terrorism coverage.

Policyholders with in-force policies as of November 26, 2002 have a minimum of 30 days, from the receipt of notice from the insurer, to review the new terrorism coverage and accept or reject the new coverage and premium.

## The TRIA in Summary

The TRIA, in summary, provides for all of the following:

- Requires all commercial property and casualty insurers to make available terrorism coverage for losses resulting from certified acts of terrorism
- Voids existing terrorism exclusions on policies in force as of November 26, 2002, to the extent that those provisions exclude losses insured under the act
- Does not currently affect personal lines coverage
- Does impact workers' compensation policies, although mandatory coverage is not changed because workers' compensation policies have never excluded losses from terrorist acts or war
- Requires insurers to provide policyholders with a clear and conspicuous disclosure of the premium charged for terrorism coverage and also a disclosure of the federal share of compensation under the act
- Requires participating insurers to retain some terrorism losses through a deductible and coinsurance (10% of losses exceeding the insurer's deductible)

# Unit Test Fifteen

1. Under a commercial property policy, which of the following is considered a direct loss?
   A. Loss of business profits due to destruction of the premises by fire
   B. Loss of rental income due to destruction of the building by fire
   C. Loss of use of a building damaged by fire
   D. Expenses to rent temporary office space following a fire

2. Under the terms of a property insurance policy, an insured who suffers a fire loss has which of the following rights?
   A. If desired, the insured may give the damaged property to the insurance company for full payment of the loss.
   B. If dissatisfied with the settlement offer, the insured may notify the insurance company of the intent to hire an appraiser.
   C. If desired, the insured may abandon damaged property to the insurer.
   D. If dissatisfied with the settlement offer, the insured may hire an independent adjuster.

3. Which of the following losses involving water damage is covered under the building and personal property coverage form with basic causes of loss?
   A. Merchandise in a retail store catches fire and sets off an automatic sprinkler system, resulting in damage to property.
   B. Water from a sewer backs up through a building's drains, causing severe water damage.
   C. A dam breaks, causing flood damage to a building and its contents.
   D. A window is left open, and rain causes extensive damage to the building's contents.

4. Which of the following is an insurable physical peril to valuable personal property?
   A. Inherent vice
   B. Theft
   C. Wear and tear
   D. Gradual deterioration

5. Which of the following losses is covered by a broad causes of loss form?
   A. Fire started by firemen to create a fire break
   B. Storms that disrupt power, closing the business
   C. Furniture destroyed by the manager's dog in the office
   D. Arson fire set by a disgruntled employee

6. The form of coverage for business risks that is most similar to additional living expense for homeowners is
   A. extended period of indemnity
   B. business income
   C. extra expense
   D. loss of rents

7. Which of the following statements regarding business income coverage is CORRECT?
   A. It automatically covers extra expenses the insured incurs because of the loss.
   B. It covers extra expenses to the extent they reduce the business interruption loss.
   C. It provides a steady source of profits to a business following a loss.
   D. It can be added to the commercial property policy without charge.

8. A business income coverage form provides insurance for
   A. cancellation of a lease
   B. additional living expenses
   C. lost profits
   D. noncontinuing expenses

9. Which of the following is NOT required of an insured following a loss under the commercial property policy?
   A. Protect the property from further damage
   B. Give prompt written notice of the loss to the insurer
   C. Provide an inventory of damaged property
   D. Provide financial statements and evidence of lost profits

10. Under the provisions of the building and personal property coverage form, the insurer may take possession of damaged property under which of the following conditions?
   A. Upon written notice to the insured of its intention to do so
   B. With permission of the insured and payment of the agreed or appraisal value to the insured
   C. At its own option and by paying the agreed or appraisal value to the insured
   D. Before payment of loss under the policy

11. The building and personal property coverage form insures which of the following items of property?
   A. Money
   B. Evidence of debt
   C. Antique furniture
   D. Licensed passenger automobiles

12. An insurance company must notify an insured of its decision as to how it will handle an insured loss within how many days?
   A. 10
   B. 30
   C. 45
   D. 60

13. All of the following coverages are included in the building and personal property coverage EXCEPT
   A. buildings
   B. appurtenant structures
   C. personal property of the insured
   D. personal property of others

14. Which of the following is insured under a building and personal property coverage form that meets the policy's coinsurance requirement?
   A. Trees and shrubs
   B. Earthquake
   C. Falling objects on driveway
   D. All of the above

15. The subrogation clause in a building and personal property coverage form allows the insurance company to
   A. reduce the policy's face value to allow for the building's depreciation
   B. deny a claim for a loss caused by a careless action of the insured
   C. take over the insured's rights against the parties responsible for the loss
   D. revoke the contract upon written notice

16. The abandonment clause of a building and personal property coverage form allows the insured to do which of the following?
   A. Abandon the premises when a loss is in progress
   B. Abandon the premises to the insurer following a loss
   C. Abandon damaged property to the insurance company and claim a total loss
   D. Nothing that would abandon the premises to the insurer after the loss

17. The broad cause of loss form includes each of the following perils EXCEPT
    A. theft
    B. wind
    C. lightning
    D. sprinkler leakage

18. Under the commercial property policy's conditions, what happens to the insured's rights and duties if he or she dies?
    A. The policy becomes null and void.
    B. The policy must be terminated with 30 days notice.
    C. The insurer assumes the insured's duties until the estate is settled.
    D. The duties are transferred to the insured's legal representative.

19. A property policy's coverage can extend to each of the following EXCEPT
    A. money and securities
    B. office equipment
    C. production machinery
    D. merchandise

20. When does a builder's risk policy terminate?
    A. When the building is occupied
    B. 90 days after completion
    C. When the purchaser accepts the property
    D. At the earliest of the above times

# Unit Test Fifteen Answers & Rationale

1. **C.** Loss of profits and rents and extra expenses are considered consequential or indirect losses.

2. **B.** A property policy provides that the insured may not abandon the property to the company. If an insured is not satisfied with a settlement, he may invoke the policy's appraisal condition, which calls for each party to hire an appraiser, with the appraisers selecting an umpire to settle losses.

3. **A.** Water damage coverage is not provided for backup of sewers or drains except by endorsement. Flood damage is included only on separate policies. For water damage to be covered, there first must be exterior damage to the building. Discharge of a sprinkler system was caused proximately by fire, a covered peril, in the situation described in answer A.

4. **B.** All property insurance policies exclude nonfortuitous losses, such as inherent vice, wear and tear and gradual deterioration of property.

5. **D.** Intentional losses caused by an insured are excluded under property policies, but those caused by others (for instance, members of the public and employees) are covered under fire insurance.

6. **C.** Extra expense coverage insures the extraordinary expenses an insured incurs following a loss to maintain a business. This coverage is most similar to the additional living expense coverage designed to maintain a family's standard of living.

7. **B.** The business income form without extra expense coverage still provides coverage for extra expenses, but only to the extent that they reduce the loss otherwise payable under the policy.

8. **C.** Business income coverage does not apply to losses due to lease cancellation or to expenses that do not continue following a loss. Additional living expense is a homeowners coverage.

9. **D.** Unless a business income loss is claimed, the insured need not furnish financial statements in the event of a property loss.

10. **C.** The determination of how a loss is settled always is left to the insurer, without any specific consent or permission of the insured.

11. **C.** Some of the property the BPP form does not cover includes money and securities, evidences of debt and motor vehicles licensed for road use.

12. **B.** The BPP form's loss payment condition requires that the insurer give 30 days' notice of how it intends to settle a loss, as well as alternatives open to the insured.

13. **B.** Homeowners policies, not commercial property forms, provide appurtenant structures coverage.

14. **A.** The BPP form's coverage extensions apply only if a coinsurance percentage of 80% or more is in effect on the policy, although the coinsurance clause does not apply to the losses included under the extensions. Coverage may be extended to the insured's outdoor property, including trees and shrubs.

15. **C.** Subrogation provides a transfer of the insured's right of recovery against another party to the insurer in exchange for payment of losses for which the other party is primarily responsible.

16. **D.** A property policy's abandonment clause prohibits an insured from abandoning the property to the insurer following a loss. This clause arises in the context of a commercial property policy as well as a homeowners policy.

17. **A.** Theft coverage is included only under the special cause of loss form, which is issued on an open perils basis.

18. **D.** When an insured dies, the insurance company remains obligated to pay any covered losses, and all duties under the policy, including premium payment and notification of loss, are transferred to the insured's legal representative.

19. **A.** Money and securities are specifically excluded personal property under a commercial property policy. Coverage for such items typically is secured using a crime insurance policy.

20. **D.** A builder's risk form provides that coverage terminates at the earliest of the policy expiration or cancellation date, when the owners accept the property, when the insured's interest ceases, when the insured abandons the construction, 90 days after construction is completed, or when the building is occupied in whole or in part or put to its intended use.

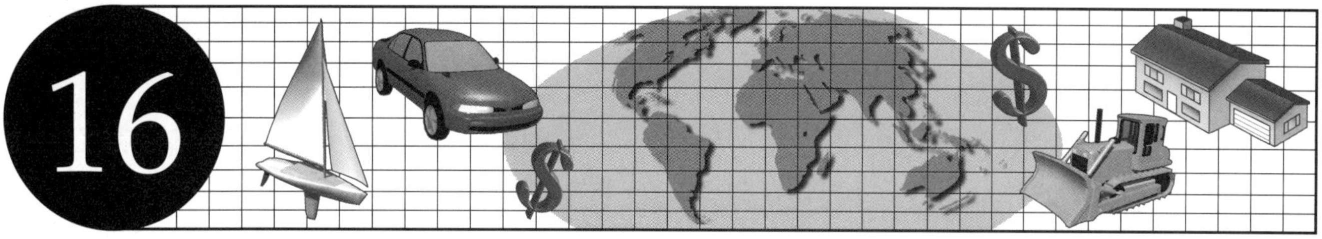


# Businessowners Policy

## INTRODUCTION

Almost 30 years ago, insurance agents and policyholders sought a better method to deal with the exposures of small businessowners. Personal lines policies were being offered as a package or bundle of needed coverages, but commercial policies were still modular, needing to be built section by section. In addition, the rating system was cumbersome and time consuming. All of this required a level of sophistication and technical knowledge that was lacking among policyholders and some newer agents, who were likely to specialize in small business accounts. Originally an insurance company developed the businessowners policy (BOP), but the ISO soon came up with its own version.

Today, major insurance companies generally offer their own BOP-type policies, with names specific to those companies, but most pattern their forms after the ISO policy. The discussion that follows is based on the ISO policy. Although no company uses the form without modification, it remains a good way to study individual company forms that follow similar formats.

## UNIT OBJECTIVES

When you have completed this unit, you should be able to:

- identify the business owners policy's purpose and unique characteristics;
- determine the types of businesses eligible for coverage under the BOP;
- describe the property the BOP does and does not cover;
- explain the additional coverages the BOP provides;
- discuss the BOP's extensions of coverage;
- distinguish between the standard and the special BOP and describe each form's causes of loss;
- describe the optional coverages available under the BOP; and
- discuss the BOP liability coverages and compare them with the coverage the CGL policy provides.

# Purpose and Characteristics (BP 00 03 07)

The **Businessowners Policy (BOP)** is a package policy providing most of the property (both direct and indirect), crime and liability coverages small and medium-sized businesses require. (The property coverages are similar to the building and personal property coverage form and the business income coverage discussed in Unit 15). However, the BOP automatically includes many of the coverages available only by endorsement in the CPP program.

**Test Topic Alert!**

The businessowners policy provides coverage similar to that of the commercial policy for small and medium-size businesses. However, the BOP does not cover businesses related to autos, bars, and banks.

## Eligibility

The BOP was designed for businesses that represent relatively low hazards and more innocuous exposures. Therefore, eligibility is restricted to apartment buildings, offices, eligible wholesalers, mercantile risks, and service or processing occupancies. Additional restrictions limit the size of the business that qualifies for coverage. For instance, sales are limited to $3 million, and the maximum floor area for mercantile, service, office, or wholesale risks is 25,000 square feet. Four new categories were included recently for eligibility under the BOP: contractors, restaurants (simple food preparation facilities only), convenience stores with gasoline pumps, laundries, and dry cleaners.

## Policy Outline

Every BOP is a self-contained contract that includes the following parts:

- businessowners Declarations;
- businessowners common policy Conditions;
- standard or special property coverage form;
- businessowners liability coverage form; and
- endorsements as required.

Many of the BOP's basic policy provisions are the same as the provisions discussed in Unit 15 for commercial property insurance. This unit will note the differences.

## Declarations

One of the BOP's unique features is that common coverages are included in the form, rather than being attached to it as policy endorsements. Coverage only applies if it has been activated by a check mark in the Declarations. Listing the optional coverages on the Declarations Page alerts policyholders to important coverages that are available, but which they have not purchased.

**Test Topic Alert!**

The BOP can be purchased with either the standard or special coverage for property. The purchaser selects the coverage by noting the choice in the Declarations.

As noted, the BOP may be purchased with either standard or special coverage for the property, indicated on the Declarations. The two forms may not be combined, so if both buildings and personal property are included, they must be insured with the same form. Most of the coverages provided in the two forms are identical. The major differences lie in the covered causes of loss, discussed below. Minor differences also exist in the availability of optional coverages.

## Businessowners Common Policy Conditions (BP 00 09 01)

The BOP is issued with a common policy conditions form that details the 12 conditions that apply regardless of whether coverage is purchased on a standard or a special basis. (Many of these conditions are identical to those discussed in previous units). Both the property and liability sections of the policy contain additional conditions that pertain specifically to that coverage.

The BOP's common policy conditions follow:

- Cancellation
- Changes
- Concealment, misrepresentation, or fraud
- Examination of the insured's books and records
- Inspections and surveys
- Insurance under two or more coverages
- Liberalization
- Other insurance
- Premiums
- Premium audit
- Transfer of rights of recovery against others
- Transfer of the insured's rights and duties under the policy

### Property Coverages

Both standard and special businessowners policies provide two coverages:

- Coverage A—Building(s); and
- Coverage B—Business Personal Property.

A limit of insurance for each coverage is shown on the Declarations.

The standard deductible is $500, also noted in the Declarations.

**Coverage A—Building(s)**

The BOP covers the replacement cost of the buildings at the premises described in the Declarations, including completed additions, fixtures, permanently installed machinery and equipment, personal property of a landlord in rented units, and personal property used to service or maintain the premises. If the buildings are not covered by other insurance, BOP coverage also includes additions under construction, building alterations and repairs and materials, supplies, equipment and temporary structures on or within 100 feet of the premises being used to make alterations, repairs or additions to buildings or structures.

**Coverage B—Business Personal Property**

The BOP policy covers replacement cost of the business personal property the insured owns and uses for business purposes at the premises described in the Declarations and within 100 feet while in a vehicle or out in the open. Also included for coverage are:

- similar property the insured holds that belongs to others but does not exceed the amount for which the insured is legally liable, including the value of labor, materials and charges furnished, performed or incurred by the insured;
- tenant's improvements and betterments, meaning the insured's use of or interest in fixtures, alterations, installations or additions comprising a part of the building the insured occupies but does not own; and
- leased personal property for which the insured has a contracted responsibility to insure.

**Property Not Covered**

The businessowners policy does not cover:

- aircraft, automobiles, motor trucks, and other vehicles subject to motor vehicle registration;
- bullion, money, and securities;
- contraband, or property in the course of illegal transportation or trade;
- land, water, growing crops, and lawns;
- watercraft (including motors, equipment and accessories) while afloat;
- outdoor fences, radio, or television antennas, including satellite dishes and the wiring, masts, or towers;
- exterior signs and other outdoor property unless insured under optional coverages:
  - accounts, bills, food stamps, accounts receivable unless otherwise covered by the policy; or
  - computers that are permanently installed or designed to permanently installed in aircraft, watercraft, motor truck or other vehicle subject to motor vehicle registration.

## Additional Coverages under Standard Form

The BOP standard form includes 11 additional coverages:

### *Debris Removal*

The BOP covers the cost of removing debris of covered property that results from an insured loss. The most the insurer pays is 25% of the amount of the direct loss, plus the deductible for that loss or damage. However, if the debris removal expense exceeds this amount, or if the combined amount of the direct loss and the debris removal expense exceeds the policy limit, the company pays up to an additional $10,000.

### *Preservation of Property*

When covered property is moved from the premises to protect it from damage by a covered cause of loss, coverage applies for 30 days while that property is being moved or is located at a temporary location.

### *Fire Department Service Charge*

The policy pays up to $1,000 for the cost of fire service to protect covered property.

### *Business Income*

One of the singular features of the BOP policy is the automatic inclusion of indirect loss coverage as an additional coverage. If business operations are suspended due to a covered loss at the described premises, the policy pays for loss of business income during the period of time the property is being restored. Coverage applies for up to 12 months following a loss and is paid on the basis of the actual loss the insured sustains, in addition to any limits indicated in the declarations. Payroll expenses, however, are paid only 60 days following the date of loss.

### *Extra Expense*

Another important automatic feature of the BOP is the inclusion of extra expense coverage. Both the business income and extra expense coverage the BOP provides are similar to the CPP program's separate coverage forms.

✓ ***Take Note:*** One of the BOP's characteristics is the automatic inclusion of business income and extra expense coverage. Because the coverage is provided on an actual loss sustained basis, it eliminates the possibility that an insured might not purchase this valuable and necessary coverage.

### *Pollutant Clean-Up and Removal*

The company pays the cost to extract pollutants from land or water at the described premises if the release or discharge was caused by a covered loss during the policy period. The most that the policy pays is $10,000 in any 12-month period.

### *Civil Authority*

Business income and extra expense is extended to include loss caused by action of a civil authority that prevents access to the insured premises when there has been a direct loss to property other than at the described premises, such as an adjacent location. The cause of the loss at that location must be covered had it occurred at the insured location.

### *Money Orders and Counterfeit Paper Currency*

The policy pays up to $1,000 for loss due to acceptance of counterfeit currency or dishonored money orders.

### *Forgery and Alteration*

Loss due to forgery or alteration of an insured's check, draft, promissory note or similar item is covered up to $2,500, including legal expenses that may result from the insured's refusal to honor these items when he or she suspects that they have been altered.

### *Increased Cost of Construction*

When buildings are insured under the policy on a replacement cost basis, the company pays up to $10,000 for the additional loss caused by the increased costs the insured incurs in complying with an ordinance or a law that regulates the construction or repair of buildings or with a zoning or land use law.

### *Exterior Building Glass*

Direct physical loss to glass that is part of a covered building's or structure's exterior is treated as a loss to the building or structure, including any necessary temporary repairs or boarding up of openings. This is not an additional amount of insurance; therefore, it is included in the limit of liability shown in the declarations.

## Additional Coverages under Special Form

The BOP special form includes all eleven of the above additional coverages, plus the following.

**Collapse** The policy covers collapse of a building or structure if the collapse is caused by any of the specified causes of loss identified in the policy, hidden decay, hidden insect or vermin damage, weight of people or property, weight of rain that collects on a roof or use of defective materials or methods in the construction, remodeling, or renovation of the building or structure.

**Water Damage, Other Liquids, Powder, or Molten Material Damage**

The cost to tear out and replace a part of an insured building due to damage from water, other liquid, powder or molten material is included. Coverage does not apply to the defect that caused the loss or damage.

## Coverage Extensions

Both BOPs provide six extensions of coverage in addition to the limits of liability shown in the policies.

**Business Personal Property at Newly Acquired or Constructed Premises**

A limit of up to $100,000 applies to personal property located at any premises the insured acquires during the policy period. Coverage ends after the policy expires, 30 days after the insured acquires the new premises, or when the values are reported to the company, whichever is earlier.

**Personal Property Off Premises**

A $5,000 limit applies to personal property other than money and securities, valuable papers, and records or accounts receivable located off the insured premises. This includes personal property while in transit and at temporary locations the insured does not own, lease, or rent.

**Outdoor Property**

Insurance can be extended to apply to damage to outdoor fences, radio and television antennas (including satellite dishes), signs (other than those attached to buildings), trees, shrubs, and plants caused by the perils of fire, lightning, explosion, aircraft, or riot or civil commotion. The total amount of coverage is $2,500 under this extension, but a limitation of $500 applies to any one tree, shrub or plant.

**Personal Effects**

The insured may extend coverage up to $2,500 for loss of personal effects, including those that officers, partners or employees own. Coverage does not apply to loss due to theft or to loss of tools or equipment used in the insured's business.

**Valuable Papers and Records**

The limit for loss or damage to valuable papers and records in a single occurrence at the insured premises is $10,000.

Loss or damage to valuable papers and records away from the insured premises is limited to $5,000. Coverage is provided for the cost of researching, replacing or restoring lost information, including information stored on electronic or magnetic media for which no duplicates exist.

**Accounts Receivable** Loss or damage to accounts receivable records that causes accounts to become uncollectable is covered up to $10,000 on premises and $5,000 off premises.

## Quick Quiz 16.1

1. What are the two primary coverages the BOP provides?

   A. ________________

   B. ________________

2. What two additional coverages does the special BOP provide that the standard form does not?

   A. ________________

   B. ________________

3. What 6 coverage extensions are available under the BOP?

   A. ________________________________________

   B. ________________________________________

   C. ________________________________________

   D. ________________________________________

   E. ________________________________________

   F. ________________________________________

### *Answers*

1. *building; business personal property*
2. *collapse; water damage*
3. *personal property at newly acquired premises; personal property off premises; outdoor property; personal effects; valuable papers and records; accounts receivable*

# Perils Insured against and Exclusions

## Standard BOP (BP 00 01 01 97)

The following perils and exclusions, which have been described previously under cause of loss forms in the last unit, appear in the standard BOP:

**Perils**

- Fire
- Lightning
- Windstorm or hail, not including frost or ice
- Explosion, not including rupture due to pressure, expansion, or swelling
- Smoke
- Aircraft or vehicles
- Riot, riot attending a strike, or civil commotion
- Vandalism or malicious mischief
- Sprinkler leakage
- Sinkhole collapse
- Volcanic action
- Transportation of property

✓ ***Take Note:*** Property in transit also is covered for collision, derailment, or overturn of a transporting conveyance; stranding or sinking of vessels; and collapse of bridges, culverts, docks, or wharves.

**Exclusions**

- Enforcement of ordinance or law
- Power failure
- Earth movement
- Governmental action
- Nuclear hazard
- War and military action
- Water damage (flood and sewer backup)

## Special BOP (BP 00 02 12 99)

The special businessowners policy, the more popular of the forms, insures against risks of direct physical loss except those items excluded specifically, as presented earlier under Cause of Loss—Special Form in Unit 15:

- Consequential loss
- Smoke, vapor, or gas
- Steam apparatus
- Frozen plumbing
- Dishonesty
- False pretense
- Exposed property
- Collapse (except as provided under the additional coverage)
- Pollution
- Other losses (wear and tear, rust, corrosion, fungus, decay, etc.)
- Weather conditions, acts or decisions of others, negligent work

Special exclusions and limitations apply to the business income, extra expense, valuable papers and records, and accounts receivable coverages.

## Optional Coverages

**Employee Dishonesty**

When designated in the declarations, the BOP covers loss of money or other business personal property caused by the dishonest or fraudulent acts of the named insured's employees. Claims are paid once an employee either admits to the act or is convicted. Coverage is for an amount not exceeding the limit of liability shown in the Declarations and subject to the conditions that apply generally to crime insurance (as discussed in Unit 8).

**Test Topic Alert!**

The BOP may cover losses of money or other business personal property caused by the dishonest or fraudulent acts of the insured's employees.

**Outdoor Signs**

When designated in the Declarations, coverage is provided for loss to all exterior signs that are the insured's property or the property of others in the insured's care, custody or control. The property must be on the premises described in the Declarations, and coverage is for direct physical loss. Although broad, coverage for exterior signs excludes wear and tear, corrosion or rust, latent defect, or mechanical breakdown.

**Interior Glass**

When such coverage is designated in the Declarations, the policy applies to all exterior grade floor and basement glass, including encasing frames and all lettering or ornamentation on the frames, that are the insured's property or the property of others in the insured's care, custody, or control in the building described in the declarations. Property is protected against risks of direct physical loss for glass, excluding wear and tear, latent defect, corrosion, and rust.

**Burglary and Robbery**

When burglary and robbery coverage is designated in the Declarations, this policy insures against loss by burglary and robbery to:

- business personal property, excluding money and securities, on the described premises for an amount not to exceed 25% of the limit of liability of Coverage B (business personal property);
- money and securities while in or on the described premises or within a bank or savings institution for an amount not to exceed the limit shown in the Declarations for Inside the Premises;
- money and securities while en route to or from the described premises, bank or savings institution, or within the living quarters of the custodian of such funds for an amount not to exceed the limit shown in the Declarations for Outside the Premises.

Various exclusions and conditions applicable to burglary and robbery coverage have been presented in Unit 8. The following property is subject to the additional limitations indicated:

- Fur and fur garments are covered up to an aggregate of $2,500 in any one occurrence.

- Jewelry, watches, watch movements, jewels, pearls, precious and semiprecious stones, gold, silver, platinum, and other precious alloys or metals are covered up to an aggregate of $2,500 in any one occurrence. This limitation does not apply to jewelry and watches valued at $100 or less per item.
- Patterns, dies, molds, and forms are limited to $2,500.

**Mechanical Breakdown** When mechanical breakdown is designated in the declarations, the BOP covers loss from an accident to an object (as defined in the policy) that the insured owns, leases or operates. (Additional information about this type of coverage will be presented in Unit 17, Boiler and Machinery Insurance.)

Because the special BOP covers burglary and robbery as part of theft, the optional coverage under that form applies to money and securities.

**Deductibles** The insurer will not pay for a loss in any one occurrence until the amount of loss or damage exceeds the deductible shown in the Declarations. Under Optional Coverages of Burglary and Robbery, Employee Dishonesty, Interior Glass and Outdoor Signs, as well as under Additional Coverage–Exterior Building Glass, the Optional Coverage Exterior Building Glass deductible shown in the Declarations will be applied. This will not increase the standard deductible shown in the Declarations. The deductible provision does not apply to losses under business income, extra expense, civil authority and fire department service charge coverages. A 72-hour time deductible under business income and civil authority coverages applies, however.

## Business Liability Coverage (BP 00 06 01 97)

**Business Liability** The insurer pays on the insured's behalf all sums that the insured becomes legally obligated to pay as damages because of bodily injury, property damage, personal injury, or advertising injury caused by an occurrence to which the insurance applies.

**Right and Duty to Defend** The insurer has the right and duty to defend any claim or suit against the insured seeking damages payable under the policy, even though the suit's allegations may be groundless, false, or fraudulent. The insurer may investigate and settle any claim or suit as it deems expedient. The insurer is not obligated to pay any claim or judgment or to defend any suit after the applicable limit of the insurer's liability has been exhausted by payment of judgments or settlements.

✓ ***Take Note:*** The insurer's right to defend a claim or suit against its insured is common in the context of insurance coverage. It entails both a right and a duty on the insurer's part. First, the insurer is not obligated to pay any claim made against the insured until the claim is proven valid. The claimant may need to sue the insured to prove its claim. If the claimant proves its claim, the insurer must pay to satisfy the judgment unless it appeals the verdict. On the other hand, the insurer has an obligation to its insured to defend it from claims and lawsuits. Therefore, if the insured is sued, the policy provides legal counsel to defend the insured and pays court for legal representation costs and filing fees. If the claimant obtains a verdict against the insured, the insurer—not the insured—pays any sum of money awarded to the claimant.

**Supplementary Payments**

The insurer pays, in addition to the applicable limit of liability, costs to defend and provide first aid as common to liability insurance. This amount is paid outside of the limits of liability.

**Medical Payments**

The insurer pays up to the limit stated in the Declarations for reasonable medical expenses incurred by any person who requires medical services because of an accident arising out of business operations. The policy pays medical expenses without regard to liability or negligence, but only if the person or event was one the insurer would insure under general liability coverage. This does not cover medical expenses arising out of automobile accidents.

The medical expenses must be incurred within one year after the accident and must result directly from the accident. The incident must be reported within a reasonable time period after the incident occurs.

**Test Topic Alert!**

The BOP pays the medical expenses a person incurs as the result of an accident arising out of the insured's business operations. The expenses must be incurred within one year of and result directly from the accident.

**Exclusions**

The businessowners liability policy contains many of the same exclusions and limitations included in the CGL policy discussed in Unit 5. The BOP excludes the following liabilities:

- Expected or intended injury
- Contractual liability
- Liquor liability
- Workers' compensation
- Employer's liability
- Pollution
- Aircraft, auto or watercraft
- Mobile equipment
- War
- Professional services
- Damage to property
- Damage to the insured's product
- Damage to the insured's work
- Impaired property
- Recall of products, work, or impaired property
- Personal or advertising injury (coverage limitations)
- Advertising injury (coverage limitations)

Additional exclusions apply to the medical expense coverage under the policy. Coverage does not apply to a(n):

- insured;
- person hired to do work for or on behalf of an insured or an insured's tenant;
- person injured on that part of the insured's premises he normally occupies;
- person eligible to receive workers' compensation or other similar benefits;
- person injured while taking part in athletics;
- person injured within the products or completed operations hazard; or
- peril insured under the business liability coverage; or
- war, insurrection, rebellion, or revolution.

## Conditions

The BOP contains most of the policy conditions that form a part of the property and liability coverage parts of the CPP.

## Endorsements

A number of endorsements are available to customize the BOP according to a policyholder's needs. Some of the more common endorsements follow.

- **Additional insured endorsements.** Several endorsements cover additional entities under the insured's policy.
- **Limitation of coverage to designated premises or projects.** Sometimes an insurer will not provide coverage on a comprehensive basis and requires a policy modification to make coverage applicable to only certain locations or activities.
- **Hired and nonowned auto liability.** If coverage is not provided on a business auto policy (usually because the insured has no owned automobile exposures), the coverage for employee use of automobiles in the insured's business and the insured's use of borrowed or rented autos may be provided in the BOP.
- **Spoilage coverage.** This endorsement provides direct damage coverage for spoilage of perishable stock, such as food products.
- **Ordinance or law.** This endorsement extends building coverage under the standard or special form to include loss to the undamaged portion of the building or structure.
- **Utility services—direct damage.** This endorsement provides coverage due to interruption of water, communication, and power services if the loss occurs off premises.
- **Earthquake.** Coverage is extended under either the standard or special form to apply to loss due to earthquake.
- **Professional liability endorsements.** A variety of endorsements is available for selected professional liability exposures, such as barbers, beauticians, funeral directors, opticians, printers and veterinarians.

## Quick Quiz 16.2

1. What characteristic of the BOP standard form distinguishes it from the special form?

 ______________________________

 ______________________________

2. Under the BOP's burglary and robbery optional coverage, what are the limitations on:

 Fur and fur garments? $ ________
 Jewelry and watches? $ ________
 Patterns, dies, molds and forms? $ ________

3. Why is the burglary and robbery optional coverage available only under the standard BOP form?

 ______________________________

 ______________________________

4. What are some examples of professions that may obtain their professional liability coverage from a BOP?

 ______________________________

 ______________________________

## *Answers*

1. *The standard BOP form is a named perils form, while the special BOP is an open perils policy.*
2. *$2,500; $2,500; $2,500*
3. *Theft is a covered peril under the Special BOP (not excluded) and is not a named peril under the Standard BOP form.*
4. *Barbers, beauticians, funeral directors, opticians, printers, veterinarians*

# Unit Test Sixteen

1. Which of the following statements regarding the BOP's business income coverage is CORRECT?
   A. It pays the net income that the insured would have received had no loss occurred.
   B. It guarantees a profit for the insured in the event of a loss.
   C. It pays only continuing expenses.
   D. It pays whether or not a direct loss has occurred.

2. Under the businessowners policy, which of the following coverages is mandatory?
   A. Boiler and machinery
   B. Money and securities
   C. Burglary and robbery
   D. Buildings or personal property

3. Coverage A (Buildings) of the businessowners policy covers all of the following EXCEPT
   A. installed machinery
   B. maintenance equipment
   C. office furniture
   D. outdoor fixtures

4. Which of the following is eligible for a businessowners policy?
   A. Farmer
   B. Retail store
   C. Auto dealer
   D. Industrial repair service

5. The businessowners policy includes which of the following optional coverages?
   A. Workers' compensation
   B. Boiler and machinery
   C. Business auto
   D. Products liability

6. Which of the following is eligible for the BOP?
   A. Automobile dealer
   B. Restaurant
   C. Farm
   D. Manufacturer

7. The BOP automatically includes each of the following coverages EXCEPT
   A. property
   B. products and completed operations
   C. liability
   D. boiler and machinery

8. Mandatory coverage for the BOP includes
   A. glass
   B. liability
   C. crime
   D. boiler and machinery

9. Which of the following have always been eligible for coverage under the businessowners policy?
   A. Restaurant
   B. Contractor
   C. Laundry
   D. Apartment

10. Which of the following is a distinctive feature of the businessowners policy?
    A. Coverage that includes property and liability
    B. Activation of certain coverages on the Declarations Page
    C. Coverage for buildings on an open perils basis
    D. Availability of optional coverages

11. The businessowners policy excludes which of the following property?
    A. Vehicle subject to registration
    B. Personal property of others
    C. Permanently installed machinery and equipment
    D. Tenant's improvements and betterments

12. All of the following are additional coverages under the businessowners policy EXCEPT
    A. preservation of property
    B. business income
    C. debris removal
    D. trees, shrubs, and plants

13. How much is the amount provided under the BOP's additional coverage for increased cost of construction?
    A. $1,000
    B. $2,500
    C. $5,000
    D. $10,000

14. Coverage for pollutant clean-up and removal under the BOP is limited to
    A. $1,000
    B. $5,000
    C. $10,000
    D. No coverage is available for pollutant clean-up and removal.

15. Under the BOP, coverage for personal property located at newly acquired locations is limited to how many days?
    A. 10
    B. 30
    C. 60
    D. 90

16. The coverage extension for outdoor property under the BOP includes all of the following causes of loss EXCEPT
    A. explosion
    B. riot or civil commotion
    C. windstorm
    D. aircraft

17. Coverage for accounts receivable on the insured's premises is limited to what amount under the BOP?
    A. $1,000
    B. $2,500
    C. $5,000
    D. $10,000

18. The special BOP does NOT exclude coverage for losses due to which of the following?
    A. Consequential damages
    B. Dishonesty
    C. Pollution
    D. Theft

19. When activated by an entry on the BOP's Declarations Page, burglary and robbery coverage is limited to which of the following?
    A. 10% of Coverage A
    B. 25% of Coverage B
    C. 50% of Coverage B
    D. 100% of Coverage B

20. What is the limit for expensive jewelry and watches under the BOP's burglary and robbery coverage?
    A. $500
    B. $1,000
    C. $2,500
    D. $5,000

21. How much is the standard deductible under the BOP?
    A. $250
    B. $500
    C. $1,000
    D. No deductible exists under the BOP.

22. The waiting period or deductible under the BOP's business income coverage is how many hours?
    A. 24
    B. 48
    C. 72
    D. 96

# Unit Test Sixteen Answers & Rationale

1. **A.** The BOP's business income coverage pays actual business income loss and necessary expenses to resume operations. This includes reduction in gross earnings and loss of rents less noncontinuing expenses.

2. **D.** The BOP must provide Coverage A Buildings or Coverage B Personal Property.

3. **C.** Installed machinery, equipment used to maintain the premises and outdoor fixtures all are included under the BOP definition of *building*.

4. **B.** Businessowners policies were designed for insureds who present relatively low hazards and more innocuous exposures. A retail store, as such an exposure, is eligible for the BOP subject to restrictions on sales and square footage.

5. **B.** The BOP's optional coverages include employee dishonesty, outdoor signs, interior glass, burglary and robbery, mechanical breakdowns (boiler and machinery), and money and securities.

6. **B.** Restaurants recently were added to the BOP's eligibility list.

7. **D.** Boiler and machinery coverage (mechanical breakdown), an optional coverage under the BOP, must be selected by the insured.

8. **B.** Businessowners policies automatically include both property (buildings or personal property) and liability coverages.

9. **D.** Restaurants, contractors, convenience stores, laundries, and dry cleaners recently were added to the BOP eligibility list. Apartments have always been eligible.

10. **B.** One of a BOP's distinguishing features is that optional coverages are included in the policy form, but they must be activated by checking a box on the Declarations Page.

11. **A.** The BOP includes a relatively short list of property not covered, but automobiles, motor trucks and other vehicles subject to motor vehicle registration clearly are excluded.

12. **D.** The BOP's additional coverages are debris removal, preservation of property, fire department service charge, business income, extra expense, pollutant clean-up and removal, acts of a civil authority, money orders and counterfeit paper currency, forgery or alteration, increased cost of construction, exterior building glass, collapse, and water damage.

13. **D.** The limit under the BOP's increased cost of construction additional coverage is $10,000.

14. **C.** The limitation for pollutant clean-up and removal under the BOP's additional coverage is $10,000.

15. **B.** Coverage for newly acquired locations under the BOP's coverage extensions is limited to 30 days.

16. **C.** Outdoor property is included in the BOP's coverage extensions for the perils of fire, lightning, explosion, aircraft, or riot or civil commotion.

17. **D.** Under the BOP's coverage extensions, accounts receivable coverage is provided up to $10,000 on premises and $5,000 off premises.

18. **D.** The BOP special form is an open perils policy that contains no exclusion for loss due to theft. The other listed causes are excluded specifically under the form.

19. **B.** When burglary and robbery optional coverage has been activated in the BOP, coverage is limited to 25% of the limit that applies to Coverage B Business Personal Property.

20. **C**. Jewelry, watches, watch movements, jewels, pearls, precious and semiprecious stones, gold, silver, platinum, and other precious alloys and metals are covered up to $2,500 in the aggregate under the burglary and robbery optional coverage. The limitation does not apply to items valued at $100 or less.

21. **B**. The BOP standard deductible is $500, but this amount may be increased and a rate credit applied.

22. **C**. Business income coverage begins 72 hours following a loss to covered property under the BOP.

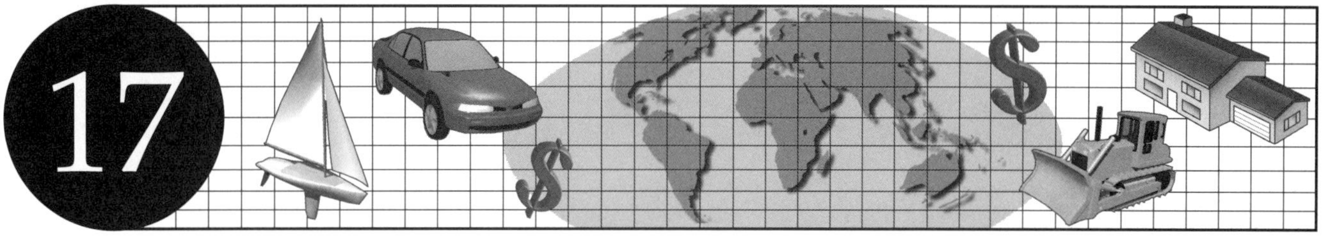


# Boiler and Machinery Insurance

## INTRODUCTION

Boiler and machinery insurance is highly specialized. It usually covers unique hazards that generally are excluded from other forms of commercial property insurance. The classification can be a bit misleading because boiler and machinery insurance can include steam boilers as well as pressure containers, refrigeration systems and units, engines, turbines, generators, and electric motors. The types of property insured are equipment whose operation involves force, pressure, or energy as a significant factor. The insurance company's inspection of the insured property generally is an important condition of the insurance.

## UNIT OBJECTIVES

When you have completed this unit, you should be able to:

- understand the basic differences between the various types of boiler and machinery coverage forms;
- describe a covered object and identify what types of objects are insured on various boiler and machinery forms;
- explain the concept of *accident* as it pertains to boiler and machinery coverage; and
- describe the distinctive way limits are applied in the boiler form.

# Policy Forms

Boiler and machinery coverage is one of the oldest forms of insurance. A small number of insurers specialize in the coverage and use their own forms. Whether issued on a monoline basis or as part of the CPP program, a boiler and machinery policy provides essentially the same protection. The forms reviewed in this unit are the ISO boiler and machinery coverage part of the CPP program. The boiler and machinery insurance policy includes:

- boiler and machinery Declarations;
- boiler and machinery coverage form;
- one or more object definition and time element forms; and
- endorsements.

Three boiler and machinery forms exist. Two are designed for smaller businesses, and one suits the needs of most insureds.

The boiler and machinery coverage form describes the covered property, its location, the causes of loss covered, coverage extensions, exclusions and conditions.

## Object Definition Forms

The object definition forms describe in detail what property is and is not covered. A business owner may select from six object definition forms, depending on the type of equipment used in the business. One or more of the following object definition forms can be attached to the boiler and machinery coverage form:

### *Object Definition no. 1—Pressure and Refrigeration Objects (BM 00 26 06 95)*

Includes coverage for boilers, fired vessels, electric steam generators, steam piping and valves, unfired vessels, refrigerating and air conditioning vessels and piping, small compressing and refrigerating units, and air conditioning units.

### *Object Definition no. 2—Mechanical Objects (BM 00 27 06 95)*

Includes coverage for engines, pumps, compressors, fans, blowers, gear wheels, enclosed gear sets, wheels and shafting, deep-well pumps, and miscellaneous machines.

### *Object Definition no. 3—Electrical Objects (BM 00 28 06 95)*

Includes rotating electrical machines, transformers, induction feeder regulators, miscellaneous electrical apparatus, and solid state rectifier units.

### *Object Definition no. 4—Turbine Objects (BM 00 29 06 95)*

Includes turbines, combustion and other parts of a gas turbine unit, components on any shaft of a driving machine, and mechanical or hydraulic governing mechanisms.

### *Object Definition no. 5—Comprehensive Coverage (BM 00 30 06 95, excluding production machinery)*

Includes all types of insurable boiler and machinery objects, with the exception of production machinery.

### *Object Definition no. 6—Comprehensive Coverage (BM 00 31 06 95, including production machinery)*

The trend in boiler and machinery coverage has been toward the use of the comprehensive forms.

## Time Element Forms

Three **indirect loss coverage endorsements** (**time element forms**) also apply to the boiler and machinery coverage form:

- business interruption;
- extra expense; and
- consequential damage.

The business interruption and extra expense forms are similar to those presented elsewhere in this text in discussions regarding property coverages. Consequential damage coverage provides indemnity for the actual loss of insured property due to spoilage resulting from lack of power, light, heat, or refrigeration at the described premises caused by an accident to an insured object. The insured object is defined in the object definition form(s) attached to the boiler and machinery policy.

## Boiler and Machinery Coverage Form (BM 00 25 06 95)

**Coverage** The insurer pays for direct damage to covered property if a loss results from a covered cause of loss. Covered property includes any property that the insured owns or that is in the insured's care, custody, or control and for which the insured is legally liable.

In addition to paying for loss to this property, the insurer defends the insured against any claim or suit alleging liability for damage to the property, subject to the defense and the supplementary payments provisions.

✓ ***Take Note:*** An interesting feature of boiler forms is the automatic inclusion of coverage for damage to property in the insured's care, custody, or control. This form of coverage usually is excluded in property and liability forms.

## Covered Causes of Loss: *Accident* Defined

Insured losses are accidents to covered objects. The covered objects are those described in the object definition form(s) attached to the policy and identified in the declarations. Objects must be in use or connected and ready for use at the location specified for them at the time of the accident.

As defined in the policy, an **accident** is a sudden and accidental breakdown of the object or a part of the object. At the time the breakdown occurs, it must manifest itself by physical damage to the object that necessitates repair or replacement. If a turbine is covered, for instance, an accident would be a sudden and accidental tearing asunder—that is, an accidental breaking of the turbine or electric generator that is part of the object.

If an initial accident causes other accidents, they all are considered a single accident.

None of the following meets the above definition of an accident:

- Depletion, deterioration, corrosion, or erosion
- Wear and tear
- Leakage at any valve, fitting, shaft seal, gland packing, joint, or connection
- Breakdown of any vacuum tube, glass tube, or brush
- Breakdown of any electronic computer or electronic data processing equipment
- Breakdown of any structure or foundation supporting the object or any of its parts
- Functioning of any safety or protective device

If a strike, riot, civil commotion, act of sabotage, or vandalism results in an accident, this insurance applies. However, the War and Military Action exclusion and resultant condition still apply.

## Limits of Insurance

The boiler and machinery policy imposes a single limit per accident. This includes all direct damage to property that results from a covered accident. Within the limit are sublimits for the following items:

- With respect to damage to covered property, the insurer pays the reasonable extra cost to:
  - make temporary repairs;
  - expedite permanent repairs; and
  - expedite permanent replacement.

- $25,000 for expediting expenses; or, what is left of the Limit of Insurance after payment of loss for Covered Property damaged by an accident, whichever is less.
- $25,000 for hazardous substance clean-up or repair or replacement of contaminated property;
- $25,000 for ammonia contamination damage; including salvage expense; and
- $25,000 for water damage, including salvage expense.

**Test Topic Alert!**

The expediting expenses sublimit covers the cost of temporary repairs and efforts to return the property to use as quickly as possible.

## Coverage Extensions

The Boiler and Machinery policy provides two extensions of coverage in addition to the limits of liability noted in the policy.

### *Automatic Coverage for Newly Acquired Property*

The insurer automatically covers accidents to objects at newly acquired property. This automatic coverage begins on the day the insured acquires the property and continues for 90 days. The insured must give the insurer written notification of the new property within 90 days. The property must be in use and of a type described in the Declarations, and the amount of coverage is within the limits on the Declarations Page. The insurer is not liable, however, for consequential damage, business interruption, or any other indirect loss resulting from an accident to an object.

Also, the insured must agree to pay an additional premium.

### *Defense and supplementary payments*

The insurer promises to settle or defend a claim or suit if brought against the insured due to an accident that caused damage to another person's property in the insured's care, custody or control.

The insurer also pays defense costs the insured incurs, costs the insured incurs at the insurer's request, including up to $100 a day because of lost earnings, and certain interest costs charged against the insured. These costs are in addition to the limit of insurance.

## Exclusions

The following common exclusions apply to this coverage:

- ordinance or law;
- nuclear hazard;
- war or military action; and
- a delay in, or an interruption of, business activity.

In addition, a boiler and machinery policy excludes certain causes of loss commonly provided under a property insurance policy:

- explosion, other than explosion of a steam boiler, a steam generator, steam piping, a steam turbine, a steam engine, a gas turbine, or moving or rotating machinery caused by mechanical breakdown or centrifugal force;
- fire or explosion that occurs at the same time as an accident or as a result of it;
- an accident that results from fire or explosion;
- water damage caused in extinguishing a fire;
- lightning;
- flood; and
- earth movement, including earthquake, landslide, and mudslide.

Other exclusions specifically related to boiler and machinery coverage and equipment include a(n):

- combustion explosion outside the object;
- accident that is the direct or indirect result of a combustion explosion;
- accident to an object while being tested; and
- lack of power, light, heat, steam, or refrigeration.

## Conditions

The following conditions apply to boiler and machinery coverage forms:

- loss conditions;
- general conditions; and
- those common conditions that apply to property and liability coverages.

## Quick Quiz 17.1

1. What are the four forms attached to a CPP when boiler coverage is added?

   A. ____________________
   B. ____________________
   C. ____________________
   D. ____________________

2. What is the broadest object definition that can be included on a boiler policy?

   ______________________________________________
   ______________________________________________

3. What are the three indirect loss forms that can be included on a boiler policy?

   A. ____________________
   B. ____________________
   C. ____________________

4. On a boiler and machinery policy, all of the following are optional coverages EXCEPT

   A. expediting expense
   B. extra expense
   C. actual cash value
   D. business interruption

5. What is the maximum amount the insurer pays for an ammonia contamination loss under the unendorsed boiler policy?

   A. $5,000
   B. $10,000
   C. $15,000
   D. $25,000

## *Answers*

1. *boiler and machinery declarations; boiler and machinery coverage form; object definition form; endorsements*
2. *Object Definition no. 6 (comprehensive coverage including production machinery)*
3. *business interruption; extra expense; consequential damage*
4. ***A.** Expediting expense is included in the per accident limit, although there is a sublimit of $25,000 that applies to this coverage.*
5. ***A.** Coverages on losses arising from expediting expense, hazardous substance clean-up, ammonia contamination, and water damage are all limited to $25,000.*

# Boiler and Machinery Policies for Small Businesses (BM 00 40 06 95; BM 00 45 06 95)

The policies designed for small businesses provide essentially the same coverages as those for other organizations. The differences lie mainly in the eligibility requirements, the coverage extensions, the limits, and some of the object definitions.

Eligibility is limited to businesses that have property values of less than $5 million. Manufacturers and processors, as well as insureds with high-pressure boilers, are not eligible for coverage under the small business policy.

Unlike its counterpart for larger businesses, the small business policy automatically includes coverage for business income and extra expense. The coverage is limited to 25% of the limit of insurance and applies as additional insurance.

Coverage sublimits for these policies are as follows:

- $25,000 for expediting expenses, or what is left of the Limit of Insurance after payment of loss for Covered Property damaged by an accident;
- $25,000 for hazardous substance clean-up or repair or replacement of contaminated property;
- $25,000 for ammonia contamination damage, including salvage expense; and
- $25,000 for water damage, including salvage expense.

Objects are defined as boiler and pressure vessels and air conditioning units.

✓ ***Take Note:*** The need for boiler and machinery coverage among small business owners often is created by lease agreements. Air conditioning units and other types of equipment that a landlord furnishes but requires a tenant to insure may be covered by the small business boiler and machinery policy. The policy provision that extends coverage to another person's property in the insured's care, custody, or control is important in these situations.

## Endorsements

In addition to endorsements that add business income and other time element coverages, boiler and machinery policies can be endorsed to raise the sublimits for certain coverages, such as expediting expenses and ammonia contamination, to remove exclusions and to extend or modify coverage.

# Unit Test Seventeen

1. The broadest object definition under a boiler and machinery policy is which object definition number?

   A. No. 1—Pressure and Refrigeration Objects
   B. No. 3—Electrical Objects
   C. No. 5—Comprehensive Coverage
   D. No. 6—Comprehensive Coverage

2. All of the following represent insured objects under a boiler and machinery policy EXCEPT

   A. pressure vessels
   B. sailing vessels
   C. electrical objects
   D. mechanical objects

3. The current trend in insuring the various objects subject to boiler and machinery losses is to use

   A. scheduled coverage
   B. comprehensive coverage
   C. object definitions
   D. specific coverage

4. All of the following are indirect loss coverages available under boiler and machinery forms EXCEPT

   A. business income
   B. business interruption
   C. consequential damage
   D. extra expense

5. Consequential damage coverage under a boiler and machinery policy insures which of the following?

   A. Loss of use of premises damaged by a boiler explosion
   B. Extra expenses incurred in securing substitute equipment
   C. Loss of income associated with a boiler and machinery loss
   D. Indemnity for loss of insured property caused by spoilage

6. The boiler and machinery coverage form provides which of the following coverages?

   A. Damage to property of others
   B. Damage to property the insured owns
   C. Defense costs for suits arising out of damage to property of others
   D. All of the above

7. Which of the following is a covered cause of loss in a boiler and machinery form?

   A. Explosion to a boiler
   B. Mechanical breakdown of an object
   C. Accident to an object
   D. Tearing asunder of a machine

8. The definition of the term *accident* includes all of the following EXCEPT

   A. breakdown
   B. tearing apart
   C. explosion
   D. leakage of a valve

9. The limit under a boiler and machinery policy applies per

   A. occurrence
   B. accident
   C. year
   D. object

10. Expediting expense provides coverage for all of the following costs EXCEPT to
    A. make temporary repairs
    B. expedite permanent repairs
    C. expedite replacement objects
    D. settle or defend a claim or suit

11. What is the sublimit for ammonia contamination under the Boiler and Machinery policy?
    A. $1,000
    B. $5,000
    C. $10,000
    D. $25,000

12. When an insured acquires property during the policy period, accidents to objects at that location are covered under the boiler and machinery policy for how many days?
    A. 30
    B. 60
    C. 90
    D. Any number of days

13. Which of the following is NOT excluded under the Boiler and Machinery policy?
    A. Flood
    B. Earthquake
    C. Fire
    D. Boiler explosion

14. All of the following are distinctive features of the small business boiler and machinery policy EXCEPT it
    A. cannot be applied to manufacturers
    B. automatically includes business interruption
    C. has few sublimits
    D. uses object definition forms

15. Which of the following is NOT an endorsement to boiler and machinery policies?
    A. Increased limit on expediting expense
    B. Business interruption
    C. Fire and lightning
    D. Extra expense

# Unit Test Seventeen Answers & Rationale

1. **D.** Object definition No. 6 Comprehensive Coverage includes production equipment, which applies to all types of insurable machinery and objects.

2. **B.** Pressure and refrigeration objects, mechanical objects, electrical objects, turbine objects and production machinery all may be insured under a boiler and machinery policy.

3. **B.** The current trend in boiler policies is to provide coverage on a comprehensive or blanket basis without specifying the types of objects to which coverage applies.

4. **A.** The term *business income* is not used in boiler and machinery policies.

5. **D.** Unlike its use in other types of property insurance, consequential loss coverage under the boiler and machinery policy is designed specifically to insure for loss of property due to spoilage.

6. **D.** The boiler and machinery policy applies to the insured's property as well as to property of others, including the cost to defend suits the property owners bring.

7. **C.** The only covered cause of loss in a boiler and machinery form is accident to an object.

8. **D.** Some of the boiler and machinery form exclusions are leakage of a valve or fitting, depletion, deterioration, corrosion or erosion, wear and tear, breakdown of any vacuum tube, glass tube or brush, breakdown of electronic or computer equipment and malfunction of a safety or protective device.

9. **B.** A boiler and machinery policy imposes a single limit per accident.

10. **D.** Expediting expense provides coverage for temporary repairs, to expedite permanent repairs and to expedite permanent replacement.

11. **D.** The sublimit for ammonia contamination under the boiler policy—$25,000—is included in the per-accident limit.

12. **C.** The boiler and machinery policy provides automatic coverage on newly acquired property for 90 days from the time the insured acquires it.

13. **D.** Boiler explosion is one of the primary reasons people purchase boiler and machinery policies because standard property policies do not cover that cause of loss.

14. **D.** One of the distinguishing features of the boiler policy designed for smaller businesses is the use of a comprehensive object definition.

15. **C.** Because standard property policies provide fire and lightning coverages, they are not needed under the boiler and machinery policy.

# 18

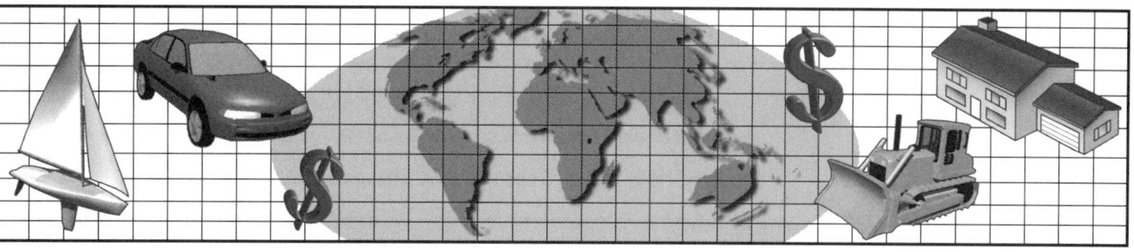

# National Flood Insurance

## INTRODUCTION

Historically, private insurers have considered floods an uninsurable peril. In 1968, Congress enacted the Housing and Urban Development Act, which included the National Flood Insurance Program. Since then, the program has undergone several major changes in how flood insurance is made available to the public. Beginning in 1983, flood insurance policies could be purchased from private insurers or from the federal government.

Currently, more than 100 private insurance companies participate in the Write Your Own flood program. These companies issue policies, collect premiums, and handle claims. They are paid a servicing fee for performing these tasks. However, the federal government fully backs (reinsures) the program, so no company is exposed to an underwriting loss for its participation in the national flood insurance program. The Federal Insurance Administration administers the program under the Federal Emergency Management Agency (FEMA).

## UNIT OBJECTIVES

When you have completed this unit, you should be able to:

- explain how a location becomes eligible for national flood insurance;
- distinguish between the emergency and regular programs of the National Flood Insurance Program (NFIP);
- describe the coverage a flood insurance policy provides; and
- describe the property covered and excluded under a flood policy.

FIGURE 18.1 Emergency Program Limits

| | Building | Contents |
|---|---|---|
| Single-family home | $ 35,000 | $ 10,000 |
| Other residential structures | $100,000 | $100,000 |
| Nonresidential structures | $100,000 | $100,000 |

## Eligibility

For land to qualify for national flood insurance, the community in which it is located must meet certain requirements. To participate in the **National Flood Insurance Program (NFIP)**, a community must demonstrate that it is willing to enact land-use restrictions in special flood hazard areas identified by the federal government. These areas have been so-designated because flooding is expected to occur once every 100 years. In other words, a 1% or greater chance exists that the area will suffer a flood.

Two programs are available under the flood insurance program. The emergency program provides coverage while a community determines the flood plain and develops ordinances to prohibit future building in an area subject to flooding. Then, after the community has accomplished these tasks, the regular program provides coverage. Rate maps prepared by the government distinguish between emergency and regular program areas. These maps are referred to as **flood insurance rate maps (FIRM)**.

**Test Topic Alert!**

The **Federal Emergency Management Agency (FEMA)**, is the national agency that monitors the flood insurance program.

### Emergency Program

After a community (1) has agreed to, but has not yet completed, the process to adopt flood control measures, including zoning ordinances that prohibit new construction in the flood plain, and (2) has requested federal assistance and participation in the flood program, residents of the community can participate in the emergency program. The rates property owners pay are subsidized. The federal government also subsidizes the program if losses exceed premiums. Profits exceeding of costs and service fees must be turned over to the federal government. The maximum coverage that may be purchased is shown in Figure 18.1.

**FIGURE 18.2 Regular Program Limits**

| | Building | Contents |
|---|---|---|
| Single-family home | $250,000 | $100,000 |
| Other residential structures | $250,000 | $100,000 |
| Nonresidential structures | $500,000 | $500,000 |

### Regular Program

To qualify for the **regular program**, the community must have implemented the controls that it planned to adopt in the flood control program it submitted to become eligible for the emergency program. Limits are higher in the regular program than in the emergency (see Figure 18.2).

## Policy Forms and Provisions

The NFIP issues its standard flood policy in three versions. One covers residential structures (dwelling form), one covers nonresidential or commercial property (general property form), and one covers residential condominiums (residential condominium building association policy).

Coverage is on an actual cash value basis, but replacement cost coverage can be purchased for one-family to four-family residences and residential condominiums. Replacement cost coverage is not available under the general property form for commercial structures. Because full insurable limits may exceed the maximum amounts of insurance available from the NFIP, the policies do not contain coinsurance provisions.

**Test Topic Alert!** Any licensed property and casualty insurance agent can sell flood insurance policies, but an agent does not have binding authority.

### Definition of Flood

A flood is defined as a general and temporary condition of partial or complete inundation of normally dry land from:

- overflow of inland or tidal waters;
- unusual and rapid accumulation or run-off of surface waters from any source;

- mudslides and other abnormal flood-related erosions of shorelines; or
- the collapse or destabilization of land along the shore of a lake or another body of water resulting from erosion or the effect of waves or water currents exceeding normal, cyclical levels.

## Perils Excluded

The following perils and losses are excluded from coverage:

### Indirect Losses

No coverage is provided for loss of use or loss of access to the premises. Also, no coverage is available for loss of business income or extra expenses or for any other type of economic loss.

### Losses from Perils Other than Flood

Coverage does not apply to loss due to fire, theft, windstorm, explosion, earthquake, rain (whether or not wind-driven), snow, sleet, hail, water spray, land sinkage, landslide, freezing, thawing, or the pressure or weight of ice or water. Furthermore, no coverage is available for water damage, moisture, mildew, mold, or mudslide from any condition confined to the insured's building or from any condition within the insured's control. Any ensuing loss caused by or that results from one of these perils is not covered. Land subsidence, sewer backup, and seepage of water are excluded unless certain conditions are met.

### Losses from Flood Occurring Under Certain Circumstances

No coverage is available for a loss already in progress, a loss confined to the insured's premises (a flood must affect two adjacent properties or cover two acres of land), a loss caused by the insured's modification of the property that materially increases the risk of flooding, an intentional loss, a loss caused by power interruption on the premises, or a loss to any building or contents located on federal land.

✓ ***For Example:*** Blackacre is privately owned land that covers 10 acres. A heavy rainfall causes the small river that runs through the property to swell, flooding most of the adjoining land. The water, however, is entirely contained within Blackacre's boundaries. Under these circumstances, its owner is entitled to coverage from a flood policy. Although the flood is confined to a single property (which would be grounds for denying coverage), the flood covers at least two acres of land.

## Property Covered

The flood policy covers both buildings and personal property. The definition of a building is very specific. Coverage is provided for a walled and roofed structure that is principally above ground and affixed to a permanent site. The definition includes buildings under construction and mobile or manufactured homes on permanent foundations.

Materials and supplies used to alter or repair a structure also are covered if they are located in an enclosed structure or on adjoining premises. If these items are located in an open structure, they are covered if the insured has taken steps to secure them so they will not float.

Coverage includes $750 for the cost of sandbags, temporary fill for levees, pumps, and wood to protect the building from flood damage. The insurance applies to these types of losses even if the insured property does not actually sustain a loss, as long as flooding has occurred in the area. The deductible does not apply to this coverage.

Coverage on personal property applies to household goods as well as merchandise, stock held for sale, materials and supplies, furniture, fixtures, and machinery and equipment the insured owns and uses for nonresidential purposes. No coverage is available for the personal property of others. A $250 aggregate limit applies to jewelry, fine art, and furs. (If additional limits are needed for this type of property, they can be arranged under an inland marine floater policy.)

If the insured is a tenant, up to 10% of the limit for contents may be applied to improvements made at the insured's expense.

The policy also covers expenses for the removal of debris. This coverage applies not only to the removal of covered property that has been damaged, but also to the removal of debris such as mud, trees and other items that may have floated into the building during a flood. In addition, removal of the insured's property that may have floated to another premises is covered.

Also, coverage of $15,000 applies to increased cost of compliance with flood plain management ordinances or laws that regulate the repair or rebuilding of property damaged in a flood. This is not an additional amount of insurance.

## Property Excluded

All three flood forms contain lengthy lists of items that are not covered. In some cases, the exclusions pertain to property that typically is not covered by a property insurance policy, such as money, aircraft and vehicles. In addition, no coverage is provided for:

- personal property in the open;
- contents, machinery, building equipment, finished walls, floors, ceilings or other improvements in a basement with its floor below grade on all sides;
- fences, retaining walls, seawalls, swimming pools (indoor or outdoor), bulkheads, wharves, piers, bridges, or docks;
- land, lawns, trees, shrubs, plants, or growing crops;

- animals, livestock, birds, or fish;
- underground structures or equipment, including wells and septic systems;
- walks, driveways or other surfaces outside a building's foundation walls; or
- containers such as gas and liquid tanks.

**Test Topic Alert!** No coverage is provided for losses resulting from a flood that is already in progress on the flood insurance policy's effective date.

## Property Removed

Coverage applies for up to 45 days when insured property must be relocated because it is threatened by a covered peril. Unlike removal coverage in other property insurance policies, this protection extends only to loss due to flood while removed from the premises. Also, the policy covers up to $500 for the cost of removing the property.

## Effective Date

During the first 30 days after a community becomes eligible for flood insurance, an individual's policy becomes effective at 12:01 am of the day following the date he or she applied for the policy and paid the premium.

After that first 30-day period, a policy becomes effective on the 30th calendar day after the applicant completes the application and pays the premium. This should serve as an impetus not to wait until flooding is imminent before calling the insurance agent.

**Test Topic Alert!** Coverage becomes effective on the 30th calendar day after the date of application and payment of premium. This also is true for any increase in coverage.

Flood policy premiums are considered fully earned when issued. If the insured cancels the policy midterm, he receives no refund of premium unless the insured has sold the property.

✓ ***Take Note:*** The 30-day waiting period under flood insurance policies is very important. Without such a provision, applicants might purchase coverage only when flooding is imminent, creating a situation of adverse selection for the program.

## Deductible

The minimum deductible for a standard policy under the regular program is $750, depending on the location of the property in a flood zone and the nature of construction. A preferred risk policy under the regular program offers a minimum deductible of $500. The deductible for a standard policy under the emergency program is $1,000. Deductibles apply separately to the building and debris removal and to the contents and debris removal. Thus, damage to a building and contents covered by a standard policy under the regular program results in a deductible of $1,500.

## Increased Cost of Compliance Endorsement

The Increased Cost of Compliance provision is available for NFIP policies written or renewed on or after June 1, 1997. The endorsement is designed to help flood insurance policyholders take the steps required to reduce future flood damage to their homes or businesses.

The new coverage, mandated under the **National Flood Insurance Reform Act of 1994**, helps to offset costs associated with flood-proofing, elevating, demolishing or relocating buildings that are substantially damaged or subject to repetitive flood loss.

### Coverage D—Increased Cost of Compliance

The limit of liability under this Coverage D (Increased Cost of Compliance) is $20,000. This coverage is only applicable to policies with building coverage (Coverage A) and is in addition to the building limit you selected on your application and appears on the Declarations Page. No separate deductible applies. The maximum amount collectible under this policy for both Coverage A (Building Property) and Coverage D (Increased Cost of Compliance), however, cannot exceed the maximum permitted under the Act.

The Increased Cost of Compliance coverage is adjusted separately from the flood damage claim. The insured can only file a claim for the increased costs associated with repairing the property to flood-safe standards if the insured's community determines that the structure has been substantially or repetitively damaged. The determination is made when the insured applies for a building permit to begin repairing the flood-damaged structure or during a post-flood survey by local building officials.

Some communities include a repetitive loss provision in the floodplain management ordinances. This could trigger eligibility for the Increased Cost of Compliance coverage if a property owner has filed at least two flood insurance claims over the past 10 years with damage averaging 25% of the market value of the property each time.

## Federal Encouragement to Purchase Flood Insurance

Flood insurance coverage is required if property is located in a flood hazard area and a federal lending institution holds a loan on the property. Despite this requirement, the number of eligible people who purchase national flood insurance is very low. Some people have the mistaken belief that flood insurance is unnecessary because federal assistance will subsidize their flood losses. The process of obtaining federal assistance is long and tedious, and federal assistance is available only in about 50% of flooding situations. Therefore, the purchase of flood insurance at an average annual premium of $300 is a wise risk management decision for most individuals and businesses.

## Quick Quiz 18.1

1. What role do private insurance companies play in providing flood coverage under the National Flood Insurance Program?

   ______________________________

   ______________________________

2. Name two important differences between the NFIP's emergency and regular programs.
   A. ______________________________
   B. ______________________________

3. If a flood is confined to the insured's one-acre premises, is the loss covered under NFIP?

   Yes _____ No _____

4. When property is threatened by flood damage, it may be removed from the premises and covered for up to __________ days.

5. The waiting period before a flood policy takes effect is __________ days if the community has been eligible for flood insurance for at least 30 days.

## Answers

1. *Private carriers may participate in the provision of National Flood Insurance under the Write Your Own flood program.*
2. *Two distinguishing features of the Emergency and Regular Programs are the community eligibility rules and available insurance limits.*
3. *No. In order to be considered a flood, the policy requires that the flood affect two adjacent properties or cover two acres of land.*
4. *45*
5. *30*

# Unit Test Eighteen

1. Flood insurance covers which of the following?
   A. Accumulation of water from a heavy rain
   B. Normal basement seepage
   C. Inundation of an insured's property only
   D. Only residential property

2. Which of the following statements regarding flood insurance is CORRECT?
   A. It is available only through the government.
   B. It can be written on any property anywhere.
   C. It is written by private insurance companies.
   D. It is available only along rivers.

3. Which of the following is considered a flood?
   A. Subsidence
   B. Mudslide
   C. Landslide
   D. Sewer overflow

4. What does FEMA provide?
   A. Subsidized rates for flood insurance
   B. Low-interest home improvement loans
   C. Community support flood insurance
   D. Grants-in-aid

5. Which of the following is excluded from flood insurance?
   A. Overflow of inland waters
   B. Surface water run-off
   C. Mudslide
   D. Sewer backup

6. Which of the following statements describes flood insurance accurately?
   A. It provides federal assistance to communities.
   B. It involves federal coordination of all relief efforts.
   C. Private insurance companies collect premiums and fund losses.
   D. It provides subsidized premiums for residents of eligible communities.

7. Which of the following is always covered under a flood insurance policy?
   A. Continuous basement seepage
   B. Sewer backup
   C. Landslide
   D. Removal of mud

8. Which of the following does flood insurance cover?
   A. Flood from burst pipes
   B. Seepage
   C. Sewer backup
   D. Tidal wave

9. Which of the following defines a 100-year flood?
   A. Flooding occurs only once each century.
   B. A 100% chance of flooding exists.
   C. No flooding has occurred in more than 100 years.
   D. A 1% or greater chance of flooding exists.

10. Flood insurance rate maps are prepared by
    A. the federal government
    B. insurance companies
    C. local banks
    D. the state flood control board

11. What is the maximum limit that can be purchased on residential property under the emergency program?

    A. $10,000
    B. $35,000
    C. $100,000
    D. $250,000

12. If a private insurer participating in the NFIP's Write Your Own flood program generates a profit on flood insurance, which of the following statements is CORRECT?

    A. It may keep the profit to offset administrative costs.
    B. It must turn the profit over to the federal government.
    C. It must share the profit with other Write Your Own Flood companies.
    D. It must use the profit to enhance flood control efforts in its area.

13. What is the maximum limit on contents located in a residential structure under the regular program?

    A. $10,000
    B. $100,000
    C. $250,000
    D. $500,000

14. All of the following are types of standard flood policies available under the NFIP EXCEPT

    A. general property form
    B. dwelling form
    C. apartment form
    D. residential condominium form

15. For which of the following reasons is a coinsurance clause NOT included in a standard flood policy?

    A. The policy is issued by the government rather than by a private insurance company.
    B. The insured should not be punished for flood losses because they are acts of God.
    C. The maximum amount of insurance may be less than the property's full replacement value.
    D. Insurance companies do not write the forms and therefore have no control over coinsurance clauses.

16. What is the amount of coverage provided under a flood policy for the cost of sandbags and temporary fill?

    A. $250
    B. $500
    C. $750
    D. $1,000

17. What coverage is provided for jewelry, watches and furs under the standard flood policy?

    A. Unlimited
    B. Limited to $250
    C. Limited to $1,000
    D. A flood policy does not cover these items.

18. How much does a standard flood policy include for ordinance or law coverage?

    A. $1,000
    B. $5,000
    C. $10,000
    D. $15,000

19. When property is removed from the insured premises because it is threatened by a covered peril, coverage applies at the place the property is located temporarily for how many days?

    A. 5
    B. 10
    C. 30
    D. 45

20. When an applicant applies for coverage under the flood program, a mandatory waiting period before coverage takes effect is how many days?

    A. 3
    B. 10
    C. 30
    D. 45

21. How much is the standard deductible under the flood insurance program?

    A. $100
    B. $250
    C. $500
    D. $750

# Unit Test Eighteen Answers & Rationale

1. **A.** The definition of a flood under the National Flood Insurance Program is a general and temporary condition of partial or complete inundation of normally dry land from overflow of inland or tidal waters, unusual and rapid accumulation or run-off of surface waters from any source, mudslides and other abnormal flood-related erosions of shorelines, or the collapse or destabilization of land along the shore of a lake or another body of water resulting from erosion or the effect of waves or water currents exceeding normal, cyclical levels.

2. **C.** Although the federal government still issues policies directly for flood insurance, private insurers also participate in the NFIP under the Write Your Own flood program. Flood coverage is available in any designated flood hazard area.

3. **B.** The definition of a flood under the National Flood Insurance Program is a general and temporary condition of partial or complete inundation of normally dry land from overflow of inland or tidal waters, unusual and rapid accumulation or run-off of surface waters from any source, mudslides and other abnormal flood-related erosions of shorelines, or the collapse or destabilization of land along the shore of a lake or another body of water resulting from erosion or the effect of waves or water currents exceeding normal, cyclical levels.

4. **A.** FEMA, which administers the National Flood Insurance Program, is responsible for all aspects of the program under the auspices of the Federal Insurance Administration.

5. **D.** A flood policy specifically excludes backup through sewers unless certain conditions are met.

6. **D.** The federal flood program provides subsidized rates (the rates are not actuarially sound) for all residents of eligible communities.

7. **D.** The definition of a flood under the National Flood Insurance Program is a general and temporary condition of partial or complete inundation of normally dry land from overflow of inland or tidal waters, unusual and rapid accumulation or run-off of surface waters from any source, mudslides and other abnormal flood-related erosions of shorelines, or the collapse or destabilization of land along the shore of a lake or another body of water resulting from erosion or the effect of waves or water currents exceeding normal, cyclical levels.

8. **D.** The definition of a flood under the National Flood Insurance Program is a general and temporary condition of partial or complete inundation of normally dry land from overflow of inland or tidal waters, unusual and rapid accumulation or run-off of surface waters from any source, mudslides and other abnormal flood-related erosions of shorelines, or the collapse or destabilization of land along the shore of a lake or another body of water resulting from erosion or the effect of waves or water currents exceeding normal, cyclical levels.

9. **D.** The definition of a 100-year flood has nothing to do with how often flooding occurs, but rather the likelihood that a flood will occur understood as a percentage; in this case, the likelihood is 1% or greater.

10. **A.** The federal government prepares flood insurance rate maps (FIRMs), which distinguish between regular and emergency flood hazard areas.

11. **C.** The maximum limit for single-family homes under the emergency plan is $35,000, but for other residential structures the limit is $100,000.

12. **B.** While private insurers may participate in the NFIP, their function is limited to issuing policies and writing checks, although they bear no

risk of loss. Therefore, if they profit from flood insurance, they owe that money to the federal government.

13. **B**. Under the regular program, the maximum limit on contents of a residential structure is $100,000.

14. **C**. The National Flood Insurance Program currently offers three coverage forms. One covers residential structures (dwelling form), one covers nonresidential or commercial property (general property form) and one covers residential condominiums (residential condominium building association policy).

15. **C**. Because flood policies may be issued only up to certain defined maximum limits, it would be unfair to policyholders to impose coinsurance requirements when the amount of available insurance may be less than the properties' full insurable value.

16. **C**. Additional coverage provided under the flood policy pays up to $750 for the cost of sandbags, temporary fill for levees, pumps, and wood to protect the building from flood damage.

17. **B**. An aggregate limit of $250 applies to jewelry, fine art, and furs under the flood insurance policy.

18. **D**. Under the flood policy, $15,000 may be applied to the increased cost of compliance with flood plain management ordinances or laws that regulate the repair or rebuilding of property damaged in a flood. It is not additional insurance.

19. **D**. The removal coverage under the flood policy applies for 45 days, the longest period provided under removal coverage in any standard property insurance policy.

20. **C**. A mandatory 30-day waiting period is imposed for new coverage under a flood insurance policy in the regular program.

21. **D**. The standard deductible under the flood insurance program is $750.

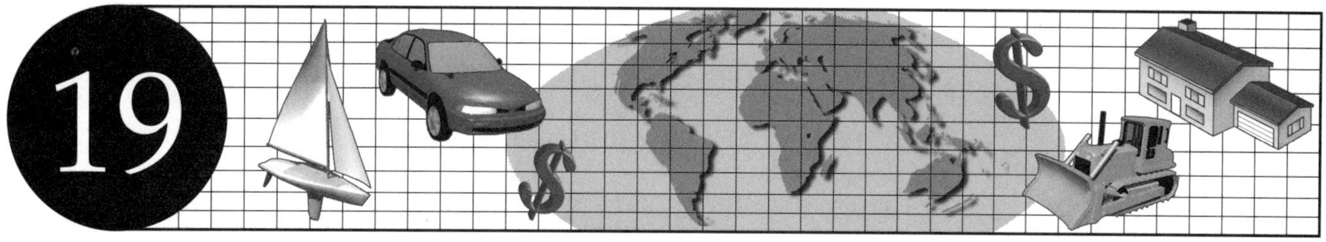


# Farm Coverage

## INTRODUCTION

This unit is based on the ISO farm program, which is a part of the commercial package policy (CPP). Many of the leading writers of farm insurance use independently developed policies. Nevertheless, a discussion of the ISO program provides a sound basis for understanding the various policies in use today.

The ISO farm coverages can be written as a farm combination policy that includes property and liability coverages, with a package discount on the property coverage. The farm coverage part also can be included in the CPP if it is combined with at least one other coverage part. When written for a family who lives on and works their own land, the farm coverage part ordinarily is issued as a separate farm combination policy. If the named insured is a business that has other operations in addition to farming, its farm exposures can be insured through the farm coverage part and added to the same CPP that covers the insured's nonfarming operations. For insurance purposes, the term *farm* also means ranch.

## UNIT OBJECTIVES

When you have completed this unit, you should be able to:

- state the distinctive exposures of farms and ranches and why a separate policy is needed to cover those operations;
- distinguish between the coverages provided under the farm portfolio policy, the homeowners policy, and the commercial general liability and commercial property coverage forms;
- describe the property the farm policy does and does not cover;
- differentiate between the covered causes of loss on the farm form and in commercial property policies;
- explain the unique coverages the farm liability coverage form provides;

- discuss the optional coverages available under the farm liability coverage; and
- describe the farm inland marine coverage forms.

# The Farm Policy

In 1998, the ISO completed the most substantial revision to the farm program since its inception. While still providing coverage using a farm portfolio policy, the previous farm forms were replaced with five new separate forms:

- Farm Property—Farm Dwelling, Appurtenant Structures and Household Personal Property coverage form;
- Farm Property—Farm Personal Property coverage form;
- Barns, Outbuildings and Other Farm Structures coverage form;
- Farm Property—Causes of Loss form; and
- Farm Property—Additional Coverages, Conditions, and Definitions—other Farm Provisions form.

## Farm Property Coverage Form (FP 00 12 01 98)

Four coverages, designated A through D, are available under the farm property—farm dwelling, appurtenant structures and household personal property coverage form. These coverages approximate Coverages A through D of the homeowners policy discussed in Unit 12, so this section highlights only the differences between that policy and the farm form.

### Coverage A—Dwellings

Coverage A insures the policyholder's dwelling, structures attached to the dwelling, and materials and supplies on the premises intended for use in construction, alteration, or repair of the dwelling or attached structures. However, Coverage A of the farm form can also cover dwellings on residential premises away from the insured location as long as a premium is shown on the Declarations for those dwellings. If not otherwise covered under the farm policy, outdoor equipment used primarily for the service of the covered dwelling, its grounds or appurtenant structures also is covered, even while located away from the premises temporarily. Covered property does not include land, water, or trees, shrubs, or plants.

### Coverage B—Other Private Structures Appurtenant to Dwelling

Coverage B of the farm form insures other private structures used in connection with the dwelling. The form permits the insured to apply, as an additional amount of insurance, 10% of the Coverage A limit to structures used solely as private garages. Other private structures and additional coverage on a private garage (when the 10% limit is not adequate) can be provided by entering a limit of insurance in the declarations. However, to avoid covering business property, farm Coverage B excludes coverage for farm buildings and other business-related exposures. The wording excludes barns or farm outbuildings or structures other than private garages that the named insured uses principally for farming purposes.

Coverage B in the homeowners policies is meant to cover other structures of the type usually found on residential premises, such as a detached garage or a storage building that shelters equipment normally used to maintain the residential premises. For farm coverage, care must be exercised in determining whether Coverage B applies to particular structures. For instance, a garage adjacent to the dwelling used as both a garage and a machine shop does not qualify because it is not a structure used solely as a private garage.

Another provision in the Coverage B farm form that differs from anything found in homeowners policies is the special limit of $250 per occurrence on outdoor radio and television antennas and towers and satellite dishes. A higher limit for such property may be indicated in the declarations.

### Coverage C—Household Personal Property

Coverage C in the farm form is similar in most respects to Coverage C in the homeowners policy. However, the farm Coverage C excludes farm personal property other than office fixtures, furniture and equipment. Thus, coverage is provided for a farm office located in the home. The excluded farm personal property must be insured using a different form.

Coverage C contains an extension of coverage that insures loss to contents of a freezer or refrigerated unit on the residence premises. The loss must be caused by the change in temperature that results from the interruption of electrical service due to damaged generating or transmission equipment or from damage caused by mechanical or electrical breakdown of the refrigeration system. The insured must maintain refrigeration equipment in proper working order. The limit of this coverage is $500, and the deductible does not apply. This extension, intended for food for the farm family's use, does not apply to farm personal property or to property the named insured does not own.

### Coverage D—Loss of Use

Coverage D of the farm property form, like Coverage D of the homeowners policy, provides additional living expense for loss of use of living quarters in the residence premises, as well as the fair rental value of any portion of the dwelling or appurtenant structures covered under Coverage B that is rented to others. This coverage does not provide business interruption or extra expense coverage for farm operations.

## Farm Property—Farm Personal Property Coverage Form (FP 00 13 09 03)

The farm personal property coverage form provides two coverages: Coverage E—scheduled farm personal property and Coverage F—unscheduled farm personal property.

### Coverage E—Scheduled Farm Personal Property

Coverage E can be used to insure 18 classes of farm personal property on a scheduled basis. To be covered, the property must be itemized, and limits must be shown on the declarations. Other types of property not listed also may be scheduled with a specific limit of coverage for each class. If the insured wants blanket coverage on farm personal property, it can be provided under Coverage F (see below).

Coverage E provisions consist largely of descriptions of the types of property that can be insured under each class. Certain items are subject to specific coverage limitations. Losses under Coverage E are settled on an actual cash value basis, not to exceed the actual cost to repair or replace the damaged or destroyed property. Some of the types of property insured under Coverage E are grain, hay, farm products, farm machinery, equipment and supplies, livestock and other animals, portable buildings and structures, and computers used as aids in farm management.

The types of property excluded from coverage are threshing machines, tractors, combines, corn pickers, hay balers, harvesters, cotton pickers, crop driers, potato diggers and pickers, and saw mill equipment.

Also excluded are automobiles, aircraft, watercraft, motorcycles, mobile homes, and house trailers.

**Test Topic Alert!**

Losses under Coverages E and F are settled on an actual cash value (ACV) basis that does not exceed the actual cost to repair or replace the damaged or destroyed property.

✓ ***Take Note:*** Many of the categories of property under Coverage E contain limitations. For instance, although livestock is insured, coverage is limited to basic or broad perils only, and no coverage is available for livestock in a common carrier's care, custody, or control.

### Coverage F—Unscheduled Farm Personal Property

In contrast with Coverage E, Coverage F provides blanket coverage on unscheduled farm personal property. A single limit of liability insures all farm personal property not excluded. Coverage F is activated simply by indicating a limit for this coverage on the farm declarations. To discourage underinsurance, Coverage F is subject to an 80% coinsurance clause that works in the usual manner, with one important difference: the coinsurance provision excludes up to $100,000 of property purchased within the last 30 days.

Losses under Coverage F are settled on an actual cash value basis not to exceed the actual cost to repair or replace the damaged or destroyed property.

Property coverage under Coverage F is determined by the property's presence on or away from the insured location. All items of farm business property are covered while on the insured location. The policy definition of *farm business property* includes animals, equipment, supplies, and products of farming or ranching operations, including but not limited to feed, seed, fertilizer, livestock, poultry, grain, produce and agricultural machinery, vehicles, and equipment. Several types of property are excluded from this broad definition, such as household property, racehorses, crops, and automobiles. Most of the excluded property may be insured elsewhere in the farm policy.

Away from the insured location, the only classes of property covered are (1) grain, ground feed, fertilizer, fodder, hay, herbicides, manufactured and blended livestock feed, pesticides, silage, straw, threshed beans and threshed seeds (except while being stored or processed); (2) livestock, except while in transit by common or contract carrier or at public stockyards, sales barns, or sales yards; (3) farm machinery and equipment; and (4) farm implements, tools and supplies. The insured property is subject to the overall limit for Coverage F.

**Coverage F Contrasted with Coverage E**

Coverage F is written with a single blanket limit, in contrast to a separate limit for each class of property or item scheduled under Coverage E. The blanket approach of Coverage F is less complicated and less likely to leave the insured inadequately protected. As long as the amount of insurance under Coverage F satisfies the 80% coinsurance requirement, Coverage F covers most of the insured's farm personal property.

Under Coverage E, if the limit for a particular class of property or item is inadequate, the insured is underinsured for that item even if the total amount of insurance for all items is sufficient.

**Test Topic Alert!**

Property under Coverage E must be scheduled and is subject to a separate limit of coverage for each class of property. In contrast, Coverage F provides a single blanket limit on unscheduled property.

Some types of farm personal property can be insured only under Coverage E. For example, animals other than livestock, such as racehorses, show horses, show ponies, poultry, bees, fish, and worms, must be scheduled under Coverage E in order to be insured. For that reason, the policyholder may wish to schedule certain property under Coverage E and the remaining property under Coverage F. The division of property between Coverage E and Coverage F also may depend on the underwriter's wishes.

An insured who wants to retain a portion of the loss can use Coverage E to insure the specific items the insured wishes to cover. An alternative would be to use Coverage F and exclude the classes of property the insured does not wish to insure.

## Barns, Outbuildings, and Other Farm Structures Coverage Form (FP 00 14 09 03)

**Coverage G—Farm Buildings and Structures**

Coverage G's principle purpose is to insure farm buildings and structures other than dwellings for a single blanket limit shown in the Declarations. In addition, other items can be covered for separate limits:

- barns, granaries, cribs, hog houses, and silos described individually whether attached to buildings or not;
- portable buildings and structures;
- all fences (other than field and pasture fences), corrals, pens, chutes, and feed racks;
- outdoor radio and television equipment, antennas, masts, and towers;
- tenants' improvements and betterments; and
- building materials and supplies for use in building, altering, or repairing farm buildings or structures kept on or adjacent to the insured location.

Property not covered includes:

- land, water, field, and pasture fences;
- below-ground foundations of buildings and structures;
- pilings, piers, wharves, and docks; and
- the cost of excavation, grading, filling, and back-filling.

**Test Topic Alert!**

Losses under Coverage G can be settled at replacement cost or on an actual cash value basis.

Coverage G can be arranged at replacement cost or at actual cash value. If replacement cost is chosen, it must be indicated expressly in the Declarations.

### *Extensions of Coverage*

Coverage G provides two extensions of coverage: First, $1,000 of coverage is provided for power and light poles, outside wiring and attachments (such as switch boxes and other electrical equipment mounted on poles) on the insured location and owned by the named insured. This limit applies in addition to the regular limit of insurance and in excess of the applicable deductible. If a specific limit for this coverage is scheduled in the policy, the $1,000 extension applies in addition to that amount.

The second extension provides up to $100,000 of the Coverage G limit to insure loss to new, permanent farm structures at the insured location, including building materials and supplies, as long as the structures are not insured otherwise. The only covered causes of loss for this extension are fire, lightning, windstorm, hail, aircraft, vehicles, explosion, riot or civil commotion, smoke, and vandalism. This extension ends when (1) the insured reports values to the insurer, (2) 60 days pass after materials and supplies are first delivered or (3) the policy expires, whichever date is the earliest.

✓ ***Take Note:*** Insureds should be encouraged to advise their agents and confirm coverage whenever they contemplate additional construction rather than relying on this automatic coverage. Not only are the covered perils restricted, but the amount of insurance also is part of, not in addition to, the Coverage G limit. If a loss involves the newly constructed structure and other structures insured under Coverage G, the amount of insurance might be insufficient.

## Quick Quiz 19.1

1. The farm property coverage form provides what four coverages?

   A. ____________________
   B. ____________________
   C. ____________________
   D. ____________________

2. What two coverages does the farm personal property coverage form provide?

   A. ____________________
   B. ____________________

3. What are some of the differences between the scheduled farm personal property and the unscheduled farm personal property coverages?

   ____________________
   ____________________

4. Which of the following types of property may be insured under Coverage G (farm buildings and structures)?

   A. Barns
   B. Portable buildings and structures
   C. Fences
   D. All of the above

### *Answers*

1. *Coverage A—Farm Dwelling, Coverage B—Appurtenant Private Structures, Coverage C—Household Personal Property, Coverage D—Loss of Use*
2. *Coverage E—Scheduled Farm Personal Property, Coverage F—Unscheduled Farm Personal Property*
3. *Under Coverage E the limits are specified by class while under Coverage F they are issued on a blanket basis, only certain types of property qualify for*

*coverage under Coverage E while Coverage F may be applied to a broader range of property*

4. **D.** *The Farm Buildings and Structures form applies to barns, granaries, cribs, hog houses, silos, portable buildings and structures, fences other than field or pasture fences, corrals, pens, chutes, feed racks, outdoor radio and TV equipment, antennas, masts, towers, tenant's improvements and betterments, and building materials and supplies for use in building, altering, or repairing farm buildings or structures.*

## Coverage Extensions

Five coverage extensions are available under the farm personal property coverage form.

### Property in Transit by Common or Contract Carrier

Coverage is extended to apply to farm personal property in a common or contract carrier's custody for up to $1,000. A higher limit may be specified in the Declarations. Loss resulting from the transportation of farm personal property is limited to the coverages the broad and basic forms provide (discussed later in this unit). The $1,000 transit coverage is part of, not in addition to, the applicable limit.

### Covered Property Away From the Insured Location

This extension provides up to 25% of the limit shown in the declarations for miscellaneous equipment while away from the insured location or 10% for other types of property. The extension is part of, not in addition to the applicable limit of insurance. The extension does not apply to livestock or individually insured farm machinery, vehicles or equipment, property stored or being processed in manufacturing plants, public elevators, warehouses, commercial drying plants, or seed houses; in public sales barns or public sales yards; or in transit by common or contract carrier.

### Replacement Machinery and Vehicles and Newly Purchased Equipment

This extension provides up to 30 days automatic coverage for farm machinery, a vehicle or equipment purchased as a replacement for an individually scheduled item of farm machinery, vehicle, or piece of equipment. The limit for such replacement equipment is $75,000 in addition to the amount of insurance provided on the item being replaced.

✓ ***For Example:*** A farmer owns a tractor that is scheduled for a limit of $20,000 and buys a new tractor to replace it. Because the limit for replacement equipment is $75,000 in addition to the amount of insurance covering the equipment being replaced, the total amount of insurance available to cover the new tractor is $95,000.

The amount payable in the event of a loss during the 30-day period would not exceed the actual cash value of the replacement item. Coverage does not extend beyond the end of the policy period and is excess over any other insurance on the newly acquired property.

**Additional Machinery and Vehicles and Newly Purchased Equipment**

The fourth extension provides 30 days automatic coverage on newly purchased items of farm equipment, machinery, and vehicles that are not replacements for items already scheduled. The $100,000 limit for this extension of coverage does not apply to automobiles and other vehicles designed primarily for road use (other than farm wagons and farm trailers), watercraft, aircraft, liquefied petroleum, manufactured gas, fuel and their containers, brooders, fences, windchargers, windmills and their towers and any item purchased as a replacement for an item already scheduled on the policy. As with replacements, coverage does not extend beyond the end of the policy period and is excess over any other insurance on the newly acquired property.

**Additional Acquired Livestock**

If livestock is declared and described specifically in the declarations or if a separate limit of insurance per class (such as sheep) is shown in the declarations, coverage for additional livestock is provided for up to 30 days from the date of acquisition. The limit of liability is the actual cash value of the newly acquired livestock, but not more than 25% of the total amount of insurance for livestock shown for Coverage E in the Declarations.

# Covered Causes of Loss

Three levels of coverage may be purchased under the farm property form: basic, broad, and special. The property coverage form contains the covered causes of loss for the farm property form, which resemble a combination of commercial property and homeowners forms. There are important differences between coverage under a farm policy and the coverage under both commercial property and homeowners policies. These are due to the particular exposures farmers and ranchers face. This section emphasizes the covered causes of loss unique to the farm property form.

## Basic Causes of Loss

The basic covered causes of loss follow:

- Fire or lightning
- Windstorm or hail
- Explosion
- Riot or civil commotion

- Aircraft
- Vehicles
- Smoke
- Vandalism
- Theft
- Sinkhole collapse
- Volcanic action
- Collision (coverages E and F only)
- Earthquake loss to livestock
- Flood loss to livestock

## Conditions and Limitations

The last three perils are not found in the basic covered causes of loss either in commercial property or homeowners forms. The collision peril applies only to covered farm machinery and livestock. Farm machinery is covered against loss or damage resulting from collision with another object or by upset or overturn of the machinery. Collision is defined to exclude collision with the roadbed or ground.

However, coverage on farm machinery does not protect against damage:

- to tires or tubes unless the damage coincides with other damage to the machinery;
- caused by contact between a tractor and an implement during towing, hitching or unhitching; and
- caused by foreign objects taken into a farm machine or harvester.

The collision peril covers livestock for loss caused by collision or overturn of the vehicle on which the livestock is being transported, as well as by running into or being struck by vehicles on public roads. The peril does not cover loss caused by a vehicle the insured owns or operates that strikes the livestock or collides with the vehicle on which the livestock is being transported.

✓ ***Take Note:*** Earthquake and flood coverages apply only to livestock.

The other basic covered causes of loss are subject to terms that generally resemble either homeowners or commercial property causes of loss, but with some differences. For instance, the farm property form's fire or lightning peril does not cover damage to buildings or contents usual to a tobacco barn if the damage results from the use of an open fire for curing or drying tobacco in the barn and occurs during or within the five days following the curing or drying. Also, the farm property form's aircraft and vehicle perils do not have the usual exclusion of loss resulting from damage by a vehicle the named insured owns or operates. The windstorm or hail peril does not apply to loss of livestock or poultry caused by running into streams, ponds, or ditches, or against fences or other objects, or from smothering or fright from freezing or smothering in blizzards or snowstorms. Nor does the windstorm or hail peril apply to dairy or farm products in the open other than hay, straw, and fodder.

## Broad Causes of Loss

The broad covered causes of loss include all of the basic causes of loss plus the following:

- Electrocution of covered livestock
- Attacks on covered livestock by dogs or wild animals
- Accidental shooting of covered livestock
- Drowning of covered livestock from external causes
- Loading and unloading accidents
- Breakage of glass or safety glazing material
- Falling objects
- Weight of ice, snow, or sleet
- Sudden and accidental tearing apart, cracking, burning, or bulging of a steam or hot water heating system, an air conditioning or automatic fire protective system or an appliance for heating water
- Accidental discharge or leakage of water or steam from within any part of a system or an appliance containing water or steam
- Accidental discharge or leakage of water or steam as a direct result of the breaking or cracking of any part of a system or an appliance containing water or steam
- Freezing of a plumbing, a heating, an air conditioning or an automatic fire protective system or of a household appliance
- Sudden and accidental damage from artificially generated electrical currents (applicable to coverages A, B, C, and D only)

### Conditions and Limitations

The first five covered causes of loss protect against loss of or damage to covered livestock only. The electrocution peril does not cover electrocution of animals other than livestock as defined. The peril of attacks on covered livestock by dogs or wild animals is subject to an exclusion of loss or damage to sheep or caused by dogs or wild animals owned by persons residing on the insured location. The accidental shooting of covered livestock peril does not include loss or damage caused by the named insured, any other insured, employees of the named insured, or other residents of the insured location. The drowning peril does not apply to swine younger than 30 days old.

The peril of loading and unloading accidents covers death or necessary destruction of livestock resulting from accidents that occur while livestock is being unloaded from or loaded onto transport vehicles. Loss due to disease is excluded.

The remaining broad covered causes of loss are comparable to either the commercial property or homeowners version of these perils.

## Special Causes of Loss

The special causes of loss are risks of direct physical loss other than losses specifically excluded. This level of coverage corresponds to the coverage provided by the special causes of loss form used in commercial property policies.

### General Exclusions

Most exclusions in the farm property form are similar to those found in commercial property and homeowners forms. Only the exclusions distinctive to the farm property form are discussed here.

The farm property form contains eight general exclusions that apply no matter which causes of loss the insured chooses. Seven of these exclusions are virtually identical to the exclusions discussed with regard to commercial property insurance:

- Building ordinance
- Earth movement
- Governmental action
- Nuclear hazard
- Power failure
- War and warlike actions
- Water damage

One important difference is that the farm property form's power failure exclusion is worded to allow for the refrigerated products coverage discussed in connection with Coverage C.

An additional exclusion in the farm property form applies to loss or damage resulting from an act committed by or at the direction of any insured with the intent to cause a loss. This is identical to a property exclusion in the homeowners forms.

**Test Topic Alert!**

The farm property form contains eight general exclusions that apply regardless of the causes of loss the insured chooses. Seven are identical to the exclusions found in commercial property insurance. The eighth applies to loss or damage committed by or at the direction of the insured with the intent to cause a loss.

### Other Exclusions

The named perils listed in the basic and broad form coverages contain exclusions and limitations similar to those in the commercial property basic and broad forms, but often with a change that reflects the different exposures farming operations present. For instance, explosion excludes loss or damage resulting from the explosion of alcohol stills, in addition to steam boilers, steam pipes, steam engines and steam turbines. In the farm property form, 23 numbered exclusions limit the open perils coverage in addition to the nine general exclusions. The majority of the 23 numbered exclusions are identical to or closely resemble the exclusions and limitations in the commercial property or homeowners special causes of loss forms. However, some of the 23 exclusions are unique to the farm property form to account for farm exposures not anticipated under commercial property policies.

In most cases, the exclusions not found in commercial forms are the same as those that limit the farm property basic and broad causes of loss, such as:

- fire resulting from the use of an open fire for curing or drying tobacco;
- windstorm or hail damage to dairy or farm products in the open, other than hay, straw or fodder;
- collision peril exclusions; and
- rupture or bursting caused by expansion of the contents of any building or structure if the expansion is caused by or results from water.

Because of the open perils nature of the coverage, a lengthy exclusion is needed for loss or damage sustained by farm machinery to clarify the exclusion of wear and tear losses, such as the exclusion of damage caused by foreign objects being taken into any farm machine or mechanical harvester.

Finally, an exclusion applies to loss of or damage to livestock, poultry, bees, fish, worms, other animals, hay and trees, shrubs, plants, and lawns. This is because only basic or broad coverage is available on those types of property, similar to other provisions in the farm property form that limit coverage on hay and trees, shrubs, plants and lawns to certain causes of loss.

## Additional Coverages

Apart from the coverage extensions in Coverages A through G, the farm property form contains several additional coverages, grouped according to the coverage forms (A through G) to which they apply.

### *Applicable to Coverages A, B, C, D, E, F, and G*

The first group, consisting of debris removal, reasonable repairs, property removed for safekeeping and fire department service charges, applies to Coverages A, B, C, D, E, F, and G.

Debris removal coverage resembles that provided in the commercial property building and personal property form, except that an additional 5% of the applicable limit (instead of an additional $10,000) is available when the limit becomes exhausted by a combination of property loss and debris removal expense or the debris removal exceeds the 25% of covered-loss-plus-deductible limit.

The additional coverage for damage to property removed from a residence endangered by a covered cause of loss is comparable to the preservation of property coverage in the building and personal property form. Fire department service charge coverage, like that the building and personal property form provides, is payable in addition to the policy limits and is not subject to any deductible. The farm property form states no limit for this coverage, whereas a $1,000 limit applies in the building and personal property form.

### Applicable to Coverages A, B, C, and D

The second group of additional coverages, which applies to Coverages A, B, C, and D only, consists of two coverages that resemble additional coverages under the homeowners policy: Removal of Fallen Trees as well as Credit Cards and Fund Transfer Cards, Forgery, and Counterfeit Currency.

### Applicable to Coverages E and F

An additional coverage that applies to Coverages E and F only covers the cost, up to $2,000, to research, replace, or restore lost information in farm operations records damaged or destroyed by a covered cause of loss. A higher limit for this coverage may be selected and shown in the Declarations. No deductible applies to this additional coverage.

The additional coverage collapse applies when the broad or special covered causes of loss are in effect. This collapse coverage is identical to that offered by commercial property and homeowners forms.

The final additional coverage is $10,000 pollutant clean-up and removal. This same coverage is found in the commercial property form.

## Optional Property Coverages

Several additional property coverages are available under the farm property coverage form. Most of the optional coverages offered in homeowners policies are available in the farm property coverage form.

One important coverage option is extra expense insurance applicable to Coverages E, F, and G. This coverage pays the necessary expenses the named insured incurs to resume normal farming operations following direct damage to covered property by a covered cause of loss. Extra expense can be vital to farmers.

✓ ***For Example:*** A barn standing on a dairy farm is destroyed by fire, leaving the cows without shelter and the farmer without milking equipment. The farmer must make immediate arrangements to shelter and milk these cows. Extra expense insurance pays the expenses incurred in resuming the dairy's normal operations.

The coverage, subject to whatever limit of insurance is shown for it in the declarations, is not limited by the policy expiration or the percentage of coverage available in any 30-day period, nor is it subject to any Deductible.

The other important coverage for farms and ranches is disruption of farming operations. This form of business income coverage can be a substantial loss exposure for those who derive most or all of their income from farming.

Coverage resembles the commercial property program's business income form and includes loss of income and continuing normal operating expenses.

## Quick Quiz 19.2

1. Under the farm policy's coverage extensions, what are the limits for each of the following coverages?

   Property in transit by common or contract carrier: $__________

   Covered property away from the insured location:__________% for miscellaneous equipment and __________ % for other types of property.

   Replacement/newly purchased machinery and equipment: $__________

   Additional/newly purchased machinery and equipment: $__________

   Additionally acquired livestock:__________% or ACV for up to __________ days

2. What three causes of loss are included in the farm policy's basic causes of loss form but not in either the homeowners or commercial property policy?

   A. __________
   B. __________
   C. __________

3. Under the broad causes of loss form, to what type of property do the following perils apply?

   Electrocution __________
   Attacks by dogs or wild animals __________
   Accidental shooting __________
   Drowning from external causes __________
   Loading/Unloading accidents __________

4. What two optional property coverages should be recommended to farmers and ranchers concerned about a suspension of their farm or ranch operations?

   A. __________
   B. __________

## *Answers*

1. *$1,000; 25%; 10%; $75,000; $100,000; 25%; 30 days*
2. *Collision (Coverage E and F), Earthquake to livestock, Flood to livestock*
3. *Livestock*
4. *Extra Expense and Disruption of Farming Operations*

# Farm Liability Coverage Form (FL 00 20 09)

Like the ISO farm property coverage form, the ISO farm liability coverage form contains elements of both commercial liability and personal liability insurance. In format, the farm liability form resembles the commercial general liability coverage form with separate coverage sections for bodily injury and property damage liability, personal and advertising injury liability and medical payments. However, many provisions of the commercial general liability coverage form are amended to match the personal liability coverage found in the homeowners policy or to address the specific liability exposures of farming operations. The explanations that follow are confined to the more significant differences between the farm liability form and the commercial general liability coverage form.

## Business Pursuits Other than Farming

Farming is the business liability exposure that the farm liability form is intended to insure. Consequently, the farm liability form contains business pursuits and professional services exclusions similar to homeowners liability coverage, but the definition of business is specific to a farmer's needs.

### Definitions

***Business***

A **business** is a trade, a profession, an occupation, an enterprise or an activity, other than farming or custom farming, that a person engages in for the purpose of monetary or other compensation.

***Farming***

**Farming** is the operation of an agricultural or aquacultural enterprise and includes the operation of roadside stands, on farm premises, maintained solely for the sale of farm products produced principally by the insured. Unless specifically indicated in the declarations, farming does not include:

- retail activity other than that described above; or
- mechanized processing operations.

The definitions in the farm liability form clarify that the business pursuits exclusion does not exclude farming or the operation of roadside stands for selling farm products produced principally by the named insured. Some business activities, however, such as the sale of seeds, fertilizers, or sprays, are not covered and require special treatment.

The farm liability form, like the commercial general liability coverage form, automatically includes products liability insurance, an indispensable coverage for farmers. However, the farm liability form does not have a separate products-completed operations aggregate limit. The farm general aggregate limit applies to all claims, including those within the products-completed operations hazards.

### *Custom Farming*

**Custom farming** is the performance of specific planting, cultivating, harvesting, or similar specific farming operations by an insured, at a farm that is not an insured location, when the performance is for, and under the direction or supervision of, the farm's owner or operator or the owner or operator's authorized representative. Custom farming does not include:

- operations conducted at a premises the insured rents, leases or controls;
- operations for which no compensation in money or goods is received; or
- a neighborly exchange of services.

Though the business pursuits exclusion does not exclude custom farming—that is, farming operations the insured performs for others for a charge under a contract or an agreement—in large measure it is excluded by another provision. Custom farming is excluded if the named insured's receipts from custom farming exceed $2,000 during the 12 months immediately preceding the date of the occurrence for which coverage is sought. If the named insured's custom farming receipts could exceed that amount in a year, full coverage is available by endorsement for an additional premium.

### *Crop Dusting*

Because of the special hazards associated with applying herbicides and pesticides to crops by aircraft, insurers do not want to cover such operations under the farm liability form. Consequently, the farm liability form excludes bodily injury or property damage resulting from any substance released or discharged from an aircraft. If coverage for such operations is needed, it must be arranged separately. Some independently developed forms offer limited coverage for aircraft spraying performed by independent contractors.

### *Other Pollution Exposures*

The farm liability form contains the same pollution exclusion found in the commercial general liability coverage form. By endorsement, this exclusion can be modified to allow limited coverage for discharge of smoke or farm chemicals, liquids, or gas used in normal farming or agricultural operations. However, the limited pollution endorsement does not alter the exclusion of injury resulting from discharge of substances from aircraft.

### *Farm Employer's Liability*

In states where farm workers are not subject to workers' compensation laws, farmers need to purchase workers' compensation insurance. In about half the states, farm workers are not subject to workers' compensation laws and can therefore sue their employers for job-related injuries resulting from the employers' negligence. The farm liability form, like the commercial general liability form, excludes both workers' compensation obligations and liability for bodily injury to the insured's employees. However, employer's liability insurance, covering the insured's liability for farm workers' job-related injuries, can be added to the farm liability form by endorsement for an additional premium. The same endorsement can be used to write farm employees' medical payments coverage.

✓ ***Take Note:*** Like the commercial general liability form, the farm liability form excludes workers' compensation obligations and liability for bodily injury to the insured's employees. Job-related injuries can, however, be covered by employer's liability insurance. This may be added to the farm liability form by endorsement.

## Other Exclusions Not Found in Either the CGL or Homeowners Forms

A few other exclusions specific to the nature of farm operations are not found in either the CGL or homeowners forms:

- use of any animal, with or without an accessory vehicle, to provide rides for a fee or in connection with a fair, charitable event or a similar function;
- use of any animal in a racing, speed, or strength contest or a prearranged stunting activity at the site designated for the contest or activity (use of mobile equipment in such a manner also is excluded, as it is in the CGL);
- rental or holding for rental of an insured location (this also is excluded in homeowners policies, but they allow coverage for rental on an occasional basis as a residence);
- losses out of any premises where a building or structure is being constructed, other than a dwelling to be occupied by the insured or a farm structure for the insured's use; and
- bodily injury to any insured (this could be a troublesome exclusion given the broad definition of the term insured; for instance, anyone who uses an insured vehicle on the insured's premises with the insured's permission is included as an insured and if such a person is injured, this exclusion seems to apply).

### Optional Liability Coverages

Several optional liability coverages are available:

- Coverage may be extended to two-, three- or four-family dwellings.
- The following may be added as additional insureds:
  - partners or co-owners; and
  - nonrelated residents.
- The following types of additional premises may be added:
  - farm premises rented to others;
  - farm premises maintained by the insured, the insured's spouse or residents of the insured's household;
  - additional residence premises maintained by the insured, the insured's spouse or residents of the insured's household; and
  - one-, two-, three-, or four-family residences rented to others.
- Coverage may be included for owned snowmobiles not subject to motor vehicle registration.
- Watercraft liability can be included for watercraft not included automatically in the farm liability coverage form.
- Business pursuits coverage for the insured's liability arising while employed by others in nonfarm jobs may be included.
- Coverage can be added for custom farming when the annual receipts exceed $2,000.

## Farm Inland Marine Coverage Forms

Two inland marine floater forms are available for use with the farm coverage part: the **mobile agricultural machinery and equipment coverage form** and the **livestock coverage form**. These classes of property can be insured under the farm property coverage form through Coverage E or Coverage F, but when an insured wishes to insure these classes of farm business property and no others, ISO rules call for the insurance to be written through the separate inland marine forms.

### *Mobile Agricultural Machinery and Equipment Coverage Form*

The mobile agricultural machinery and equipment coverage form insures eligible equipment for special causes of loss subject to policy limitations and exclusions.

### *Livestock Coverage Form*

The livestock coverage form is a named peril form, insuring loss resulting in the death or destruction of livestock caused by the basic causes of loss (except vehicles). Livestock coverage may be extended to include death or destruction by accidental shooting, drowning, electrocution, attack by dogs or wild animals, loading or unloading accidents and building collapse.

## Quick Quiz 19.3

1. The performance of specific farming operations by an insured at other than an insured location is referred to as __________ __________.

2. What are four of the optional liability coverages that may be included in a farm policy?

   A. ____________________
   B. ____________________
   C. ____________________
   D. ____________________

3. Why would an insured wish to purchase a separate inland marine form for mobile agricultural equipment or livestock?

   ______________________________________________________________
   ______________________________________________________________

### *Answers*

1. *Custom farming*
2. *Coverage for two-, three- or four-family dwellings; additional insureds; additional covered residence premises; owned snowmobiles; watercraft liability; business pursuits from nonfarming activities; custom farming when receipts exceed $2,000 per year*
3. *When no other farm coverages are required, the insured may wish to cover only mobile agricultural equipment or livestock. Separate forms are available for this purpose. The coverages provided are similar to those under Coverage E and Coverage F if included in the Farm Portfolio Policy.*

## Crop-Hail Insurance

Growing and harvested crops are an important item of insurable property in the United States. In years past, the US government was the only organization willing to provide insurance coverage for farmers and ranchers who suffered losses due to adverse weather, drought, pests, and other production problems. Recently, private insurers have become more involved in the provision of crop insurance.

### Coverage Provided

The coverage provided by crop insurance usually applies to the reduced yield of a crop following a loss.

✓ ***For Example:*** A wheat farmer may have 1,000 acres of wheat that he anticipates will sell for $2.00 per acre. Following a severe storm in which the crop is damaged, the most the farmer can expect to sell for is $0.25 per acre. Crop insurance is designed to cover the difference between the $2.00 last revenue and $0.25 actual revenue per acre.

When underwriting crop insurance, there are many unique features that must be considered. First, weather conditions vary by region. Some crops are routinely affected by hail, while for others this is an unusual event. Second, the type of crop is a factor in underwriting. Some crops are more susceptible to damage and disease. Depending on the location of the crop and the time of year, some may be damaged by weather conditions such as frost while others may resist this damage.

Crop insurance was originally issued on a named perils basis. Thus, the term *crop-hail insurance* came to characterize the type of coverage provided. Recently, multi-peril crop insurance coverage has replaced crop-hail insurance.

## Providers of Crop Insurance

In the early days, only the US government was a market for crop-hail insurance. This situation has changed substantially in the last decade.

Crop coverage is currently provided by:

- private insurers;
- the Federal Crop Insurance Corporation (FCIC); and
- state crop-hail funds.

The trend of insurers has been from the government to private carriers, although the federal government maintains a predominant role in the provision of crop insurance in the United States.

### *Private Insurers*

Most crop insurance is currently provided by private carriers who are stock, mutual, or reciprocal insurers. Private insurers generally offer broad **multi-peril crop insurance coverage (MPCI)** that includes losses due to adverse weather conditions (e.g., wind, hurricanes, and tornadoes), flood, drought, insect damage, and other causes of loss.

### *Federal Crop Insurance Corporation*

The US Department of Agriculture also participates in providing crop insurance through its subsidiary, the **Federal Crop Insurance Corporation (FCIC)**. This coverage is all risk in nature (versus the named perils coverage of crop-hail insurance) and is sold through licensed agents. The FCIC is now a partnership between the federal government and private carriers. The FCIC also reinsures some of the multi-peril crop coverage written by private carriers.

### State Crop Hail Funds

Several states experimented with state run crop-hail insurance plans. Most experienced financial difficulty and other problems, leading to their demise. Only one state—Montana—maintains a state crop hail fund.

## The Crop Insurance Market

Farming and ranching continues to be a significant segment of the United States economy. In some states, it is the largest portion of economic activity. The government has played a major role in increasing the market for crop insurance by continually adding to the list of crops that may be insured.

### Size of the Market

Since the government has emphasized risk management principles for the farmer and rancher, crop insurance premiums have increased substantially. Much of the recent growth in crop insurance premiums can be attributed to changes in federal crop insurance guidelines, inflation, and the tendency of lenders to require crop insurance when making agricultural loans. Nearly all multi-peril crop insurance is currently written through private carriers, with the federal government serving as reinsurer.

### Concentration by Region

Every state sells crop insurance, but the vast majority of coverage is still written in the Midwestern states. Iowa, Kansas, Nebraska, Minnesota, and North Dakota account for over 80% of the crop insurance market.

### Concentration by Crop

There are over 200 different crops eligible for crop insurance, and the list is growing daily. However, the majority of crop insurance premiums are derived from a somewhat narrow list of crops:

- corn;
- cereal grains (such as wheat);
- soybeans;
- tobacco; and
- cotton

Nearly any crop with a commercial market value may be insured. Other crops that are eligible, but do not constitute a major share of the market, include wine grapes, fruit trees, nut trees, beans, potatoes, and sugar beets. Hay and grasses may also be insured.

## Crop Hail Insurance Actuarial Association

Although it is no longer a viable organization, the **Crop Hail Insurance Actuarial Association (CHIAA)** was a pioneer in the collection and dissemination of data regarding crop insurance in the United States.

### *Origin and Purpose*

As with many new forms of insurance, crop insurance rates were not actually sound until some time after the coverage began to be sold. Statistics were recorded on a regional basis, but there was no organization with overall authority to set rates and prices. In the 1940s the Crop Hail Insurance Actuarial Association was formed (CHIAA). CHIAA was provided with the regional statistics in an attempt to assimilate the data and promulgate countrywide rates. CHIAA was designed to operate for crop insurance pricing and rating much as the ISO does for other lines of property and casualty insurance.

### *Structure of CHIAA*

In 1974 the parent company of CHIAA opened its membership to other companies who underwrote crop insurance and formed the National Crop Insurance Association (NCIA). NCIA provided services to member insurers that included research and training. In some cases, the NCIA duplicated the services offered by CHIAA. In 1989, the two organizations consolidated their operations and became National Crop Insurance Services (NCIS). Today, NCIS is responsible for gathering, preparing, and publishing crop insurance rating information and insurance coverage forms. NCIS is supported by its member crop insurance companies who provide data and are assessed for the organization's expenses. NCIS is governed by a Board of Directors and operates as a non-profit, volunteer organization.

### *Limits to NCIS (CHIAA) Data*

Since NCIS is an advisory organization, similar to ISO, carriers are not required to provide data. Therefore, the information contained in the NCIS database may not be reflective of the entire crop insurance industry. Distortions may occur in the data due to regional weather factors, the use of large deductibles, and the fact that hail is only a portion of the damage that crops may suffer. NCIS statistics are still considered more reliable than those gathered by FCIC since that data favors hail losses.

### *NCIS (CHIAA) Rating Philosophy*

The NCIS uses a rating basis that considers:

- inclusion of the maximum number of years' experience;
- the smallest feasible geographic units (township rating); and
- frequent revision of rates based on seasonal activity.

In order to determine rates, the NCIS considers loss experience as far back as records have been kept. Rates are not collected on a statewide basis, but are focused on the township (or county) level. Without rating at the local level, crop insurance was fraught with adverse selection since farmers in areas that had not experienced losses often felt the coverage was unnecessary. Rates are also based on the experience for different crops because some are more vulnerable to perils like windstorm and hail.

## Crop Insurance Coverage

As the market and availability of crop insurance has changed, so have the coverage options available to the insured.

### *Insurable Interest*

The measure of insurable interest is typically the financial loss that could result to the insured if the property is injured or destroyed. In crop insurance, the landowner has an insurable interest in crops grown on the land. In addition, a tenant farmer may have an insurable interest in crops grown on the land of another person. The contracts and agreements between the tenant farmer and the owner of the land may also create an insurable interest for both parties and both may be entitled to purchase crop insurance.

### *Policy Forms*

Although NCIS issues specimen or sample policies, crop insurers are free to use any form they choose, subject to regulatory approval. Therefore, there are no standard crop insurance forms.

### *Policy Term and Coverage Period*

Crop insurance may be issued on an annual or a seasonal basis. Coverage is typically issued based on the growing season of the crop involved. Coverage may not take effect until the crop is visible above the ground or until a certain number of leaves are present in a crop such as citrus or fruit trees. Coverage is subject to a waiting period, typically the day after application is made. Coverage terminates when the crop is harvested or on a specified date. Coverage for certain crops, such as wheat, barley, rye, or fruit crops may terminate on a specific calendar date. These time limits are important for determining coverage under a crop insurance policy.

### *Coverage Amount*

Limits for crop insurance are usually stated as a dollar amount per acre. The amount of a loss is usually the decline in the anticipated yield of the crop. There is effectively a 100% coinsurance clause in a crop insurance policy. Therefore, the insured must be able to anticipate what the actual amount of the crop yield will be and then determine an insurance amount. Most insureds choose amounts of insurance less than 100% of the insurable amount, which equates to a percentage of retention.

✓ ***For Example:*** If the actual value of a crop is $400 per acre and the amount of insurance is $200 per acre, and the yield is $160 per acre, the insured can collect 50% of the decrease in the yield since the insured value was 50% of the anticipated actual value.

### *Excess of Loss—Deductibles*

Crop insurance may be written with no deductible or with some type of deductible. A policy with no deductible is not a viable option for the insured from an economic standpoint. Crop insurance deductibles are usually written on an excess over basis, meaning that no loss will be paid up to a certain dollar amount and then only the excess will be paid. Typical deductibles in crop insurance are:

- excess over 5% loss;
- excess over 10% loss; and
- excess over 20% loss.

Some policies also have a **disappearing deductible**, meaning that there is a deductible for smaller losses, but the deductible "disappears" for larger losses.

### *Perils Covered*

There are two basic methods of providing crop insurance. One is a named perils basis that covers hail and other perils such as fire, lightning, and windstorm. Multi-peril crop insurance policies cover on an "all risk" basis, subject to policy exclusions. Multi-peril crop insurance is not available for all crops in all areas.

### *Losses Not Covered—Exclusions*

Crop insurance does not apply until a crop is visible above the ground. In addition, crop insurance policies may contain exclusions for losses or damage:

- that take place prior to the effective date and hour of the policy;
- due to a peril that is not insured;
- due to the failure of the insured to cut, dig, pick, pull, or harvest mature crops;
- due to the harvester's inability to recover that portion of the crop;
- of a crop in which the insured does not have an insurable interest;
- to buds, blooms, or blossoms of a crop;
- to leaves, vines, bushes, stalks, or squares of any crop except to the extent that the crop is affected; or
- to trees or bushes of any nut or fruit crop.

Most policies also contain nuclear and contamination exclusions.

### *Policy Provisions*

Crop insurance policies contain miscellaneous provisions similar to those contained in other property and casualty policies such as:

- concealment, misrepresentation and fraud;
- other insurance;
- loss conditions;
- suit against the insurer;
- abandonment; and
- subrogation.

# Unit Test Nineteen

1. Separate farm forms were created for which of the following reasons?
   A. Companies are unwilling to write farm risks.
   B. Farms often are located in rural areas.
   C. Farms combine personal and business exposures.
   D. Farms represent substantial fire hazards.

2. Coverage A Dwelling of the farm property form insures all of the following EXCEPT
   A. attached structures
   B. materials and supplies located on the premises
   C. contents in farm structures
   D. dwellings away from the insured location

3. Unlike homeowners policies, the farm property form limits coverage for outdoor antennas under Coverage B to how much?
   A. $100
   B. $250
   C. $500
   D. $1,000

4. Which of the following situations is NOT covered under Coverage C of the farm property form?
   A. The food in a freezer spoils when an electrical storm interrupts power.
   B. The furniture in the insured's den, also used as the farm office, is damaged in a fire.
   C. The property of a guest visiting the insured is stolen during a social gathering.
   D. Refrigerated produce being held for sale at a roadside stand spoils when lightning strikes a power pole on the premises and interrupts the electrical supply.

5. The farm property coverage form insures which of the following in addition to household personal property?
   A. Animal mortality
   B. Crop insurance
   C. Loss of use
   D. Business interruption

6. Which of the following describes the difference between Coverage E and Coverage F of the farm personal property coverage form?
   A. Coverage F is less expensive than Coverage E.
   B. Coverage E is scheduled, and Coverage F is blanket.
   C. Coverage E is special form, and Coverage F is named perils.
   D. Coverage F may be included only when Coverage E is written.

7. Which of the following statements regarding Coverage F is CORRECT?
   A. An 80% coinsurance provision applies.
   B. Coverage is not provided for newly acquired property.
   C. Coverage applies only at the described premises.
   D. Coverage includes automobiles.

8. Certain types of property may be included only under Coverage E of the farm program. These types of property include all of the following EXCEPT
   A. racehorses
   B. poultry
   C. fish
   D. cattle

9. Coverage G Farm Buildings and Structures is designed to cover which of the following?
   A. Structures attached to the farm dwelling
   B. Field and pasture fencing
   C. Private garages on the insured premises
   D. Barns and other farm structures

10. Farm property coverages are provided on which of the following bases?
    A. Actual cash value basis
    B. Replacement cost basis
    C. Replacement cost basis for private structures and ACV for farm buildings
    D. Replacement cost basis for all structures if indicated in the declarations

11. An insured farmer has a limit of $100,000 on Coverage E Scheduled Farm Personal Property. Last week, the insured purchased a new piece of equipment valued at $60,000, and before reporting the acquisition to the insurance agent, a fire destroyed the equipment. How much coverage does the farm policy provide?
    A. $50,000
    B. $60,000
    C. $100,000
    D. Nothing—the item needed to be reported and scheduled in order to be covered

12. All of the following cause of loss forms are available under the farm program EXCEPT
    A. basic
    B. broad
    C. special
    D. commercial

13. In addition to the basic causes of loss covered in the homeowners program, the farm basic causes of loss form includes all of the following perils EXCEPT
    A. theft
    B. collision
    C. electrocution
    D. earthquake loss to livestock

14. Which of the following statements is CORRECT under the broad causes of loss form?
    A. Coverage provided is identical to that of the comparable form in the homeowners program.
    B. Coverage is broader than that provided by the comparable form in the homeowners program.
    C. Coverage is provided automatically for earthquake and flood for all property.
    D. Coverage is included for death of livestock and other animals from any cause.

15. The farm property program includes which of the following optional coverages?
    A. Loss of use
    B. Disruption of farming operations
    C. Debris removal
    D. Pollutant clean-up

16. The farm liability form includes coverage for which of the following activities?
    A. All of the insured's business activities
    B. Only farm business activities
    C. Custom farming and all other activities
    D. The insured's farm business and nonbusiness activities

17. Products liability is which of the following under the farm liability form?
    A. Included
    B. Excluded
    C. Included on a claims-made basis
    D. Limited to $100,000

18. What is the limit on receipts for custom farming activities under the farm liability form?

    A. $1,000
    B. $2,000
    C. $3,000
    D. $5,000

19. Which of the following is an exclusion contained in the farm liability form, but not in either the CGL or homeowners form?

    A. Professional services
    B. Bodily injury to any insured
    C. Workers' compensation
    D. Intentional injuries

20. The two inland marine forms available under the farm program include coverage for which of the following?

    A. Livestock and crops
    B. Crops and mobile agricultural equipment
    C. Mobile agricultural machinery and equipment and livestock
    D. Portable buildings and mobile agricultural equipment

# Unit Test Nineteen Answers & Rationale

1. **C.** Farms do not qualify for coverage under either personal lines or commercial lines forms because they combine business and nonbusiness exposures.

2. **C.** Contents in farm structures are covered under either Coverage E or Coverage F of the farm program.

3. **B.** A special limit of $250 per occurrence applies to outdoor radio and television antennas and towers and satellite dishes under the farm other structures form.

4. **D.** Coverage C of the farm property form covers for household personal property, including furnishings in a farm office located in the home. Coverage for property of others resembles that in homeowners policies. An extension of coverage applies to the contents of a freezer or refrigerator due to interruption of electrical power, but only to food intended for use by the family, not to food held for sale.

5. **C.** The farm property coverage form includes loss of use coverage as Coverage D, similar to that provided under a homeowners policy.

6. **B.** Coverage E provides coverage only for those categories of property listed in the form, while coverage F provides blanket coverage.

7. **A.** Because Coverage F provides blanket coverage, an 80% coinsurance clause applies. Coverage includes newly acquired property and property off premises. Automobiles are excluded.

8. **D.** Certain types of property may be insured using Coverage E only. Examples are animals other than livestock, such as racehorses, show horses and show ponies, poultry, bees, fish, and worms.

9. **D.** Coverage A insures structures attached to the farm dwelling. Field and pasture fencing is specifically excepted from the coverage provided under Coverage G. Private garages are insured under Coverage B.

10. **D.** Similar to homeowners policies, the farm program insures all real property for replacement cost unless the insured has specifically selected actual cash value (ACV) and the policy has been endorsed.

11. **B.** The farm policy provides an extension of coverage for newly acquired additional machinery and equipment up to a maximum of $100,000. In this case, the actual cash value of the equipment was $60,000. Coverage applies for 30 days.

12. **D.** The causes of loss are the same under the farm program as the commercial property and homeowners policies: basic, broad, and special. In addition, an earthquake cause of loss form may be added to the policy.

13. **C.** The farm basic causes of loss form adds coverage for collision under Coverages E and F, as well as earthquake loss to livestock and flood loss to livestock. Electrocution is included under the broad causes of loss form.

14. **B.** Due to the inclusion of electrocution of covered livestock, attacks on livestock by domestic or wild animals, accidental shooting of livestock, drowning of covered livestock, and loading and unloading accidents, the list of covered perils on the farm form is broader than that on the homeowners policy.

15. **B.** Loss of use is included automatically in a farm policy. Debris removal and pollutant cleanup are included as additional coverages. Disruption of farming operations is optional coverage and must be added by endorsement.

16. **B.** The intent of the farm liability section is to provide business-type coverage only for farm operations. If the insured operates other businesses, he or she must purchase a separate CGL policy or add that coverage to the farm policy.

17. **A.** Products liability, an important coverage for farm operations, is included automatically under farm policies, as it is under homeowners policies.

18. **B.** Custom farming is excluded under farm liability if the receipts from such operations exceed $2,000 during the 12 months immediately preceding the date of the occurrence for which coverage is sought.

19. **B.** No such broad exclusion exists under either the CGL or the homeowners policy that prohibits coverage for bodily injury to any insured. This exclusion can be problematic for a farm policyholder.

20. **C.** Farm inland marine coverage, which may be included under a farm package policy, can insure mobile agricultural machinery and equipment and livestock.

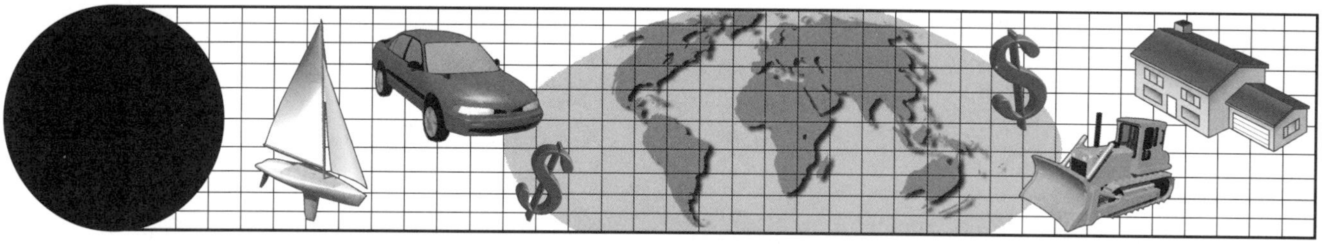

# Property and Casualty Final Exams

Remember to read the entire question before selecting an answer. Some of the responses may seem correct, but a careful reading may prove otherwise. Words like "all," "may," "shall," "not," and "except" can change the answer. All questions have a single correct response and are based on information found in this text.

# Casualty Insurance Final Exam Questions

1. Collision insurance covers which of the following perils?
   A. All damage to an auto struck by the insured, if the insured is legally liable
   B. Upset of the auto without a deductible applying
   C. Direct loss to the auto caused by collision with another object
   D. Collision of the covered vehicle with a large animal

2. Physical damage coverage of an auto policy applies to which of the following?
   A. The hubcaps on the vehicle
   B. A typewriter in the auto
   C. A detachable radio that is in the insured's home
   D. A residence rented to the insured

3. An insured burns his or her own car. The loss is NOT covered under an auto policy because
   A. the loss must be accidental
   B. the loss must be overt
   C. arson is specifically excluded
   D. fire damage is excluded

4. Which of the following statements best describes subrogation?
   A. The insurance company may recover costs from another party assuming the other party was responsible for the accident.
   B. An insured can collect for his loss from his own insurance company and also from a responsible third party.
   C. The claimant can collect from the insured and his own insurer.
   D. The insurance company may collect from the negligent party on behalf of the insured.

5. Which of the following statements is a provision or requirement of an insurance policy?
   A. The insured must cooperate with all companies and, when requested, assist in making settlements.
   B. The insured has a duty to cooperate, which includes attendance at hearings and trials.
   C. The insured may make settlements without the approval of the insurance company.
   D. The insured may provide a waiver to a claimant as long as it is negotiated following a loss.

6. How do insolvency or bankruptcy affect an insured's policy coverage?
   A. Any policy in effect prior to the bankruptcy or insolvency is void.
   B. There is no effect on a liability policy.
   C. All policies issued prior to the bankruptcy are canceled.
   D. Only those policies in effect at the time are void.

7. Which of the following statements concerning automobile physical damage insurance losses is CORRECT?

   A. The insurer has the option of paying the insured the actual cash value of the automobile or the cost to repair or replace the car with one of a like kind or quality.
   B. The insured has the option of requesting a cash settlement or having the automobile repaired.
   C. The insured is obligated to replace the vehicle in order to receive payment.
   D. Losses are paid on the basis of market value subject to a stated limit.

8. An auto policy would provide coverage if an insured were driving his or her auto in all of the following places EXCEPT

   A. Alberta, Canada
   B. Paducah, Texas
   C. Mexico City, Mexico
   D. Honolulu, Hawaii

9. If an insured hits a garbage can while parallel parking, which part of an auto policy would cover the damage to the car?

   A. Medical payments
   B. Collision
   C. Comprehensive
   D. Liability

10. Which of the following is NOT an insured's duty in the event of a loss under a crime policy?

   A. Notify police
   B. Place the perpetrator under arrest
   C. Provide a list of missing items
   D. Keep records of insured property

11. Which of the following is a definition of theft?

   A. Loss of property
   B. Any act of stealing
   C. Wrongful taking of property, leaving visible signs of forcible entry
   D. Mysterious disappearance

12. The phrase *robbery or hold-up*, as used in burglary and robbery insurance, means the felonious taking of property in which of the following ways?

   A. By someone using a scheme, trick, or device designed to deprive the owner of the property
   B. From within an insured premises, safe or vault, by actual force and violence, leaving visible marks of forced entry
   C. From insured premises left unguarded and accessible without evidence of forced entry
   D. By use of or threat of the use of violence with the means to carry it out

13. The term *burglary*, as used in burglary and robbery insurance, means the felonious taking of property in which of the following ways?

   A. From within an insured premises, safe or vault, leaving visible marks of forced entry
   B. From a custodian, by violence or threats of violence, or from his person or direct custody, if he has been killed or rendered unconscious
   C. From an armored car or the employee of an armored car
   D. By the threat of violence to someone inside or outside the insured premises

14. A discovery period in a crime insurance policy stipulates which of the following?

    A. The insured must discover who committed the crime to have coverage.
    B. All losses discovered during the policy's term will be covered, regardless of when they occurred.
    C. A loss must be discovered within a specified time after the termination of the policy.
    D. A loss must be discovered prior to the expiration of the policy.

15. The practice of indemnifying *default of performance* is called

    A. indemnification
    B. insurance
    C. suretyship
    D. sistership

16. A $25,000 Employee Dishonesty Coverage Form has been in force for 8 years. A loss of $80,000 caused by a bookkeeper is discovered and the claim presented to the company. What would the insurer pay?

    A. Nothing, because a bookkeeper is not covered
    B. $25,000
    C. $80,000
    D. $10,000

17. All of the following are responsibilities of the insured in virtually all crime policies, EXCEPT to

    A. report theft losses to the police
    B. hire and pay for an appraiser
    C. report the loss to insurance company within 4 months
    D. keep records of all insured property

18. A Commercial General Liability (CGL) policy would cover which of the following losses?

    A. Theft of a customer's property from inside the premises
    B. An insured's employee injured by a falling elevator
    C. A woman entering the insured's store and tripping over a vacuum cleaner
    D. Injury to the insured's employee while leaving the premises

19. A laundromat would purchase bodily injury and property damage coverage in order to protect against which of the following occurrences?

    A. Damage to a customer's property caused by shrinkage
    B. Former employees leaving and opening competing laundromats, causing loss of customers
    C. The loss of revenues if the electricity goes off as a result of the utility's negligence
    D. Injury to a customer who slips on water from a leaking washer

20. Which of the following statements best characterizes waiver?

    A. The intentional giving up of a known right.
    B. A discharge from further liability under an insurance policy.
    C. The same as estoppel.
    D. The same as warranty.

21. Which of the following terms describes the deliberate failure to reveal material facts that would affect the validity of an insurance policy?

    A. Inducement
    B. Concealment
    C. Collusion
    D. Rebating

22. Legally enforceable contracts require all of the following EXCEPT

    A. offer and acceptance
    B. consideration
    C. legal purpose
    D. insurable interest

23. During the application process, statements made by applicants that they claim are true to the best of their knowledge are

    A. warranties
    B. concealments
    C. representations
    D. waivers

24. The term *insurable interest* refers to the

    A. relationship between the insured and the agent
    B. carrying charges a person pays when he finances the purchase of insurance
    C. amount of insurance that a person carries
    D. extent of the financial loss a person may suffer as a result of the occurrence of a contingency

25. An employee of an insured is injured on the job. Coverage would be provided under which of the following products?

    A. CGL
    B. BOP
    C. Workers' compensation
    D. Fidelity bond

26. Which kind of risk only has the potential for loss or no loss?

    A. Insurance
    B. Pure
    C. Speculative
    D. Retained

27. Which of the following is NOT covered under Commercial General Liability insurance?

    A. An employee who is injured on an escalator in the store
    B. A shopper who accidentally walks through a plate glass window in the store
    C. A shopper who trips on a bucket left by a janitor
    D. A patron who is injured after choking on food in a restaurant

28. A salesperson and a client are injured in the salesperson's office. Whose injuries are covered under the salesperson's Commercial General Liability policy?

    A. Salesperson
    B. Client
    C. Both
    D. Neither

29. If a claim is valid, the insurer may do which of the following?

    A. Reduce premiums
    B. Deny the claim and request resubmission
    C. Pay the claim to the extent of the limits of liability
    D. Pay part of the claim only

30. Which of the following constitutes valid consideration?

    A. Warranties
    B. Premiums
    C. Statements
    D. Representations

31. Which of the following contracts can be legally enforced?

    A. One in which one party pays money and the other agrees to perform a service
    B. One that violates public policy
    C. One in which the insured has no insurable interest in the property
    D. One to destroy property owned by another

32. The Commercial General Liability (CGL) policy includes all of the following types of limits EXCEPT

    A. aggregate
    B. personal injury
    C. occurrence
    D. combined

33. The conditions section of an insurance policy does which of the following?

    A. Lists the obligations of the insured and the insurance company
    B. Alters the general provisions of the insuring agreement
    C. Eliminates uninsurable perils
    D. Covers unique insurable exposures of the insured

34. An insurance contract can be modified by which of the following?

    A. Condition
    B. Addendum
    C. Memorandum
    D. Endorsement

35. The holder of a CGL policy moves to a new location during the policy term. Which of the following statements about coverage at the new location is CORRECT?

    A. It begins when the insurance company is notified.
    B. It is automatic until the end of the policy term.
    C. It is automatic for 30 days after the move.
    D. It is determined pro rata at both locations.

36. The Premises Burglary Coverage Form covers which one of the following perils?

    A. Robbery of a store clerk
    B. Theft from the insured premises
    C. Mysterious disappearance of merchandise
    D. Burglary when the premises are closed

37. A CGL policy provides coverage against liability arising from all of the following EXCEPT

    A. ownership of the premises
    B. maintenance of the premises
    C. injury to employees
    D. conduct of business operations

38. Products coverage pays for which of the following?

    A. Expenses involved in recalling a product
    B. Damages to a product
    C. The cost of rebuilding a faulty product
    D. Injury to a person caused by a faulty product

39. Which of the following accidents would be covered under a CGL policy?

    A. An insured truck strikes a pedestrian.
    B. An insured boat rams another boat.
    C. A customer of an insured is killed while flying in a company plane.
    D. A customer is injured by a box dropped by an employee.

40. Workers' compensation insurance would cover all of the following employees EXCEPT one injured

    A. on the job due to own negligence
    B. on the job due to an unsafe workplace
    C. when an employer fails to make necessary repairs
    D. at a sporting event attended with other employees

41. Shoplifting is classified as which of the following?

    A. Robbery
    B. Burglary
    C. Theft
    D. Malicious mischief

42. What is the primary difference between a claims-made and occurrence form of a CGL policy?

    A. The claims-made form provides coverage only for events that take place during the policy period.
    B. The claims-made policy provides coverage for claims first made during the policy period.
    C. The occurrence form provides coverage for claims that occur after the expiration of the policy using a tail.
    D. The occurrence form is issued with an aggregate limit and the claims-made form is not.

43. Suretyship can be provided by all of the following EXCEPT

    A. individual
    B. corporation
    C. trusts
    D. casualty company

44. Which of the following statements about accidents is CORRECT?

    A. They are identifiable in time and place.
    B. They include losses caused intentionally by the insured.
    C. They include occurrences.
    D. They must take place during the policy period.

45. A surety bond protects which of the following parties?

    A. Principal
    B. Contractor performing the work
    C. Surety
    D. Obligee

46. In addition to providing coverage for damage to a third party's property, a liability policy will pay all of the following expenses EXCEPT

    A. defending a claim
    B. investigating a claim
    C. negotiating a claim
    D. paying opposing counsel

47. Uninsured motorist coverage in an auto policy provides payments for which of the following?

    A. Bodily injury to other parties
    B. Bodily injury to the insured
    C. Physical damage to the auto
    D. Bodily injury to the uninsured driver

48. Which of the following statements about an auto policy's Medical Payments coverage is NOT correct?

    A. It covers all reasonable medical expenses incurred within the specified period up to coverage limits.
    B. It pays regardless of who caused the accident.
    C. It covers bodily injury sustained within 5 years.
    D. It covers family members and other persons injured while occupying the insured auto.

49. An insured has an auto policy with Damage to Your Auto coverage. After an accident, the insured must do all of the following to recover the loss EXCEPT

    A. secure an estimate of damages
    B. protect the insured automobile against further loss
    C. notify the police if the auto is stolen
    D. submit to a medical exam

50. Supplementary transportation coverage begins 48 hours after a theft, provided the insured's auto policy includes theft coverage. This coverage will pay which of the following amounts?

    A. Up to $3 a day for 10 days
    B. Up to $20 a day with a maximum of $600
    C. Up to $30 a day for 10 days
    D. Up to $20 a day for 30 days

51. Which of the following statements regarding coverage for custom farming in a farm liability policy is CORRECT?

    A. It is not included.
    B. It carries a maximum limit of $100,000.
    C. It is included without limitation.
    D. It is included if receipts are less than $2,000.

52. When farm liability coverage is provided under a combination policy, which of the following statements is CORRECT?

    A. Both business and nonbusiness pursuits are covered.
    B. Coverage applies only to farm operations.
    C. Nonbusiness pursuits are not covered.
    D. There is a sublimit on nonfarm business pursuits.

53. Under the liability section of the Personal Auto Policy, which of the following is NOT considered an insured person?

    A. The 13-year-old child of an insured who takes the car without permission
    B. The guest of the insured who uses the vehicle with the permission of the insured
    C. The employee who drives a delivery truck for an employer
    D. The employee of an insured who works as a domestic servant and runs errands using the insured's car

54. Which of the following coverages is included under the Protection and Indemnity portion of a marine insurance policy?

    A. Workers' compensation for crew members
    B. Liability for damage to another vessel
    C. Property damage to a vessel owned by the insured
    D. Property damage to a vessel leased by the insured

55. Which coverage is automatically included under Section II of a Homeowners policy?

    A. Personal injury
    B. Bodily injury to employees
    C. Additional residences rented to others
    D. Damage to property of others

56. To change the terms of a liability policy, which of the following must be attached to the contract?

    A. Conditions
    B. Binder
    C. Endorsement
    D. Declaration

57. If an insured has minimum financial responsibility limits under an automobile policy, which of the following statements regarding coverage on an out-of-state vacation trip is NOT correct?

    A. It will automatically adjust to the limits in each state the vehicle enters.
    B. It will apply to no fault benefits when entering a state with that type of law.
    C. It will not cover the insured while driving out of state.
    D. It will increase if the coverage limits in the other states are higher.

58. Automobile comprehensive coverage insures all of the following perils EXCEPT

    A. collision
    B. glass breakage
    C. fire
    D. theft

59. Coverage for legal fees paid by an insurance company is included in which of the following?

    A. Defense cost provision
    B. Supplementary payments
    C. Limits of liability
    D. Settlement options

60. A Commercial General Liability policy will pay expenses to defend all of the following suits EXCEPT

    A. bodily injury in which the insured is legally liable
    B. property damage that may be groundless
    C. injury to an employee
    D. advertising injury

61. An auto policy's Bodily Injury and Property Damage coverage will pay for

    A. damage to the insured's garage caused by the insured's car
    B. intentional injuries to a passenger caused by the insured
    C. damage to the insured's own vehicle caused by an accident with another car
    D. unintentional injury to a pedestrian caused by the insured's car

62. An Employee Dishonesty Coverage Form is purchased to provide protection for the

    A. principal
    B. employer
    C. employee
    D. insurer

63. A toy manufacturer with a Commercial General Liability Policy would have coverage for all of the following exposures EXCEPT a

    A. customer in a showroom who severs a finger examining a new toy
    B. child who is injured playing with a toy at home
    C. toy that is manufactured and sold in China
    D. display of toys that falls on a child inside a manufacturer's showroom

64. An employee of a drugstore broke into the store on New Year's Day at 2:15 pm and stole three cartons of cigarettes. Which of the following reasons excludes the theft from coverage based on the Premises Burglary Coverage Form?

    A. It occurred during daylight hours.
    B. It was committed by an employee.
    C. It involved property rather than money.
    D. It did not include force or the threat of force.

65. Which of the following statements regarding workers' compensation is NOT correct?

    A. It covers work-related injuries.
    B. An injured employee can still sue a negligent third party.
    C. An employee can sue an employer whenever he wants.
    D. An employee must accept the benefits specified by law.

66. Which of the following persons would NOT be considered an insured under a Personal Auto Policy?

    A. The named insured's 10-year-old child who is permitted to start the car in the driveway
    B. The named insured's child while away at college
    C. The named insured's spouse who resides in the household
    D. The named insured's employee while working for the insured

67. The Supplementary Payments section of an auto policy covers all of the following EXCEPT

    A. premiums for bonds
    B. legal expenses to handle the claim
    C. costs of investigating the claim
    D. hospital expenses

68. Which of the following auto policy coverages would pay for damage to a traffic light owned by the city?

    A. Bodily Injury
    B. Property Damage
    C. Physical Damage
    D. Collision

69. A passenger injured in an automobile may recover under all of the following coverages EXCEPT

    A. liability
    B. collision
    C. medical payments
    D. uninsured motorist

70. Loss that occurs when someone enters the premises by breaking a window is which of the following?

    A. Burglary
    B. Robbery
    C. Theft
    D. Not covered

71. Loss that occurs when someone leaves the premises after-hours by breaking a window is considered which of the following?

    A. Theft
    B. Burglary
    C. Robbery
    D. Mysterious disappearance

72. Loss that occurs when someone is mugged taking a deposit to the bank is considered which of the following?

    A. Theft
    B. Burglary
    C. Robbery
    D. Larceny

73. Loss that occurs when jewelry is shoplifted from a department store is considered which of the following?

A. Burglary
B. Robbery
C. Theft
D. Mysterious disappearance

74. A Premises Burglary Coverage Form covers which of the following situations?

A. An armored car driver who is robbed after leaving the premises
B. A shop foreman who returns in the evening and takes some equipment home
C. An employee who enters the premises with a key and takes some milk
D. A customer who breaks a window and enters the premises when closed

75. While examining a toy in the manufacturer's warehouse, a child cuts a finger. The toy manufacturer would be covered if its insurance policy includes which of the following products?

A. Commercial General Liability
B. Workers' Compensation
C. Building and Personal Property Coverage Form
D. Employment Practices Liability

76. Insured A borrowed Insured B's auto. Insured B had an auto policy with limits of 100/300/25. Insured A had a car with an auto policy of 50/100/10. Insured A had an accident while driving Insured B's car and caused a $118,000 injury to a person. How much will Insured B's policy pay?

A. $59,000
B. $100,000
C. $118,000
D. $300,000

77. Using the information provided in Question 76, with respect to Insured A's policy, what clause or coverage would apply?

A. Subrogation
B. Assignment
C. Bodily Injury
D. Collision

78. Workers' compensation provides all of the following EXCEPT

A. rehabilitation benefits
B. death benefits
C. indemnity benefits for less income
D. coverage for non-occupational diseases

79. The CGL policy provides coverage against liability arising from all of the following EXCEPT

A. ownership of the premises
B. maintenance of the premises
C. use of the premises
D. injuries to employees

80. Collision or upset insurance covers which of the following?

A. All damage to an auto struck by an insured, providing the insured is legally liable
B. Direct loss to an auto caused by collision with another object or by upset of an auto, subject to the deductible amount stated in the policy
C. The pain and suffering of the policyholder when an accident occurs
D. Damage to an auto caused by fire, theft or collision with another object

81. All of the following injuries would be covered under auto medical payments coverage EXCEPT

A. injury to the occupant of another vehicle
B. injury to the insured's child who was a passenger in the insured's vehicle
C. injury to the insured's spouse from driving into a pole
D. injuries to a passenger in the insured's vehicle

82. Exclusions written into casualty insurance policies eliminate coverage of all for the following EXCEPT

A. perils covered by other policies
B. uninsurable perils
C. catastrophic perils
D. human perils

83. All of the following supplementary payments are provided by an auto policy's bodily injury coverage EXCEPT

A. the cost of investigating an accident
B. the premium for a bail bond
C. all of the insured's lost earnings during attendance at a hearing or trial
D. the premium for an appeal bond

84. An insured, with an auto policy containing Bodily Injury/Property Damage liability limits of 50/100/50, negligently runs into the back of a car and injures the driver and passenger. The driver suffers injuries and loss of income of $45,000, and the passenger suffers medical expenses of $95,000. How much will the insured's policy pay?

A. This is considered one occurrence, so the insurer will pay no more than $50,000 for one person and no more than $100,000 total for bodily injury.
B. This is considered one occurrence, but both persons will receive payment for their injuries since the amount is less than $100,000 for each.
C. This is considered two occurrences, so the limits of 50/100 apply separately to driver and passenger; each can collect for their injuries since the amount for each one is less than $100,000.
D. This is considered two occurrences, so the limits of 50/100 apply to the injuries suffered by the driver and the passenger up to a total of $200,000.

85. An auto liability policy covers all of the following EXCEPT

A. all family members of the insured
B. all family members who reside in the insured's house
C. any friend of the named insured who has permission to use the auto
D. a coworker who uses the auto on company business

86. General liability insurance protects business liability exposures caused by all of the following EXCEPT a(n)

A. customer of the insured
B. employee of the insured
C. owner of the business
D. partner of the insured

87. Which of the following statements regarding changes in exposures during the term of a CGL policy is CORRECT?

    A. They are covered if added to the policy by endorsement.
    B. They are covered automatically until the end of the policy period.
    C. They are not covered until the policy renews.
    D. They are not covered until an additional premium is paid.

88. The right to investigate and settle a personal liability claim rests with the

    A. insured
    B. insurer
    C. claims adjusting company
    D. courts

89. General liability policies provide coverage for damage to which of the following kinds of property?

    A. Rented by the insured for a short period of time.
    B. Leased long-term by the insured.
    C. Borrowed, without cost, by the insured.
    D. Stored by a customer on the insured's business premises.

90. Which of the following statements about Coverage E Personal Liability of the Homeowners policy is NOT correct?

    A. It is issued on a single limit of liability basis.
    B. It is issued to cover personal activities.
    C. It is not issued to react to professional activities.
    D. It includes medical payments coverage.

91. A general liability policy is issued effective January 1 with a Bodily Injury limit of $100,000. On March 1, a loss occurs and is settled for $20,000. How much insurance would be available for a loss that occurs one month prior to the policy's expiration date?

    A. $120,000
    B. $100,000
    C. $80,000
    D. $50,000

92. An insured is successfully sued for negligence, and the court awards the plaintiff $300,000. If the insurance company is charged $15,000 for defending the suit, and the limit of liability on the insured's policy is $250,000, how much will the insurer pay?

    A. $250,000
    B. $265,000
    C. $300,000
    D. $315,000

93. The duties of the insurance company in the event of a loss to the insured are explained in which of the following sections of an insurance policy?

    A. Declarations
    B. Conditions
    C. Exclusions
    D. Insuring Agreement

94. The claims-made form will cover which of the following losses?

    A. Accidents happening before the retroactive date
    B. Accidents happening after the retroactive date
    C. Accidents happening after the policy period
    D. Accidents happening after the extended reporting period

95. A business is sued because a wall constructed on its property 12 years ago collapsed and injured a child last week. Which of the following statements is NOT correct?

A. The current insurance company is obligated to defend the insured.
B. Coverage is provided under the premises and operations section of the CGL policy.
C. Coverage is provided under the completed liability section of a CGL policy.
D. The current insurance company must defend the insured if the case is arbitrated.

96. Which of the following situations would be covered by a General Liability Policy?

A. Manufacturing exhaust kills a crop of tomatoes in a nearby field.
B. An employee drives his or her auto into the employer's garage door.
C. An employee's finger is injured in an electric pencil sharpener.
D. A surfboard falls off a shelf and injures a shopper.

97. Which of the following would protect a policyholder for assumed liability under a construction contract to install water lines for the city?

A. Independent contractors
B. Insured contracts
C. Contractual liability
D. Completed operations

98. All of the following are considered to be supplementary payments under a CGL policy EXCEPT

A. payment for an appeal bond
B. cost of legal defense
C. cost of bail bonds
D. medical payments for an injured customer

99. If a manufacturer is forced to recall a product from the market, its Products and Completed Operations coverage would cover which of the following?

A. Claims for damages caused by loss of use of the recalled product
B. Expenses incurred in the recall operation
C. Costs of repairing or remedying the product
D. The damages resulting from the recall are excluded under a CGL policy

100. All of the following are excluded under a CGL policy EXCEPT

A. a loss involving the use of a licensed vehicle
B. a loss to property being transported by the insured
C. injuries suffered by an employee of the insured at a job site
D. loss of use of property that has not been damaged but is caused by the insured's negligence

## Casualty Insurance Answers & Rationale

1. **C.** Coverage for collision in an auto policy is designed to cover damage to the insured's auto that results from collision with another object or upset, e.g., rolling the car over by taking a corner too fast. Collision pays whether the insured is at fault or not. A deductible applies to collision losses. Hitting a large animal is considered a comprehensive loss under an auto policy.

2. **A.** The physical damage section of an auto policy applies to parts of the auto such as hubcaps. It does not apply to personal property in the auto such as a typewriter. A detachable radio that is in the home of the insured would be covered under a homeowners policy. Damage to a residence would be covered under auto liability, not physical damage.

3. **A.** The auto policy does not specifically exclude arson. However, the insuring agreement for physical damage states that the insurer will pay for direct and accidental damage to the covered auto. Accidental damage requires that the damage be unforeseen and unintended from the standpoint of the insured.

4. **A.** Subrogation means the insurer's right to recover payment. If the insured has the right to recover from a negligent third party but instead collects from his own insurer, the insurer will pay the insured but then may collect from the negligent third party.

5. **B.** Insurance policies require that the insured cooperate, but only with his own insurance company. The policy also imposes a duty to cooperate that includes attendance at hearings and trials, but not in making settlements. The insured must do nothing to impair the insurer's rights under the policy, including issuing waivers.

6. **B.** In a liability policy, the financial insolvency of the insured does not relieve the insurer of any obligation under the policy. This provision states that the insurer is still responsible for making a settlement or defending the insured even if he or she declared bankruptcy. Consequently, an insured's insolvency or bankruptcy has no effect on the policy.

7. **A.** The limit of liability section of the physical damage section states that the insurer will pay the lesser of the actual cash value or the amount necessary to repair or replace the property. The insured does not have a choice in the matter. The insured is under no obligation to actually repair the vehicle since the policy is issued on an actual cash value basis.

8. **C.** An auto policy would provide coverage while driving in the United States of America, its territories or possessions, Puerto Rico, or Canada. Because Mexico is usually not part of this coverage territory, accidents or losses occurring in Mexico generally will not be covered.

9. **B.** Collision covers upset or impact with another vehicle or object, including a garbage can. Exceptions would include being struck by a falling object or missile, or striking an animal.

10. **B.** The policy requires notification of the police to report the crime. Although there is no specific requirement to keep records, proof of ownership may be required. Thus, records must be maintained to show what was stolen. The insured is under no obligation to arrest anyone.

11. **B.** Theft is a broad term meaning the taking of property belonging to someone else or any act of stealing, whether by robbery, burglary, or larceny.

12. **D.** Robbery specifically requires the taking of property from someone by force or threat of force, and falls under the generic definition of theft.

13. **A.** Burglary or safe burglary requires the forcible entry into or exit from the premises or safe with visible signs of entry.

14. **C.** All crime insurance forms provide that the insurer will pay for a loss that otherwise would be covered if it is discovered no later than 1 year from the end of the policy period. This is because theft of some kinds of property, which are not used on a daily basis, may not be discovered for some time.

15. **C.** Suretyship in its broadest sense covers all forms of obligation to pay the debt or answer for the default of another. This includes both fidelity and surety bonds. Surety bonds specifically provide that the surety agrees to answer to the obligee for the nonperformance or default of the principal. A fidelity bond will reimburse an employer for loss up to the amount of the bond, sustained by reason of any dishonest act of an employee covered by the bond.

16. **B.** The Employee Dishonesty Coverage Form indicates that for each occurrence the insurer will only pay up to the limits of insurance shown on the Declarations Page. The form defines an occurrence as all loss caused by or involving one or more employees, whether the result of a single act or a series of acts. Therefore, because the limit of insurance is $25,000, this is all the company will pay for the loss whether it happened all at once or over a period of time.

17. **B.** According to the Crime General Provisions Form, the insured must report the loss to the local law enforcement agency and to the insurance company within specific time periods, and must maintain records of all insured property. Hiring and paying for an appraiser, however, is part of the Arbitration Clause, used when there is a disagreement as to the value of a first party loss.

18. **C.** In the Commercial General Liability Coverage (CGL) policy, the insurer agrees to pay those sums that the insured becomes legally obligated to pay as damages owing to bodily injury, personal injury or property damage. That would apply to the situation described in choice C, presuming the insured was legally liable. Choice A would be covered under a bailee's customers policy and choices B and D under workers' compensation insurance.

19. **D.** An insured purchases liability coverage to insure against claims from third parties who are injured by conditions on the insured's property or by the insured's operations. Only choice D describes a situation in which a person suffers bodily injury or property damage.

20. **A.** Waiver is willingly giving up a known right. It may be intentional or unintentional.

21. **B.** If an applicant is aware of material facts that may affect the underwriting of the policy, the applicant is obligated to disclose this to the agent or insurer. If the applicant fails to disclose important information, a policy may be cancelled or a claim denied under the doctrine of concealment.

22. **D.** All legally enforceable contracts, including insurance policies, must contain four elements: offer and acceptance, consideration, competent parties, and legal purpose. Although an applicant for insurance must demonstrate insurable interest in the insured for a policy to be underwritten, it is not one of the essential elements of contracts generally.

23. **C.** Representations are statements made by applicants that are true to the best of their knowledge. If those statements are made a part of the contract they become warranties. Warranties must be absolutely true.

24. **D.** Insurable interest in property and casualty insurance means having a relationship to property such that if that property is damaged, destroyed, or lost, a person will suffer a pecuniary or monetary loss. Such an interest can arise by owning property, having a mortgage or lien on property or having care, custody, or control of other people's property. Most states require that such an interest be present in order to take out a policy. The principles of property and casualty insurance also require that an insurable interest be present at the time of a loss.

25. **C.** To protect against claims for injuries to employees, a business owner must purchase workers' compensation coverage. A Commercial General Liability (CGL) and a Business Owners

Policy (BOP) provide coverage for bodily injury and property damage if an insured is legally liable to others. A fidelity bond applies to losses due to employee dishonesty.

26. **B.** Risk means the uncertainty regarding financial loss. There are only two types of risk: pure and speculative. Pure risk has no potential for gain since either a loss occurs or it does not. Speculative risk involves a chance of gain as well as loss. Only pure risks are insurable.

27. **A.** The situations described in choices B, C, and D are the reasons a business owner would buy liability insurance. The purpose of CGL insurance is to protect a business against claims arising out of premises, the business it conducts, products it makes or sells or operations in progress or completed. Workers' compensation coverage is available for injuries to employees.

28. **B.** Liability policies are designed to cover the insured's liability to others, not to cover injury to the insured or to his own property. Therefore, the insured's liability policy would pay for bodily injury to the client if the insured is legally liable. It would also defend the insured in a lawsuit brought against the insured.

29. **C.** If a claim is valid, the presumption is that the insured performed all duties as spelled out in the conditions section of the policy and notified the company and completed the proof of loss within the required time. Therefore, the insurer will pay for the claim up to the limits of insurance.

30. **B.** In order to have a valid contract, there must be consideration from both parties. Consideration by the insured includes the promise to pay premium. Consideration by the insurer is its promise to pay if the insured suffers a loss described in the policy.

31. **A.** To make any contract enforceable, four elements must be present: offer and acceptance, consideration, competent parties, and legal purpose. Also, insurable interest must be shown at the time of writing the application and loss. Contracts that are against public policy, to destroy another's property or in which no insurable interest exists are not legally enforceable.

32. **D.** CGL policies have a personal injury limit, a per occurrence limit and an annual aggregate limit.

33. **A.** The Conditions section lists the obligations of the insured and insurer. The other major parts of an insurance policy are Declarations, Insuring Agreement, and Exclusions.

34. **D.** An endorsement is used to modify an insurance contract by adding or deleting coverages specific to that policy. It may be added at the beginning of the policy or during the policy's term.

35. **B.** Absent any exclusion to the contrary, a CGL policy covers all exposures of the insured whether premium is indicated or not. Newly acquired exposures are covered automatically, subject to premium adjustment at the end of the policy period by audit.

36. **D.** A Premises Burglary Coverage form covers actual or attempted burglary, that is, the taking of property from inside the premises by a person unlawfully entering or leaving the premises as evidenced by marks of forcible entry or exit. Therefore, the premises must have been closed for burglary to have occurred. This coverage form also provides coverage for actual or attempted robbery of a watchperson.

37. **C.** The CGL policy provides liability coverage if a business owns or rents the property where it is doing business, i.e., if it maintains the premises. It also provides coverage for injuries or damages arising in the course of a business' daily operations. It does not cover injury to employees.

38. **D.** Products and Completed Operations exposures are covered under CGL policy. The products coverage applies if a product manufactured or sold by a business causes bodily injury or property damage to a third party if the insured is legally liable. The policy specifically excludes

coverage for damages claimed for any loss, cost, or expense incurred by the insured or others for the loss of use, withdrawal, recall, inspection, repair, replacement, adjustment, removal, or disposal of the insured's product or work. The policy also excludes property damage to the insured's product arising out of it or any part of it.

39. **D.** A CGL policy excludes bodily injury or property damage arising out of the ownership, maintenance, use, or entrustment to others of any aircraft, auto, or watercraft owned or operated by, or rented or loaned to any insured. It would cover injuries to a customer that were sustained while on the business's premises.

40. **D.** Workers' compensation insurance provides coverage on the basis of employer liability without fault. If an employee is injured during the course of his employment, the employer's workers' compensation insurer must pay. This is true whether or not the employer or employee was negligent. However, there is no coverage for injuries to employees that occur away from work and not in the course of employment, such as at an athletic event.

41. **C.** As previously noted, robbery and burglary have very specific requirements. In contrast, the definition of theft is very broad and includes any act of stealing. Shoplifting involves taking property that does not belong to one and is therefore considered theft.

42. **B.** A claims-made policy provides coverage for claims during the policy period. In contrast, a claim can be submitted after the policy has expired under an occurrence form, provided the injuries or damage occurred during the policy period.

43. **C.** Suretyship is the process of guaranteeing the performance or honesty of someone. Today surety and fidelity bonds are generally provided by insurance companies that have decided to add this type of policy to their product list. However, an individual can also provide a suretyship.

44. **A.** Accidents can be identified as to time and place in contrast to an occurrence, which includes an accident but also includes events which happen over a period of time. Accidents, as well as occurrences, must be unintentional from the standpoint of the insured.

45. **D.** There are three persons or entities involved in surety bonds. For example, a developer who wants to have an apartment building constructed is the obligee, that is, the one to whom an obligation is owed and the one protected by the bond should a contractor fail to perform. The contractor is the principal, that is, the one who has or owes an obligation. The third party, then, is the *surety*, or the one who guarantees that a contractor will perform according to the contract.

46. **D.** The insuring agreement requires the insurer to defend any suit seeking bodily injury or property damage. It also agrees to investigate and settle any claim or suit at its discretion. Under Supplementary Payments, the insurer agrees to pay all expenses incurred in defending any claim or suit. There is no obligation for the insurer or insured to pay opposing counsel unless such costs are part of a judgment rendered against the insured.

47. **B.** Uninsured motorist coverage pays only for bodily injury to the persons defined in the policy as insureds, if they are injured by someone having no insurance or by a hit-and-run driver. Family members are covered even as pedestrians. Damage to the insured's auto is covered by the insured's collision coverage under the physical damage section of the policy.

48. **C.** The Medical Payments coverage of a Personal Auto Policy pays reasonable expenses incurred for necessary medical and funeral services because of accidental bodily injury sustained by an insured. Coverage applies without regard to fault or negligence. Only those medical expenses incurred within 3 years will be covered. Covered persons include family members and other persons who are injured while in the insured auto.

49. **D.** Under Damage to Your Auto coverage, the insured must notify the police if the car was stolen and take reasonable steps after a loss to protect the covered auto and its equipment from further loss. In order to attempt to determine a settlement, the insured will have to obtain an estimate of the damage to the vehicle. There is no requirement under Damage to your Auto for medical exams.

50. **B.** As part of the auto policy's section on coverage for damage to the insured's auto, the insurer promises to pay up to $20 a day to a maximum of $600 for transportation expenses incurred by the insured if the insured's auto is stolen and if the insured had purchased Comprehensive/Other Than Collision coverage. Such coverage does not begin until 48 hours after the theft and ends when the covered auto is returned to use, the insurer pays for the loss, or the limit is reached, whichever comes first.

51. **D.** Coverage for custom farming is included under the farm liability policy only if receipts do not exceed $2,000 in the 12 months prior to the occurrence for which coverage is sought.

52. **A.** The farm policy can be written as a combination of business and personal coverages. Therefore, farm liability includes coverage for farming operations and for the personal exposures of the farmer and his family. Other business pursuits, however, are not automatically included under farm liability and must be added by endorsement.

53. **C.** Family members and others who use autos with a reasonable belief that they are entitled to do so are covered under the PAP; actual permission need not be given for coverage to apply. Domestic employees who use autos while working for the insured would also be covered. However, an employee who uses a delivery truck will not be covered.

54. **A.** The Protection and Indemnity portion of a marine policy provides workers' compensation insurance for crew members and includes coverage for bodily injury to passengers and others injured as a result of the operation of a vessel.

55. **D.** Section II of a Homeowners policy automatically includes damage to property of others to a limit of $1,000. Coverage for personal injury and workers' compensation coverage for domestic employees both must be added to the homeowners policy by endorsement. Additional residences rented to others may be covered by attaching an endorsement with appropriate premium charged.

56. **C.** An endorsement is the attached form that changes the terms of a policy. It may be attached at the beginning of the policy or added during the policy's term.

57. **C.** Auto policies are considered to be extra territorial because they automatically adjust to changes in the laws of the various states as the vehicle enters and leaves each area.

58. **A.** The physical damage portion of a PAP has two sections: Collision and Comprehensive (also known as Other Than Collision). Comprehensive coverage provides for fire, theft, vandalism, being struck by a falling object or a missile, and hitting or being hit by an animal.

59. **B.** The insuring agreement requires the insurer to defend any suit seeking bodily injury or property damage. It also agrees to investigate and settle any claim or suit at its discretion. Under Supplementary Payments, the insurer agrees to pay all expenses incurred in defending any claim or suit. There is no obligation for the insurer or insured to pay opposing counsel unless such costs are part of a judgment rendered against the insured.

60. **C.** The CGL policy stipulates that the insurer has the right and duty to defend any suit seeking recovery for bodily injury or property damage or because of personal injury or advertising injury, if the claim would be covered by the coverage form and if the insured were negligent. The policy does not stipulate that the insurer will only defend suits that have some basis. In other

words, insurers will defend even if the suit is false or groundless.

61. **D.** The Liability section provides protection when the insured unintentionally either injures someone or damages someone else's property. It will pay all sums that the insured becomes legally responsible for due to his negligence. Only choice D shows injury or damage that is to someone other than the insured and is not intentional.

62. **B.** The Employee Dishonesty Coverage form is purchased by the employer to protect itself against the possibility of employees stealing money, securities, or other property from the business. The employer is the obligee, and the employees are principals.

63. **C.** The CGL policy provides protection for Premises and Operations as well as Products and Completed Operations. The Premises coverage will provide protection while a guest is on the premises, as in choice A and D. The Products and Completed Operations provides protection away from the insured premises, as in choice B. Although coverage is worldwide in nature, products must be manufactured domestically and suits brought in the coverage territory.

64. **B.** While this situation may appear to be a burglary, it is not covered under the Premises Burglary Coverage Form because the form excludes coverage for any acts by employees, directors, trustees, or representatives of the insured. The Employee Dishonesty Coverage form would provide coverage in this situation.

65. **C.** Workers' compensation laws are designed to provide benefits for employees injured during the course of employment. The employee must accept the benefits specified by statute and may not sue his or her employer. However, the employee may sue a negligent third party (i.e., for an injury caused by equipment owned by the employer but manufactured by someone else).

66. **D.** Under a PAP, an insured includes the named insured, relatives of the named insured who reside in the named insured's household (by blood, marriage, or adoption, including a ward or foster child), and those using the vehicle with the reasonable belief they are entitled to do so. However, there is no coverage provided under a PAP for bodily injury sustained by an insured's employee. It is important to note that the policy does not exclude a nonlicensed relative of the named insured residing in the home. Coverage would be extended to the 10-year-old child. A person away at college is generally considered a resident of the household, as long as such person has not established an independent residence.

67. **D.** Depending on the state, hospital expenses for the insured or passengers would be handled under medical payments or no fault insurance. The Supplementary Payments Section would cover the cost of investigation and legal expenses.

68. **B.** Damage to a traffic light is property damage. The liability coverage section pays for bodily injury and property damage if an insured is legally liable for the injury or damage.

69. **B.** Collision only pays for damage to the insured's automobile owing to striking or being struck by another object (with the noted exceptions for Other than Collision). The injured passenger can recover for medical expenses through the insured's medical payments coverage (without regard to fault), the insured's bodily injury liability section (if the operator was at fault), or through Uninsured Motorist coverage if the third party was at fault but did not carry liability insurance. However, the injured party cannot collect for medical bills under both the liability section and medical payments coverage of the policy.

70. **A.** Burglary or safe burglary requires the forcible entry into or exit from the premises or safe with visible signs of entry.

71. **B** Burglary or safe burglary requires the forcible entry into or exit from the premises or safe with visible signs of entry.

72. **C** Robbery specifically requires the taking of property from someone by force or threat of force, and falls under the generic definition of theft.

73. **C** Theft is a broad term meaning the taking of property belonging to someone else or any act of stealing, whether by robbery, burglary, or larceny.

74. **D.** The fact that the loss was caused by a customer-turned-burglar has no impact on coverage, because Premises Burglary only requires forcible entry into or exit out of the premises. Employees committing acts of burglary are specifically excluded from the coverage, so protection should be provided through an employee dishonesty form or fidelity bond.

75. **A.** To cover bodily injury or property damage to others, the manufacturer must have a liability policy such as a Commercial General Liability (CGL) policy. Since the injury happened on the insured's premises, it would be a Premises and Operations exposure and not a Products and Completed Operations exposure even though the child was handling a product. If the injured person only claimed medical expenses and the insured had purchased Coverage C of the CGL, the insurer would pay under the Medical Payments section. If a claim were made for bodily injury, medical payments will only apply if the injury would be covered under the liability section.

76. **B.** Insured B's auto policy will only pay up to the policy limits of $100,000 regardless of the number of insureds. Insured B's policy is primary since B's car was involved in the accident. However, assuming that Insured A is named in the suit and is legally liable A's policy would pay the remaining $18,000.

77. **C.** The injury in this situation would be covered by Insured A's policy under the Bodily Injury portion of the liability coverage.

78. **D.** Although workers' compensation covers occupational diseases arising out of employment, it does not cover non-occupational diseases or illness. Workers' compensation does provide medical expense benefits, rehabilitation benefits, and indemnity for loss of income. It also provides two types of death benefits: burial expense and survivors' benefits.

79. **D.** A CGL policy does not provide coverage to employees injured while working. It does, however, provide coverage for someone who owns the land and the building thereon as well as for someone who only maintains the premises, such as a tenant or someone who only uses some part of the premises.

80. **B.** Direct loss to an auto owing to upset or collision with another object is subject to Collision coverage. Choice A would be covered under the liability section of the insured's auto policy for property damage to others. Choice C would be covered by the negligent driver's liability insurance or by the insured's uninsured motorists coverage. Choice D would be covered under comprehensive coverage, also known as Other than Collision coverage.

81. **A.** Injuries to the insured, family members or any passenger in the insured's car are covered by medical payments coverage. Occupants in other vehicles who are injured might receive compensation for their injuries under the policy's liability coverage.

82. **D.** Generally, exclusions are written into a policy because the perils are uninsurable, such as catastrophic events like war or flood. Exclusions are also written because the premium does not contemplate the exposure, such as auto coverage under a homeowner's policy.

83. **C.** If an insurer requires the insured to attend a hearing or trial, the insured may only receive up to $200 for lost earnings as a supplementary payment. An auto policy will provide certain supplementary payments, including the cost of investigating an accident, the premium for a bail bond and the premium for an appeal bond.

84. **A.** This accident would be considered one occurrence even though two persons were injured. The insured's policy limits apply once per occurrence. Therefore, the driver can collect the full amount of injuries, $45,000, since it is less than $50,000. The passenger can collect only $50,000 and not $95,000 because $50,000 is the limit per person. Finally since the limit is $100,000 for all persons, the driver can collect $45,000 and the passenger $50,000.

85. **D.** Under a PAP, an insured includes the named insured, relatives of the named insured who reside in the named insured's household (by blood, marriage, or adoption, including a ward or foster child), and those using the vehicle with the reasonable belief they are entitled to do so. However, there is no coverage provided under a PAP for bodily injury sustained by an insured's employee. It is important to note that the policy does not exclude a nonlicensed relative of the named insured residing in the home. Coverage would be extended to the 10-year-old child. A person away at college is generally considered a resident of the household, as long as such person has not established an independent residence.

86. **A.** General liability exposures come about through the operation of a business, whether because of the conduct of the business owner or employees, for which the business owner is vicariously liable. General liability insurance does not cover liability exposures caused by a customer.

87. **B.** In a CGL policy, the premium shown on the Declarations Page is an advance premium and a deposit. At the close of an audit period, the insurer will compute the earned premium for the period based on the exposures that were dropped or added during the year. As a result, new exposures are automatically insured without notice required with one significant exception: if an insured forms a new organization or acquires a new organization, the insurer will provide coverage for 90 days or the end of the policy period, whichever is earlier.

88. **B.** All liability policies stipulate that the insurer can investigate and settle any claim or suit that the insurer decides is appropriate.

89. **D.** A CGL policy provides protection for injury or damage caused by the insured to someone else or to property or persons other than the insured. The CGL will exclude damage to property that the insured owns, rents, or occupies; premises that the insured sells, gives away, or abandons; property loaned to the insured; and personal property in the insured's care, custody, or control.

90. **D.** Section II of the homeowners policy includes neither medical payments nor coverage for professional liability as part of the form. This section is written on a single limit basis and its forms are used to provide protection for personal activities, such as homeownership or apartment occupancy, and day-to-day activities.

91. **B.** The limit of liability applies per occurrence, so the full limit, $100,000, is available for each occurrence. Because no aggregate limit is indicated, each occurrence will have the same limit of liability available.

92. **B.** The insurer would pay $250,000, the policy's limit of liability to the plaintiff, plus defense costs of $15,000, or a total of $265,000. Any supplementary payments, such as defense costs, are paid in addition to the limit of liability. The insured would be responsible for $50,000, the amount of the claim exceeding the limit of liability.

93. **B.** The Conditions section contains the duties and responsibilities of the insured and insurer.

94. **B.** The CGL policy is issued on either an occurrence basis or a claims-made basis. The claims-made form means that the policy that is in effect when the accident occurred and the claim is made will pay. Claims-made forms may have a retroactive date that would be some time prior to the effective date of the policy such. The claims-made form that is in effect when the claim is made

will pay, but only if the occurrence was after the retroactive date.

95. **C.** The insurance policy currently in effect will provide protection to the business owner rather than the policy in effect 12 years ago. Protection is provided under premises and operations rather than products and completed operations. The company must defend the insured, whether the case goes to trial or arbitration.

96. **D.** Because a guest is injured on the premises, the loss would be covered under a Premises and Operations exposure under the CGL. Choice A is considered pollution; choice B is personal auto; and choice C is workers' compensation.

97. **B.** A CGL policy excludes coverage for liability that the insured assumes in a contract or agreement. However, coverage will apply if there is an insured contract, e.g., lease of premises, sidetrack agreement, easement, or license agreement in connection with vehicle or pedestrian private railroad crossings at grade, any other easement agreement, indemnification of a municipality as required by ordinance, except in connection with work for a municipality and elevator maintenance agreement. Insured contracts also include any other contract or agreement pertaining to the insured's business under which the insured assumes the tort liability of another to pay damages owing to bodily injury or property damage to a third person as long as the agreement is made prior to the injury or damage. In this question the insured would have coverage because the contract with the city would be considered an insured contract.

98. **D.** Under a CGL policy medical payments are covered separately in the liability section and are not part of the supplementary payments. Supplementary payments include the items listed in choices A, B, and C.

99. **D.** The CGL policy excludes damages claimed for any loss, cost or expense incurred by the insured or others for the loss of use, withdrawal, recall, inspection, repair, replacement, adjustment, removal, or disposal of the insured's product or work or impaired property because of a known or suspected defect, deficiency, inadequacy, or dangerous condition in it.

100. **D.** The CGL policy contains exclusions for the items in choices A, B, and C. However, loss of use of damaged property and loss of use of property that has not been physically injured are both included under the definition of property damage.

# Property Insurance Final Exam Questions

1. The HO-3 Special Form includes all of the following standard exclusions EXCEPT

   A. war
   B. inherent vice
   C. breakage
   D. wear and tear

2. An endorsement is a form attached to a policy that

   A. modifies the contract
   B. lists the duties of the insured and the insurer
   C. lists the perils and property that are not covered
   D. contains that insurer's promise to pay for loss

3. A cracked hot-water heater would be covered under which of the following policies?

   A. HO-1 only
   B. HO-2 only
   C. HO-2 and HO-3
   D. HO-1 and HO-2

4. After completing a flood insurance application and paying the premium, an insured must normally wait how many days before the policy is effective?

   A. 0
   B. 3
   C. 15
   D. 30

5. When must insurable interest be present in order for an insured to be paid for a loss?

   A. During the term of the policy
   B. Just prior to the loss
   C. At the time of the loss
   D. On the first effective day of the policy

6. Which of the following best describes the purpose of coinsurance?

   A. To obtain a rate credit
   B. To have a rate penalty
   C. To obtain a claims credit
   D. To include a partial deductible

7. If an insured's dog bites a neighbor on the neighbor's property, which of the following would pay for the neighbor's injury?

   A. Insured's homeowners policy under the liability section
   B. The neighbor's homeowners policy
   C. Insured's homeowners policy under the property section
   D. Insured's homeowners policy under the dwelling section

8. If the insured's parent gave a house to the insured, which of the following statements is CORRECT?

   A. The insured can buy insurance under the interment clause.
   B. The insured can buy insurance because he has an insurable interest.
   C. The insured's parent retains the policy on the house.
   D. The insured's parent automatically assigns the policy to the insured under the inheritance clause.

9. In the event of the lapse of a homeowners insurance policy, the mortgagee can do which of the following if the insured can no longer pay the premiums?

   A. Cancel the policy
   B. Require proof of loss from the insured
   C. Pay premiums for insured
   D. Nothing

10. Coverage D of the homeowners policy includes which of the following?

    A. Personal property of others
    B. Medical payments to others
    C. Additional living expense
    D. Plants, shrubs, and trees

11. Which of the following is NOT an other structure as defined under Coverage B of a homeowners policy?

    A. Fence
    B. Outdoor shed
    C. Unattached garage
    D. Tree

12. Which of the following people can demand the appraisal procedure?

    A. The insurer only
    B. The insured only
    C. Both the insurer and the insured
    D. A third-party claimant

13. While talking to the company president at a cocktail party, an insured notices that a very expensive diamond is missing from her ring. The loss would be covered under which of the following?

    A. Burglary
    B. Robbery
    C. Theft
    D. Personal articles floater

14. A person uses a key to enter a building in the dead of night and then breaks into a closet and takes two leather coats that the owner had for sale but always locked up at night to protect from burglars. The loss would be considered which of the following?

    A. Burglary
    B. Robbery
    C. Theft
    D. Mysterious disappearance

15. While fishing, a watch falls off the insured's wrist to the bottom of a lake. The loss would be considered which of the following?

    A. Robbery
    B. Theft
    C. Mysterious disappearance
    D. None of the above

16. A bookstore closes at 9:00 pm. Hours later, a person breaks a back window, reaches in, opens the back door and takes two collectible books valued at $61,000 each. The loss would be considered which of the following?

    A. Burglary
    B. Robbery
    C. Theft
    D. Mysterious disappearance

17. A clerk opens a store at 9:30 am.Just after putting the cash drawer into the cash register, someone who had broken into the store during the night puts a knife to the clerk's throat and steals all the cash in the cash drawer. The loss would be considered which of the following?

    A. Burglary
    B. Robbery
    C. Theft
    D. None of the above

18. Which of the following is a cause of loss included in the DP-1 Basic policy?

    A. Theft
    B. Lightning
    C. Windstorm
    D. Earthquake

19. Exclusions in an insurance policy are used for which of the following purposes?

    A. To reduce the potential for fraudulent claims
    B. To help control physical and moral hazards
    C. To eliminate uninsurable perils
    D. To provide a benefit for insurance companies

20. Which of the following statements about open perils coverage is CORRECT?

    A. It includes unusual losses and losses from any cause.
    B. It includes losses resulting from perils not specifically excluded.
    C. It places the burden of proof on the policyholder in the event of a loss.
    D. It is not available for commercial risks.

21. Under Section I of a homeowners policy, if an article that is part of a pair or set is lost, the insurance company will pay the insured

    A. the value of the single item only
    B. a reasonable and fair proportion of the total value of the pair or set
    C. for the loss of the total pair or set, but only after confiscation of the remainder of the pair or set
    D. for the loss of the pair or set as a whole

22. All of the following exclusions apply to property coverage under homeowners forms EXCEPT

    A. earthquakes
    B. water damage
    C. neglect
    D. collapse

23. The Building and Personal Property Coverage Form covers all of the following property EXCEPT

    A. completed additions to the insured building
    B. indoor and outdoor fixtures of the insured building
    C. machinery and equipment
    D. money, notes and securities

24. In insurance, which of the following is considered waiver?

    A. Material representation
    B. Discharge from further liability under an insurance policy
    C. Suspension of a policy right
    D. Intentionally giving up a right

25. An insurance contract does which of the following?

    A. Eliminates risk by accumulating funds
    B. Makes risk predictable by transferring funds
    C. Eliminates risk by transferring funds
    D. Transfers risk by accumulating funds

26. If an insured's car catches fire during a vacation trip, how much would an HO-3 policy pay for personal property carried in the automobile?

    A. Nothing, because coverage is only on premises
    B. 10% of the normal coverage limit
    C. 50% of the normal coverage limit
    D. 100% of the normal coverage limit

27. Deductibles are used for all of the following purposes EXCEPT to

    A. reduce the cost of insurance
    B. increase the insured's caution
    C. eliminate small losses
    D. eliminate losses due to uninsurable perils

28. A policy may be amended only with which of the following?
    A. Endorsement
    B. Declarations
    C. Warranty
    D. Condition

29. All of the following perils are common exclusions in the personal articles floater EXCEPT
    A. war
    B. breakage
    C. vermin
    D. insects

30. Each of the following is considered an occurrence in insurance EXCEPT
    A. being struck by a falling object
    B. slipping on icy pavement
    C. illness due to repeated exposure to chemicals
    D. being intentionally hit by a worker

31. *Unforeseen and unintended* best describes which of the following?
    A. Hazard
    B. Accident
    C. Peril
    D. Risk

32. Which part of the policy lists the perils covered?
    A. Declarations Page
    B. Insuring Agreement
    C. Conditions section
    D. Exclusions section

33. What term best describes a building which contains nothing and in which no normal activities are taking place?
    A. Absent
    B. Vacated
    C. Vacant
    D. Unoccupied

34. Which of the following statements best describes subrogation?
    A. The insurer claims the insured's right to sue a third party.
    B. The insurer claims the right to collect damages from the insured.
    C. The insured claims the right to collect from a third party.
    D. The insurer claims the right to collect from a third party.

35. In an appraisal matter between the insured and the insurer, the cost of the umpire is paid by which of the following people?
    A. Insured
    B. Insurer
    C. Court
    D. Both parties divide the costs

36. An insured had an HO-3 policy with a Coverage A limit of $75,000 and rented a cottage that suffered $10,000 of wind damage. The insured's HO-3 would pay
    A. $0
    B. $1,000
    C. $7,500
    D. $10,000

37. Damage to trees and shrubs would be covered if which of the following perils caused the damage?
    A. Windstorm
    B. Hail
    C. Lightning
    D. Rain

38. When an insurance company sues a negligent third party to recover a loss paid to an insured, the insurer is exercising its right of
    A. assignment
    B. arbitration
    C. estoppel
    D. subrogation

39. Coverage C—Personal Property of the homeowners policy would cover?

    A. a collection of tropical fish belonging to the insured's children
    B. a garden tractor that the insured can ride
    C. a neighbor's television set dropped while the insured was carrying it home to watch the Super Bowl
    D. clothing belonging to a college student who rents the insured's extra bedroom while attending school

40. An insured has a homeowners policy with a Coverage A limit of $160,000. Lightning completely destroys the home, which has a replacement cost of $140,000. The insured will receive how much?

    A. $0
    B. $120,000
    C. $140,000
    D. $160,000

41. Under a farm insurance policy, coverage is usually included for all of the following EXCEPT

    A. farm animals
    B. mobile agricultural equipment
    C. household personal property
    D. grain and hay

42. How would a loss be adjusted under a homeowners policy with coverage of less than 80% of the replacement cost on the dwelling?

    A. Greater of actual cash value or a proportionate share of the loss based on the policy limits compared to 80% times the replacement cost
    B. Cost to repair
    C. Cost to replace
    D. 100% of the loss

43. If an insured does not file a proof of loss following a loss, what recourse does a mortgagee have?

    A. File a proof of loss on its own
    B. Sue the insured
    C. Apply for a waiver of subrogation
    D. None

44. Under a Farm Property Broad Causes of Loss form, coverage is

    A. identical to that of the Farm Property Basic Causes of Loss form
    B. broader than the Farm Property Basic Causes of Loss form
    C. identical to the basic covered causes of loss in commercial property forms
    D. identical to the basic covered causes of loss in homeowners forms

45. Company X and Company Y each carry $100,000 Building and Personal property coverage on a building. If there is a $10,000 loss, how much would each company pay?

| | Company X | Company Y |
|---|---|---|
| A. | $0 | $10,000 |
| B. | $5,000 | $5,000 |
| C. | $10,000 | $10,000 |
| D. | $10,000 | $0 |

46. A homeowner buys homeowners policies from two different insurance companies. If a loss by fire occurs, the payment of the loss will be on what kind of basis?

    A. Pro rata
    B. First policy effective
    C. Equal shares
    D. Excess

47. Which of the following is found on the Declarations Page of a homeowners policy?

    A. Named insured's occupation and annual income
    B. Policy's exclusions
    C. Perils insured against
    D. Amount of insurance

48. Which of the following statements about the principle of indemnity is CORRECT?

    A. It provides a means by which a claimant can be paid for a loss.
    B. It permits the insured to collect from both the insurance company and the person responsible for the loss.
    C. It encourages the purchase of policies with face values larger than the value of the protected property.
    D. It provides for an insured to be restored financially in the event of a loss.

49. The owner of a $500,000 commercial building buys a $300,000 policy with an 80% coinsurance clause. In the event of a $200,000 loss, how much will the insured collect?

    A. $120,000
    B. $150,000
    C. $200,000
    D. $300,000

50. Which of the following statements about a personal articles floater attached to a homeowners policy is NOT correct?

    A. There is usually no deductible.
    B. Worldwide coverage is provided except for fine art.
    C. The insured must report all newly acquired property that is to be covered within 60 days.
    D. There are exclusions for wear and tear, insects, war, and nuclear hazard.

51. All of the following Cause of Loss forms are used in commercial property insurance EXCEPT

    A. Classified
    B. Basic
    C. Broad
    D. Special

52. All of the following are examples of insurable interest EXCEPT a

    A. person's interest in the improvements he has added to a leased apartment
    B. person's interest in the home he owns
    C. dry cleaner's interest in customer clothing in his custody, care, or control
    D. person's interest in property she hopes to inherit from an uncle

53. If an HO-2 (Broad Form) has a coverage limit of $50,000 on the dwelling, the standard amount of Personal Property coverage applicable is

    A. $20,000
    B. $25,000
    C. $30,000
    D. $50,000

54. Which of the following is part of the formula for calculating the actual cash value of a dwelling?

    A. Purchase price
    B. Original market value
    C. Assessed value
    D. Replacement cost

55. After a loss covered by a homeowners policy, the insured must do all the following EXCEPT

    A. file a notice of loss by certified mail
    B. file a proof of loss within 60 days
    C. separate damaged and undamaged personal property
    D. furnish a complete inventory of the damaged property

56. Which of the following is a document that shows a change in the policy after its effective date?

    A. Proposal
    B. Binder
    C. Policy
    D. Endorsement

57. Which of the following is a short-term document that evidences coverage and some policy terms?

    A. Proposal
    B. Binder
    C. Policy
    D. Endorsement

58. Which of the following statements about the Businessowners policy (BOP) is NOT correct?

    A. It is used by small and medium businesses.
    B. It excludes contractors, restaurants, certain convenience stores, and laundries from eligibility.
    C. It automatically includes many coverages that are available only by endorsement in the CPP program.
    D. It provides coverage for buildings and business personal property.

59. Which of the following forms provides open perils (except flood, earthquake, landslide, and war) for buildings and broad form coverage on contents?

    A. HO-1 Basic Form
    B. HO-2 Broad Form
    C. HO-3 Special Form
    D. HO-8 Modified Form

60. Which of the following forms provides actual cash value coverage on a dwelling and its contents?

    A. HO-1 Basic Form
    B. HO-2 Broad Form
    C. HO-3 Special Form
    D. HO-8 Modified Form

61. Which of the following forms provides specified perils on contents and no dwelling coverage?

    A. HO-3 Special Form
    B. HO-4 Tenant's Form
    C. HO-6 Condominium Form
    D. HO-8 Modified Form

62. Which of the following forms provides basic causes of loss coverage and actual cash value on building and contents?

    A. HO-3 Special Form
    B. HO-4 Tenant's Form
    C. HO-6 Condominium Form
    D. HO-8 Modified Form

63. Under the personal articles floater, which of the following classes of property is insured on a valued basis?

    A. Musical instruments
    B. Silverware
    C. Jewelry and furs
    D. Fine art

64. Which of the following is covered under a homeowners policy?

    A. The family auto
    B. Accident and health
    C. Personal liability
    D. Subrogation

65. Which insurance principle is applied when an insured is reimbursed for a loss or losses actually sustained?

A. Insurable interest
B. Indemnity
C. Subrogation
D. Coinsurance

66. A house has an actual cash value of $200,000 and a replacement cost of $300,000. To make sure that the replacement cost provision of a homeowners policy applies, how much should the minimum policy amount for the dwelling be?

A. $160,000
B. $200,000
C. $240,000
D. $300,000

67. In insurance, the term *risk* refers to?

A. accuracy with which a loss can be predicted
B. specific cause of an individual loss
C. probability that a loss will occur
D. uncertainty regarding financial loss

68. Lightning strikes a restaurant, and the resulting fire damages the building and much of the dining area furniture. The building and contents are owned and insured by Karen O'Leary. Jack Martin has been renting the building and its contents from Ms. O'Leary. The restaurant is closed for one month for repairs following the fire. Ms. O'Leary's Buildings and Personal Property Coverage Form with Special Form Cause of Loss will cover which of the following?

A. The cost to rebuild with current building code compliance
B. The building and contents loss
C. Ms. O'Leary's loss of rental income
D. Mr. Martin's loss of income

69. Internal limitations on property covered under a homeowners policy include which of the following?

A. Antiques and fine art
B. Money, jewelry, and furs
C. Furniture and clothes
D. Appliances and equipment

70. Mr. Brown insured his health food store building and contents under a Building and Personal Property Coverage Form with Broad Form Cause of Loss. In the event of a loss due to fire, which of the following will be covered?

A. The money in the register
B. The stock of granola and wheat germ
C. The unpaid bills on the counter
D. The accounts receivable kept in the office

71. Ms. Smith rents an apartment from Mr. Jones. She has an HO-4, and he has a fire policy on the building. Due to Ms. Smith's negligence, a fire on the stove does fire damage to the ceiling in her apartment. Whose insurance will ultimately pay the claims?

A. Part I of her policy
B. Part II of her policy
C. Part I of his policy
D. Part II of his policy

72. A basic homeowners policy will provide coverage for

A. the insured's property and the property of others
B. theft of items from a parked, unoccupied vehicle
C. personal Injury Protection (PIP)
D. all of the above

73. Which of the following insurance products covers mechanical breakdown of an air compressor?

A. General property form
B. BOP—general liability form
C. Boiler and Machinery coverage
D. Comprehensive General Liability

74. What is Section I of the homeowners policy?

A. Policy jacket
B. Declarations Page
C. Property section
D. Liability section

75. Under Section II Liability Coverage of the homeowners policy, the insurer will pay for all of the following losses EXCEPT

A. bodily injury to the insured's guest while on the insured's premises
B. medical expenses incurred by a neighbor who is bitten by the insured's dog
C. bodily injury to the insured's child who is injured in their backyard
D. medical expenses incurred by the insured's guest who slips and falls after spilling a drink

76. Which of the following statements about the boiler and machinery policy is CORRECT?

A. It provides coverage for fire damage to the insured's building caused by a boiler explosion.
B. It encourages loss control by providing for suspension of coverage on dangerous or defective objects.
C. Both.
D. Neither.

77. Named perils are found in which Cause of Loss Form?

A. Basic Form
B. Broad Form
C. Both
D. Neither

78. What provision determines contested amounts of a loss between the insurer and insured?

A. Pro rata liability
B. Proof of loss
C. Arbitration
D. Appraisal

79. An apartment house is valued at $500,000. The policy covering it is for $300,000 with an 80% coinsurance clause. If a $100,000 loss is sustained, the policy most likely would pay how much?

A. $60,000
B. $75,000
C. $80,000
D. $100,000

80. Which of the following best describes a homeowners policy?

A. Package policy for property and liability coverage
B. Comprehensive policy for anyone owning property
C. Policy to protect the interests of a loss payee
D. Property policy offering optional liability coverage

81. Who is the Builder's Risk policy designed for?

A. Owners of property on which a building is being constructed
B. Contractors who are building structures for others
C. Both
D. Neither

82. Which of the following perils is the homeowners policy NOT intended to cover?

    A. Destruction of a neighbor's property by the insured's dog
    B. Theft of a bicycle left in the front yard overnight
    C. Lightning damage to an expensive cactus on the insured's property
    D. Erosion under a house causing the foundation to crack

83. All homeowners policies contain a standard deductible clause of how much?

    A. $100
    B. $250
    C. $500
    D. $750

84. Which of the following coverages is provided by HO-4?

    A. For built-in appliances
    B. For furniture in a furnished apartment
    C. Open perils for personal property
    D. Actual cash value settlement losses

85. Which of the following statements regarding the HO-3 policy is CORRECT?

    A. It is issued for a 1-year period.
    B. It is issued for the length of the mortgage.
    C. It provides coverage on an open perils basis.
    D. Voluntary property damage may be added by endorsement.

86. Under a homeowners policy, Coverage A provides which of the following coverages?

    A. Dwelling
    B. Medical Payments to Others
    C. Loss of use
    D. Personal Liability

87. Which of the following is a policy written to cover personal property only?

    A. HO-1
    B. HO-3
    C. HO-4
    D. HO-8

88. In order to collect for a covered loss the insured must do certain things. Which of the following is something the insured is NOT obligated to do?

    A. Give written notice of the loss to the company
    B. Protect the property from further damage
    C. Furnish an inventory of damaged and undamaged property
    D. Secure appraisals from contractors for repair

89. All of the following perils are insured under a Dwelling Policy DP-1 Basic Form EXCEPT

    A. fire
    B. lightning
    C. internal explosion
    D. vandalism and malicious mischief

90. Which of the following statements regarding Dwelling policies is CORRECT?

    A. They do not provide special form cause of loss coverage.
    B. They do not automatically include theft coverage.
    C. They may only be written for owner-occupants.
    D. They are no longer used since the advent of homeowners coverage.

91. Faulty wiring causes a fire that destroys a building. The faulty wiring would be considered which of the following?

    A. Peril
    B. Indirect cause
    C. Risk
    D. Hazard

92. Bob has a homeowners policy with a $1,000 deductible. A small fire causes damage of $750. How much will the insurer pay?

    A. $0
    B. $250
    C. $750
    D. $1000

93. Ace Insurance Company and Acme Insurance Company each insure the same building for the same amount. In the event of a partial loss Acme will pay how much of the loss?

    A. Nothing, because second named companies are always excess coverage
    B. 50%
    C. 100%, but has the right of subrogation against Ace Insurance Company
    D. One third because the insured is the third party to the contract and must bear part of the loss

94. Tom owns an apartment building and permits a tenant to operate a fireworks supply business from it. If Tom does not disclose this information when applying for dwelling coverage, this would be considered which of the following?

    A. Fraud
    B. Estoppel
    C. Concealment
    D. Waiver

95. If an HO-2 has a coverage limit of $150,000 on the dwelling, how much would the standard amount of Other Structures coverage be?

    A. $10,000
    B. $15,000
    C. $25,000
    D. $75,000

96. Which of the following situations is NOT covered by a Dwelling Building and Contents DP-1?

    A. Smoke from the fireplace damages carpeting in the insured's dwelling
    B. A low flying aircraft damages the roof on insured's dwelling
    C. Tools are stolen from the insured's garage during a vacation
    D. Hail damages the insured's freshly painted exterior walls

97. Which of the following statements about dwelling coverage are NOT correct?

    A. The basic policy does not cover theft.
    B. It does not cover vacant buildings.
    C. It is used when homeowners insurance is unavailable.
    D. Farm dwellings are excluded from coverage.

98. Broad form coverage on personal property is provided by all of the following EXCEPT

    A. Tenant's HO-4
    B. Dwelling Building and Contents Broad Form (DP-2)
    C. Dwelling Building and Contents Special Form (DP-3)
    D. HO-3

99. A dwelling policy is most often used to provide coverage

A. better than that available under a homeowners policy
B. for a home that is not eligible for a homeowners policy
C. at a lower price than a homeowners policy
D. when the insured cannot obtain full coverage on the dwelling

100. The Dwelling Building Special Form (DP-3) provides open perils coverage on

A. the dwelling
B. personal property
C. all property coverage
D. none of the property covered under the policy

# Property Insurance Answers & Rationale

1. **C.** The HO-3 Special Form has exclusions that include war, inherent vice and wear and tear, but not breakage.

2. **A.** An endorsement is a form attached to a policy that modifies the contract to fit special circumstances. The insurance company must approve this modification in writing.

3. **C.** Sudden and accidental tearing apart, cracking, burning or bulging of a steam or hot-water heater system, an air conditioning system, automatic fire protective sprinkler system or an appliance for heating water is a broad form peril specifically listed in HO-2 for buildings and personal property. It would be included in HO-3 coverage for the building and listed in HO-3 for personal property.

4. **D.** There is a 30-day waiting period after completing the application and paying the first premium before a flood policy becomes effective. This is to discourage the common tendency to wait until a flood is imminent before applying for flood insurance.

5. **C.** In the context of property and casualty insurance, insurable interest must be present at the time of loss. Insurable interest means that one will suffer a financial loss should some insurable event occur. State law may also require that insurable interest be present to purchase a policy.

6. **A.** The purpose of coinsurance, which is often a part of commercial property policies, is to encourage insureds to carry insurance close to the value of the property. If an insured carries insurance close to the property's full value, the rate per $1,000 of property value will be less.

7. **A.** In this case, the liability section of a homeowners policy, Section II, will pay a neighbor if the insured becomes legally liable for the damages. Liability is extended to damage or injury caused by the insured's pets.

8. **B.** The insured now has an insurable interest (because if the house is destroyed he or she will suffer a loss) and can therefore buy a policy. The parent, unless currently holding a mortgage on the property, no longer has insurable interest.

9. **C.** The mortgage clause provides that the mortgagee has certain rights under the policy. The insurer must notify the mortgagee of any change to the policy, including a lapse of coverage. The mortgagee then can pay any premium due to the insurer, charging the amount back to the property owner.

10. **C.** Coverage D protects against Loss of Use, that is, consequential or indirect loss. This includes additional living expenses over and above normal expenses in the event of a loss.

11. **D.** Coverage B of a homeowners policy provides coverage for other structures. Other structures are things constructed on the land other than the dwelling, which is covered under Coverage A. Items such as fences, pools, outdoor sheds, and unattached or detached garages are constructed on the land. Trees fall outside this definition.

12. **C.** Property policies provide that in case of a dispute between the insured and the insurer as to the dollar value of lost or damaged property, either party may initiate the appraisal process. On the other hand, disputes as to whether coverage is applicable is not a subject for the appraisal process; such disputes are determined ultimately by a court.

13. **D.** In the situation described here, there appears to have been no opportunity for a theft; rather the stone apparently dropped out somewhere, and as such this is a mysterious disappearance. Such a loss would be covered under a scheduled personal articles floater.

14. **C.** Although this might appear to be a burglary, burglary requires visible signs of forced

entry into or exit out of the premises. Because a key was used, no force was needed to enter the premises. It would not be considered a robbery because force was not used to take personal property from someone. The loss would therefore be considered a theft, which includes any act of stealing.

15. **D.** The loss cannot be classified as theft or robbery because there was no wrongful criminal taking. It is also not a mysterious disappearance because there is no mystery about what happened to the watch because it is known to have fallen into the lake.

16. **A.** This is a burglary because the store is closed and there is a breaking and entering into the premises (the inside of the outside wall) and property is taken.

17. **B.** Robbery is the use of violence or threat of violence to take property from someone, which is what is described here. It does not make any difference that the person broke into the store overnight; the money was taken from a person by violence.

18. **B.** The DP-1 policy provides coverage only for fire, lightning and internal explosion. However, the optional ECE endorsement would include coverage for windstorm.

19. **C.** Exclusions are designed to limit the applicability of the policy to certain conditions, that is, no coverage will apply if the loss occurs owing to the specified situation. For example, property policies will not pay if the insured neglects to protect property from further damage after a loss. Exclusions also eliminate uninsurable risks, such as war and flood. Although they provide rate credits to policyholders, they provide no direct benefit to insurers.

20. **B.** Open perils provides broader coverage for physical loss or damage, except for the causes of loss that are specifically excluded. All policies, including open perils forms, will contain exclusions both of types of property and types of perils. The burden of proof in the event of loss is on the insurer.

21. **B.** One of the conditions of most property policies is the pair or set clause. In this clause, the insurer states that it will pay to repair or replace the lost or damaged part, to restore the pair or set to its value before the loss or to pay the difference in the value before and after the loss. The insurer will only pay for the value of the entire pair or set if the entire set is lost or damaged. There is an exception for fine art objects, for which the insurer will pay the value of the pair or set and take the remaining part.

22. **D.** General exclusions include loss due to earthquakes, water damage and neglect, among others. Limited coverage for loss due to collapse is available as an additional coverage.

23. **D.** The Building and Personal Property Coverage Form covers additions to the insured building as well as its fixtures. Machinery and equipment are also covered. However, accounts, bills currency deeds, evidences of debt, money, notes and securities are not covered.

24. **D.** Waiver is the intentional relinquishment of a right. If, for example, an insurer has an opportunity to deny coverage for a claim and decides not to do so, it has waived its right to reassert the denial at a later time.

25. **D.** Insurance is considered a social device for transferring risk to the insurance company. The insurer in turn accumulates the premiums and pays for losses as they occur. Such a device does not reduce the overall risk, because the insurer does not prevent risks from occurring; the insurer solely compensates insureds for risks that have happened.

26. **D.** The HO-3 policy will provide 100% of on-premises coverage off the premises unless the property involved was regularly located at a secondary premises, such as a seasonal residence.

27. **C.** Because the insurer does not have to pay for the small loss or the claims-handling

expenses, it can reduce the amount of premium charged, thus reducing the cost of insurance. Because the insured has to pay for such small losses, he or she theoretically will be more careful about taking care of the property. Choice D is a rationale for exclusions, not deductibles.

28. **A.** An endorsement is attached to change or modify the wording or coverage in a policy. It either narrows or broadens coverage depending on what the insured or insurer is trying to accomplish.

29. **B.** The personal articles floater provides coverage for direct physical loss to described property. There are some exclusions that apply to property covered by the floater, e.g., wear and tear, insects or vermin, war, and nuclear hazard. Breakage is only excluded under certain floaters and for specific categories of property.

30. **D.** An accident can be identified as an event that is sudden and unexpected as to time and place. This would include choices A and B. The term *occurrence* is more inclusive and refers not only to accidents but also to events that occur over a period of time, as in choice C. Thus, only the intentional battery described in choice D would not be considered an occurrence.

31. **B.** An accident is a sudden unanticipated event that causes loss or damage. The result is unforeseen and unexpected by the person injured and it takes place without the insured's foresight, expectation, or intent.

32. **B.** The perils or causes of loss are either included in a policy or attached as separate forms. In either event, they detail the circumstances under which coverage will be provided and are examples of insuring agreements in a policy.

33. **C.** A vacant building has no contents or normal household or business activities occurring in it. An unoccupied building has contents, but no normal household or business activities are taking place in it.

34. **A.** Property and liability policies include a condition referred to as subrogation, which is designed to keep the insured from being able to collect twice for the same loss. If the insured receives a settlement from his insurer and also has a right to recover against a third party who negligently caused the loss, the policy indicates that this right of recovery is transferred to the insurer.

35. **D.** Appraisal is a condition in property and casualty policies that establishes the procedures in case of a dispute between the insured and insurer as to the value of property lost or damaged. Either side can invoke the procedure, but both sides pick an appraiser and each pays the cost of its own appraiser. Both appraisers must then agree on an umpire. If the appraisers cannot agree on a value for the property, they use the umpire; agreement between any two of the three determines the value of the settlement. The costs of the umpire and other costs of the procedure are divided between the insurer and insured.

36. **A.** Section I of homeowners policies pays primarily for damage to one's own property. In this case, the insured is renting a cottage that was damaged by wind. The owner of the cottage will have to look to his or her insurer for coverage. The insured has no insurable interest in the property.

37. **C.** Homeowners policies can provide additional coverages for trees, shrubs, and other plants. The covered perils are limited to fire, lightning, explosion, riot or civil commotion, aircraft, vehicles not owned or operated by a resident of the residence premises, vandalism or malicious mischief, and theft. Windstorms, hail, and rain are occurrences too common to be covered and therefore are not listed as perils for trees, shrubs and plants.

38. **D.** Property and liability policies include a condition referred to as subrogation, which is designed to keep the insured from being able to collect twice for the same loss. If the insured receives a settlement from his insurer and also has a right to recover against a third party who negligently caused the loss, the policy indicates that this right of recovery is transferred to the insurer.

39. **B.** Although Coverage C excludes motor vehicles or all other motorized land conveyances, it covers vehicles or conveyances not subject to motor vehicle registration that are used to service an insured's residence or designed to assist the handicapped. The garden tractor is designed to service the insured's premises. The policy excludes coverage for animals, birds, or fish. It also excludes the property of roomers, boarders and other tenants except those related to an insured. Finally, Coverage C does not include in the list of perils the dropping of personal property nor does it cover a neighbors' property.

40. **C.** A property policy will pay the lesser of the amount to repair, replace, or restore, but never more than the limit shown on the policy. The amount paid is up to the extent of the insurable interest or the limit of insurance. Homeowners policies pay replacement cost if the insured carries insurance to at least 80% of replacement value. In this question, the replacement cost is $140,000 and that is all the policy will pay; the property was overinsured.

41. **B.** The farm combination policy provides coverage for livestock and other farm animals under either Coverage E or Coverage F. Coverage E also covers property such as hay, grain and livestock. Household personal property is included as Coverage C under the farm property coverage form. Mobile agricultural equipment, though not usually covered, can be included in the farm package using an available inland marine form.

42. **A.** HO-1, HO-2, HO-3, and HO-5 are designed to pay replacement cost for the buildings as long as the insured is carrying 80% of replacement cost at the time of the loss. If coverage is for less than 80% the policy will pay the greater, but not more than the limit of liability, of either the actual cash value or the amount of the insurance divided by 80% of the replacement cost of the property times the cost to repair or replace, less the deductible.

43. **A.** In addition to electing to pay back any premiums due to maintain an existing policy, the mortgagee can also file a proof of loss for its insurable interest in the property. If such a proof is filed by the mortgagee but not the insured, the insured will not receive any benefits from the insurance contract.

44. **B.** Due to the inclusion of additional perils such as drowning of livestock, attacks by wild animals, and others, the coverage afforded by the farm broad causes of loss is broader than that under the basic causes of loss forms for farm property, commercial property and homeowners property.

45. **B.** The Commercial Property Conditions, which is part of the Building and Personal Property Coverage Form, provides that the insured may have other insurance that is subject to the same plan, terms, conditions, and provisions as this insurance. If there are other applicable policies, each policy will pay the pro rata share that its limit of liability bears to the total limit of liability of all policies. Thus, if Company X and Company Y each provide $100,000 of coverage (a total of $200,000), each share is half of the loss. Therefore, each will pay half of the $10,000 loss, or $5,000.

46. **A.** The Commercial Property Conditions, which is part of the Building and Personal Property Coverage Form, provides that the insured may have other insurance that is subject to the same plan, terms, conditions, and provisions as this insurance. If there are other applicable policies, each policy will pay the pro rata share that its limit of liability bears to the total limit of liability of all policies.

47. **D.** The Declarations Page contains identifying information, including the insured's name, property location, effective dates of coverage, limit of liability for the various coverages, name of mortgagee, deductibles, and a list of any endorsements. It does not contain the perils or exclusions, which are in the policy form itself. Nor does it contain the insured's occupation or annual income, because these are unimportant to identify the insurance.

48. **D.** In insurance, the principle of indemnity provides that insurance should return the insured to the financial position he was in before the loss occurred, no better and no worse.

49. **B.** The recovery would be calculated as follows:

Required amount:

$500,000 × 80% = $400,000

Recovery amount: ([policy limit / Required amount] × loss)

$$\frac{\text{Policy limit} \quad \$300{,}000}{\text{Required amount} \quad \$400{,}000} = 0.75$$

0.75 × $200,000 loss = $150,000

Any deductible would be subtracted from the $150,000 recovery.

50. **C.** The scheduled personal articles floater provides worldwide coverage for personal property. There is automatic coverage for newly acquired property, but the purchase must be reported within 30 days (60 days for fine art).

51. **A.** There are three different cause of loss forms used in commercial property insurances: basic, broad, and special. There is no classified form.

52. **D.** Insurable interest means that a person would suffer a loss if some event happened. In property and casualty insurance, this interest must be pecuniary; that is a monetary loss must result. A person can take out a policy to cover such a financial loss, which makes it an insurable interest. Such an interest can come about because of ownership whether by purchase or gift. Because this person does not have any financial interest in the property, there is no insurable interest in choice D.

53. **B.** Homeowners forms 1, 2, 3, and 8 provide that coverage for personal property is 50% of the coverage on the dwelling. This amount may be increased or decreased within limits with a comparable adjustment to the premium. In this case, $25,000 of standard personal property coverage is available (50% of $50,000).

54. **D.** Actual cash value is calculated using current replacement cost of rebuilding the structure with like kind and quality of material minus depreciation. Depreciation is a dollar amount representing the wear and tear and using up of the property.

55. **A.** The conditions section of a homeowners policy sets forth the duties of the insured after a loss. The insured's duties include prompt notice to the insurer or agent, notification of the police if loss involves a theft, protection of the property from further damage, preparation of an inventory of damaged goods, access to the damaged goods as often as the insurer reasonably requires, and a signed, sworn proof of loss statement sent within 60 days after requested by the insurer. The notice of loss and proof of loss statement do not have to be sent by certified mail.

56. **D.** If the terms in a policy are to be altered in any way, either when issued or during its effective period, this is accomplished by an endorsement attached to the policy.

57. **B.** If an applicant needs evidence of insurance immediately, before a policy can be issued, property and casualty agents generally have the authority to bind coverage. Such a binder provides temporary, short-term coverage until the actual policy is issued. Depending on state law and the requirements of the situation, a binder may be oral or written.

58. **B.** A businessowners policy provides coverage for certain small and medium businesses such as contractors, restaurants and convenience stores with gas pumps, and laundries. Coverage is provided for buildings and the business personal property.

59. **C.** HO-3 provides open perils coverage for the buildings and broad form coverage (same as HO-2) on the personal property.

60. **D.** The HO-8 Modified Form was created for insureds who did not wish to replace their structures in the event of a loss and therefore provides ACV coverage on the dwelling. Without endorsement, all HO forms provide ACV on contents.

61. **B.** The HO-4 provides broad form coverage (same as HO-2) for personal property. Because the tenant is not concerned about insuring the building, there is no dwelling coverage. There is $1,000 coverage for dwelling items included in the HO-6 policy. HO-3 and HO-8 both provide dwelling coverage.

62. **D.** HO-8 is designed to provide a homeowners package policy, but in situations where the market value of the property is well below replacement cost of the building, the building is of an unusual construction or based on the age of the property. The HO-8 provides for settlement on an actual cash value basis and it provides for basically the same peril coverage as does the HO-1, referred to as basic coverage.

63. **D.** Loss settlement in a personal articles floater varies by class of property. Fine art is insured on a valued basis, which means that the insurer and insured agree on a value before the property is insured. If there is a loss the insurer will pay the value stated in the policy. For other property, including listed stamps and coins, the insurer will pay the lesser of the actual cash value, the cost to repair or replace or the value listed in the schedule of insurance.

64. **C.** Section I of the homeowners policy provides coverage for the insured's own property; Section II provides coverage for personal liability rather than business liability exposures or auto liability exposures. While Section II provides for medical payments, these are payments to a person, other than the insured, who is injured on the insured's property or by actions of the insured without a determination of negligence. Accident and health insurance for the insured is not provided. Subrogation is not a coverage but rather a condition in a policy.

65. **B.** In insurance, the principle of indemnity provides that insurance should return the insured to the financial position he was in before the loss occurred, no better and no worse.

66. **C.** Homeowners policies will pay replacement cost for real property if the insured carries insurance equal to or greater than 80% of current replacement cost. To satisfy this requirement, the homeowners in this case should have 80% of the current replacement cost of $300,000, or $240,000.

67. **D.** Risk means the uncertainty regarding financial loss.

68. **B.** The Building and Personal Property Coverage Form only covers what the title indicates—loss of the building and personal property for Ms. O'Leary for the perils described in the Special Covered Cause of Loss form. Ms. O'Leary could have had coverage for loss of rental income if the Business Income Coverage Form was attached. Mr. Martin could also have had coverage if he had purchased a Building and Personal Property Coverage Form, a Business Income Coverage Form, an Extra Expense Coverage Form and a Covered Cause of Loss Form.

69. **B.** In a homeowners policy, there are loss limits on certain property regardless of the peril that causes the loss. Such property includes money and related items, securities, manuscripts, stamp collections, valuable papers, watercraft and related equipment, other trailers, and property used for business on premises and off premises. There are also internal limits that only apply if the property is stolen. Such property includes jewelry, watches, furs, precious and semiprecious stones,

firearms, silverware, silver-plated ware, goldware, gold-plated ware, and pewterware. There is no internal limit on furniture and clothing, appliances and equipment or fine art and antiques. Instead, there is only the limit of liability shown for Coverage C on the Declarations Page for personal property.

70. **B.** The Building and Personal Property Coverage Form describes the property covered while the Cause of Loss Forms describe the perils insured against. The Building and Personal Property Coverage Form provides coverage for the building described on the declarations page and business personal property such as furniture and fixtures, machinery and equipment, stock or merchandise, as well as personal property of others that is in the insured's care, custody, or control and within the described building. Excluded property includes: accounts (accounts receivable), bills, currency, deeds, evidences of debt, money, notes or securities. The items in choices A, C, and D would be excluded.

71. **B.** Although Mr. Jones will probably submit a claim with his own insurance company, he could collect from Ms. Smith because the loss was due to her negligence. Normally Ms. Smith's HO-4 policy, which includes Section II liability, does not cover property she owns or that is in her care, custody or control. However, it provides for fire legal liability, which means it will pay if such property is damaged by fire or smoke through her negligence. Ultimately, Ms. Smith's Section II liability will pay for the damage.

72. **A.** Homeowners policies, under Section I, provide coverage for the insured's own property and property used by the insured. Although theft coverage is included in all HO forms, there are limitations on the types of property that may be covered in an automobile, such as electronic apparatus. Personal Injury Protection (PIP) relates to no fault coverage, which is covered under auto insurance. There is also no coverage for bodily injury or medical payments to the insured.

73. **C.** The Boiler and Machinery Coverage Form is designed to provide coverage for an accident, defined as a sudden and accidental breakdown of an object. There are four definitions of object in this form, including pressure and refrigeration objects, mechanical objects, electrical objects, and turbine objects. An air compressor would qualify as an object.

74. **C.** As noted previously, Section I of the homeowners policy provides coverage for the insured's property, and Section II covers the insured's liability.

75. **C.** Section II Liability Coverages of the Homeowners Policy pays for the reasonable medical expenses for bodily injury caused by an insured's animal and for injuries sustained by guests, regardless of fault. Coverage does not apply to bodily injury sustained by the insured or the insured's family.

76. **C.** Coverage under a boiler policy may be suspended any time an inspection reveals an unsafe or hazardous condition of an insured object. This should serve to encourage good loss control on the part of the insured. Unlike other property and liability forms, the boiler form automatically covers damage to property in the insured's care, custody or control.

77. **C.** The Cause of Loss Forms used for commercial or business coverage must be attached to the Building and Personal Property Coverage Form. The Basic and Broad Forms list (or name) the perils that are covered. The Special Form is open perils.

78. **D.** See Questions 12 and 35.

79. **B.** The recovery would be calculated as follows:

Required amount:

$500,000 × 80% = $400,000

Recovery amount: ([policy limit / Required amount]) × loss

$$\frac{\text{Policy limit} \quad \$300{,}000}{\text{Required amount} \quad \$400{,}000} = 0.75$$

0.75 × $100,000 Loss = $750,000

Any deductible would be subtracted from the $75,000 recovery.

80. **A.** A homeowners policy is considered a multi-line or package policy because it requires both property coverage on the insured's own property, as well as liability coverage (for bodily injury and property damage to others).

81. **C.** Builder's Risk policies are designed for both owner-builders and contractors who are constructing buildings for others.

82. **D.** Choice A is covered under the liability section. Choice B is covered under Section I because theft is a named peril or is included under all risk coverage. Choice C is covered under additional coverages to Section I, where coverage is provided for trees, shrubs and other plants up to 5% of coverage on the dwelling but no more than $500 for any one tree, shrub, or plant. Choice D would be excluded under water damage exclusions, which includes flood, surface water, water which backs up through sewers or drains or water below the surface of the ground.

83. **B.** The standard deductible in all homeowners policies is $250. However, other deductibles are available.

84. **D.** HO-4 is for tenants and provides coverage on a broad named peril basis. It, as do all homeowners policies, provides for settlement of personal property losses on an actual cash value basis.

85. **A.** Normally a homeowners policy is issued for a 1-year period, as are most property policies. The period of coverage is not related to the life of a mortgage even though the mortgagee has protection under the policy. An HO-3 provides open perils coverage on buildings but broad form coverage on the personal property.

86. **A.** Coverage A of a homeowners policy covers the dwelling. Coverage D covers loss of use while Section II covers personal liability and medical payments to others.

87. **C.** Because the insured in a rented building has no insurable interest in the structure, tenants' policies provide only coverage for personal property.

88. **D.** Choices A, B, and C are all requirements if a loss occurs. Choice D is a requirement of the Arbitration Clause.

89. **D.** Fire, lightning and internal explosion are all insured perils under a Dwelling Policy DP-1 Basic Form. At the insured's option, vandalism and malicious mischief may be included.

90. **B.** Dwelling policies do not automatically include theft coverage since they are typically purchased by a non-occupant owner and theft is only of concern to the tenant. The coverage may be added by endorsement if needed.

91. **D.** A peril is the cause of the loss. In this case, the fire is the peril. A hazard is something that increases the likelihood of a peril occurring, such as faulty wiring. A hazard can also be something that increases the size of a loss should a peril occur, such as a pile of oily rags next to a fireplace or the faulty wiring.

92. **A.** Because the amount of the loss ($750) is less than Bob's deductible ($1,000), the insurer will not pay for any of the fire damage. If, however, the damages were more than $1,000, Bob

would pay the deductible and the insurer would pay the remaining amount.

93. **B.** Property policies generally provide for pro rata coverage if two or more policies apply to the same property for the same loss. In this case, each company provides one half of the coverage. In case of a loss, each would pay 50%.

94. **C.** Tom has the duty to voluntarily disclose material facts that may affect the underwriting of his dwelling coverage. Failure to disclose the existence of the fireworks business would be considered concealment.

95. **B.** In the homeowners forms coverage for other structures is equal to 10% of Coverage A. In this case, the standard amount of other structures is $15,000 (10% of $150,000).

96. **C.** There is no theft coverage included under any of the DP forms. However, coverage for theft of personal property may be added to a DP form by endorsement.

97. **B.** Eligible properties include dwellings (except farm dwellings) that are rented to others and vacant buildings, among others. Because it is most often used for property rented to others, the dwelling policy does not provide coverage for theft. It is used when coverage is desired but homeowners insurance is unavailable.

98. **D.** The HO-3 policy provides open perils coverage on Coverages A and B.

99. **B.** Homeowners forms are package policies that provide both property coverage and liability coverage, while dwelling forms provide only property coverage. The HO policy is usually used for an owner-occupant, while DP policies are usually written for owned property rented to others.

100. **A.** Only coverage on the Dwelling is written on an open perils basis under the DP forms.

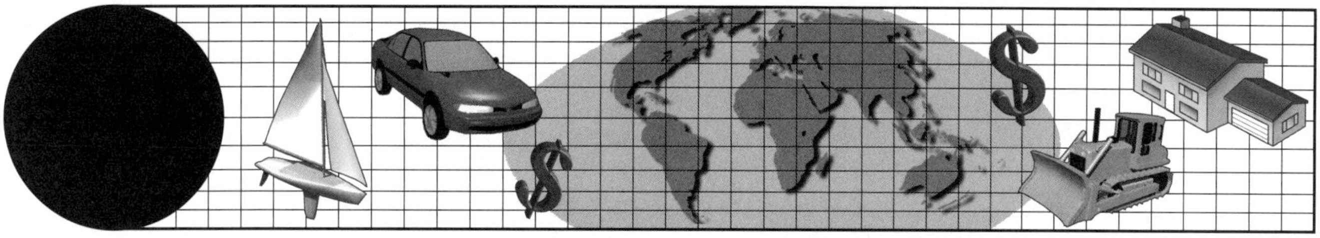

# Glossary

## A

**abandonment** The relinquishment or surrender of all rights and interests in an insured property to the insurance company. Abandonment is not permitted under most property contracts.

**acceptance** One party's agreement to the purchase offer of another party, such that a legal contract is formed and both parties are contractually bound. With an insurance contract, acceptance generally takes place when the agent binds coverage or the policy is issued. *See also* contract.

**accident** A sudden and unexpected event that results in a financial loss. *See also* occurrence.

**act of God** Accident or event resulting from natural causes, without any human intervention, that reasonable foresight or care could not have prevented, such as flood, lightning, earthquake, or storms.

**actual cash value (ACV)** The replacement (current) cost of an item minus depreciation from wear and tear or obsolescence.

**actuary** A mathematician who specializes in the field of insurance. The actuary determines, on the basis of existing experience, the rate to be charged for various lines of insurance and reserves to be set aside for payment of losses.

**additional insured** An individual or business, other than the named insured on the declarations page, who has a financial interest requiring protection under the terms of the contract, e.g., the lienholder on the loan for a car or a bank for a mortgage.

**additional living expense insurance** This is insurance coverage that pays for extra necessary living costs incurred during the time it takes to repair or replace insured property that has been damaged or destroyed by an insured peril.

**adjuster** The salaried employee of an insurance company, or an independent contractor representing an insurance company, who is responsible for determining the cause and amount of a loss, the insurance company's liability for the loss and satisfactory agreement on such from the parties involved (insured and insurer).

**admitted company** An insurer that meets the licensing criteria of the state it wishes to do business in and has received a certificate of authority. Also known as an authorized company.

**adverse selection** The tendency of insureds who present a higher probability of loss to purchase or renew insurance more often than those who present a lower probability; selection against the best interests of the insurance company (e.g., people near rivers purchasing flood insurance).

**agency** The legal principle that allows an individual or organization to represent another individual or organization.

**agent** A person licensed by the state insurance authority to sell insurance products. The agent represents the insurance company in all transactions. *See also* broker; producer.

**aggregate limit** The maximum limit of liability the company is obligated to pay for all claims within a specific time period, usually one policy year.

**agreed value coverage** This is an option for property policies by which the insured and the company agree to or stipulate to the value of property. Suspends the coinsurance clause.

**aircraft hull insurance** This provides coverage for direct loss or damage to aircraft.

**aleatory** A kind of contract in which one party may obtain greater value under the agreement than the other party and in which payment depends upon a fortuitous event. An insurance contract is an aleatory contract.

**alien insurance company** An insurance company incorporated and organized under the laws of a foreign nation, state, province or territory, rather than under the laws of the United States.

**allied lines** These are lines of insurance generally related to property insurance, such as sprinkler leakage, glass, water damage, and earthquake coverage.

**annual statement** An insurance company's yearly financial report required by various state insurance departments. Covers the calendar year period and is made according to a form agreed upon by the National Association of Insurance Commissioners.

**apparent authority** The authority the general public assumes an agent has due to his actions, regardless of whether the authority has been given to the agent by law or contract.

**appeal bond** A type of court bond that guarantees that payment of court costs and judgments on appeal when a defendant loses a suit and appeals the case.

**application** The questionnaire completed by a prospect or insurance professional that will be used during the underwriting of the policy. For contractual purposes, the application is considered the offer to purchase.

**apportionment clause** *See* other insurance clause.

**appraisal** An estimate of the value of, or the amount of loss or damage to, insured property.

**appraisal clause** The provision in an insurance policy that sets forth the duties of the insured and the insurer when there is a dispute over the amount of loss. For example, a fire insurance policy provides for appraisal at the demand of either party after a loss.

**arbitration** The process of settling differences relating to loss under an insurance policy between the insured and the insurer. Each party selects a representative who in turn selects a disinterested arbitrator whose decision or award is binding upon both parties to the insurance contract.

**arson** A felonious and deliberate act of burning property.

**assessment** An additional fixed charge or proportionate share of claims expenses sometimes levied against policyowners by an assessment mutual insurance company when premiums are insufficient to meet its costs of operations.

**assigned risk** An uninsurable individual or company that is assigned an insurance company from a pool of insurers (usually all that hold certificates of authority in a specific state). Although the company must accept the risk, it may charge an appropriate premium.

**assignment** The legal transfer of a policy-owner's rights or interests in an insurance policy to another party. The insured requests the assignment, and, barring state law, the company can either accept or reject the request.

**assumption of risk** The acceptance of the risk presented to an insured, including full responsibility for any loss that may occur.

**assured** Person for whom insurance is provided. *See* insured.

**attachment** The legal process that prevents the removal of property belonging to another party pending a court's decision concerning that property.

**attorney-in-fact** A person empowered to act for another party; the chief administrative officer of a reciprocal insurance exchange who is given authority to act on the organization's behalf; also, a person authorized to execute a surety bond on behalf of an insurance company. *See also* reciprocal exchange.

**attractive nuisance** Something that, although normally harmless, may nevertheless attract those who do not understand its uses and may cause injury. Typically this doctrine applies to children who may be attracted to things such as swimming pools or animals that can cause them harm.

**audit premium** A premium adjusted at the end of the policy term to compensate for additional exposures. Audited contracts typically include liability and workers' compensation. *See also* deposit premium.

**authorized company** *See* admitted company.

**auto policy** A policy that provides coverage for owned and nonowned vehicles, including liability, damage to the auto, medical payments and uninsured motorists coverage.

**automatic coverage** A common term for coverage provided automatically in property and liability policies (generally for a limited time and amount) for newly acquired property and changing interests and values.

## B

**bail** A security deposit that guarantees the appearance of a defendant in court for trial, forfeited if the defendant fails to appear for trial; also the act of delivering goods to another to be held in trust for a special purpose.

**bailee** A person one who has care, custody or control of another's property, usually for repair, cleaning, processing, storage or service.

**bailee's customers policy** This provides coverage for loss of or damage to property of others that is in the care, custody or control of a bailee.

**bailor** The owner of property who delivers it in trust to a bailee for a special purpose.

**banker's blanket bond** This provides protection for financial institutions and similar organizations against employee and non-employee dishonesty.

**bankruptcy** The legal process that determines and oversees the distribution of an insolvent person's or company's assets to creditors. After distribution, the person or company is relieved of all liability to these creditors, even though some payments may have been less than the full obligation.

**bankruptcy clause** Insurance policy clause which stipulates that the bankruptcy or insolvency of the insured does not relieve the insurance company of any of its obligations under the policy.

**betterment** An improvement to property that puts it in a better condition than it was before the occupancy or loss. For example, a renter's redesign of an office space to accommodate his needs. *See also* improvements and betterments coverage.

**binder** A written or oral acknowledgment of insurance in force and evidence of acceptance of the applicant's offer to purchase the insurance, whether or not premium settlement has been reached and pending issuance of the policy.

**blanket crime policy** This provides coverage against dishonesty, with money and securities coverage and forgery coverage, covering all employees.

**blanket insurance** A property or liability policy extending to more than one location, class of property or employee, without specifically naming the location, class or employee. *See also* specific insurance.

**blanket position bond** An employee dishonesty bond that covers all employees of the insured and provides protection for the insured from dishonest acts of those employees, without specifically naming the employees or their positions.

**boatowner's policy** This provides hull physical damage and liability coverage for losses arising out of the ownership, maintenance and use of a watercraft. *See also* yacht coverage.

**bodily injury (BI) liability coverage** Liability coverage that protects the insured from financial loss in the event he or she is legally liable to pay damages because of bodily injury, sickness, or disease, including required care, loss of services, and resulting death.

**boiler and machinery insurance** This provides coverage for accidental loss arising from the operation of a boiler, pressure, mechanical and electrical equipment, and machinery. Such policies may include coverage for loss to the boiler and machinery itself, for liability from damage done to other property and for loss from business interruption.

**bond** A written agreement under which the surety agrees to pay, within stated limits, for a financial loss caused to another (obligee) by the act or default of a third party (principal) or by some contingency over which the principal may have no control.

**breach of contract** The failure to comply with terms or conditions of an insurance policy that may result in restricted coverage or void the policy.

**broker** A person who, for a commission from the insurance company, solicits, negotiates, and services insurance policies on behalf of the person buying the insurance. *See also* agent; producer.

**builder's risk insurance** This provides coverage against loss to a building in the course of construction and to temporary structures, materials, and supplies incidental to that construction. May also cover the builder's machinery and equipment while on the premises.

**burglary** The forcible entry into or exit out of another premises with the intent to steal property. There must be visible signs of forced entry or exit in order for an incident to be considered a burglary.

**business auto policy** This is insurance for commercial automobile risks against legal liability, damage to vehicles, medical expenses, loss from uninsured motorists, and personal injury protection or other equivalent no fault coverage. Coverage can be extended to owned, leased, and borrowed vehicles.

**business income insurance/business interruption insurance** This provides coverage for loss of earnings that results when a business must shut down or curtail its operations after damage or destruction of property by an insured peril. Coverage applies for the length of time it takes to rebuild, repair, or replace the damaged or destroyed property so that business operations can resume.

**business pursuits endorsement** An attachment to a homeowners policy that provides liability coverage for business conducted at and away from the residence.

**businessowners policy (BOP)** A package policy designed to provide property and liability coverage for retail, service, and other small to medium-sized businesses.

## C

**camera and musical instrument dealer's form** This provides open perils coverage on a dealer's stock of musical instruments or cameras, supplies and materials. May extend to cover property in the insured's care, custody, or control.

**cancellation** The termination of a policy before the end of the policy period by the insurance company or the insured according to the terms of the policy. *See also* non-renewal; pro rata cancellation; short rate cancellation.

**carrier** *See* insurer.

**casualty insurance** The generic term for non-property insurance coverage, such as liability, crime, workers' compensation insurance, fidelity, and surety. In some states, accident and sickness insurance are considered casualty coverage.

**catastrophe** A sudden, unexpected, unavoidable, and severe calamity or disaster that involves a large population and normally generates an extraordinarily large amount of loss. Examples would include floods, earthquakes, and tornadoes.

**certificate of authority** An insurer's license to conduct the business of insurance; the legal certificate issued by a state insurance department granting an insurance company legal power and right to issue contracts of insurance within the state.

**claim** A notification given to the insurance company that a loss has occurred and that demands payment for the loss, as provided by the terms of the insurance policy.

**claimant** A person who has a claim according to the provisions of an insurance policy. *See also* first party claim; third party claim.

**claims-made coverage** A policy that provides liability coverage (usually professional or medical malpractice liability) only if a claim occurs and is reported during the policy period or any applicable extended reporting period. *See also* extended reporting period.

**class** The rates applied to similar hazard groups such as frame buildings, clerical employees, or young drivers.

**class rate** The basic factors considered for similar hazards, including classification of the risk, pure premium, and credibility.

**coinsurance clause** A provision requiring a specified amount of insurance based on the value of the insured property. There may be a penalty in the event of a partial loss if the insured fails to comply.

**collision insurance** This is automobile coverage for direct and accidental loss to the insured automobile resulting from upset or impact with another vehicle or other object, usually paid without regard to fault.

**collusion** A secret agreement and cooperation between two individuals or corporations, to the detriment of others and for fraudulent and deceitful purposes.

**combined single limit (CSL)** The combination of the liability limits of bodily injury and property damage into a single limit of liability for both. Example: $25,000 per person/$50,000 per occurrence for bodily injury and $15,000 for property damage liability is the equivalent of $65,000 ($50,000 + $15,000) combined single limit of liability for BI and PD.

**commercial blanket bond** A type of fidelity bond with a lump-sum limit that applies to each loss and collectively to all employees, no matter how many are involved in the loss.

**commercial lines insurance** A common term for insurance that pertains to business, industrial, mercantile, or manufacturing risks. *See also* personal lines insurance.

**commercial package policy (CPP)** A commercial package policy that combines commercial property, liability, and other insurance in a single package policy.

**commission** The compensation paid by an insurance company to an insurance agent or broker for sale or service of a policy.

**common carrier** The business or individual that offers transportation services for hire to the public, such as by railroad, truck, bus, or taxi.

**common law** Law derived from common usage or from court decision.

**common policy provision** The provisions common to all coverage parts under a single policy.

**compensation** Any kind of financial remuneration, such as wages, salary, fees, commissions, or awards.

**competitive state fund** A state fund that writes insurance coverage, usually workers' compensation, in competition with private insurance companies.

**completed operations liability insurance** This is bodily injury and property damage legal liability insurance that covers finished operations by the insured business. *See also* products liability insurance.

**comprehensive coverage (other than collision)** Provides auto coverage for theft, vandalism, fire and collision with a missile, falling object, and wild or domestic animal. *See also* collision.

**comprehensive dishonesty, disappearance, and destruction policy** Commonly called the 3-D policy, it is equivalent to Coverage C of the crime insurance policy.

**commercial general liability (CGL)** This provides commercial liability coverage, including premises and operations, products and completed operations and other available liability options.

**compulsory insurance** Insurance that is required by law.

**concealment** The deliberate withholding of material facts that would affect the validity of an insurance policy or a claim under the policy.

**concurrent insurance** Two or more insurance policies that cover the same property at the same location under the same terms and conditions, with the same types of coverage. *See also* other insurance provision.

**conditions** The part of an insurance policy that details the rights and duties of the insured and the insurance company in the policy.

**condominium association coverage form** A commercial package policy designed to provide property and liability coverage for a condominium owners association.

**condominium unit owners form** A commercial property policy for a unit owner of a nonresidential condominium or cooperative unit; an HO-6 homeowners form designed for owners of condominiums, cooperatives, or townhomes.

**consequential damage coverage** This provides indirect loss coverage for boiler and machinery risks that indemnifies the insured both for actual loss of specified property as well as the liability for others' loss owing to the spoilage that resulted from a lack of power, light, heat, steam, or refrigeration caused by an accident to an insured boiler or machinery.

**consequential loss** The indirect loss caused by an insured peril that occurs after and as a result of other loss, for example, the loss of profits when a business is damaged by fire and consequently must temporarily close, or the loss of perishable items that freeze when an electrical failure damages the heating system in a building.

**consideration** The inducement to complete a contract, for example, the premium paid by the insured and the promise to pay made by the insurer.

**conspiracy** The corrupt or unlawful collusion or agreement between two or more parties to do an unlawful act by concerted action or to do a lawful act by unlawful means.

**constructive total loss** A partial loss to property of a sufficient amount to make the cost of salvage or repair equal to or more than the value of the property.

**contingent business income insurance** This provides protection for the commercial risk against loss of earnings when fire or other insured peril damages a business that is not owned, operated, or controlled by the insured, such as those that supply materials and services needed by the insured for the conduct of business.

**contingent liability** This provides coverage for loss due to the destruction of the undamaged portion of a building or structure that is required by law or ordinance when damage exceeds a percentage of the property value.

**contingent loss** *See* indirect loss.

**contract** An agreement (offer and acceptance) between two parties who have legal capacity to contract that involves valuable consideration and that does not violate any statute or other legal rule.

**contract of adhesion** A contract prepared by one party, without negotiation with the other, which can either be accepted or rejected by the other party.

**contract of insurance** A legal and binding unilateral contract in which an insurance company agrees to indemnify an insured for losses, provide other benefits, or render services to or on behalf of an insured.

**contractor's equipment floater** This provides physical damage coverage for equipment used by contractors, such as bulldozers or cranes, that may be located at a temporary or permanent jobsite.

**contractual liability insurance** This provides coverage against legal liability for bodily injury or property damage assumed by the insured under a contract.

**countersignature** The signature of a licensed insurance agent or representative of an insurance company necessary in certain states to validate the contract.

**coverage** A guarantee against specific losses provided under the terms of an insurance policy; the amount and extent of insurance afforded under a contract of insurance. Often used as a synonym for insurance or insurance contract.

**credit card, forgery, and counterfeit money coverage** This provides protection, up to a specified limit, for legal liability incurred because of theft or unauthorized use of credit cards issued to the insured as well as loss to the insured caused by forgery or accepting counterfeit money in good faith.

**crop (crop-hail) insurance** This provides coverage for financial loss resulting from hail damage to growing crops. This is a federally sponsored program.

## D

**damages** The amount claimed by or awarded to an injured party as compensation for liability owing to bodily injury or property damage.

**debris removal coverage** This provides protection for reasonable expenses incurred by the insured for removal of debris after a loss caused by a covered peril.

**declarations page (dec page)** The part of an insurance policy that contains the applicant's representations and other information pertinent to the risk, on the basis of which the policy is issued.

**deductible** Policy provision that requires the insured to pay a specific amount or percentage of a loss and the insurance company to pay covered losses in excess of that amount.

**demolition** This is insurance that covers the cost of destroying a building or structure that has been partially damaged.

**deposit premium** An advance, estimated premium paid at the inception of a policy that is adjusted periodically (monthly, annually, etc.), based on actual exposures.

**depreciation** A decrease in value of property due to use, age, obsolescence, wear and tear, deterioration, etc.

**difference in conditions** This provides coverage that provides broad protection for damage to property. This form usually excludes fire and other perils covered by personal and commercial property insurance policies, but includes other perils such as earthquake and flood.

**direct loss** A loss resulting immediately and directly from an insured hazard.

**direct writer** An insurance company that sells its policies directly to insureds through insurance agents who are salaried employees or agents commissioned by that company exclusively.

**discovery period** The period of time after an insurance contract or bond is terminated within which a loss that occurred during the policy period must be discovered in order for the loss to be covered by the policy or bond.

**discrimination** The act of charging different rates to groups or individuals who represent the same risk, usually on the basis of age, sex, national origin, race, location, or occupation.

**domestic company** An insurance company that writes business in the state or province of its incorporation or charter.

**dwelling policy** A series of forms providing basic, broad or special form coverage for dwelling buildings and contents or coverage for household contents only. Usually written for owned residential property that is rented to others.

## E

**earned premium** The premium paid for the period of time a policy is in effect. *See also* unearned premium; audit premium.

**earth movement** Any sinking, shifting or rising of land, including earthquake, landslide, or mudslide.

**effective date** The date on which a policy or bond is put in force and protection is furnished. Also called the inception date.

**embezzle** The act of appropriating fraudulently and for one's own use money or other property entrusted to one's care or control.

**employer's liability coverage** This provides coverage for an employer against third-party liability claims that result from an employee's injuries. Usually part of a workers' compensation policy.

**endorsement** A written amendment attached to a policy, with the insurance company's approval, that stipulates changes to the policy's terms.

**environmental impairment coverage (pollution liability)** This provides coverage for unintentional bodily injury and property damage that arises out of the discharge, release, dispersal or escape of smoke, vapors, soot, fumes, acid, toxic chemicals, or irritants. Also provides coverage for the accidental discharge of pollutants or contaminants into or upon land, atmosphere, or any body of water.

**errors and omissions (E&O) insurance** This is professional liability insurance primarily intended for nonmedical professionals that pays for losses or for defense of malpractice suits. *See also* malpractice.

**estoppel** The legal doctrine that prevents the denial of a fact previously admitted through action or conduct.

**excess insurance** This provides coverage against loss in excess of a stated amount or in excess of coverage provided under another insurance contract.

**exclusion** A provision in an insurance policy that excludes certain risks or otherwise limits the scope of coverage; certain causes and conditions listed in the policy that are not covered.

**expense ratio** The cost of soliciting, underwriting and servicing an insurance policy by an insurer, expressed as a percentage of written premiums.

**experience modification** A factor applied to an insurance policy, usually workers' compensation, that modifies the premium based on the policyholder's loss experience.

**experience rating** A modification of the insurance rate based on the loss experience of an individual insured.

**expiration date** The date on which coverage under a policy terminates.

**exposure** The potential for loss to an item of property or to the assets of an individual, family, firm, or organization; the measure of risk to an insurer.

**express authority** The authority given to an agent or agency directly by means of the agency agreement or contract.

**extended coverage** Additional, broader protection against loss or damage to property offered in conjunction with fire insurance that usually covers the perils of windstorm, hail, smoke, explosion, riot, riot attending a strike, civil commotion, vehicles, and aircraft.

**extended reporting period** The time, under a commercial claims-made liability contract, after a policy has expired, during which the insured can still make a claim for a loss occurring within the policy period.

**extra expense insurance** This is coverage that pays for the necessary extra expenses, over and above normal expenses, to keep a business operating during the time it takes to rebuild, repair, or replace the damaged or destroyed property after a loss.

## F

**family member** A person related to the insured by blood, marriage, or adoption who is a resident of the named insured's household, including a ward or foster child.

**farmowners and ranchowners policies** This is a package policy that provides coverage for farm dwellings and their contents, personal liability, and optional coverages for farm personal property, structures, livestock, and mobile agricultural equipment.

**fidelity bond** A bond that reimburses an employer for losses caused by dishonest acts of employees, such as embezzlement, fraud, forgery, or theft.

**fiduciary** A person who occupies a position of special trust and confidence regarding the handling or supervision of the affairs or funds of another. Examples are trustees, executors, administrators, corporate directors, and insurance agents.

**fiduciary bond** A court bond executed on behalf of a person appointed by a court to a position of trust that guarantees the performance of statutory duties and proper accounting.

**fiduciary duty or responsibility** The responsibility (usually financial) that someone owes to another because of funds or other items held in trust.

**fire department service charge coverage** This provides protection in connection with fire insurance to pay (up to a specified limit of liability) fire department charges incurred if the fire department is called to save or protect insured property.

**fire** *See* hostile fire.

**fire insurance** This is coverage for losses to insured property that result from fire or lightning, as well as the resultant damage caused by smoke and water.

**fire legal liability insurance** This provides protection against legal liability that arises from a fire started by the negligence of the insured or an employee of the insured that damages property occupied by or rented to the insured.

**first party claim** A loss paid by an insurance company to its own policyholder.

**floater policy** An insurance policy that provides coverage for mobile property regardless of location.

**foreign company** An insurance company that operates in a state other than the one in which it is incorporated or chartered.

**forgery** The criminal act of falsely and fraudulently making or altering a document with intent to deprive others of some right, interest, or property by deceit.

**fortuitous event** An unintended accident.

**fraud** An intentional concealment or false representation of a material fact that intends to take something of value or to force the surrender of a right. Fraud can only be determined by a court of appropriate jurisdiction.

**furrier's block policy** This provides broad, open perils coverage on a furrier's stock of furs, including furs that have been sold to customers, but not yet delivered.

**furrier's customers policy** A policy that provides coverage for loss or damage to a customer's furs while in the care, custody, or control of a furrier for storage, repair, or cleaning.

## G

**garage insurance** This provides special protection for firms in the automobile business that offers bodily injury and property damage for premises and operations, products and completed operations, medical payments, ownership, operation, and use of owned and nonowned autos and garagekeepers coverage. It protects against loss that results from damage by insured perils to customer's vehicles in the custody of the insured for reasons such as safekeeping, storage, service, or repair.

**garagekeepers insurance** This provides collision and comprehensive (other than collision) coverage for losses to nonowned vehicles left in the insured's care, custody, or control.

**general liability insurance** This provides protection against legal liability for commercial risks arising from ownership, maintenance, or use of business premises, defects in manufactured products, and completed operations. *See also* commercial general liability.

## H

**hazard** A specific situation or condition that increases the probability or severity of a loss.

**hold harmless agreement** A contractual agreement, usually written, whereby one party assumes legal liability on behalf of the other.

**homeowners policies (HO)** A series of package policies for occupants of residential property that combines insurance for dwellings and household contents with personal liability insurance.

**hostile fire** A fire that produces a visible spark, flame, or glow and leaves the area in which it was intended to be kept.

## I

**implied authority** Authority that, although it is not expressed in a contract (express authority) is necessary to perform the duties expressly authorized.

**improvements and betterments coverage** Protection for lessees and tenants against loss to additions or changes made by them at their own cost that enhance the value of the property they occupy.

**inception date** *See* effective date.

**incidental contract** A written lease of premises; also an easement agreement, except in connection with construction or demolition operations on or adjacent to a railroad; a municipality indemnification agreement, sidetrack agreement, or elevator maintenance agreement.

**increased cost of construction insurance** This provides protection for the portion of a loss owing to changes in local building code specifications that requires modification when rebuilding after a covered loss. *See also* contingent liability from operation of building laws; demolition cost insurance.

**indemnify** To restore in whole or in part by payment, repair or replacement the situation of one who has suffered a loss.

**indemnity** The payment of an amount of money to offset all or part of an insured loss.

**independent contractor** A contractor who performs work for another but is not an employee of the party for whom the work is performed.

**indirect (contingent) loss** A loss that results from a peril, but is not directly and immediately caused by it.

**inflation guard endorsement** A endorsement to a property insurance policy that increases the amount of coverage by a stated percentage at specified times to counteract the effects of increased building costs.

**inherent vice** A characteristic in property itself that causes it to depreciate, spoil, break, become defective, disintegrate, or destroy itself.

**inland marine insurance** This provides insurance protection for cargo and shipments that do not involve ocean transit. In addition, coverage is provided for bridges and tunnels, as well as jewels, furs, collectibles and other items that may not remain at a single location.

**installation floater** This primarily insures a contractor's or owner's interest in machinery, equipment and supplies while they are in transit to the place of installation and during installation.

**insurable interest** The interest from which monetary loss will result if the peril insured against occurs; possibility of financial loss that can be protected against by insurance.

**insurance** A contractual means of transferring the risk of loss to an entity (insurer) that pools similar exposures.

**insurance company** *See* insurer.

**insurance services office (ISO)** A private, nonprofit organization that develops and provides standardized and state-specific forms, rates and inspections for its members.

**insured** Person for whom insurance is provided. *See also* assured

**insurer** An entity that grants insurance.

**insuring agreement** A clause in a policy that broadly defines and describes the scope of the coverage provided and its limits of indemnification.

## J

**jettison** The act of throwing a ship's cargo overboard of cargo from a ship to prevent further damage or sinking.

**jeweler's block policy** This provides broad, open perils coverage for a jeweler's goods and the goods of others while they are in the insured's care, custody, or control.

## L

**lapse** The termination of a policy terminated because of the nonpayment of premiums.

**larceny** The unlawful removal of personal property with the intent to deprive the rightful owner of it.

**law of large numbers** A statistical principle which states that the larger the number of observations, the more accurate and reliable a prediction will be.

**legal purpose** The concept that the purpose of a contract must be legal, moral, and in the public good. *See also* contract.

**lessee** One to whom a lease is granted; a tenant.

**lessor** One who grants a lease; a landlord.

**liability** The condition of being bound by law or contract to do something that may be enforced in the courts; obligation, usually financial; probable cost of meeting an obligation.

**liberalization clause** A clause in a policy providing that if, during the policy period, the insurance company adopts a change in the contract or there is a change in law that extends or broadens coverage, the insured will receive the benefit of this change in the same manner as if the endorsement had been made without paying an increased premium until renewal.

**limit of liability** The maximum amount an insurance company is willing to insure under a given form or contract on any particular risk; the maximum amount payable for a given loss, occurrence, or aggregate limit.

**livestock floater** A form that provides blanket or scheduled coverage on a named perils basis for certain types of livestock.

**Lloyd's of London** An association of syndicates who share similar interests that insures specialized risks. Each syndicate is made up of individual investors who become financially responsible for any incurred loss. Each person is responsible for only the share of the risk that he or she assumes.

**loss** The basis of a claim for indemnity under the provisions of an insurance policy. A loss is measured in terms of the reduced value of the property, the amount of medical and other related expenses or the amount of the claim made against an insured.

## M

**malpractice** An occurrence of professional misconduct, negligence or lack of ordinary skill when performing a professional act that makes a person liable for damages.

**malpractice insurance** A form of professional liability insurance that pays for losses or for defense of suits malpractice. *See also* errors and omissions insurance.

**market value** The amount a willing seller will accept for his or her property from a willing buyer. *See also* actual cash value.

**material fact** Information required to make an insurance underwriting decision; statement concerning an action or entity of such importance that disclosure of it would alter an underwriting decision or loss settlement.

**medical malpractice insurance** A professional liability form specifically designed for doctors, nurses, medical assistants, hospitals, or clinics.

**mini-tail** The extended reporting period, usually 60 days, that allows the insured to report any possible claim to an insurer after the expiration of a claims made contract. *See also* claims-made.

**misrepresentation** A false statement of a material fact known at the time the statement was made.

**mobile agricultural equipment floater** This provides blanket or scheduled open perils coverage for ranch and farm owners on farm machinery and equipment.

**mobile home insurance** This provides protection for the owner-occupant of a residential mobile home; similar to homeowners broad form (HO-2) coverage.

**money and securities broad form policy** This provides broad open perils coverage of commercial risks associated with money and securities both on and off premises.

**moral hazard** The effect(s) personal reputation, character, associates, personal living habits, financial responsibility, criminal history, and environment have on the risk to be insured.

**morale hazard** The effect(s) indifference concerning loss has on the risk to be insured.

**mortgage clause** A provision in or attached to fire policies covering mortgaged property that defines the mortgagee's rights and privileges under the policy.

**mortgagee** One who holds a mortgage loan on property.

**motor truck cargo insurance** This provides coverage (1) against direct loss or damage to an insured trucker's goods while they are in transit on the insured's own trucks and (2) against the legal liability of an individual or business engaged in transporting the property of others for hire.

**multi-lines** An insurance company, insurance agency or insurance agent in the business of selling and servicing more than one type of insurance, most often property and casualty insurance and life insurance.

**multi-peril policy** An insurance policy that provides coverage for several different causes of loss.

**mutual company** An insurance company that is owned by its policyholders and managed by a board of directors.

## N

**named insured** The person specifically designated by name as the insured in a policy. *See also* insured.

**named peril policy** A policy that specifies the perils insured against. *See also* open perils.

**name schedule bond** A fidelity bond that covers only the employees named on the bond.

**National Association of Insurance Commissioners (NAIC)** An association of state insurance commissioners active in the analysis of insurance regulations and in the formation and recommendation of uniform and model regulations and legislation.

**National Flood Insurance Program (NFIP)** A federal program established through the Housing and Urban Development (HUD) Act of 1968 to make flood insurance available to individuals and businesses in those flood-prone communities that adopt certain land-use and flood-loss control measures.

**nationwide marine definition** A guideline for classifying marine, inland marine or transportation insurance; includes imports, exports, domestic shipments, bridges, tunnels, and other means of transportation and communication and personal property and commercial property floater risks.

**neglect** The failure to use all reasonable means to save and preserve property before, during, and after a loss or whenever property is threatened.

**negligence** The failure to act as a reasonable and prudent person would (under the same circumstances and with the same knowledge) to prevent an accident or injury.

**no fault automobile insurance** Insurance designed to replace or limit tort liability from automobile accidents. A state's financial responsibility laws often require liability and limited medical, rehabilitation, and wage loss reimbursement for any person injured in an automobile accident.

**nonadmitted company** An insurance company that is not licensed to write business in a particular state. Also known as a surplus, excess, or excess and surplus lines (E&S) company.

**nonconcurrency** The situation in which a number of insurance policies that are intended to cover the same property against the same hazard(s) are not identical as to the extent of coverage or the interest insured.

**nonowned auto** An automobile that is borrowed or rented from others or is owned by an employee of the insured.

**nonresident agent** An insurance agent licensed in a state in which he or she does not reside.

**nonrenewal** The determination by the insurer or insured not to continue coverage after the anniversary date of the contract. *See also* cancellation.

**nuclear clause** A policy clause that relieves or reduces insurance company liability for loss caused by specific types of nuclear incidents.

## O

**occupational disease** A disease or condition of health not caused by accident but by exposure to conditions arising out of or in the course of one's employment. In many states, this includes occupational related stress.

**Occupational Safety and Health Act (OSHA)** A federal law, enacted in 1971, that mandated specific health and safety standards in places of employment.

**occurrence** A happening that takes some length of time; a series of accidents, including exposure to injurious conditions, that can be connected through common cause. *See also* accident.

**occurrence coverage** A policy that provides liability coverage for injury or loss regardless of when the claim is actually made as long as it occurred during the policy period.

**ocean marine insurance** This provides protection against loss to the insured ship and its cargo, machinery, equipment, and merchandise in transit; generally includes legal liability in the event of a collision with another ship and liability for injuries or damage to other property.

**open perils\open coverage** A common term for broad property or liability insurance coverage against risks of direct loss that is subject to specific exclusions or limitations listed in the policy. Formerly referred to as "all risk."

**ordinance or law coverage** Usually attached to a homeowners or commercial property form (HO or CPP). This provides protection for the cost of demolition, increased costs of construction or the value of undamaged property if these actions are required by a governmental authority due to a covered loss.

**ordinary payroll** An employer's payroll to all employees except officers, executives, department managers, employees under contract, and other key employees.

**other insurance clause** A provision in a policy that states what is to be done when another contract of insurance provides the same coverage or covers essentially the same property.

**owner's and contractor's protective liability insurance** This insures the legal liability of contractors and other persons for the negligent acts of independent contractors engaged by them and, in some cases, for their own negligent supervision of the work performed.

**owners, landlords and tenants liability insurance** This is business insurance designed to protect against liability for bodily injury or property damage to others arising from the ownership, maintenance, or use of premises owned or occupied by the insured.

## P

**package policies** Insurance policies that offer several coverages included in one contract.

**pair or set condition** A provision that stipulates that the loss of one item of a pair or set does not represent the loss of the entire set. Settlement of the claim is usually based on the difference in the value of the set before and after the loss.

**partial loss** A loss that does not completely destroy insured property or exhaust the insurance limits applying to that property.

**performance bond** A surety bond that guarantees that a contract will be completed per the agreed specification.

**peril** An event insured against; the cause of a possible loss.

**personal auto policy (PAP)** This provides protection for liability, medical payments and damage to the automobile for individuals and married couples and their owned and nonowned vehicles.

**personal injury coverage** This provides coverage for libel, slander, invasion of privacy, and other intentional torts.

**personal injury protection (PIP)** In a no fault state, PIP provides first-party coverage for injuries suffered by the insured in an automobile accident. *See also* no fault.

**personal liability insurance** This provides protection against legal liability arising in connection with personal, nonbusiness activities both on and off insured premises.

**personal lines insurance** This provides coverage of risks of an individual, personal, or nonbusiness nature.

**personal property** All property, other than real property, owned or used by an insured.

**personal property floater** This is a broad, open perils policy for personal property regardless of its location. It is written as a separate policy or as an endorsement to a homeowners policy.

**physical hazard** A hazard arising out of the use, condition or occupancy of the insured property.

**plaintiff** The party to a lawsuit who brings charges against another party, the defendant.

**policy** The insurance contract and all attached endorsements.

**policy period** The length of time during which the policy contract affords protection; also called the policy term.

**pollution liability** The part of a CGL contract that provides limited liability coverage in the event of necessary pollution clean-up.

**position schedule bond** A fidelity bond that covers losses due to employee dishonesty when committed by persons who occupy certain listed job descriptions.

**pool** A group of insurance companies that join together to share certain risks, such as aviation liability, on an agreed-upon basis.

**premises and completed operations** This provides business liability protection for occurrences at the business location or elsewhere due to its operations.

**premises burglary** A commercial crime form that provides coverage for burglary or attempted burglary.

**premium** The designated amount owed by the insured to the insurance company in order to keep the contract in force.

**principal** A person whose obligations are guaranteed under a bond (also called the obligor); the applicant for or subject of insurance; the one (usually the insurer) from whom an insurance agent derives authority.

**property damage** This is liability coverage that provides protection in the event of loss of property, including loss of use, owned by someone other than the insured.

**pro rata cancellation** The termination of a policy or bond with a return of premium charged for the exact time the protection was in force equal to the ratio of the total premium to the total policy period. *See also* short rate cancellation.

**pro rata liability clause** A property insurance clause that makes each company insuring the same interest in a property liable according to the proportion that its insurance bears to the total amount of insurance on the property.

**producer** A general term for an insurance sales representative.

**products liability insurance** This provides protection against legal liability for bodily injury or property damage arising after goods and products have been manufactured, handled, sold, or distributed. It includes products that have left the insured's possession and premises or, in the case of food, when it is given to a customer. *See also* completed operations liability insurance.

**proof of loss** A formal document that contains the signed and sworn statement of the insured in regard to the loss for which a claim has been filed.

**property insurance** This provides protection against loss to physical property or its income-producing ability.

**provisions** The written terms or conditions of a policy.

**proximate cause** The immediate cause that in a natural and continuous sequence, unbroken by any intervening efficient cause, brings about the loss and without which the loss would not have happened.

**pure risk** The uncertainty as to whether loss will occur; offers no chance for gain. Insurance may be provided against many types of pure risk.

## R

**rate** Cost of a given unit of insurance.

**real property** Land and generally whatever is permanently erected or growing upon or affixed to the land; property not of a personal and movable nature. *See also* personal property.

**reciprocal exchange (insurer)** An association of individuals known as subscribers, managed by an attorney-in-fact, who agree to exchange insurance risks.

**reinsurance** The act of sharing or spreading a risk that is too large for one insurer by transferring part of the risk to a reinsurer. The insurance company obtaining the reinsurance is called the ceding company; the insurance company issuing the reinsurance is called the reinsurer.

**release** A discharge from further liability under an insurance policy.

**removal coverage** This provides coverage for damage that results from property removed for its own protection from premises endangered by an insured peril.

**renewal** The continuation of coverage under an insurance policy beyond its original term.

**rental value insurance** This provides protection against loss of rental value when a building is made untenantable due to damage or destruction by an insured peril; the insured may be either the owner of the building or a tenant.

**replacement cost** The actual cost of replacing property without a deduction for depreciation. *See also* actual cash value.

**reporting forms** This is insurance written to provide for fluctuating values of property that requires payment of an advance premium, value reports made by the insured at specified times and the adjustment of earned premium.

**representation** A statement of material fact that is reasonably accepted as substantially true.

**respondeat superior** A general rule in law that a principal or employer is liable for the acts of an agent or representative performed on behalf of the principal's business.

**return premium** The amount of unused premium owed to the insured if a policy is cancelled or its face amount or rate is reduced.

**risk** The uncertainty regarding loss; a term indicating the person or property insured. *See also* pure risk; speculative risk.

**risk management** The attempt to identify, measure, control and translate pure risk and insurance problems into significant business language in order to protect future income and reduce long-range costs against accidental or unintended loss. The risk manager controls risk by accepting, reducing, eliminating, or transferring it.

**robbery** The unlawful taking of others' personal property by violence or threat of violence; a hold-up.

**robbery and safe burglary policy** This provides coverage for commercial risks to protect against loss of money, securities and other property as a result of forced entry into a safe or vault.

## S

**salvage** The damaged property recovered and sold by an insurance company to reduce its financial loss.

**schedule rating** A merit rating system whereby a standard risk is established for each classification and measured by the manual rate. If the risk is better than average, credit factors are applied to the manual rate; if the risk does not meet the standard, debit factors are applied.

**self-insurance** Provided by a non-insurance company that has the financial ability to retain the risk of loss without the use of an insurance policy.

**self-insured retention (SIR)** The amount the insured must satisfy if a loss is covered by an umbrella policy but not by any underlying insurance.

**short rate cancellation** The termination of a policy or bond by the insured before the end of the policy period, with the earned premium plus administrative expenses retained by the insurance company.

**speculative risk** The uncertainty regarding loss and gain. Speculative risks may not be insured against.

**split limits** The practice of separating Bodily Injury and Property Damage into distinct limits of liability (for example, $50,000 BI and $15,000 PD). *See also* combined single limit.

**spreading of risk** The underwriting principles that require the insurance company to spread its risk to as many geographic locations as possible.

**sprinkler leakage insurance** This provides protection against loss caused by accidental discharge of water or other substances from an automatic fire protective system, including direct loss caused by collapse or fall of tanks forming a part of the system.

**standard fire policy** This generally refers to the 1943 New York 165-line standard form, it was used in most states with statutory modifications. Provided protection against direct loss by fire, lightning, and removal.

**stated amount coverage** An amendment to the valuation provision of a property insurance policy that provides a maximum amount for payment of any loss. It is typically used in automobile insurance for older, classic, or antique automobiles.

**stock company** An insurance company owned by its stockholders. Also known as a capital company or a capital-stock company.

**subrogation** The act of assigning or substituting the rights of one party to another in collecting a debt or claim, as an insurance company is assigned an insured's rights of recovery from a third party who has caused a loss.

**surety** The party under a bond who is legally liable for the debt, default or failure of the principal to the bond.

## T

**tail** *See* extended reporting period.

**term** The period of time for which a policy or bond is written.

**theft** Any illegal act of taking or stealing, or attempting to take or steal, someone else's property, including such crimes as larceny, burglary, and robbery.

**third-party claim** An insurance claim paid by an insurance company to someone other than their own policyholder. *See also* first party claim.

**time element coverages** A common term for insurance protection against indirect loss resulting from damage to insured property, such as business interruption, leasehold interest, loss of rents, and extra expense insurance.

**tort** A civil wrong or injury for which legal action may be taken; for example, negligence or assault.

**trucker's policy** This policy protects individuals and organizations in the business of transporting property for hire; it offers bodily injury and property damage liability, physical damage coverages and trailer interchange coverage for owned and nonowned trailers.

## U

**umbrella liability insurance** This provides broadened coverage and higher limits of liability for businesses, organizations, and individuals. Supplements basic liability coverage. *See also* excess insurance.

**underinsurance** The condition of having coverage for less than the percentage of value required to satisfy the coinsurance clause of a policy.

**underinsured motorist (UIM)** This is auto coverage that provides protection in the event an insured is involved in an accident caused by another who is carrying insurance coverage lower than the amount of the damages and lower than the claimant's Underinsured Motorists coverage.

**underlying insurance** The amount of insurance required to be in effect before the next higher excess layer of insurance attaches.

**underwriting** The process of researching, evaluating and determining the insurability of a risk.

**unearned premium** The portion of an insurance premium that has not been used to provide protection to an insured. *See also* earned premium.

**uninsured motorist (UM) coverage** This is auto coverage that provides protection in the event the insured is involved in an accident where the other party is at fault, but not insured. *See also* underinsured motorist.

**unoccupied** The insured property is not currently being used but the occupant intends to return.

**utmost good faith** A requirement in a contract that there be no fraud, concealment, or misrepresentation between the contracting parties.

## V

**vacant** Property that does not contain sufficient furnishings to support its intended occupancy or use.

**valuable papers and records insurance** This provides protection against loss of papers, documents, or other means of storing information that must be recreated in the event of a loss.

**valuation clause** The provision in a policy that defines the basis for establishing the amount to be paid in the event of a loss to insured property.

**valued policy** This is a policy in which the value of the property insured and amount to be paid in case of total loss are determined at policy inception rather than at the time of the loss.

**vandalism/malicious mischief** Willful and malicious physical damage to or destruction of property.

**void** The act of cancelling a contract back to the original inception date. Effectively, the contract is rendered null, having no legal force or binding effect.

**voidable** A policy contract that can be made void at the option of one or more parties to the agreement.

## W

**warranty** A literal promise and guarantee, either expressed or implied (i.e., concerning the condition of property to be insured), made for the purpose of risk evaluation by the insurance company; if found to be untrue, may provide a basis for voiding the policy.

**workers' compensation insurance** This provides benefits to a worker or the worker's dependents for injury, disability, or disease contracted by the worker in the course of his or her employment.

## Y

**yacht coverage** This provides coverage for physical damage (Hull) and liability (Protection and Indemnity) arising out of the use of personal watercraft.

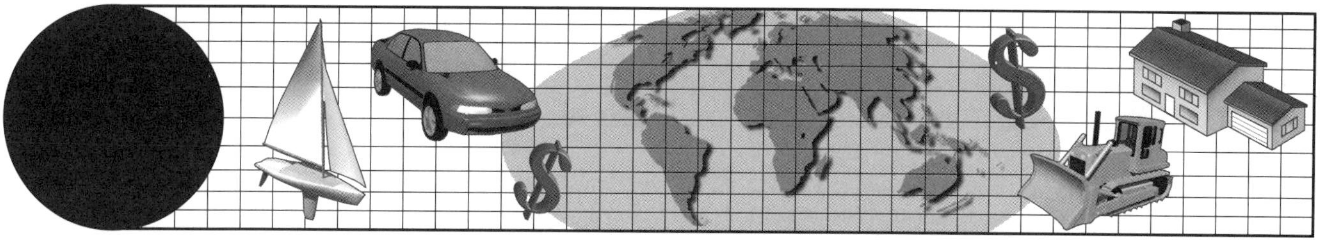

# Appendix
# Comparison of Homeowners Forms

## Part I: Section I—Property Coverages

### Limits of Liability and Perils

| | HO-2 Broad Form | HO-3 Special Form | HO-4 Contents Broad Form | HO-5 Comprehensive Form | HO-6 Unit Owners Form | HO-8 Modified Coverage Form |
|---|---|---|---|---|---|---|
| **Cov. A—Dwelling** | Refer to state rate pages for min. limits | Refer to state rate pages for min. limits | Refer to state rate pages for min. limits | Refer to state rate pages for min. limits | Refer to state rate pages for min. limits | Refer to state rate pages for min. limits |
| **Cov. B—Other Structures** | | | | | | |
| 1 or 2 family | 10% of Cov. A | 10% of Cov. A | N/A | 10% of Cov. A | N/A | 10% of Cov. A |
| 3 or 4 family | 5% of Cov. A | 5% of Cov. A | N/A | 5% of Cov. A | N/A | 5% of Cov. A |
| **Cov. C.—Personal Property** | | | | | | |
| 1 or 2 family | 50% of Cov. A | 50% of Cov. A | Refer to Declarations Page | 50% of Cov. A | Refer to Declarations Page | 50% of Cov. A |
| 3 family | 30% of Cov. A | 30% of Cov. A | N/A | 30% of Cov. A | N/A | 30% of Cov. A |
| 4 family | 25% of Cov. A | 25% of Cov. A | N/A | 25% of Cov. A | N/A | 25% of Cov. A |
| **Cov. D—Loss of Use** | 30% of Cov. A | 30% of Cov. A | 30 % of Cov. C | 30% of Cov. A | 50% of Cov. C | 10% of Cov. A |

### Additional Coverages

| | HO-2 Broad Form | HO-3 Special Form | HO-4 Contents Broad Form | HO-5 Comprehensive Form | HO-6 Unit Owners Form | HO-8 Modified Coverage Form |
|---|---|---|---|---|---|---|
| **Debris Removal** | Reasonable expense up to $500/$1,000 per tree/all trees | Reasonable expense up to $500/$1,000 per tree/all trees | Reasonable expense up to $500/$1,000 per tree/all trees | Reasonable expense up to $500/$1,000 per tree/all trees | Reasonable expense up to $500/$1,000 per tree/all trees | Reasonable expense up to $500/$1,000 per tree/all trees |
| **Reasonable Repairs** | All forms cover the reasonable cost incurred to protect property from further damage. | | | | | |
| **Lawns, Trees, Shrubs, and Plants** | $500 per tree 5% of Cov. A for all plants | $500 per tree 5% of Cov. A for all plants | $500 per tree 10% of Cov. C for all plants | $500 per tree 5% of Cov. A for all plants | $500 per tree 10% of Cov. C for all plants | $250 per tree 5% of Cov. A for all plants |
| **Fire Dept. Service Charge** | Up to $500 | Up to $500 | Up to $500 | Up to $500 | Up to $500 | Up to $500 |
| **Property Removed** | Open Perils up to 30 days | Open Perils up to 30 days | Open Perils up to 30 days | Open Perils up to 30 days | Open Perils up to 30 days | Open Perils up to 30 days |
| **Credit Card, Fund Transfer, Forgery and Counterfeit Money** | Up to $500 | Up to $500 | Up to $500 | Up to $500 | Up to $500 | Up to $500 |
| **Loss Assessment** | Up to $1,000 | Up to $1,000 | Up to $1,000 | Up to $1,000 | Up to $1,000 | Up to $1,000 |
| **Collapse** | All forms except HO-8 provide named perils coverage plus coverage for hidden decay, insect or vermin damage, weight of contents, weight of rain collected on a roof or use of defective construction material or methods. | | | | | Not Covered |
| **Landlord's Furnishings** | Up to $2,500 | Up to $2,500 | Not Covered | Up to $2,500 for named perils | N/A | Not Covered |
| **Building Additions and Alterations** | N/A | N/A | Up to 10% of Cov. C | N/A | Included under Cov. A | N/A |
| **Ordinance or Law** | 10% of Cov. A | 10% of Cov. A | 10% of Bldg. Additions and Alterations | 10% of Cov. A | 10% of Cov. A | Not Covered |
| **Grave Markers** | Up to $5,000 | Up to $5,000 | Up to $5,000 | Up to $5,000 | Up to $5,000 | Not Covered |

### Section I—Property: Perils Insured Against

| | HO-2 Cov A/B | HO-2 Cov C | HO-3 Cov A/B | HO-3 Cov C | HO-4 Cov A/B | HO-4 Cov C | HO-5 Cov A/B | HO-5 Cov C | HO-6 Cov A/B | HO-6 Cov C | HO-8 Cov A/B | HO-8 Cov C |
|---|---|---|---|---|---|---|---|---|---|---|---|---|
| Basic Form | | | | | | | | | | | X | X |
| Broad Form | X | X | | X** | N/A | X* | | | X* | X* | | |
| Open Perils | | | X | | | | X | X | | | | |

*Can be endorsed to add open perils.
**Must use HO-5 to obtain open perils coverage.

### Section I—Broad Form Perils and Exclusions

| Basic Form Perils | | Broad Form Perils (In Addition to Basic Perils) |
|---|---|---|
| Fire or Lightning | Smoke | Falling Objects |
| Windstorm or Hail | Vandalism or Malicious Mischief | Weight of Ice, Snow or Sleet |
| Explosion | Theft | Accidental Discharge or Overflow of Water or Steam |
| Riot or Civil Commotion | Volcanic Eruption | Sudden and Accidental Tearing Apart, Cracking, Burning or Bulging |
| Aircraft | | Freezing |
| Vehicles | | Sudden and Accidental Damage from Artificially Generated Electrical Current |

| Broad Form Named Perils | Standard Building and Personal Property Exclusions (All Forms) |
|---|---|
| Sudden and accidental direct physical loss caused by: | Loss caused directly or indirectly by: |
| 1. Fire or Lightning | 1. Ordinance or Law |
| 2. Windstorm or Hail | 2. Earth Movement |
| 3. Explosion | 3. Water Damage (including flood) |
| 4. Riot or Civil Commotion | 4. Power Failure |
| 5. Aircraft | 5. Neglect |
| 6. Vehicles | 6. War |
| 7. Smoke | 7. Nuclear Hazard |
| 8. Vandalism or Malicious Mischief | 8. Intentional Loss |
| 9. Theft | 9. Governmental Action |
| 10. Falling Objects | |
| 11. Weight of Ice, Snow or Sleet | |
| 12. Accidental Discharge or Overflow of Water or Steam | |
| 13. Sudden and Accidental Tearing Apart, Cracking, Burning or Bulging | |
| 14. Freezing | |
| 15. Sudden and Accidental Damage from Artificially Generated Electrical Current | |
| 16. Volcanic Eruption | |

### Section I—Property Loss Settlement

| | HO-2 Cov A/B | HO-2 Cov C | HO-3 Cov A/B | HO-3 Cov C | HO-4 Cov A/B | HO-4 Cov C | HO-5 Cov A/B | HO-5 Cov C | HO-6 Cov A/B | HO-6 Cov C | HO-8 Cov A/B | HO-8 Cov C |
|---|---|---|---|---|---|---|---|---|---|---|---|---|
| Replacement Cost | X | | X | | | | X | | X | | | |
| Actual Cash Value | | X | | X | N/A | X | | X | | X | | X |
| Cost of Repair with Current Material | | | | | | | | | | | X | |

## Part II: Section I—Personal Property

### Section I—Personal Property Limitations

| | Item Description | HO 2000 Amount | HO 1991 Amount |
|---|---|---|---|
| a. | Money, bank notes, bullion, gold, silver, platinum, coins, medals, scrip, stored value cards and smart cards. | $200 | $200 |
| b. | Securities, accounts, deeds, evidences of debt, letters of credit, manuscripts, personal records, passports, tickets and stamps. | $1,500 | $1,000 |
| c. | Watercraft of all types, including their trailers, furnishings, equipment and outboard engines or motors. | $1,500 | $1,000 |
| d. | Trailers or semitrailers not used with watercraft of all types. | $1,500 | $1,000 |
| e. | Loss by theft of jewelry, watches, furs, precious and semiprecious stones. | $1,500 | $1,000 |
| f. | Loss by theft of firearms and related equipment. | $2,500 | $2,000 |
| g. | Loss by theft of silverware, silver-plated ware, goldware, gold-plated ware, platinumware, platinum-plated ware and pewterware. | $2,500 | $2,500 |
| h. | Property, on the "residence premises," used primarily for "business" purposes. | $2,500 | $2,500 |
| i. | Property, away from the "residence premises", used primarily for "business" purposes, n/a to electronic apparatus and other property described in Categories j. and k. below. | $500 | $250 |
| j. | Electronic apparatus and accessories while in or upon a "motor vehicle", but only if the apparatus is equipped to be operated by power from the "motor vehicle's" electrical system. | $1,500 | $1,000 |
| k. | Electronic apparatus and accessories used primarily for "business" while away from the "residence premises" and not in or upon a "motor vehicle." | $1,500 | $1,000 |

## Part III: Section II—Liability Additional Coverages

| Section II Additional Coverages | | |
|---|---|---|
| A. | Claim Expenses | No limit on legal and other costs the insurer incurs. Insurer pays premiums on bonds up to Coverage E limit of liability. The insurer pays a maximum of $250 per day reimbursement to the insured for reasonable expenses while assisting in claims investigation and settlement, including loss of earnings. Insurer pays interest on judgment, including prejudgment interest. |
| B. | First Aid Expenses | No limit for firstaid expenses incurred at the time of an accident for persons other than the insured. |
| C. | Damage to Property of Others | Physical damage to property of others up to $1,000 per occurrence applies even if the insured is not legally liable. Coverage does not apply to intentional damage by an insured 13 years of age or older, property owned by an insured or property otherwise excluded by the policy. |
| D. | Loss Assessment | Loss assessments up to $1,000 when assessment results from bodily injury or property damage not excluded by the policy. |

### Section II—Liability Boat Coverage: Covered Engines and Vessels

| Coverage E—Personal Liability and Coverage F—Medical Payments to Others | | |
|---|---|---|
| *This Type of Engine or Vessel* | *With These Specifications* | *Is Covered if the Object's Relationship to the Insured Is* |
| Inboard or Inboard/Outboard Motor | ≤ 50 HP<br>> 50 HP | Rented or Borrowed<br>Borrowed |
| Outboard Motor | ≤ 25 HP<br>> 25 HP | Owned, Rented or Borrowed<br>Rented, Borrowed or Newly Acquired |
| Sailboat | ≤ 26' Long<br>> 26' Long | Owned, Rented or Borrowed<br>Borrowed |
| Any Type | In storage | Owned, Rented or Borrowed |

## Part IV: Endorsements

| Endorsements that Apply to Section I | |
|---|---|
| Additional Insured—Residence Premises (HO 04 41) | Insures a single residence owned by two or more parties. One party insures the dwelling and names the other(s) as additional insured(s) with this endorsement. Additional insureds should use the HO-4 to cover any contents, loss of use and liability exposures. |
| Building Additions & Alterations (HO 04 51) | Covers improvements and alterations made by tenants in rented properties. |
| Coverage B—Off Premises (HO 04 91) | Covers structures located away from the residence premises but used in connected with the residence. Extends coverage to 10% of Coverage A. |
| Specific Structures Away from the Residence Premises (HO 04 92) | Covers specifically described locations to be insured. Coverage is additional insurance to what is automatically provided under Coverage B. |
| Coverage C Increased Special Limits of Liability (HO 04 65) | Increases coverage of certain categories of valuable property. |
| Credit Card and Counterfeit Money Coverage—Increased Amounts (HO 04 53) | Increases limits of loss due to lost or stolen credit or fund transfer cards or the acceptance of counterfeit paper currency. |
| Earthquake Endorsement (HO 04 54) | Covers earthquakes, landslides, volcanic eruptions and earth movements that occur within a 72-hour period as if they were a single loss. |
| Inflation Guard (HO 04 46) | Provides an annual pro-rata percentage increase in the limits in Coverages A, B, C and D. |
| Mine Subsidence Coverage (Varies by State) | Covers against mine subsidence, which is lateral or vertical ground movement caused by a failure initiated at the mine level of man-made underground mines. |
| Mobilehome Endorsement (MH 04 01) | Amends the definition of "residence premises" to include the mobilehome listed in the Declarations. Also includes transportation coverage. |
| Ordinance or Law Coverage (HO 04 77) | Gives back the exclusion for loss arising from an ordinance or law that regulates the construction, repair or demolition of property. |
| Other Structures—Increased Limits (HO 04 48) | Alows an increase in the Coverage B limit beyond the 10% provided automatically. |
| Personal Property Replacement Cost (HO 04 90) | Without endorsement, losses to personal property are settled on an actual cash value basis. This endorsement changes the valuation basis for Coverage C to replacement cost, with few exceptions. |
| Refrigerated Property Coverage (HO 04 98) | Provides up to $500 of coverage for direct loss to property contained in a refrigerator or freezer if the unit experiences a mechanical failure or the power is interrupted. |
| Scheduled Personal Property Endorsement (HO 04 61) | Broader coverage for personal jewelry, furs, cameras, musical instruments, silverware, golf equipment, fine art and stamp and coin collections. Articles must be described and insured on a full value basis. Also covers mysterious disappearance, which can be an important coverage when the insured is uncertain as to whether an item was stolen. |
| Sinkhole Collapse Endorsement (HO 04 99) | Covers damage to property caused by settlement or collapse of the earth under the insured property. |
| Special Loss Settlement (HO 04 56) | Allows the insured to carry 50, 60 or 70%, instead of the customary 80%, of the replacement cost of the dwelling without affecting the replacement cost loss payment provisions. |
| Special Personal Property Coverage Endorsement (HO 05 24) | Available to HO-4 policyholders who wish to have open perils coverage on their personal property. |
| Special Computer Coverage (HO 04 14) | Provides open perils coverage for computer equipment including hardware; software, operating systems or networks, and other electronic parts, equipment, or systems. Data is not covered. |
| Windstorm or Hail Exclusion (HO 04 94) | Excludes windstorm or hail coverage for insureds who do not need this coverage. |
| Unit Owners Coverage A—Special Coverage (HO 17 32) | Amends Coverage A of the HO-6 to open perils. Also broadens Coverage D to include protection when the premises cannot be used because of any insured loss caused by an open peril. |
| Unit Owners Coverage C—Special Coverage (HO 17 31) | Amends Coverage C of the HO-6 to open perils. Also broadens Coverage D to include protection when the premises cannot be used because of any insured loss caused by an open peril. |
| Water Backup and Sump Pump Overflow Endorsement (HO 04 95) | Pays for damage up to $5,000 to property covered under Section I caused by sewer backup or sump pump overflow, including mechanical breakdown. $250 deductible applies in lieu of any other deductible. |

| Endorsements that Apply to Section II | |
|---|---|
| **Snowmobile Endorsement (HO 24 64)** | Provides liability coverage for owned snowmobiles away from the insured location. |
| **Watercraft Endorsement (HO 24 75)** | Provides liability and medical payments coverage to motorized watercraft over 25 total horse power and sailing vessels 26 feet or more in overall length. Bodily injury to an employee of an insured is excluded, as is coverage if the watercraft is used to carry passengers for a fee, is rented to others, used for business purposes or for racing. |
| **Personal Injury (HO 24 82)** | Changes the definition of "bodily injury" to include false arrest, detention or imprisonment, malicious prosecution, libel, slander or defamation of character, invasion of privacy, wrongful eviction and wrongful entry. |
| **Loss Assessment Coverage (HO 04 35)** | Provides additional coverage for loss assessment to homeowners or condominium owners over the $1,000 covered by the standard policy. |
| **Loss Assessment for Earthquake (HO 04 36)** | Covers loss assessments due to earthquake or land shock waves related to a volcano. |
| **Business Pursuits (HO 24 71)** | Extends liability coverage to any of the insured's business pursuits listed in the endorsement. The endorsement does not apply to businesses the insured owns or controls, to professional liability or to injuries to fellow employees. |
| **Incidental Farming Personal Liability Endorsement (HO 24 72)** | Covers liability and medical payments to others as a result of farming on the residence premises. The endorsement covers only inconsequential farming that is not done as a primary source of income. Coverage may also be added for incidental farming activities that are conducted away from the residence premises, such as boarding and grazing animals. |
| **Farmers Personal Liability Endorsement (HO 24 73)** | Deletes the Section II—Liability Coverages and Exclusions and replaces them with liability sections tailored to the farm operation. |

| Endorsements that Apply to Both Sections I and II | |
|---|---|
| **Permitted Incidental Occupancies–Residence Premises (HO 04 42)** | Deletes or modifies the exclusions pertaining to a business under both the policy's property and liability sections. This endorsement eliminates the exclusion for other structures used in whole or in part for business, deletes the $2,500 limitation for business property under Coverage C and eliminates the exclusion for business pursuits under the policy's liability section. |
| **Structures Rented to Others (HO 04 40)** | Coverage B excludes coverage for structures rented to anyone other than a resident of the household. This endorsement deletes that exclusion and adds coverage under the liability section for property rented to others. This can be an important endorsement for someone with a garage or another outbuilding that has been converted to an apartment. |
| **Home Day Care Coverage (HO 04 97)** | Deletes the exclusion under Coverage B for business use, eliminates the $2,500 restriction on business property under Coverage C and extends the coverage under Section II to apply to day care operations. The endorsement also changes the limit for Coverage E Liability from an occurrence limit to an annual aggregate. Requests for this endorsement receive a great deal of underwriting scrutiny. |
| **Unit Owners Rental to Others Coverage (HO 17 33)** | Provides personal property coverage, theft for most items and coverage for personal liability and medical payments to others. |

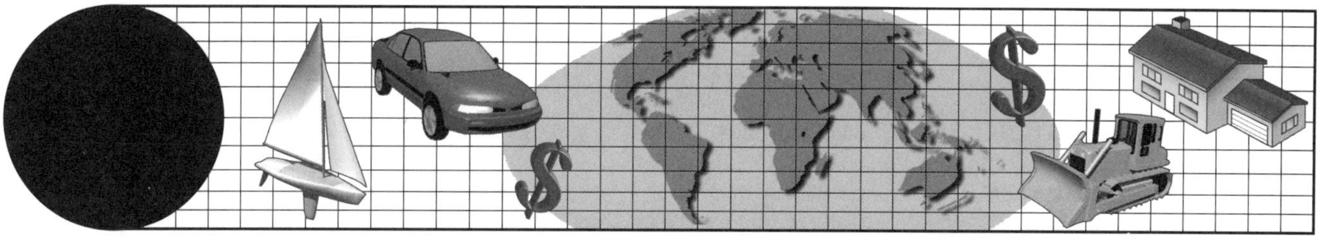

# Index

## T



## U

***Dear Student,***

What did you think of your Dearborn PASSTRAK study materials? We'd like to know!

We invite you to complete the PASSTRAK survey below. Your responses will help us to develop even better exam preparation materials. Please tear this page out of your book, fold it into thirds, seal it and mail it to us. We'll pay the postage. Your comments are greatly appreciated.

Dearborn™
Financial Services
A **Kaplan Professional** Company
30 S Wacker Drive
Suite 2500
Chicago IL 60606-7481

Book title and edition number: ______________________________

**Please rate the PASSTRAK materials using the following scale:**

1 = Poor 2 = Satisfactory 3 = Very Good

***License Exam Manual***

| | | | |
|---|---|---|---|
| Easy to read | 1 | 2 | 3 |
| Easy to understand | 1 | 2 | 3 |
| Organized | 1 | 2 | 3 |
| Up-to-date | 1 | 2 | 3 |
| Complete | 1 | 2 | 3 |
| Accurate | 1 | 2 | 3 |

***Questions & Answers***

| | | | |
|---|---|---|---|
| Challenging | 1 | 2 | 3 |
| Number of questions | 1 | 2 | 3 |
| Accurate | 1 | 2 | 3 |
| Up-to-date | 1 | 2 | 3 |
| Matches the test | 1 | 2 | 3 |

How well do you believe the PASSTRAK materials prepared you for the exam? 1 2 3

What did you like about the PASSTRAK materials?

What would you like us to do to improve the PASSTRAK materials?

Which topic or subject did you find most difficult to study?

What other Dearborn products do you use? Please check them here:

Classroom ____ AnswerPhone ____ Online Drill & Practice ____ Continuing Education Materials ____

Practice Finals ____ Diagnostic Exams ____ Course software ____ Audiotapes ____

How likely would you be to use an online product? Very likely ____ Somewhat likely ____ Not likely ____

Did you take the licensing exam? No ____ Yes ____ Date __________ Score ____

Name (optional): ______________________________

State of Residence ______ Firm ______________

May we contact you?
If so, please provide us with your phone number or email address: ______________________

You can reach us with your comments and questions at Dearborn's AnswerPhone, a toll-free service.
Securities AnswerPhone: (800) 621-9621, ext. 3598
Insurance AnswerPhone: (800) 621-9621, ext. 2444

You can also contact us at our website, www.dearborn.com.

**NOTE:** This page, when folded over and taped, becomes a postage-free envelope that has been approved by the United States Postal Service. It has been provided for your convenience.

▼ Important—please fold over and tape before mailing ▼

NO POSTAGE NECESSARY IF MAILED IN THE UNITED STATES

# BUSINESS REPLY MAIL

FIRST-CLASS MAIL PERMIT NO. 88175 CHICAGO, IL

POSTAGE WILL BE PAID BY ADDRESSEE

**ATTN FINANCIAL SERVICES MARKETING**
**DEARBORN FINANCIAL SERVICES**
**30 S WACKER DRIVE**
**SUITE 2500**
**CHICAGO IL 60606-7481**

▲ Important—please fold over and tape before mailing ▲

**NOTE:** This page, when folded over and taped, becomes a postage-free envelope that has been approved by the United States Postal Service. It has been provided for your convenience.